KU-206-816

I KNOW NOT WHAT COURSE OTHERS MAY TAKE BUT - AS FOR ME - GIVE ME LIBERTY OR GIVE ME DEATH

PATRICK HENRY (1775)

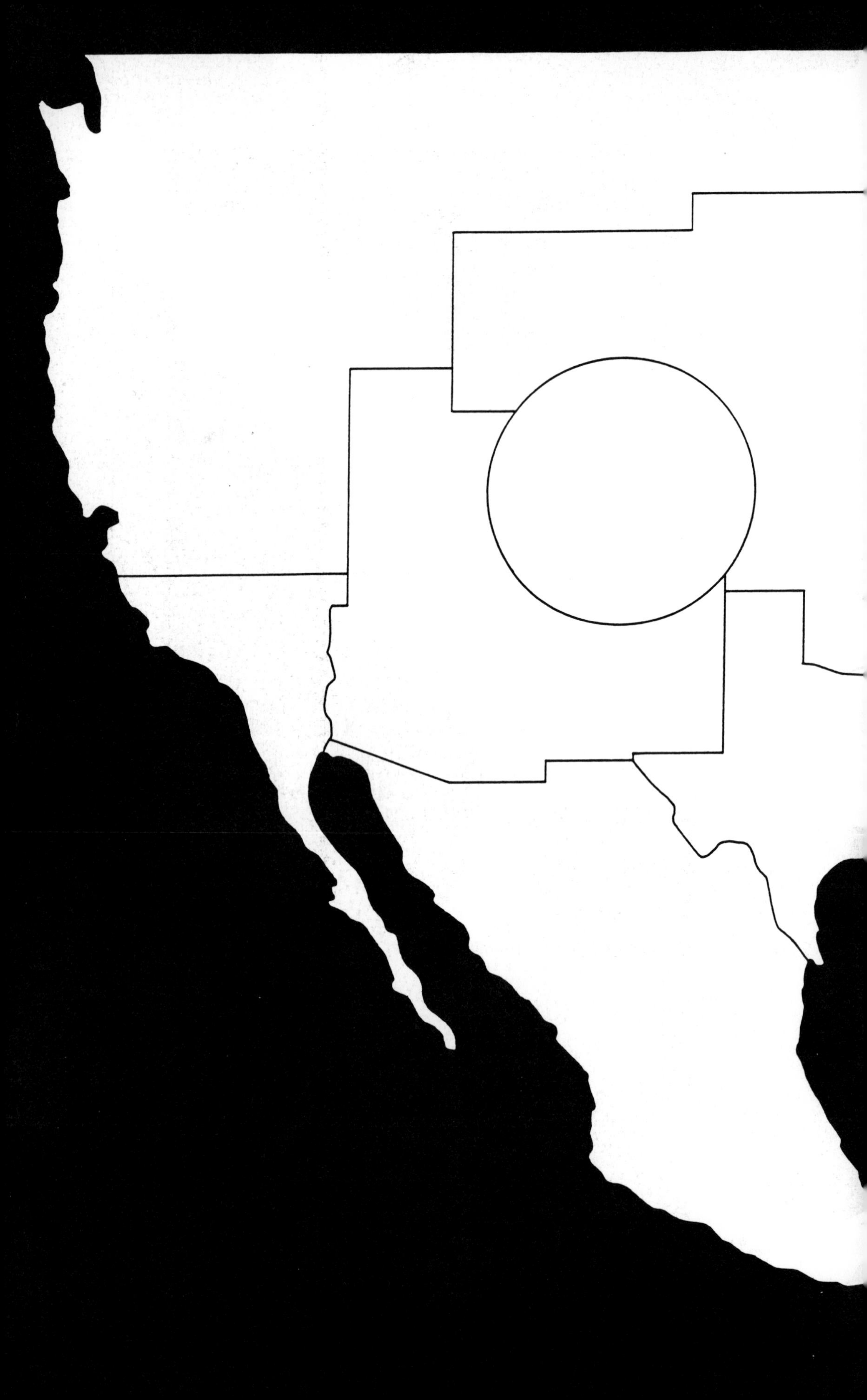

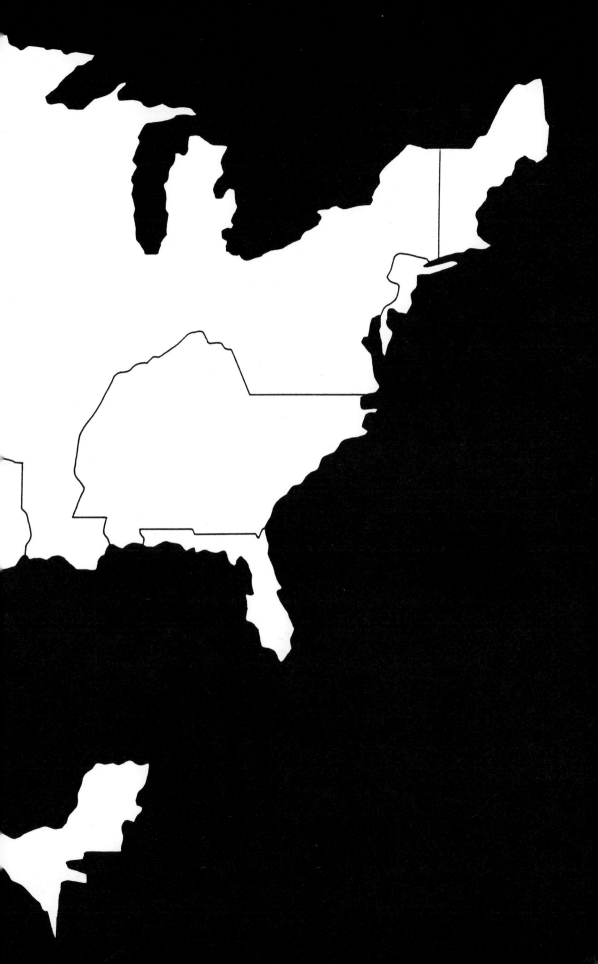

1: HOMES & GARDENS

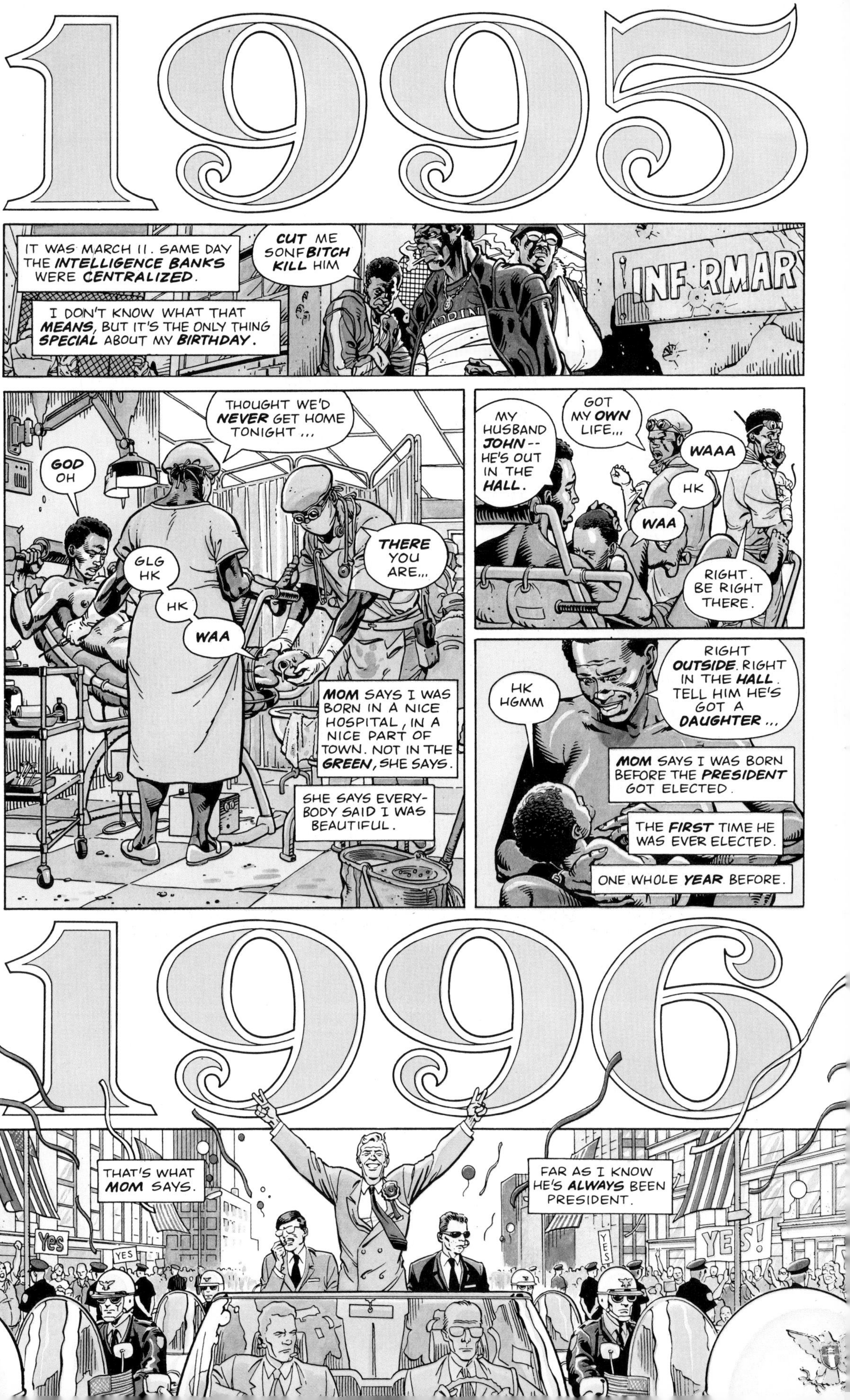
1995
IT WAS MARCH 11. SAME DAY THE INTELLIGENCE BANKS WERE CENTRALIZED.
I DON'T KNOW WHAT THAT MEANS, BUT IT'S THE ONLY THING SPECIAL ABOUT MY BIRTHDAY.
CUT ME SONFBITCH KILL HIM
INF RMARY
GOD OH
THOUGHT WE'D NEVER GET HOME TONIGHT...
GLG HK
HK
WAA
THERE YOU ARE...
MOM SAYS I WAS BORN IN A NICE HOSPITAL, IN A NICE PART OF TOWN. NOT IN THE GREEN, SHE SAYS.
SHE SAYS EVERYBODY SAID I WAS BEAUTIFUL.
MY HUSBAND JOHN-- HE'S OUT IN THE HALL.
GOT MY OWN LIFE...
WAAA
HK
WAA
RIGHT. BE RIGHT THERE.
HK HGMM
RIGHT OUTSIDE. RIGHT IN THE HALL. TELL HIM HE'S GOT A DAUGHTER...
MOM SAYS I WAS BORN BEFORE THE PRESIDENT GOT ELECTED.
THE FIRST TIME HE WAS EVER ELECTED.
ONE WHOLE YEAR BEFORE.
1996
THAT'S WHAT MOM SAYS.
FAR AS I KNOW HE'S ALWAYS BEEN PRESIDENT.
YES
YES
YES
YES!

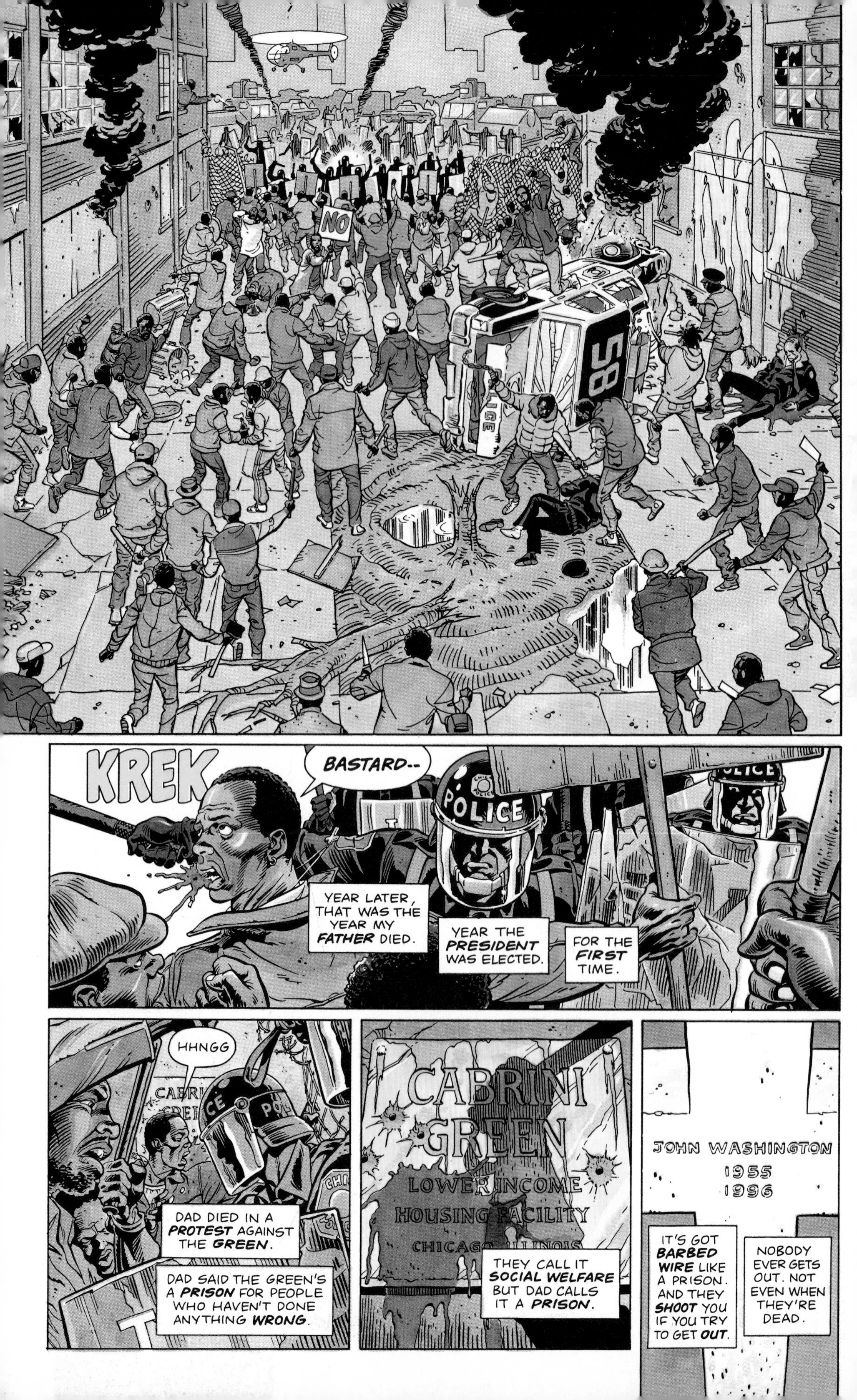

NO
58
KREK
BASTARD--
POLICE
YEAR LATER, THAT WAS THE YEAR MY FATHER DIED.
YEAR THE PRESIDENT WAS ELECTED.
FOR THE FIRST TIME.
HHNGG
DAD DIED IN A PROTEST AGAINST THE GREEN.
DAD SAID THE GREEN'S A PRISON FOR PEOPLE WHO HAVEN'T DONE ANYTHING WRONG.
CABRINI GREEN
LOWER INCOME
HOUSING FACILITY
CHICAGO ILLINOIS
THEY CALL IT SOCIAL WELFARE BUT DAD CALLS IT A PRISON.
JOHN WASHINGTON
1955
1996
IT'S GOT BARBED WIRE LIKE A PRISON. AND THEY SHOOT YOU IF YOU TRY TO GET OUT.
NOBODY EVER GETS OUT. NOT EVEN WHEN THEY'RE DEAD.

DAD NEVER GOT OUT OF THE GREEN.
2000
HELL YES
POLICE
POLICE
2001
I CAN'T SLEEP.
IT'S NOT THE NOISE. THERE ISN'T MUCH NOISE TONIGHT.
AIR'S BETTER TONIGHT. NOT MUCH COUGHING.
DICKENS, BUT HE ALWAYS COUGHS.
PD
POLICE
937F
WHUP WHUP

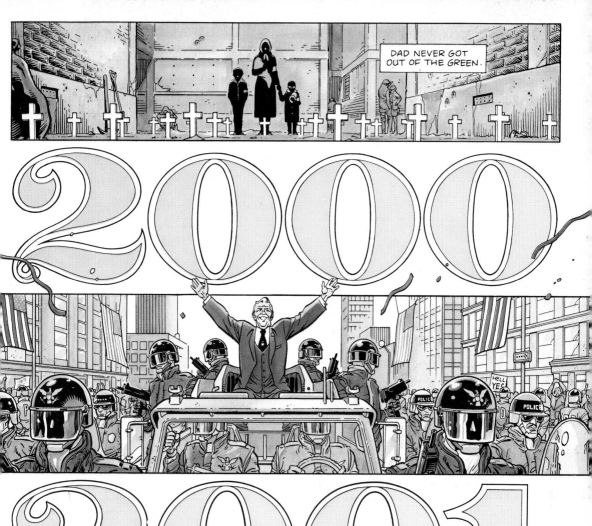

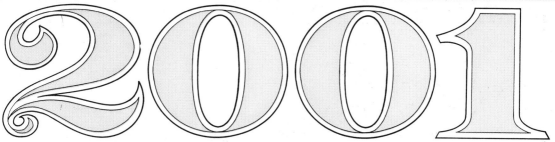

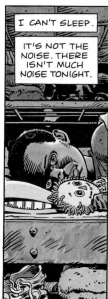

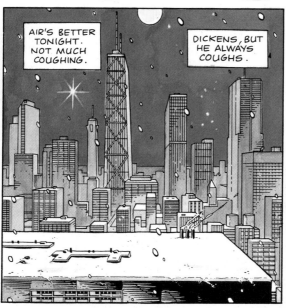

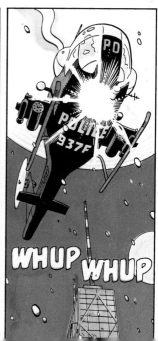

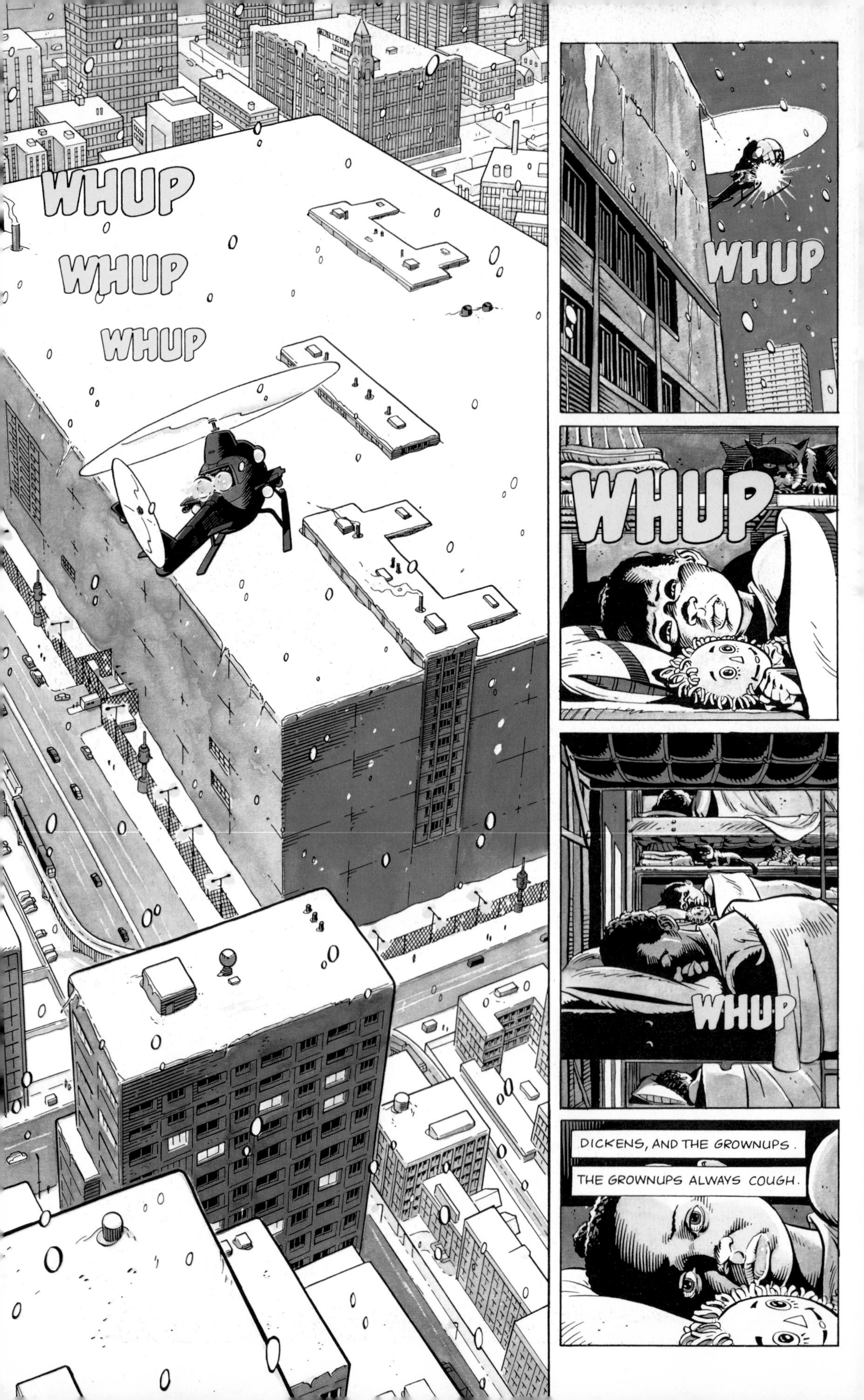
WHUP
WHUP
WHUP
WHUP
WHUP
WHUP
DICKENS, AND THE GROWNUPS.
THE GROWNUPS ALWAYS COUGH.

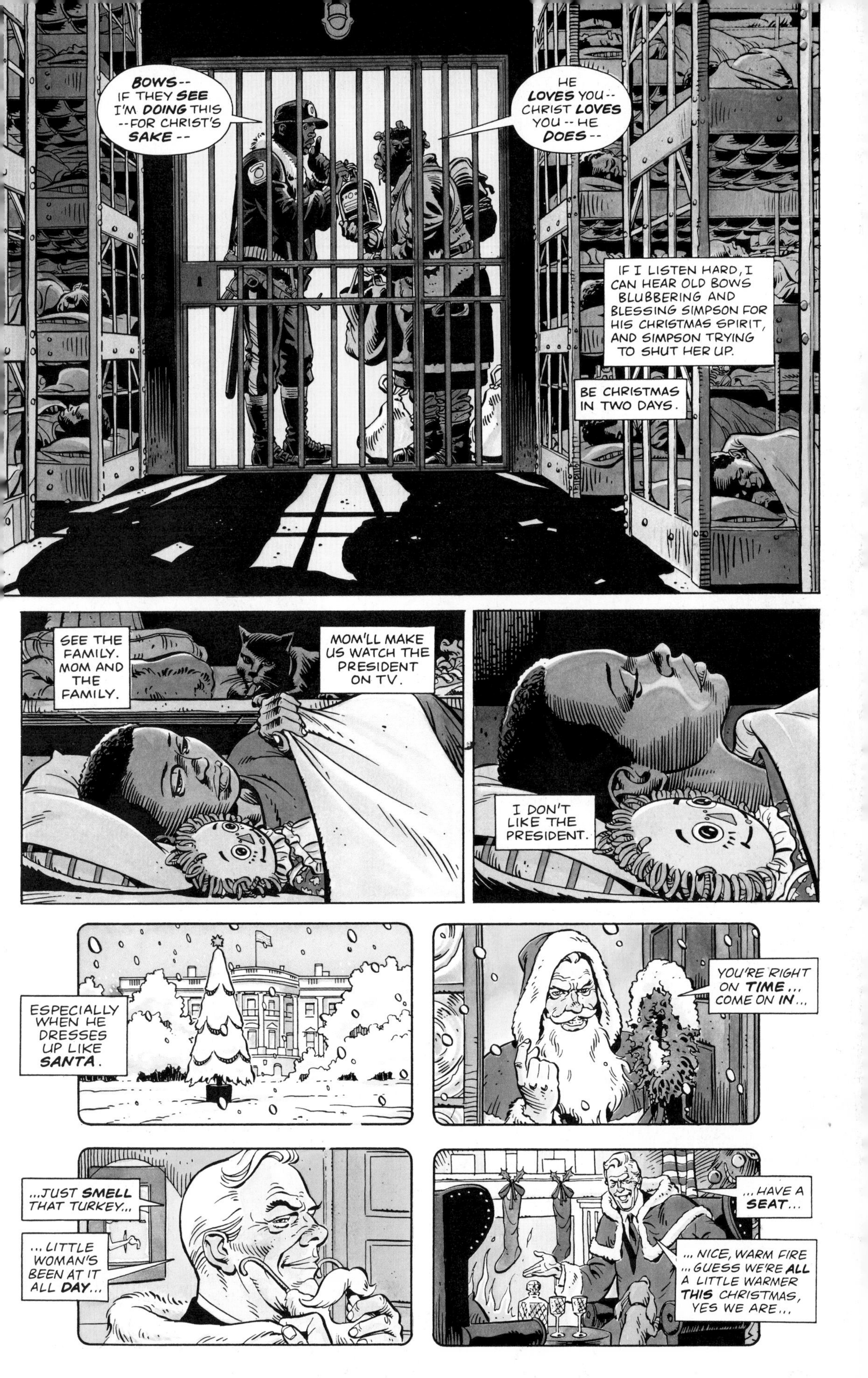
BOWS-- IF THEY SEE I'M DOING THIS --FOR CHRIST'S SAKE --
HE LOVES YOU-- CHRIST LOVES YOU -- HE DOES --
IF I LISTEN HARD, I CAN HEAR OLD BOWS BLUBBERING AND BLESSING SIMPSON FOR HIS CHRISTMAS SPIRIT, AND SIMPSON TRYING TO SHUT HER UP.
BE CHRISTMAS IN TWO DAYS.
SEE THE FAMILY. MOM AND THE FAMILY.
MOM'LL MAKE US WATCH THE PRESIDENT ON TV.
I DON'T LIKE THE PRESIDENT.
ESPECIALLY WHEN HE DRESSES UP LIKE SANTA.
YOU'RE RIGHT ON TIME... COME ON IN...
...JUST SMELL THAT TURKEY...
...LITTLE WOMAN'S BEEN AT IT ALL DAY...
...HAVE A SEAT...
...NICE, WARM FIRE ...GUESS WE'RE ALL A LITTLE WARMER THIS CHRISTMAS, YES WE ARE...

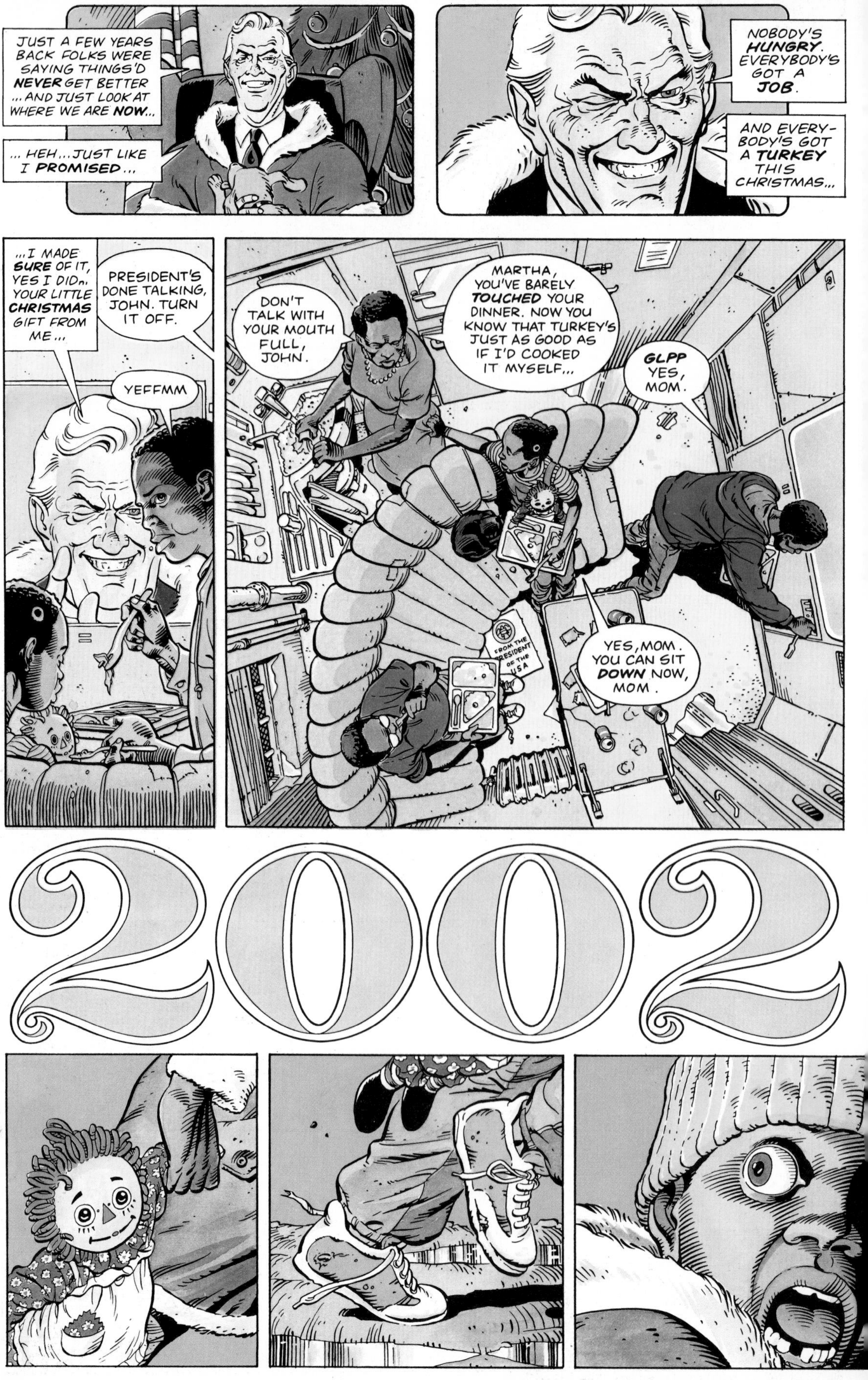
JUST A FEW YEARS BACK FOLKS WERE SAYING THINGS'D NEVER GET BETTER ...AND JUST LOOK AT WHERE WE ARE NOW...
... HEH... JUST LIKE I PROMISED...
NOBODY'S HUNGRY. EVERYBODY'S GOT A JOB.
AND EVERYBODY'S GOT A TURKEY THIS CHRISTMAS...
...I MADE SURE OF IT, YES I DID... YOUR LITTLE CHRISTMAS GIFT FROM ME...
PRESIDENT'S DONE TALKING, JOHN. TURN IT OFF.
YEFFMM
DON'T TALK WITH YOUR MOUTH FULL, JOHN.
MARTHA, YOU'VE BARELY TOUCHED YOUR DINNER. NOW YOU KNOW THAT TURKEY'S JUST AS GOOD AS IF I'D COOKED IT MYSELF...
GLPP YES, MOM.
FROM THE PRESIDENT OF THE USA
YES, MOM. YOU CAN SIT DOWN NOW, MOM.
2002

THERE'S NO **STREETS** IN THE GREEN.

NO **CARS** SO NO **STREETS**.

JUST SIDEWALKS AND SIDEWALKS AND THE **TUBE** IF YOU'RE TOO **OLD** TO **WALK** OR IF YOU'RE **CRAZY** ENOUGH TO TAKE THE **TUBE**.

SHIT

GOD LOVES

GOD LOVES

ON MY WAY TO **SCHOOL** AND **THUNDERBALLS** SEES ME **ALONE**.

DRESSED LIKE A **BOY** LIKE ALWAYS.

CRAZY TO DRESS LIKE A GIRL.

GOD LOVES

DRESS LIKE A **BOY** BUT I GUESS IT DOESN'T FOOL **THUNDERBALLS**.

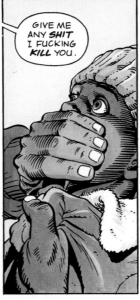

GIVE ME ANY **SHIT** I FUCKING **KILL** YOU.

I DON'T GIVE HIM ANY SHIT.

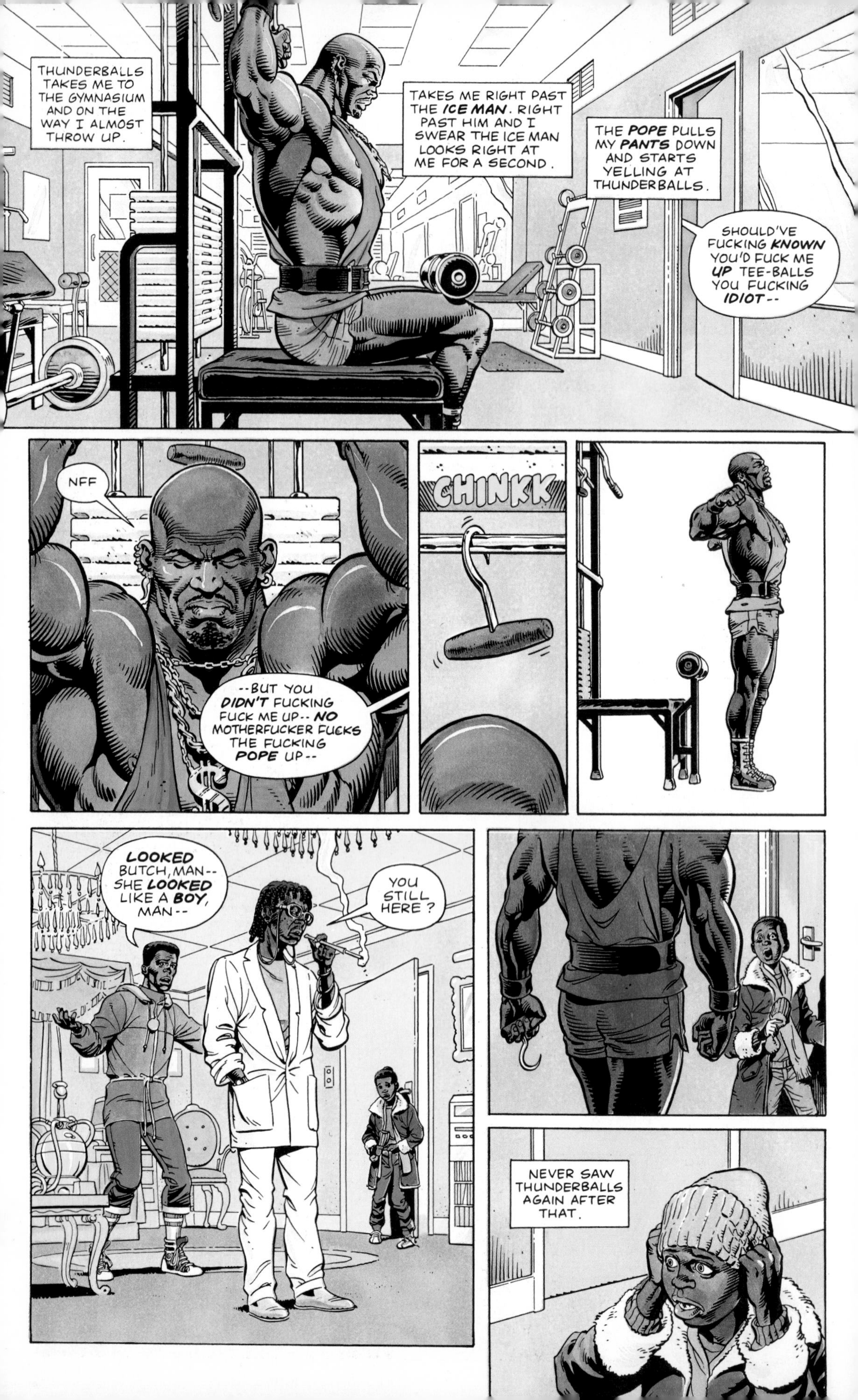
THUNDERBALLS TAKES ME TO THE GYMNASIUM AND ON THE WAY I ALMOST THROW UP.
TAKES ME RIGHT PAST THE ICE MAN. RIGHT PAST HIM AND I SWEAR THE ICE MAN LOOKS RIGHT AT ME FOR A SECOND.
THE POPE PULLS MY PANTS DOWN AND STARTS YELLING AT THUNDERBALLS.
SHOULD'VE FUCKING KNOWN YOU'D FUCK ME UP TEE-BALLS YOU FUCKING IDIOT--
NFF
--BUT YOU DIDN'T FUCKING FUCK ME UP-- NO MOTHERFUCKER FUCKS THE FUCKING POPE UP--
CHINKK
LOOKED BUTCH, MAN-- SHE LOOKED LIKE A BOY, MAN--
YOU STILL HERE?
NEVER SAW THUNDERBALLS AGAIN AFTER THAT.

2007

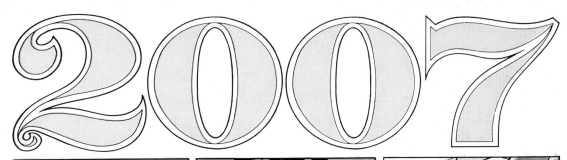

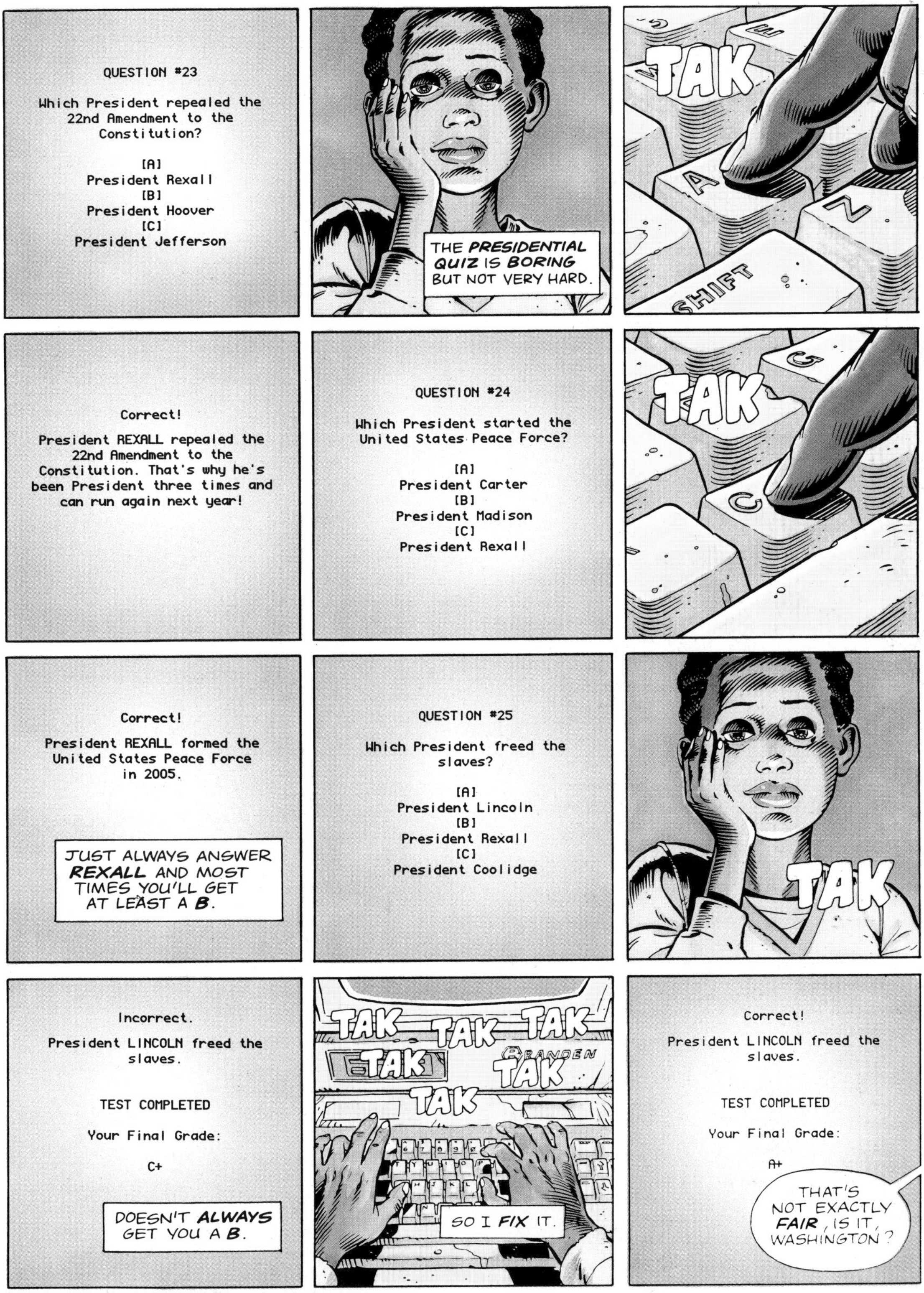
QUESTION #23
Which President repealed the 22nd Amendment to the Constitution?
[A]
President Rexall
[B]
President Hoover
[C]
President Jefferson
THE PRESIDENTIAL QUIZ IS BORING BUT NOT VERY HARD.
TAK
Correct!
President REXALL repealed the 22nd Amendment to the Constitution. That's why he's been President three times and can run again next year!
QUESTION #24
Which President started the United States Peace Force?
[A]
President Carter
[B]
President Madison
[C]
President Rexall
TAK
Correct!
President REXALL formed the United States Peace Force in 2005.
JUST ALWAYS ANSWER REXALL AND MOST TIMES YOU'LL GET AT LEAST A B.
QUESTION #25
Which President freed the slaves?
[A]
President Lincoln
[B]
President Rexall
[C]
President Coolidge
TAK
Incorrect.
President LINCOLN freed the slaves.
TEST COMPLETED
Your Final Grade:
C+
DOESN'T ALWAYS GET YOU A B.
TAK TAK TAK
TAK TAK
TAK
SO I FIX IT.
Correct!
President LINCOLN freed the slaves.
TEST COMPLETED
Your Final Grade:
A+
THAT'S NOT EXACTLY FAIR, IS IT, WASHINGTON?

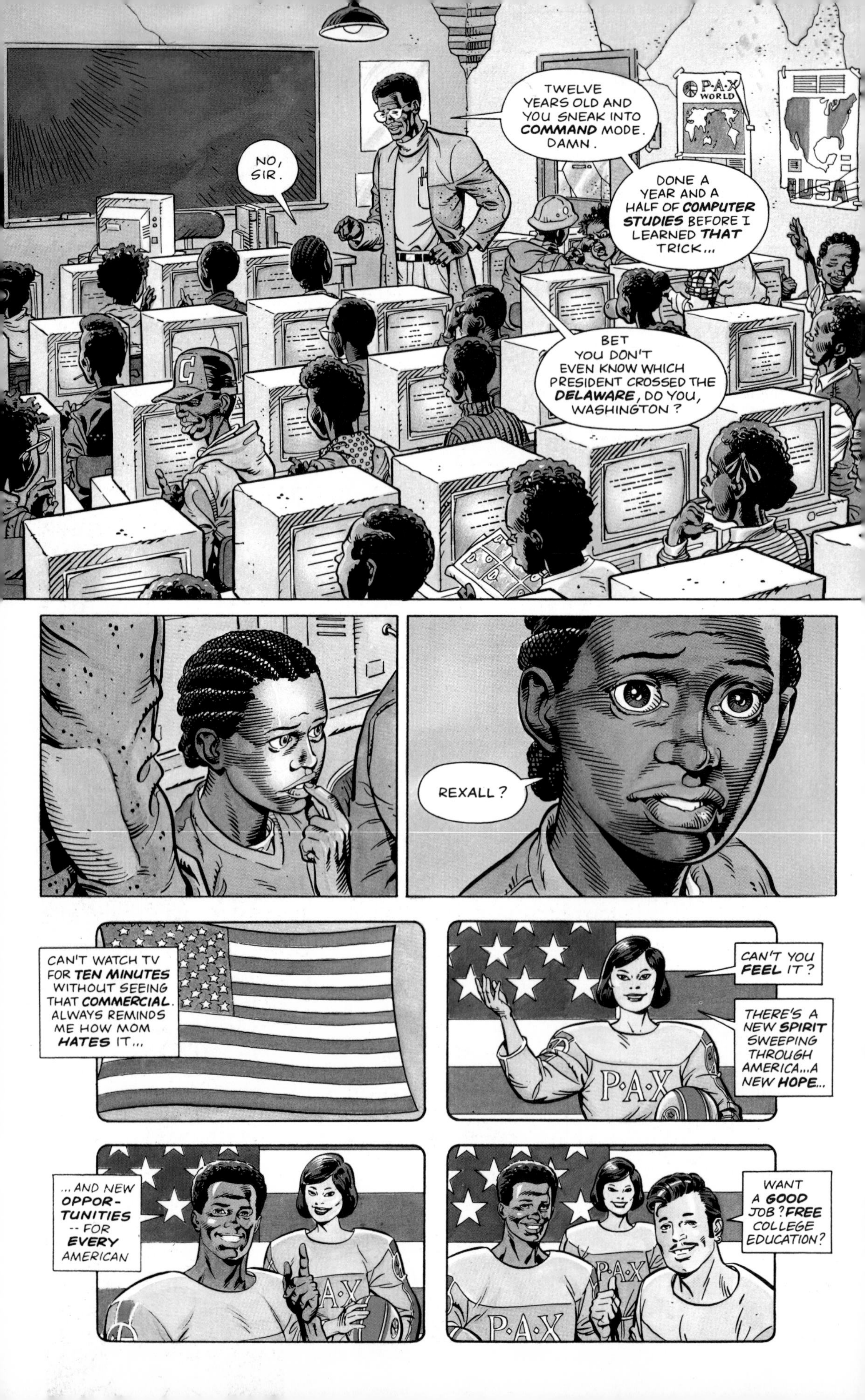

TWELVE YEARS OLD AND YOU SNEAK INTO COMMAND MODE. DAMN.
NO, SIR.
DONE A YEAR AND A HALF OF COMPUTER STUDIES BEFORE I LEARNED THAT TRICK...
BET YOU DON'T EVEN KNOW WHICH PRESIDENT CROSSED THE DELAWARE, DO YOU, WASHINGTON?
P·A·X WORLD
USA
REXALL?
CAN'T WATCH TV FOR TEN MINUTES WITHOUT SEEING THAT COMMERCIAL. ALWAYS REMINDS ME HOW MOM HATES IT...
CAN'T YOU FEEL IT?
THERE'S A NEW SPIRIT SWEEPING THROUGH AMERICA...A NEW HOPE...
P·A·X
...AND NEW OPPOR-TUNITIES -- FOR EVERY AMERICAN
WANT A GOOD JOB? FREE COLLEGE EDUCATION?

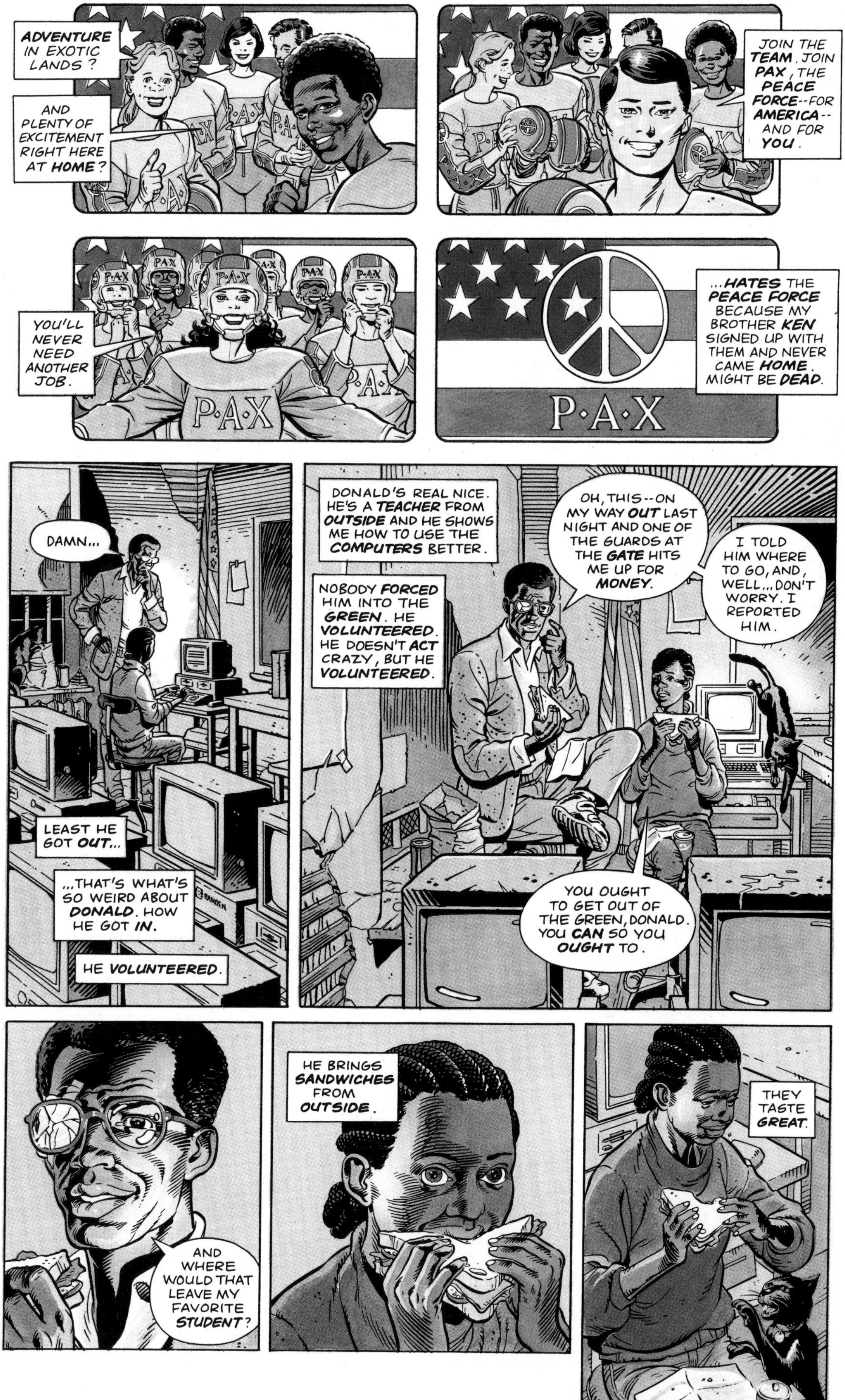
ADVENTURE IN EXOTIC LANDS?
AND PLENTY OF EXCITEMENT RIGHT HERE AT HOME?
JOIN THE TEAM. JOIN PAX, THE PEACE FORCE--FOR AMERICA--AND FOR YOU.
P·A·X
YOU'LL NEVER NEED ANOTHER JOB.
P·A·X
...HATES THE PEACE FORCE BECAUSE MY BROTHER KEN SIGNED UP WITH THEM AND NEVER CAME HOME. MIGHT BE DEAD.
P·A·X
DAMN...
LEAST HE GOT OUT...
...THAT'S WHAT'S SO WEIRD ABOUT DONALD. HOW HE GOT IN.
HE VOLUNTEERED.
DONALD'S REAL NICE. HE'S A TEACHER FROM OUTSIDE AND HE SHOWS ME HOW TO USE THE COMPUTERS BETTER.
NOBODY FORCED HIM INTO THE GREEN. HE VOLUNTEERED. HE DOESN'T ACT CRAZY, BUT HE VOLUNTEERED.
OH, THIS--ON MY WAY OUT LAST NIGHT AND ONE OF THE GUARDS AT THE GATE HITS ME UP FOR MONEY.
I TOLD HIM WHERE TO GO, AND, WELL... DON'T WORRY. I REPORTED HIM.
YOU OUGHT TO GET OUT OF THE GREEN, DONALD. YOU CAN SO YOU OUGHT TO.
AND WHERE WOULD THAT LEAVE MY FAVORITE STUDENT?
HE BRINGS SANDWICHES FROM OUTSIDE.
THEY TASTE GREAT.

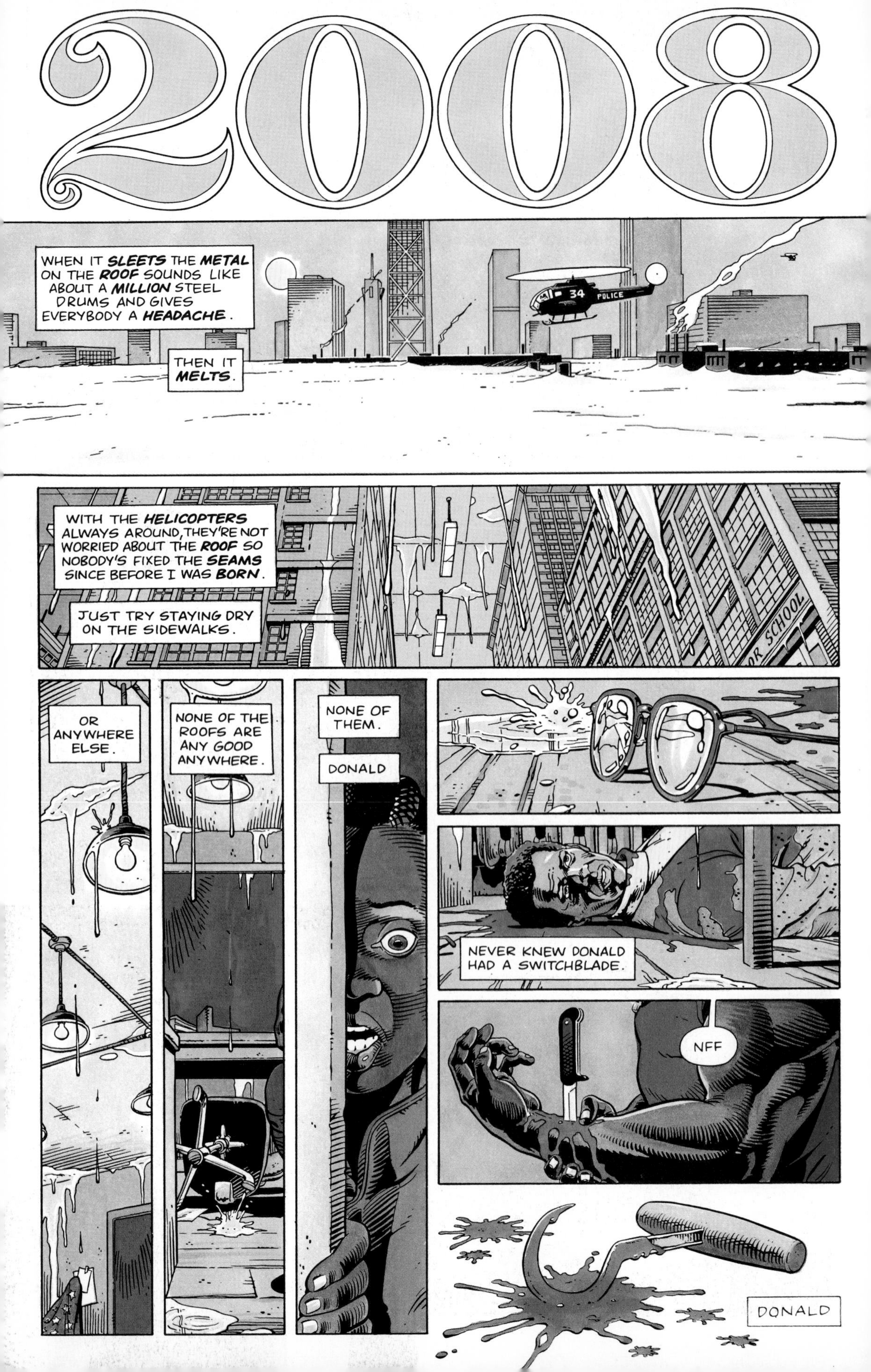
2008
WHEN IT SLEETS THE METAL ON THE ROOF SOUNDS LIKE ABOUT A MILLION STEEL DRUMS AND GIVES EVERYBODY A HEADACHE.
THEN IT MELTS.
34 POLICE
WITH THE HELICOPTERS ALWAYS AROUND, THEY'RE NOT WORRIED ABOUT THE ROOF SO NOBODY'S FIXED THE SEAMS SINCE BEFORE I WAS BORN.
JUST TRY STAYING DRY ON THE SIDEWALKS.
OR SCHOOL
OR ANYWHERE ELSE.
NONE OF THE ROOFS ARE ANY GOOD ANYWHERE.
NONE OF THEM.
DONALD
NEVER KNEW DONALD HAD A SWITCHBLADE.
NFF
DONALD

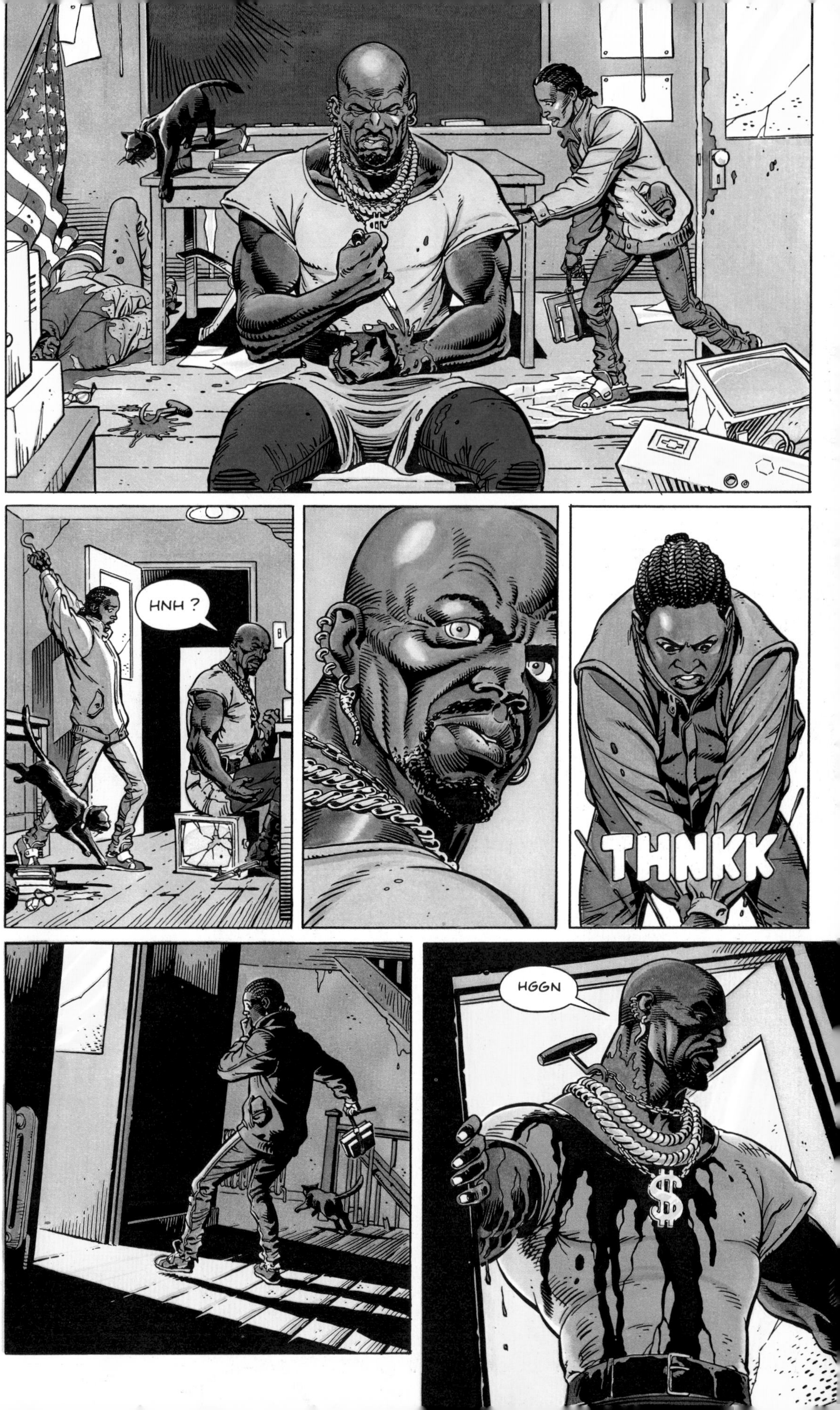
HNH ?
THNKK
HGGN

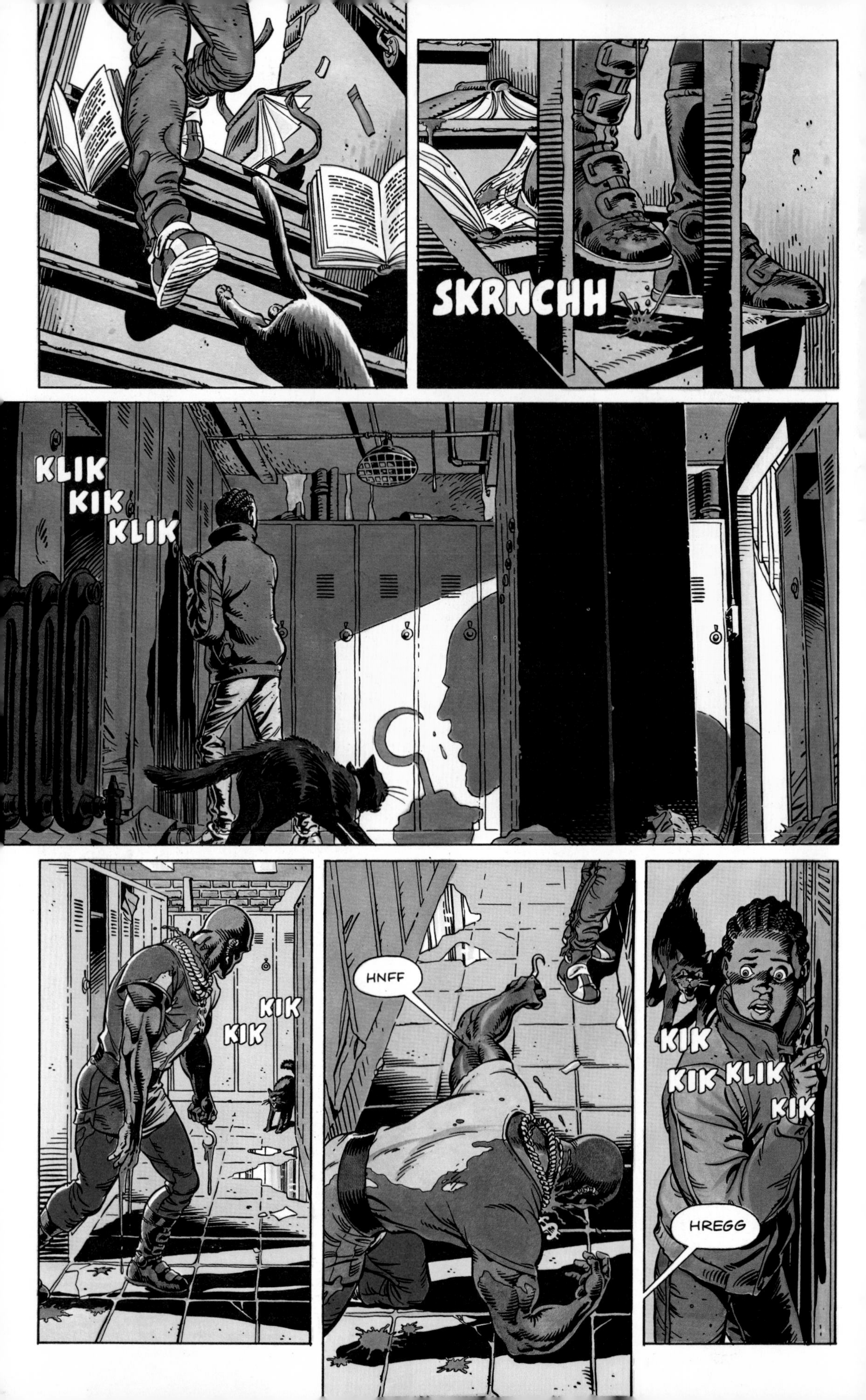
SKRNCHH
KLIK
KIK
KLIK
KIK
KIK
HNFF
KIK
KIK KLIK
KIK
HREGG

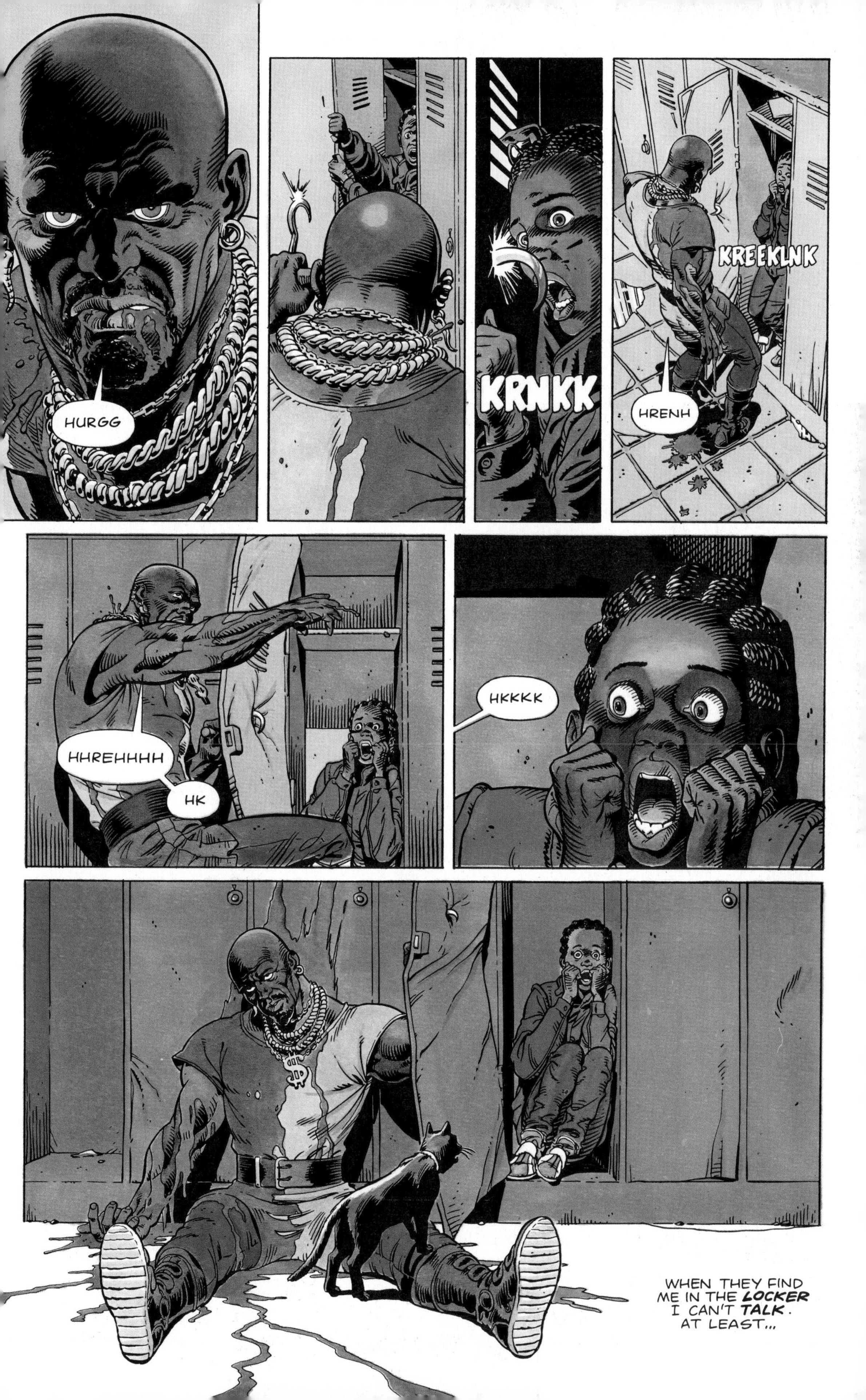

HURGG
KRNKK
KREEKLNK
HRENH
HHREHHHH
HK
HKKKK
WHEN THEY FIND ME IN THE LOCKER I CAN'T TALK. AT LEAST...

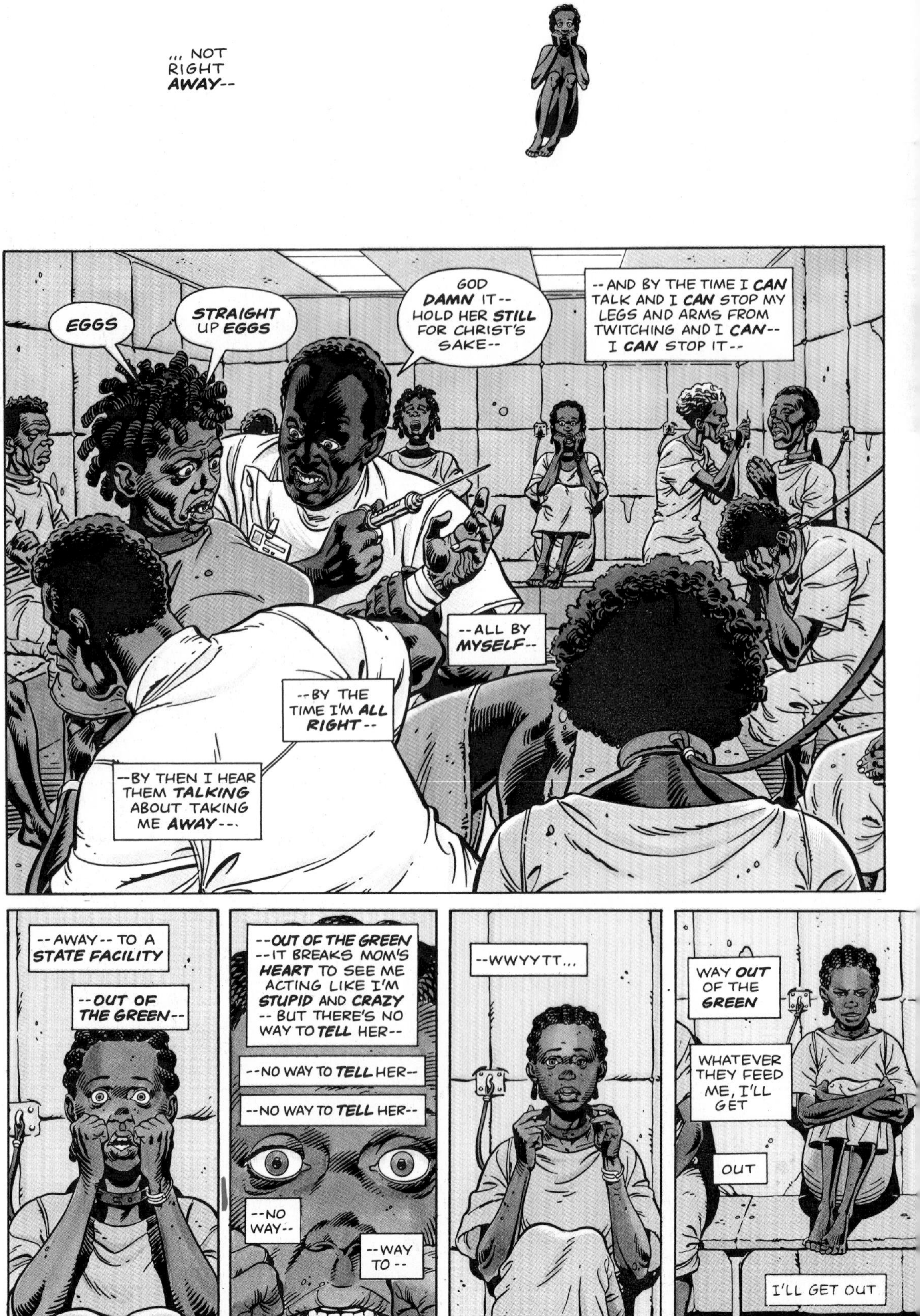

... NOT RIGHT AWAY--
EGGS
STRAIGHT UP EGGS
GOD DAMN IT-- HOLD HER STILL FOR CHRIST'S SAKE--
--AND BY THE TIME I CAN TALK AND I CAN STOP MY LEGS AND ARMS FROM TWITCHING AND I CAN-- I CAN STOP IT--
--ALL BY MYSELF--
--BY THE TIME I'M ALL RIGHT--
--BY THEN I HEAR THEM TALKING ABOUT TAKING ME AWAY--
--AWAY-- TO A STATE FACILITY
--OUT OF THE GREEN--
--OUT OF THE GREEN --IT BREAKS MOM'S HEART TO SEE ME ACTING LIKE I'M STUPID AND CRAZY -- BUT THERE'S NO WAY TO TELL HER--
--NO WAY TO TELL HER--
--NO WAY TO TELL HER--
--NO WAY--
--WAY TO--
--WWYYTT...
WAY OUT OF THE GREEN
WHATEVER THEY FEED ME, I'LL GET
OUT
I'LL GET OUT

2009

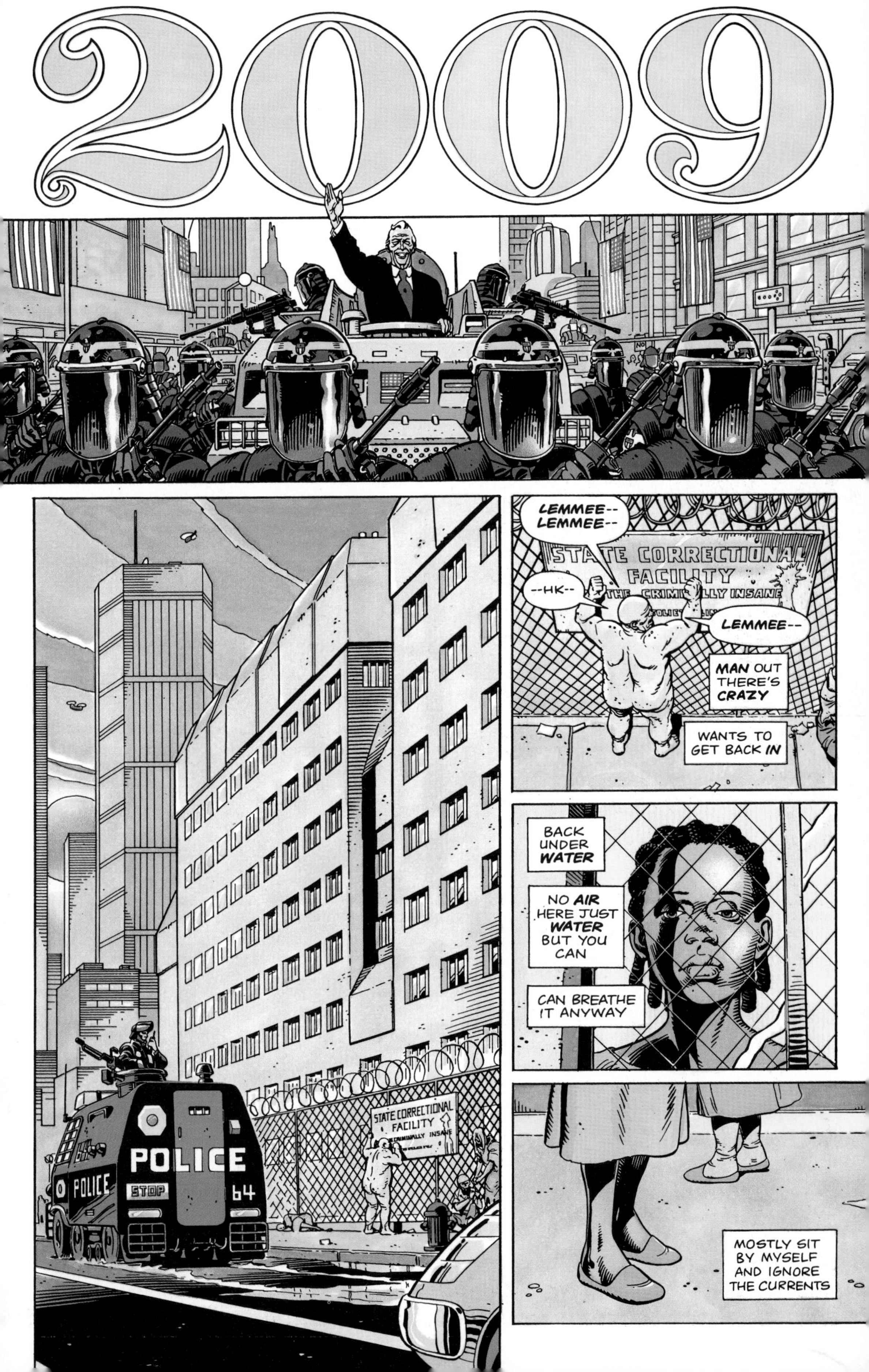

POLICE
POLICE
STOP
64
STATE CORRECTIONAL FACILITY
LEMMEE--
LEMMEE--
STATE CORRECTIONAL FACILITY
--HK--
LEMMEE--
MAN OUT THERE'S CRAZY
WANTS TO GET BACK IN
BACK UNDER WATER
NO AIR HERE JUST WATER BUT YOU CAN
CAN BREATHE IT ANYWAY
MOSTLY SIT BY MYSELF AND IGNORE THE CURRENTS

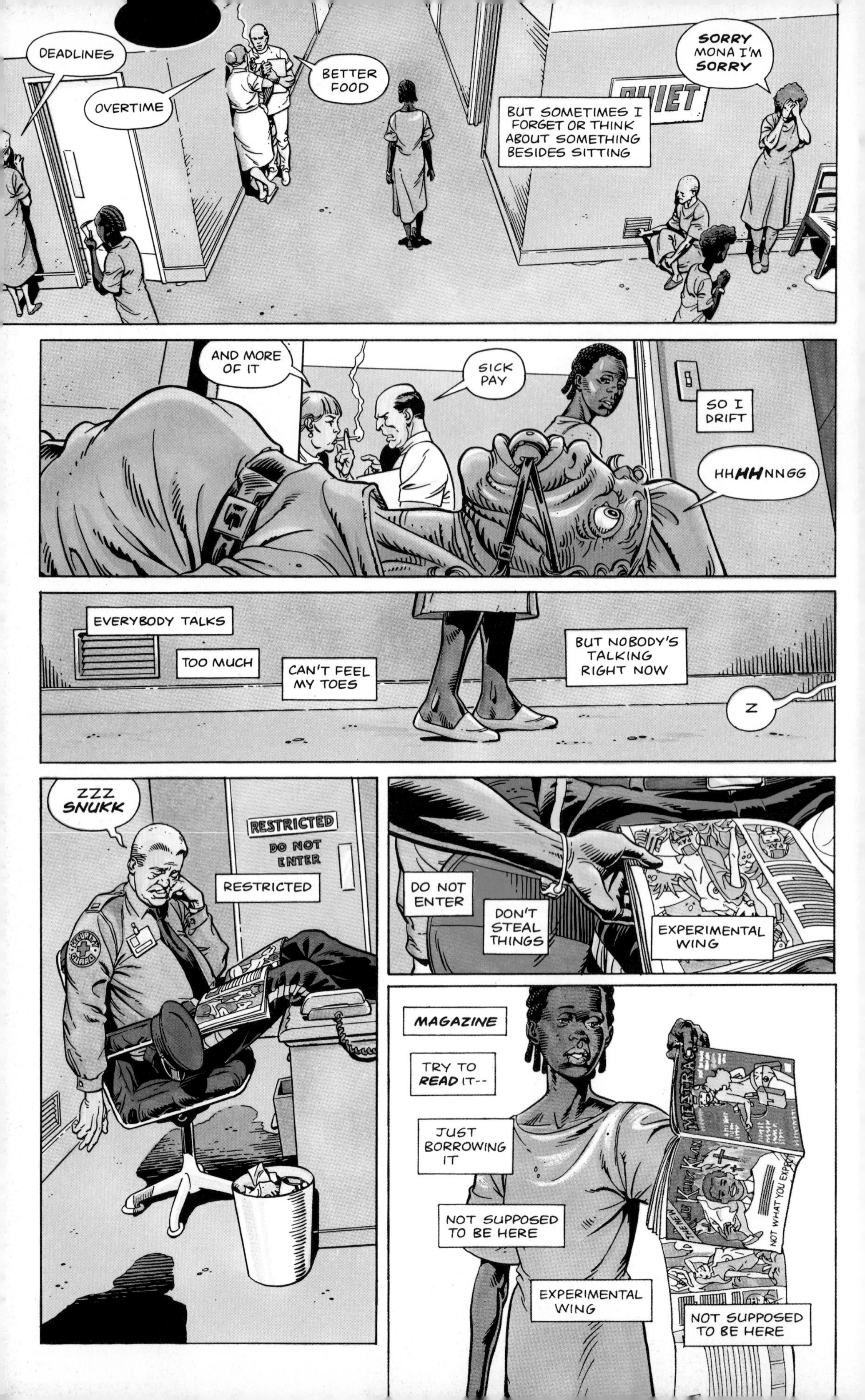
DEADLINES
OVERTIME
BETTER FOOD
SORRY MONA I'M SORRY
BUT SOMETIMES I FORGET OR THINK ABOUT SOMETHING BESIDES SITTING
AND MORE OF IT
SICK PAY
SO I DRIFT
HHHHNNGG
EVERYBODY TALKS
TOO MUCH
CAN'T FEEL MY TOES
BUT NOBODY'S TALKING RIGHT NOW
Z
ZZZ SNUKK
RESTRICTED DO NOT ENTER
RESTRICTED
DO NOT ENTER
DON'T STEAL THINGS
EXPERIMENTAL WING
MAGAZINE
TRY TO READ IT--
JUST BORROWING IT
NOT SUPPOSED TO BE HERE
EXPERIMENTAL WING
NOT SUPPOSED TO BE HERE

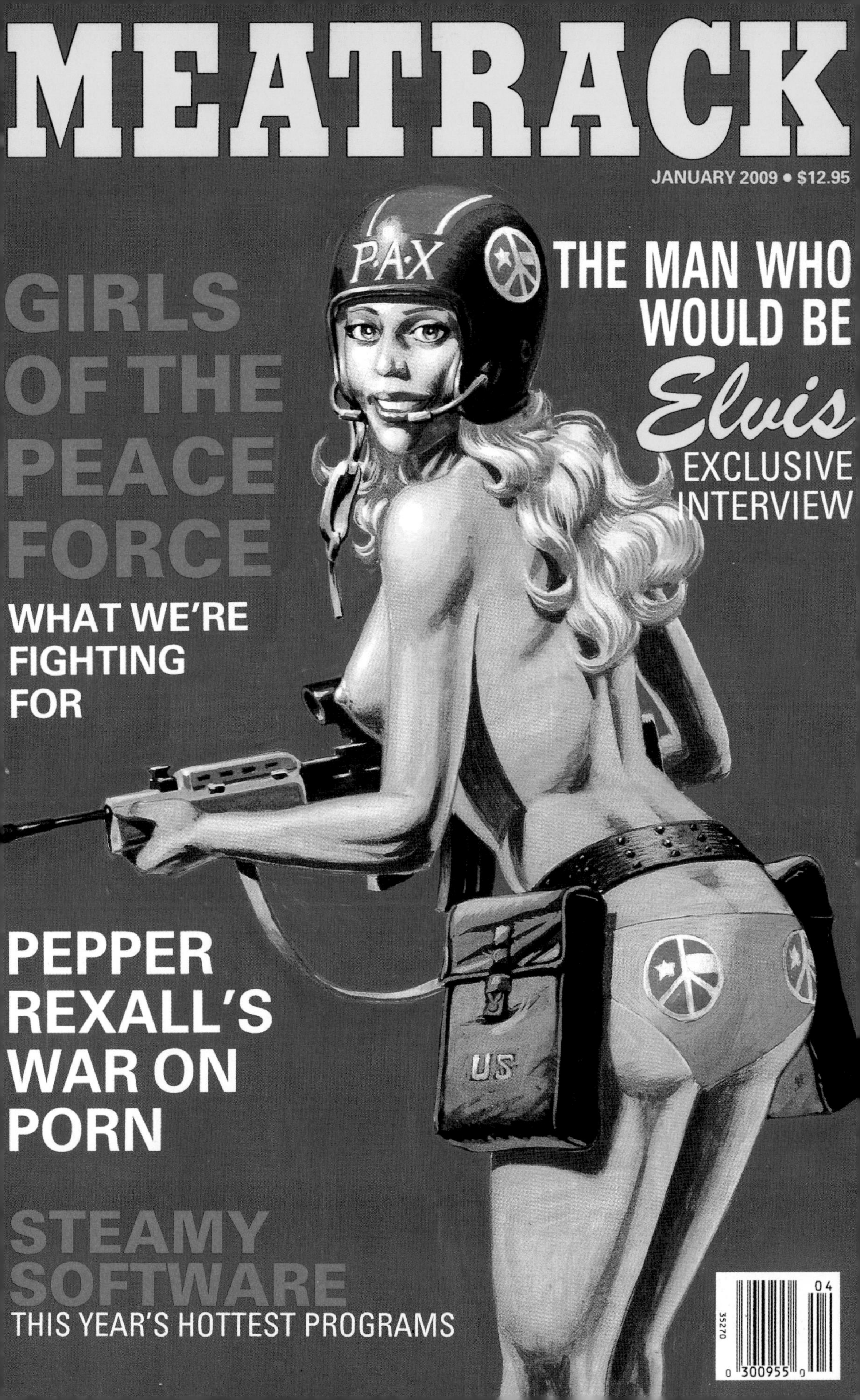

MEATRACK

JANUARY 2009 • $12.95

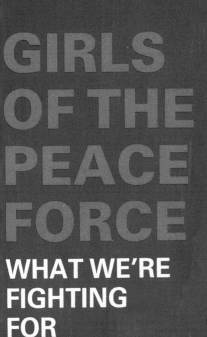

GIRLS
OF THE
PEACE
FORCE

WHAT WE'RE
FIGHTING
FOR

THE MAN WHO
WOULD BE
Elvis
EXCLUSIVE
INTERVIEW

PEPPER
REXALL'S
WAR ON
PORN

STEAMY
SOFTWARE
THIS YEAR'S HOTTEST PROGRAMS

0 300955

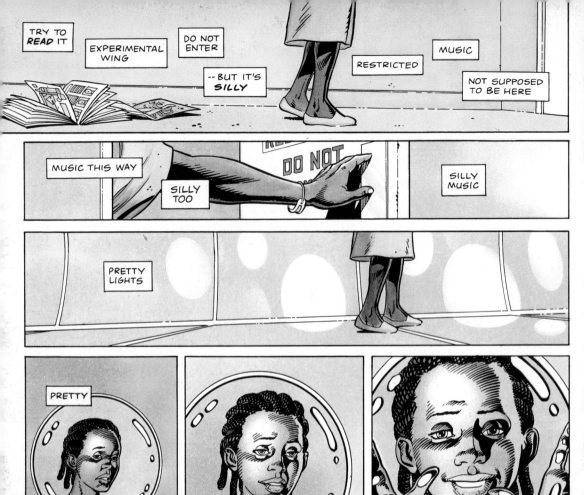

TRY TO **READ** IT

EXPERIMENTAL WING

DO NOT ENTER

-- BUT IT'S **SILLY**

RESTRICTED

MUSIC

NOT SUPPOSED TO BE HERE

MUSIC THIS WAY

SILLY TOO

SILLY MUSIC

PRETTY LIGHTS

PRETTY

RAGGEDY ANN

NOT RAGGEDY ANN

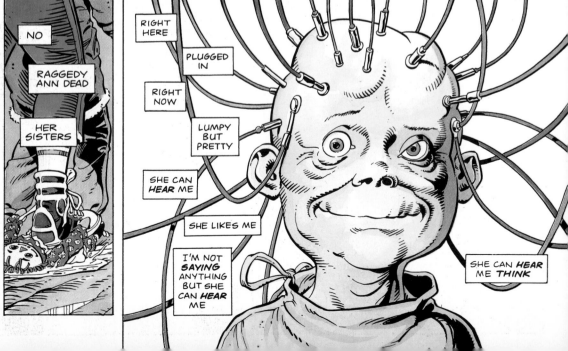

NO

RAGGEDY ANN DEAD

HER SISTERS

RIGHT HERE

PLUGGED IN

RIGHT NOW

LUMPY BUT PRETTY

SHE CAN **HEAR** ME

SHE LIKES ME

I'M NOT **SAYING** ANYTHING BUT SHE CAN **HEAR** ME

SHE CAN **HEAR** ME **THINK**

JESUS CHRIST--
--MEKKELSON I'LL HAVE YOUR ASS FOR THIS...
GOD DAMN IT
SHE CAN HEAR ME THINK
THEY'RE MEAN
BUT THE MEANEST
PRETTY
IS WHEN THEY THROW ME OUT

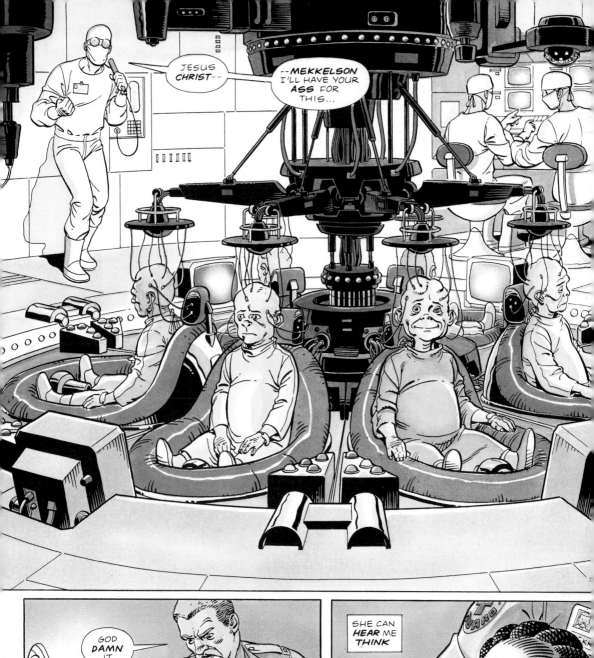

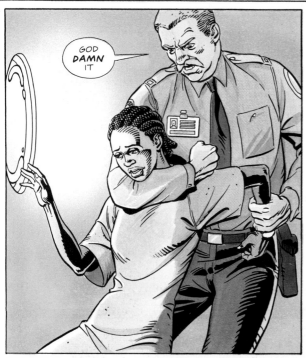

SDI Disaster

It was aimed at Libya — but the laser cannon struck the oil-rich desert of Saudi Arabia. In the greatest environmental disaster of the century, the desert is ablaze. The sky is black over the Middle East — and our closest ally may now be America's deadliest enemy.
International: Page 34

Ally turned enemy: King Xassad

A skyrocketing deficit and plummeting stock market raise new doubts about Rexonomics

Are The Good Times Over?

The Wall Street panic continues. Experts talk of a collapse of the world economy — and blame the economic policies of a presidency already plagued by growing civil unrest and condemnation by the United Nations. Is Rexall's reign finished? How bad will it get? Will we recover? **National Affairs: Page 18**

Death Clouds

The flames are a quarter mile high, a blazing field the size of Connecticut. But environmentalists warn that the real danger lies in the jet black smoke — predicting death in the many thousands worldwide as massive lethal clouds circle the earth.
Environment: Page 53

This smoke will bring death to thousands, experts say

Apache Warlord

On the Warpath

Two years ago his people suffered from unspeakable poverty and an 89% alcoholism rate. The youthful, charismatic Chief Redfeather has galvanised Apache cultural pride. But can he fulfill his promise to make the Apache Nation economically self-sufficient? **Nation: Page 20**

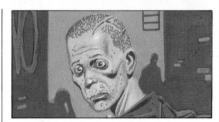

Left behind: America's mentally ill

Out in the Cold

Economic belt tightening is roughest on those who can't vote — an estimated 200,000 patients have been kicked out of U.S. mental institutions following recent budget cuts. How will they survive? THISWEEK looks at the most pathetic victims of hard times. **Lifestyle: Page 87**

National Affairs

International

Environment

Litigation

Science

Lifestyle

Departments

Cover: *Illustration by Ron Cull — THISWEEK*

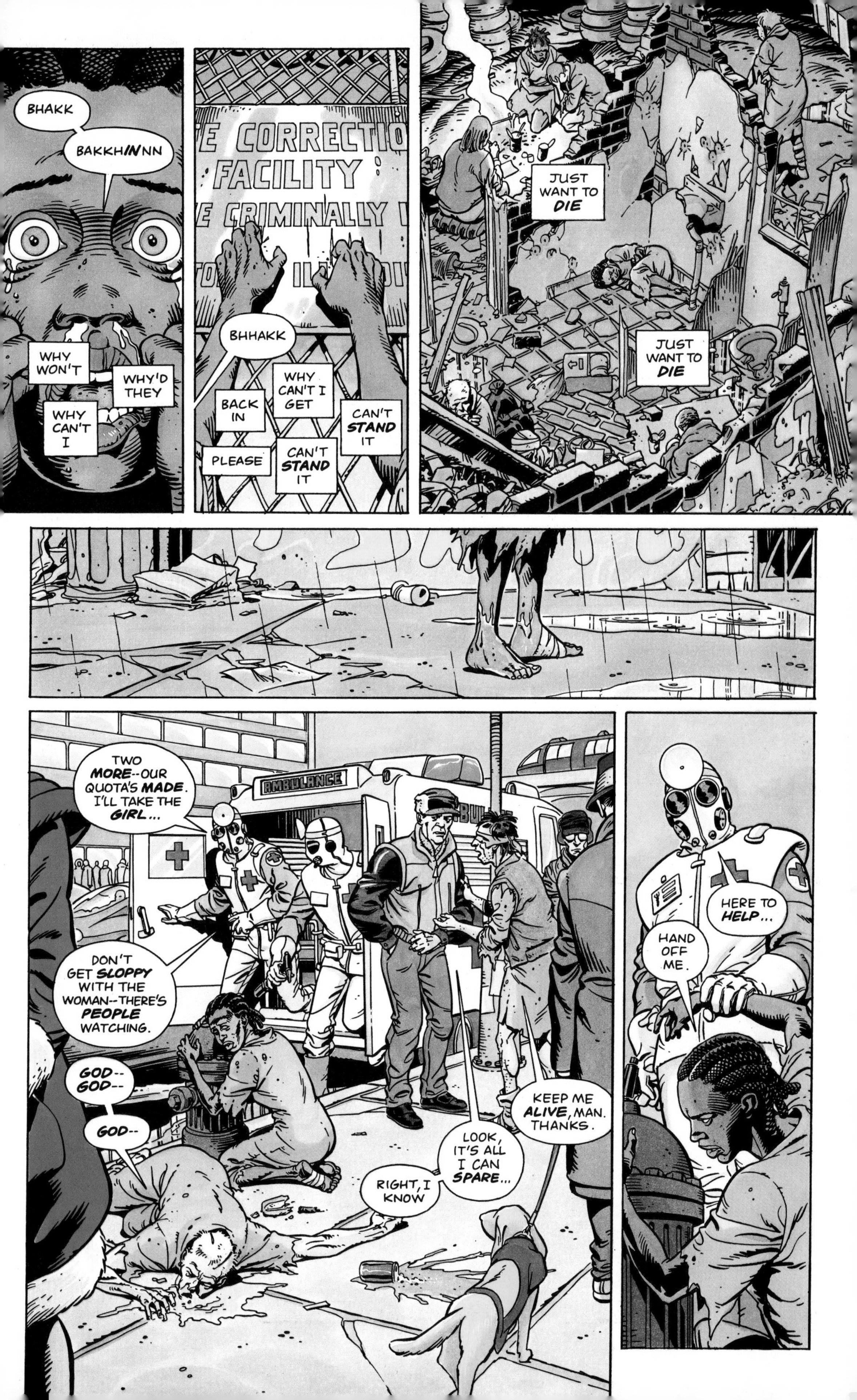
BHAKK
BAKKHINNN
WHY WON'T
WHY'D THEY
WHY CAN'T I
E CORRECTIO
FACILITY
E CRIMINALLY
BHHAKK
BACK IN
WHY CAN'T I GET
CAN'T STAND IT
PLEASE
CAN'T STAND IT
JUST WANT TO DIE
JUST WANT TO DIE
AMBULANCE
TWO MORE--OUR QUOTA'S MADE. I'LL TAKE THE GIRL...
DON'T GET SLOPPY WITH THE WOMAN--THERE'S PEOPLE WATCHING.
GOD-- GOD--
GOD--
KEEP ME ALIVE, MAN. THANKS.
LOOK, IT'S ALL I CAN SPARE...
RIGHT, I KNOW
HERE TO HELP...
HAND OFF ME.

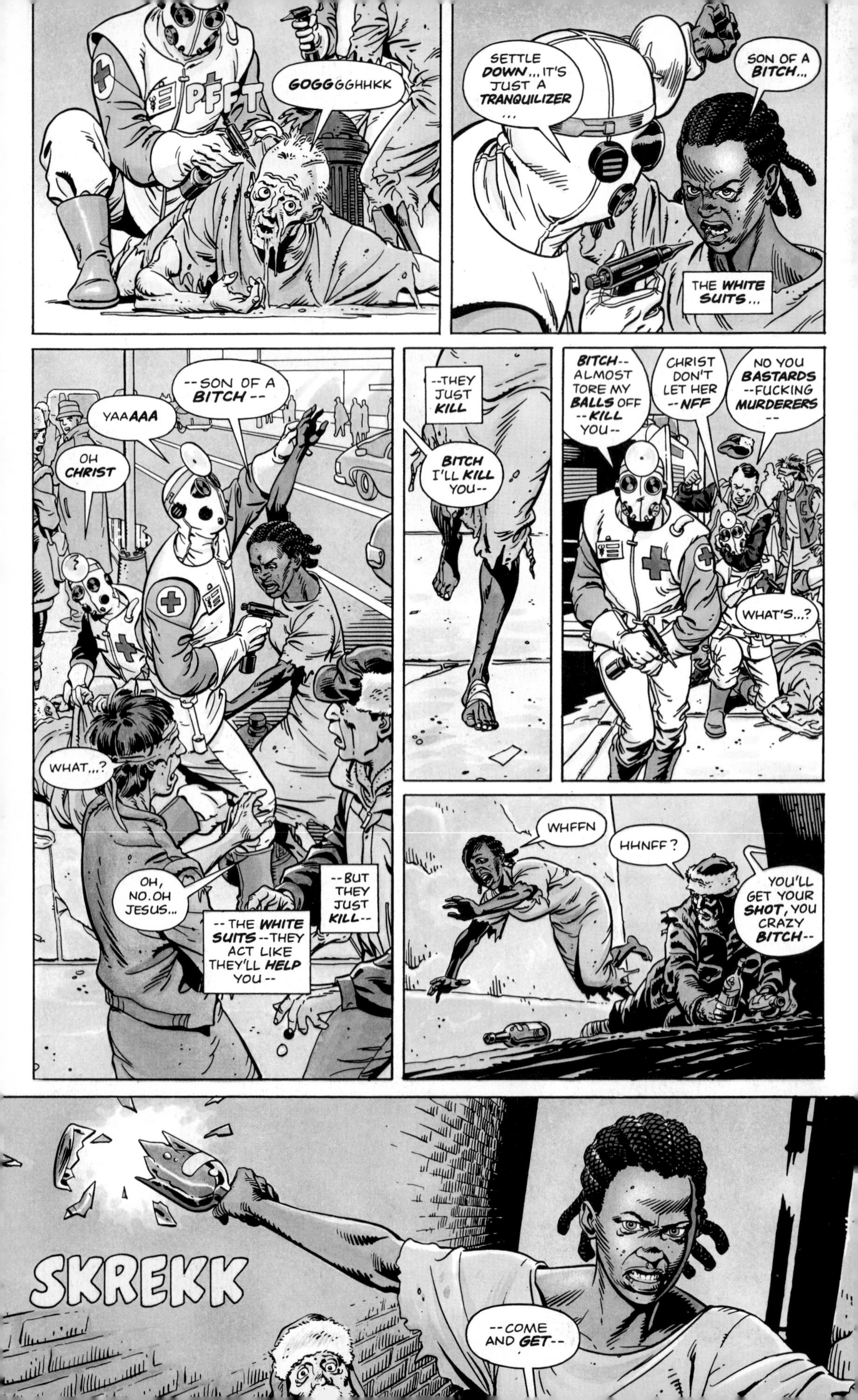
PFFT
GOGGGGHHKK
SETTLE DOWN... IT'S JUST A TRANQUILIZER ...
SON OF A BITCH...
THE WHITE SUITS...
YAAAAA
--SON OF A BITCH--
OH CHRIST
WHAT...?
OH, NO.OH JESUS...
--THE WHITE SUITS--THEY ACT LIKE THEY'LL HELP YOU--
--BUT THEY JUST KILL--
--THEY JUST KILL
BITCH I'LL KILL YOU--
BITCH--ALMOST TORE MY BALLS OFF --KILL YOU--
CHRIST DON'T LET HER --NFF
NO YOU BASTARDS --FUCKING MURDERERS --
WHAT'S...?
WHFFN
HHNFF?
YOU'LL GET YOUR SHOT, YOU CRAZY BITCH--
SKREKK
--COME AND GET--

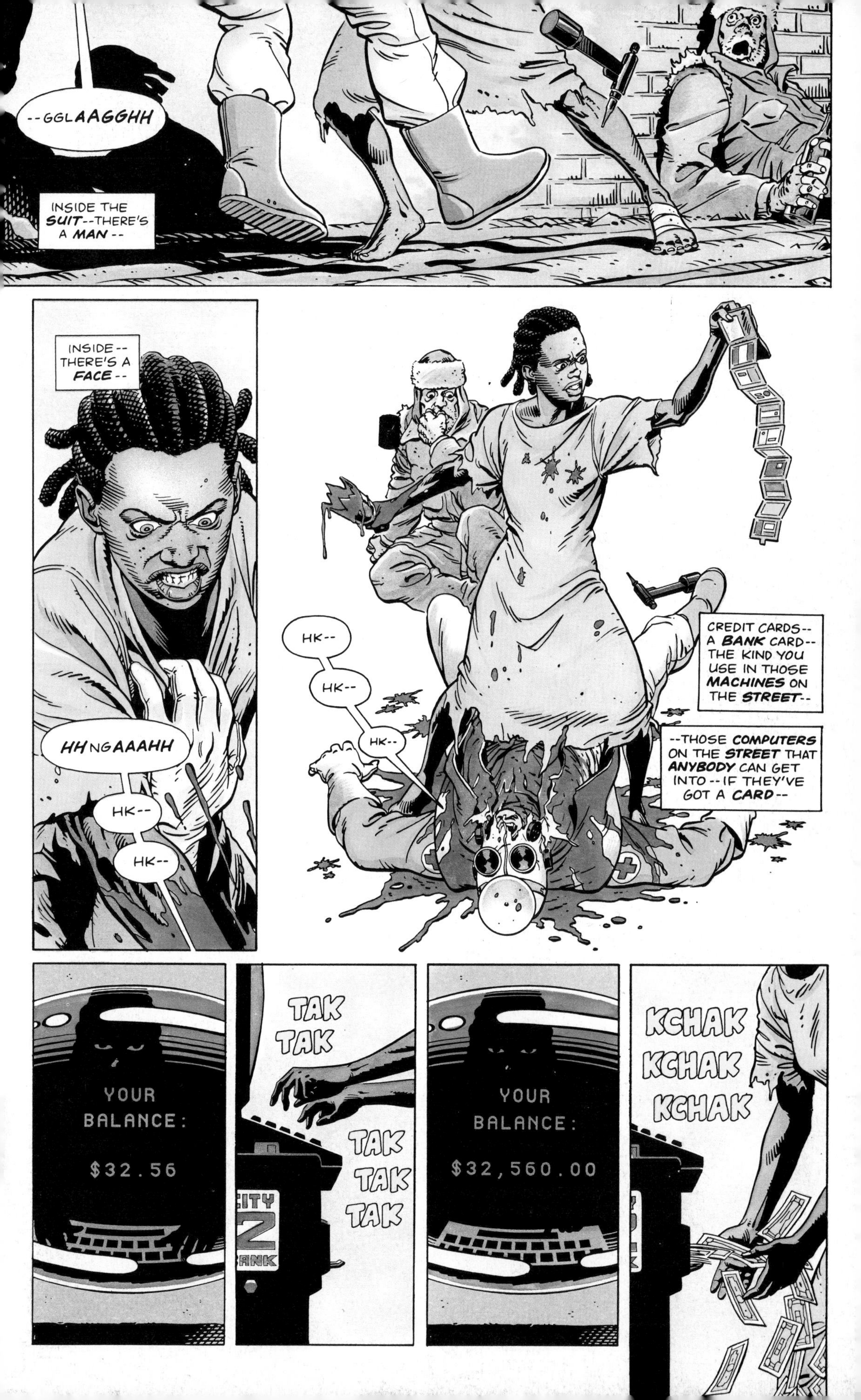
--GGLAAGGHH--
INSIDE THE SUIT--THERE'S A MAN--
INSIDE--THERE'S A FACE--
HHNGAAAHH
HK--
HK--
HK--
HK--
HK--
CREDIT CARDS--A BANK CARD--THE KIND YOU USE IN THOSE MACHINES ON THE STREET--
--THOSE COMPUTERS ON THE STREET THAT ANYBODY CAN GET INTO--IF THEY'VE GOT A CARD--
YOUR BALANCE: $32.56
TAK TAK
TAK TAK TAK
CITY 2 BANK
YOUR BALANCE: $32,560.00
KCHAK KCHAK KCHAK

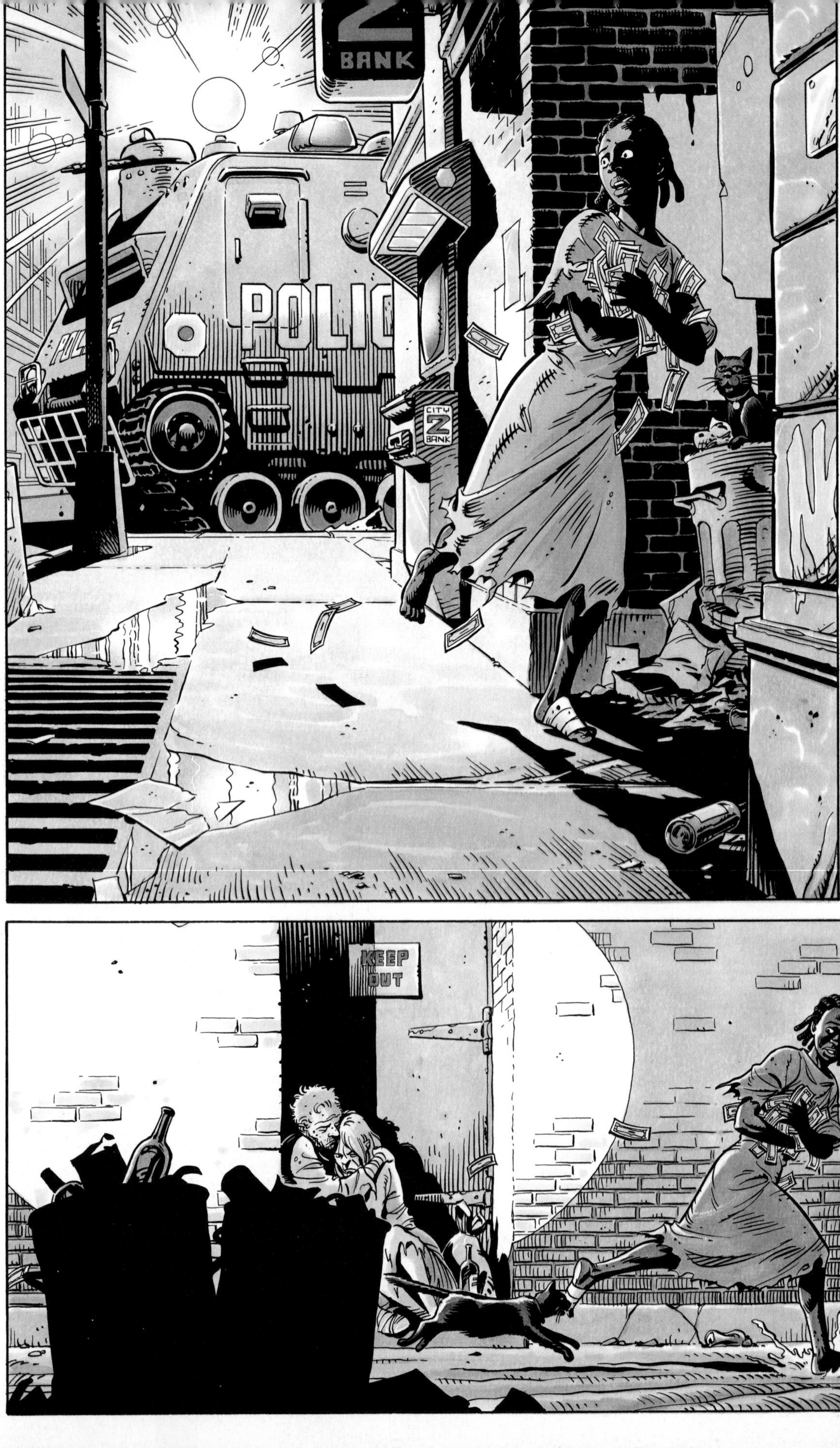
BANK
POLIC
CITY Z BANK
KEEP OUT

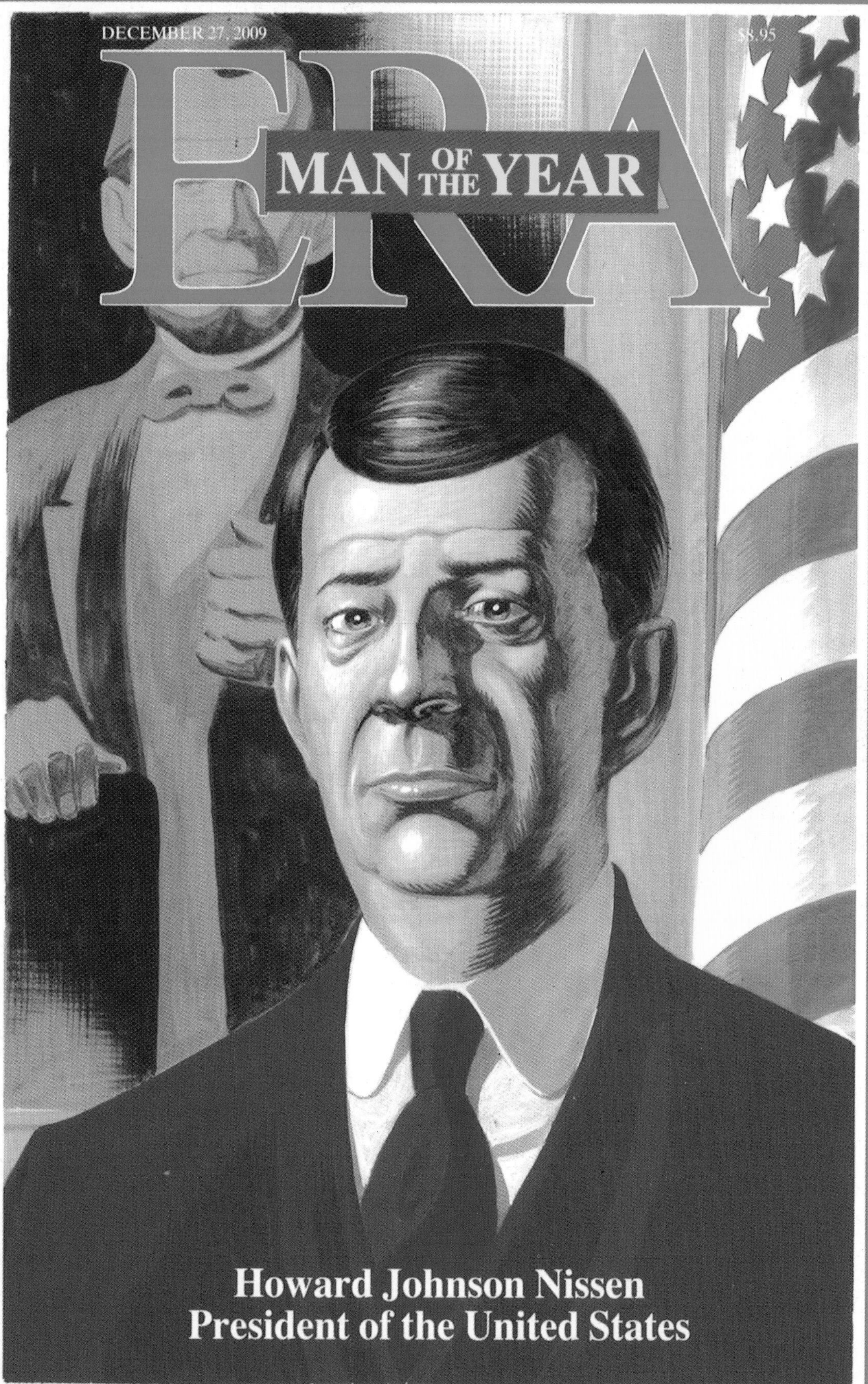
DECEMBER 27, 2009
$8.95
ERA
MAN OF THE YEAR
Howard Johnson Nissen
President of the United States

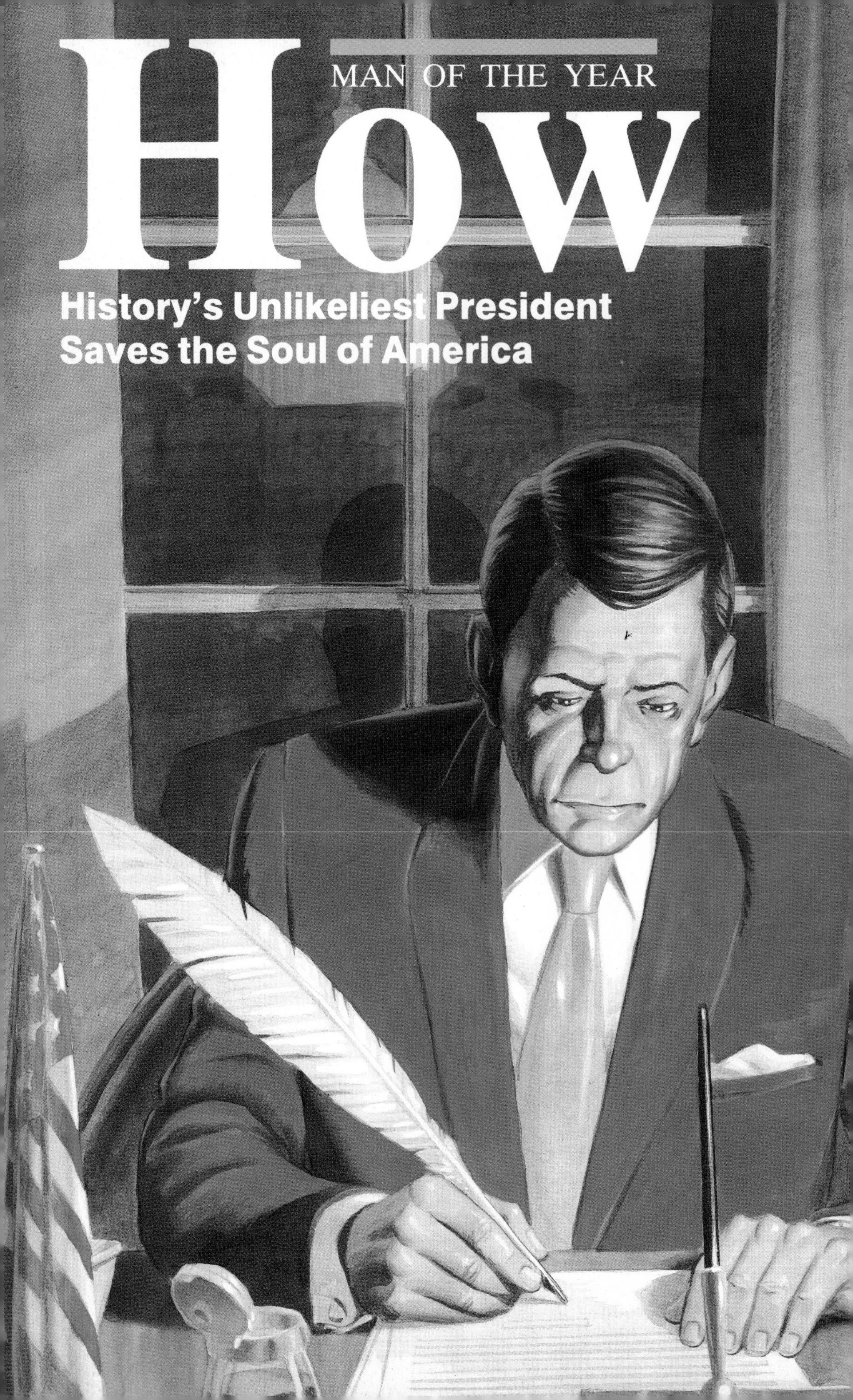
MAN OF THE YEAR
How
History's Unlikeliest President
Saves the Soul of America

May 5, 2009: A Saudi Arabian firebomb reduces the White House to a blazing shell, incapacitating President Rexall and incinerating Vice President Cargo, Attorney General Sphincter, and every member of the scandal-plagued Rexall Cabinet. Every member but one.

Acting Secretary of Agriculture Howard Johnson Nissen, home in bed with a hundred and two degree fever, rose from his bed and reached for the ringing telephone — and found himself holding the highest office in the land.

A liberal democrat only momentarily boosted into the Cabinet position by the death two weeks earlier of Secretary Placebo, Nissen had fully expected the call would end his career. It was no secret that Rexall was displeased with his militant environmentalism.

While Rexall languished in a coma from which he has yet to recover, the first new chief executive in thirteen years wasted no time in reviving America's

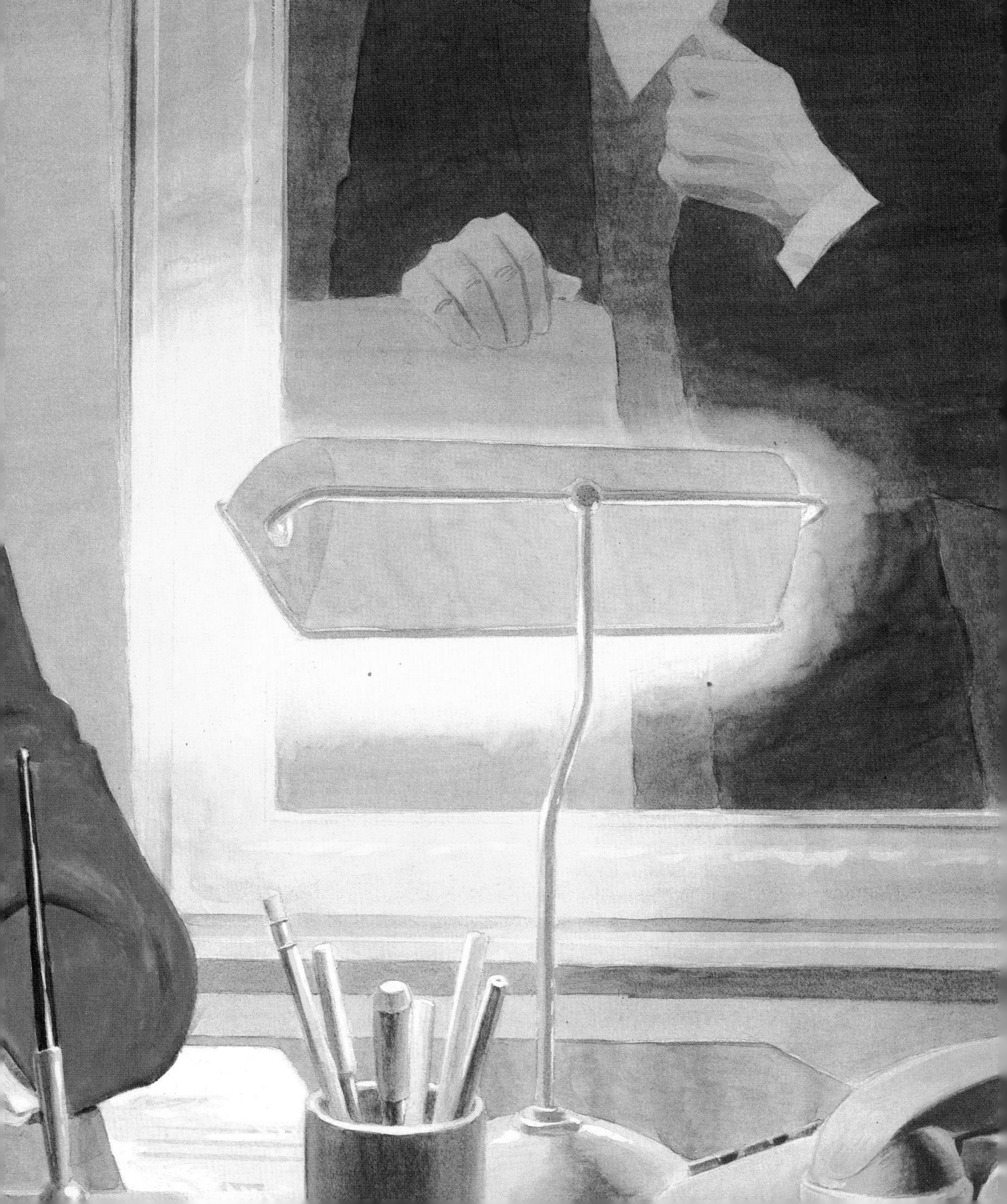

SWORDS INTO PLOWSHARES

Nissen ends months of terror at home and abroad, making peace with the Apache Nation [right], negotiating the Swords into Plowshares Disarmament Treaty with Soviet Premier Jackoff [above], and commits America to the reclamation of the Amazon Rain Forest [far right].

commitment to human rights, international peace, and environmental survival.

Even his closest friends and colleagues were stunned by the soft-spoken, mild mannered "How" Nissen. His first day in office — May 6th — began at 6:05 a.m., with an executive order pulling all Peace Force troops from poisoned No Man's Lands in Central America, Cuba, Israel, Pakistan, and Indochina, thereby ending over a decade of costly wars and paving the way for America's readmittance to the United Nations.

Those who thought they knew him learned quickly to expect the unexpected. The 150,000 PAX troops pulled from every war-torn corner of the world were not left idle. Nissen dispatched them to Brazil, to seize and surround the dying remains of the great Amazon Rain Forest, forcing U.S. hamburger corporations to cease their destruction of the world's greatest and most precious source of oxygen. The newly-fitted and expanded Environmental Protection Agency followed the troops in, and, despite repeated military attacks by Brazilian nationals and Hamburger-sponsored terrorists, EPA experts have begun the process of reforestation.

It soon became clear to all that the new president had no intention of stripping his office of the enormous power it had accumulated under Rexall's reign. Within the week the tireless Nissen had brought cries for impeachment from the Rexall Republican Congress — and shouts of joy from liberals, environmentalists, feminists, and ethnic lead-

ers. Telegrams by the thousands have reached the rebuilt White House, cheering him on with each new bold initiative. A "silent majority" never envisioned by the far Right has, a mere six months after his inauguration, canonized Howard Nissen as the saviour of the soul of America.

By early June he authored and successfully negotiated the US-Soviet Swords Into Plowshares Disarmament Treaty, compelling both nations to point their enormous laser cannons at their own territories in fixed position that can only be changed by a unanimous vote of the United Nations. By July he ended months of strife at the Aragones Refinery in the Mexican Territory, signing a handwritten treaty that granted the Apache Nation the refinery and its surround-

ing land. With the help of lobby groups and enthusiastic letter campaigns by citizens groups, he is well on his way to forcing through Congress a wide range of social and educational programs unheard-of since before the Mexican War.

Should Erwin Rexall ever rise from his bed at Walter Reed, he will be confronted with an America that scarcely resembles that which he ruled like a king.

Howard Johnson Nissen was born in 1965 in Berkeley, California, the son of Wildflower and Primrose Nissen, to whom he refers lovingly as "hopeless hippies". An only child, he attended a variety of grade and high

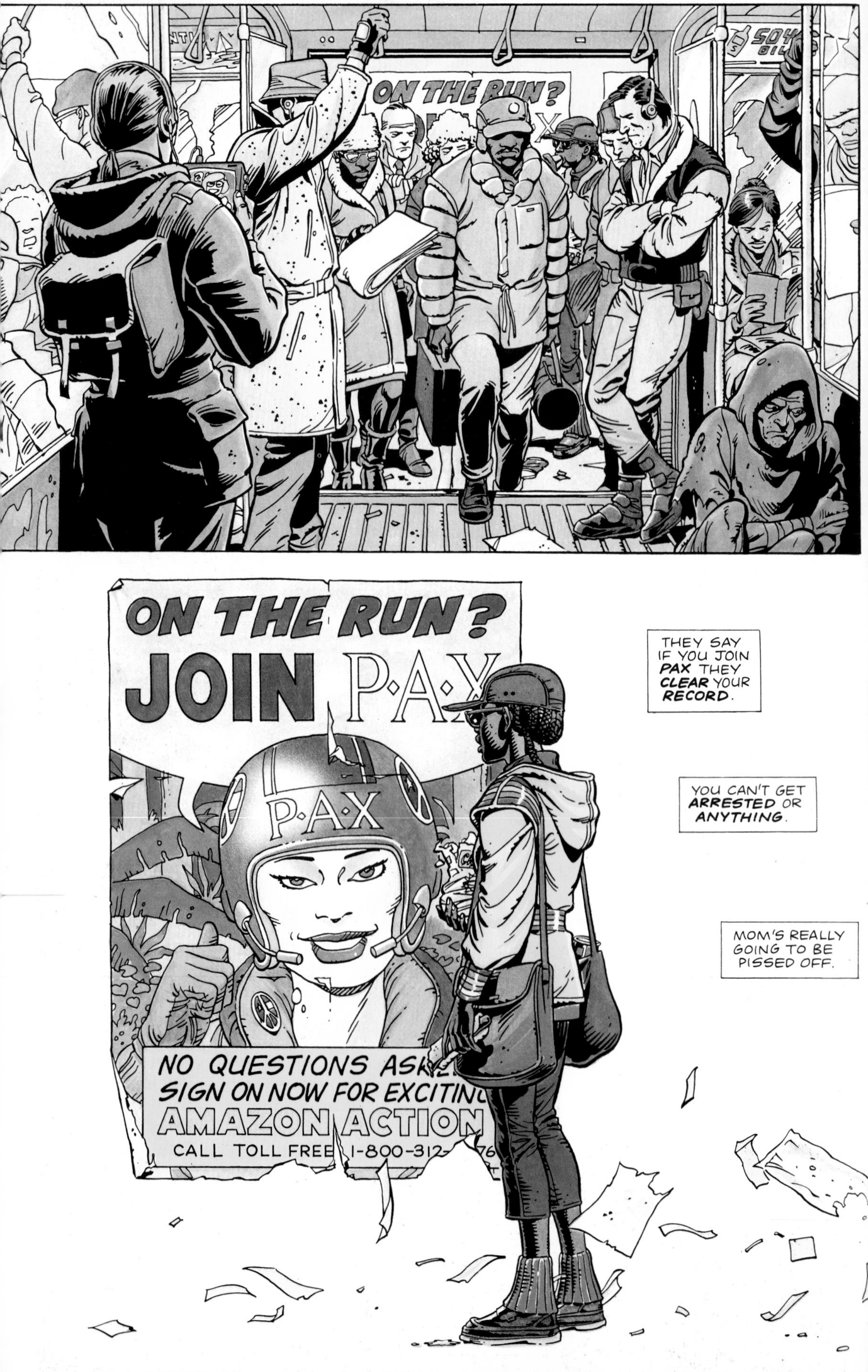
ON THE RUN?
ON THE RUN?
JOIN P·A·X
P·A·X
NO QUESTIONS ASKE
SIGN ON NOW FOR EXCITIN
AMAZON ACTION
CALL TOLL FREE 1-800-312-
THEY SAY IF YOU JOIN **PAX** THEY **CLEAR** YOUR **RECORD**.
YOU CAN'T GET **ARRESTED** OR **ANYTHING**.
MOM'S REALLY GOING TO BE PISSED OFF.

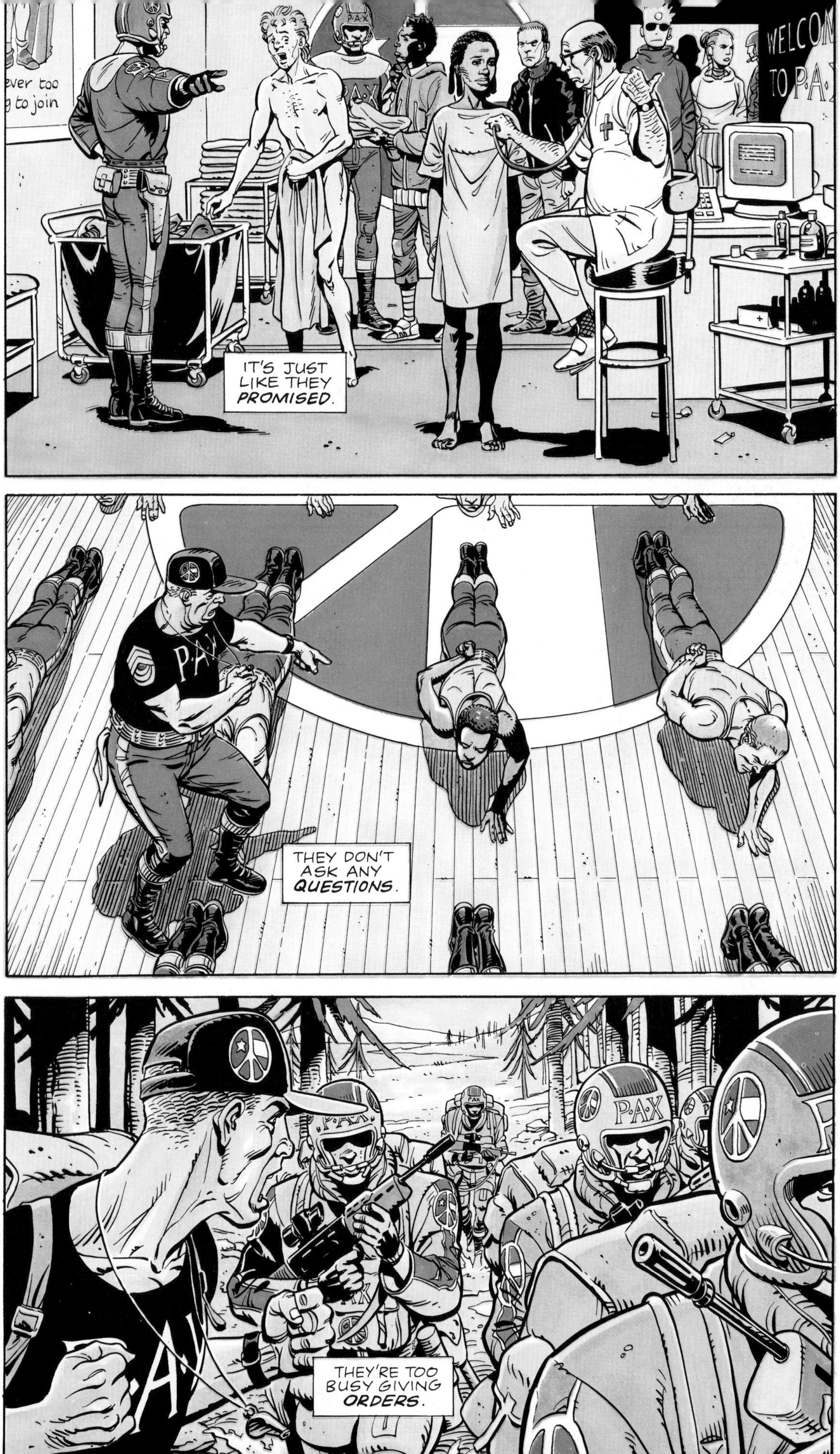
IT'S JUST LIKE THEY PROMISED.
THEY DON'T ASK ANY QUESTIONS.
THEY'RE TOO BUSY GIVING ORDERS.

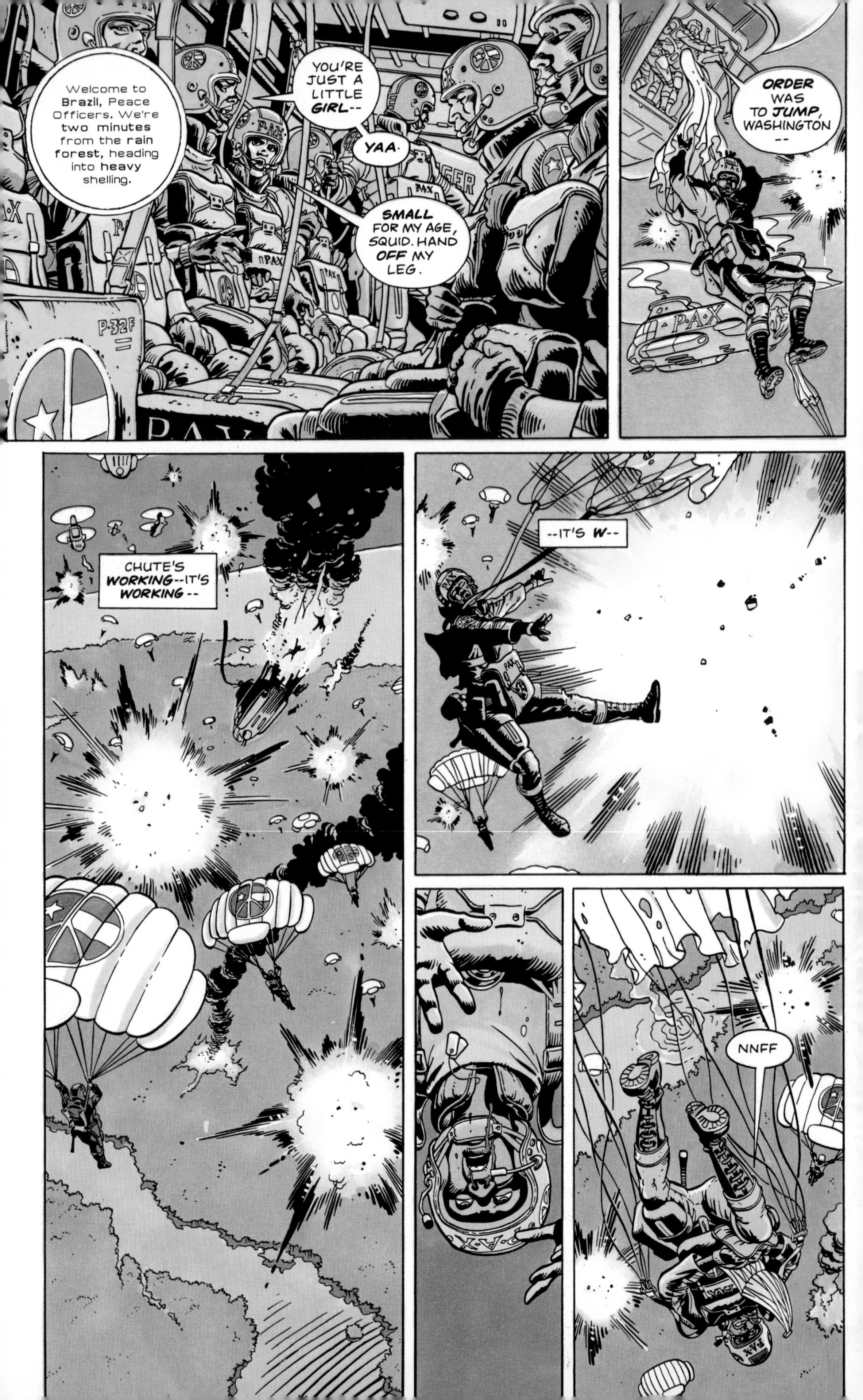
Welcome to Brazil, Peace Officers. We're two minutes from the rain forest, heading into heavy shelling.
YOU'RE JUST A LITTLE GIRL--
YAA.
SMALL FOR MY AGE, SQUID. HAND OFF MY LEG.
ORDER WAS TO JUMP, WASHINGTON --
CHUTE'S WORKING--IT'S WORKING--
--IT'S W--
NNFF

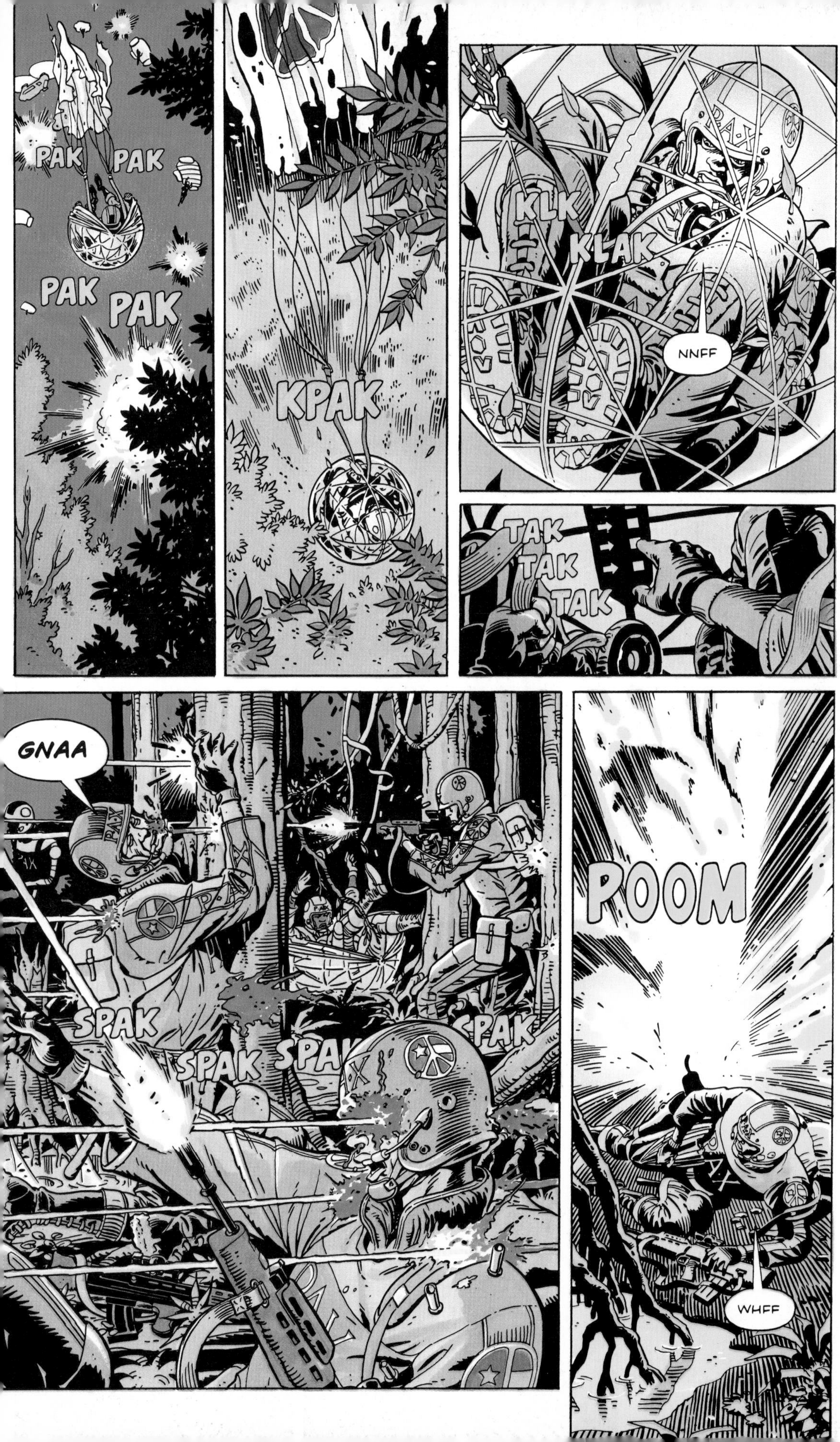
PAK PAK
PAK PAK
KPAK
KLK
KLAK
NNFF
TAK
TAK
TAK
GNAA
SPAK
SPAK
SPAK
SPAK
POOM
WHFF

BRAKA BRAKA BRAK

LIEUTENANT *MORETTI* --SIR--

SPUK SPUK SPUK

--PRIVATE *WASHINGTON* REPORTING FOR DUTY--

THEY'RE *SAUCING* THE MEN UP *FRONT* --STAY *LOW* -- GET THESE *TO* THEM--

JUST A *GIRL,* SIR-- I'LL DO IT--

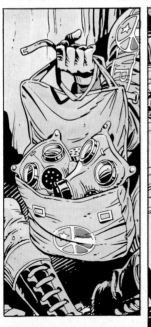

OH GOD JESUS

JESUS

SPUK

SPUK

SPUK

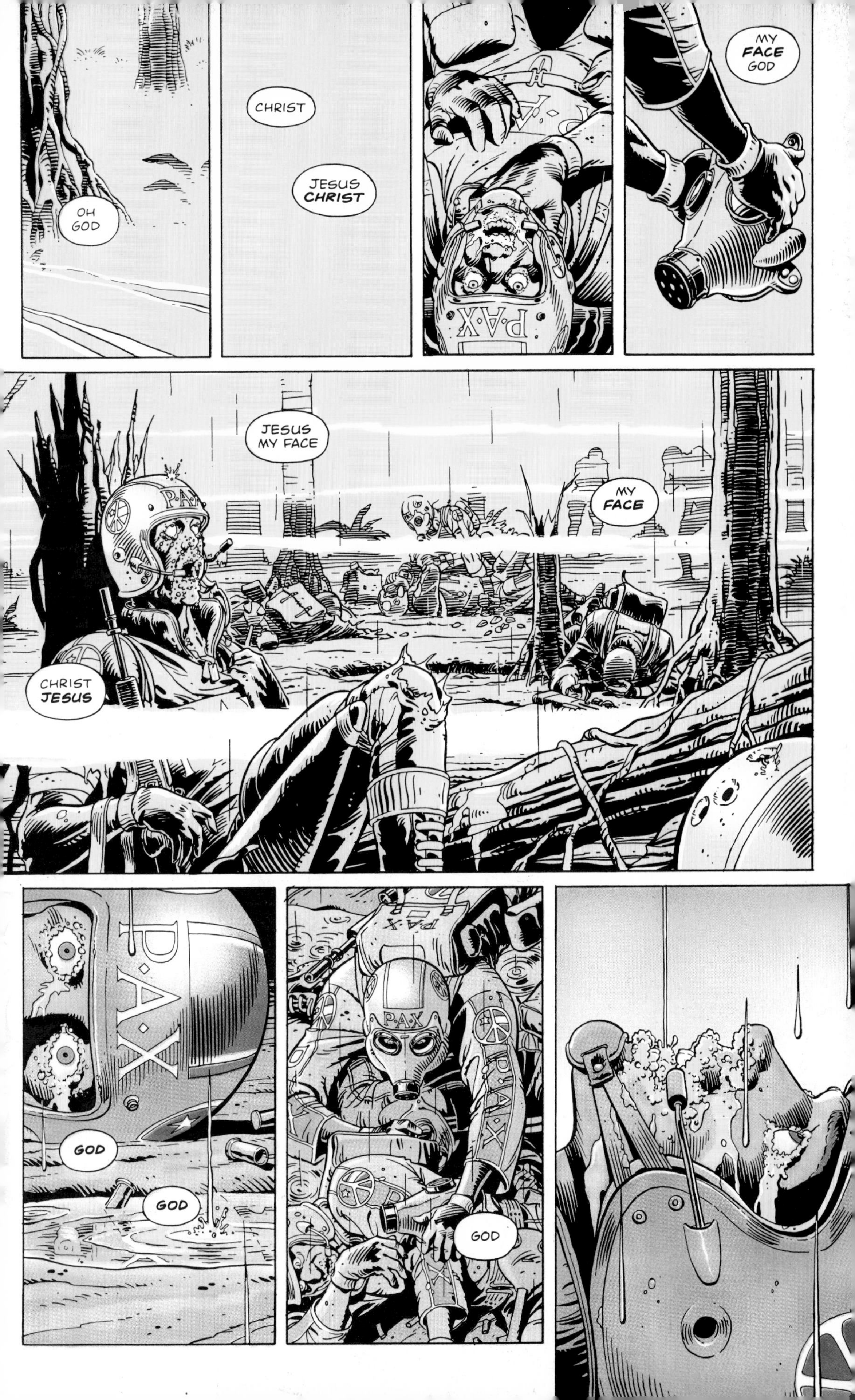
OH GOD
CHRIST
JESUS CHRIST
MY FACE GOD
JESUS MY FACE
MY FACE
CHRIST JESUS
GOD
GOD
GOD

SPLTT

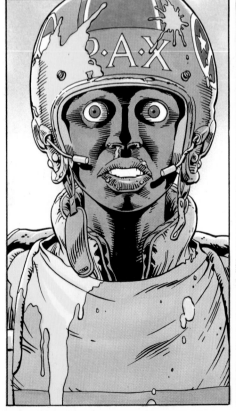

SKEE

SKEE

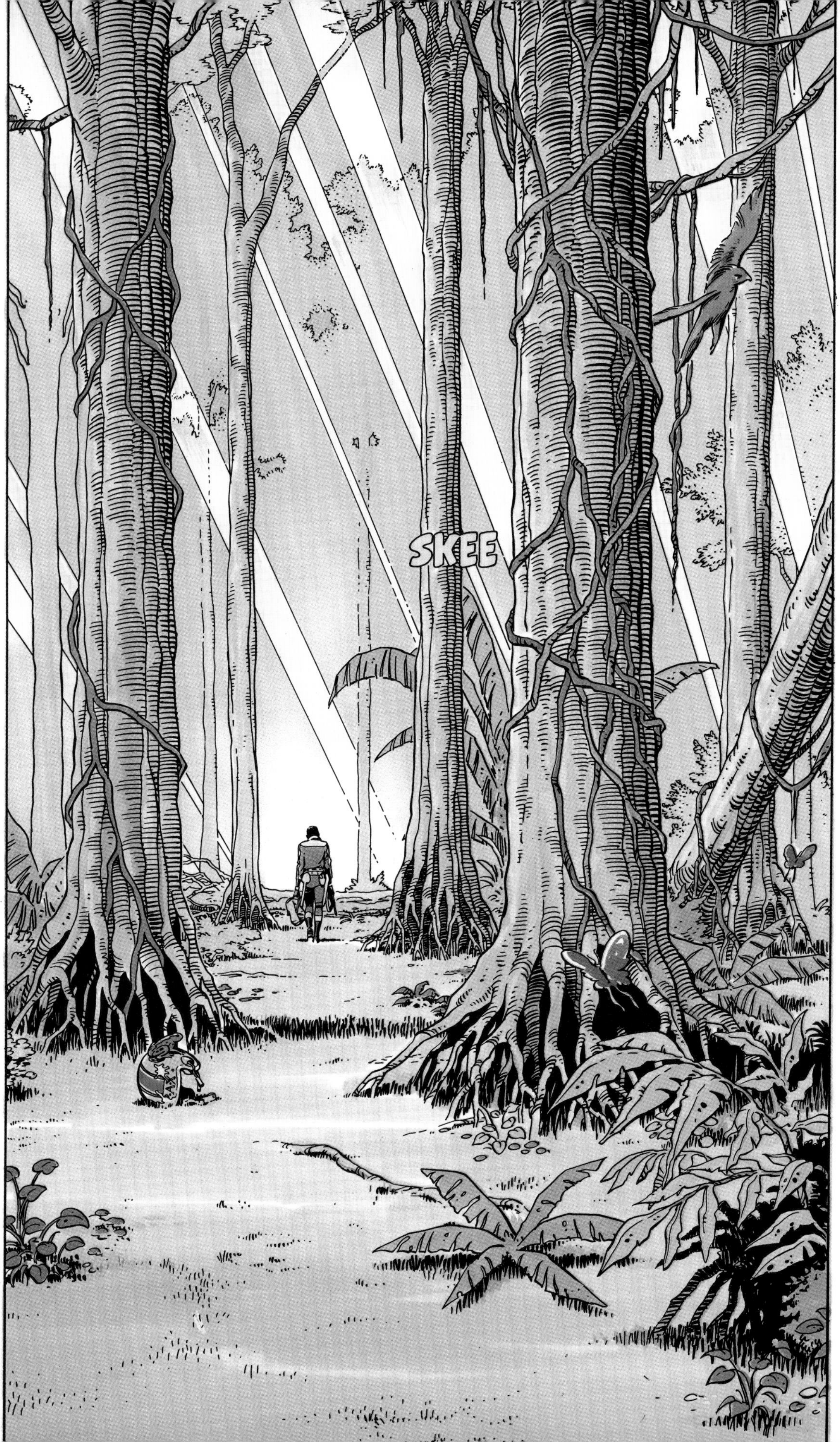
SKEE

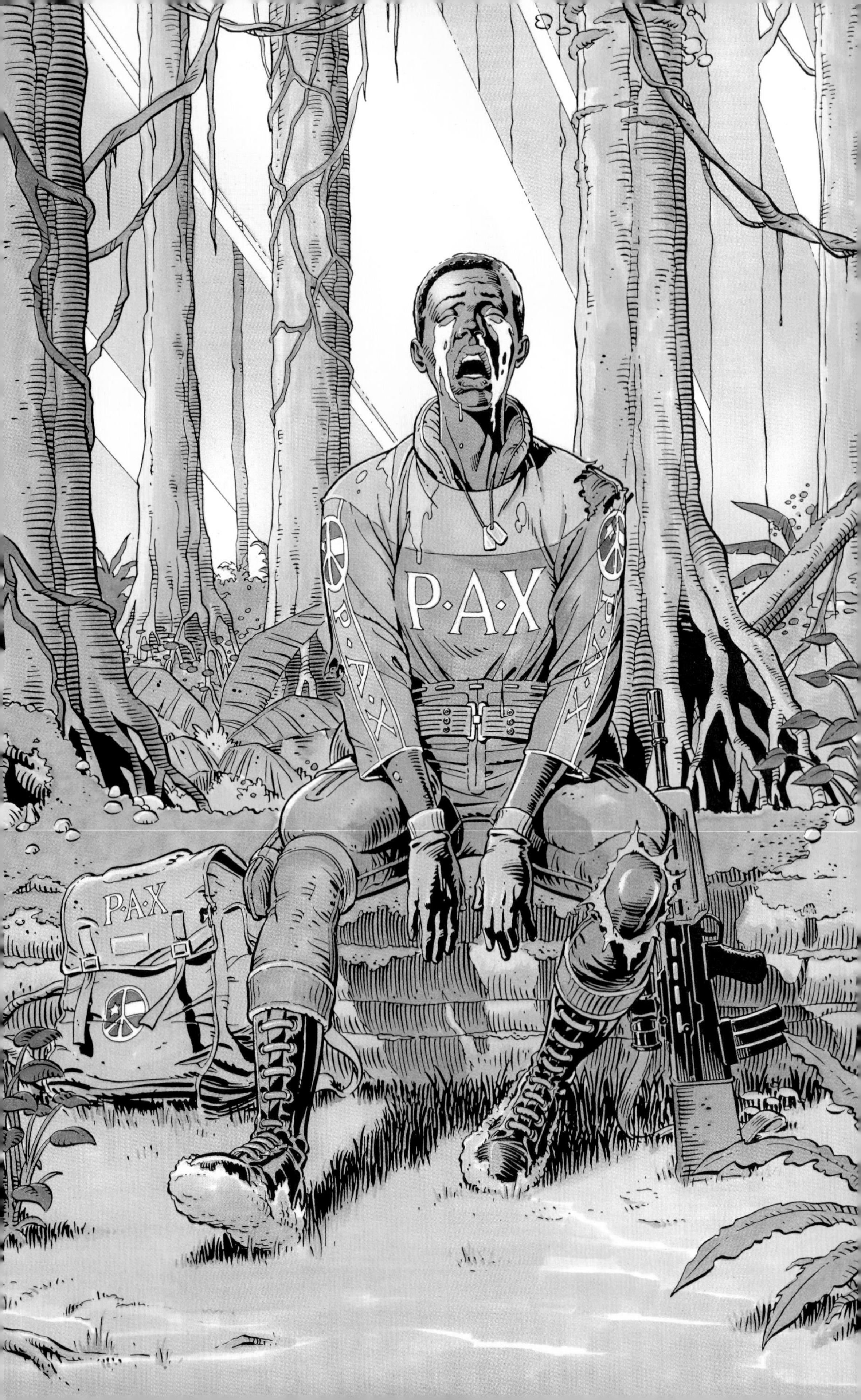
P·A·X
P·A·X

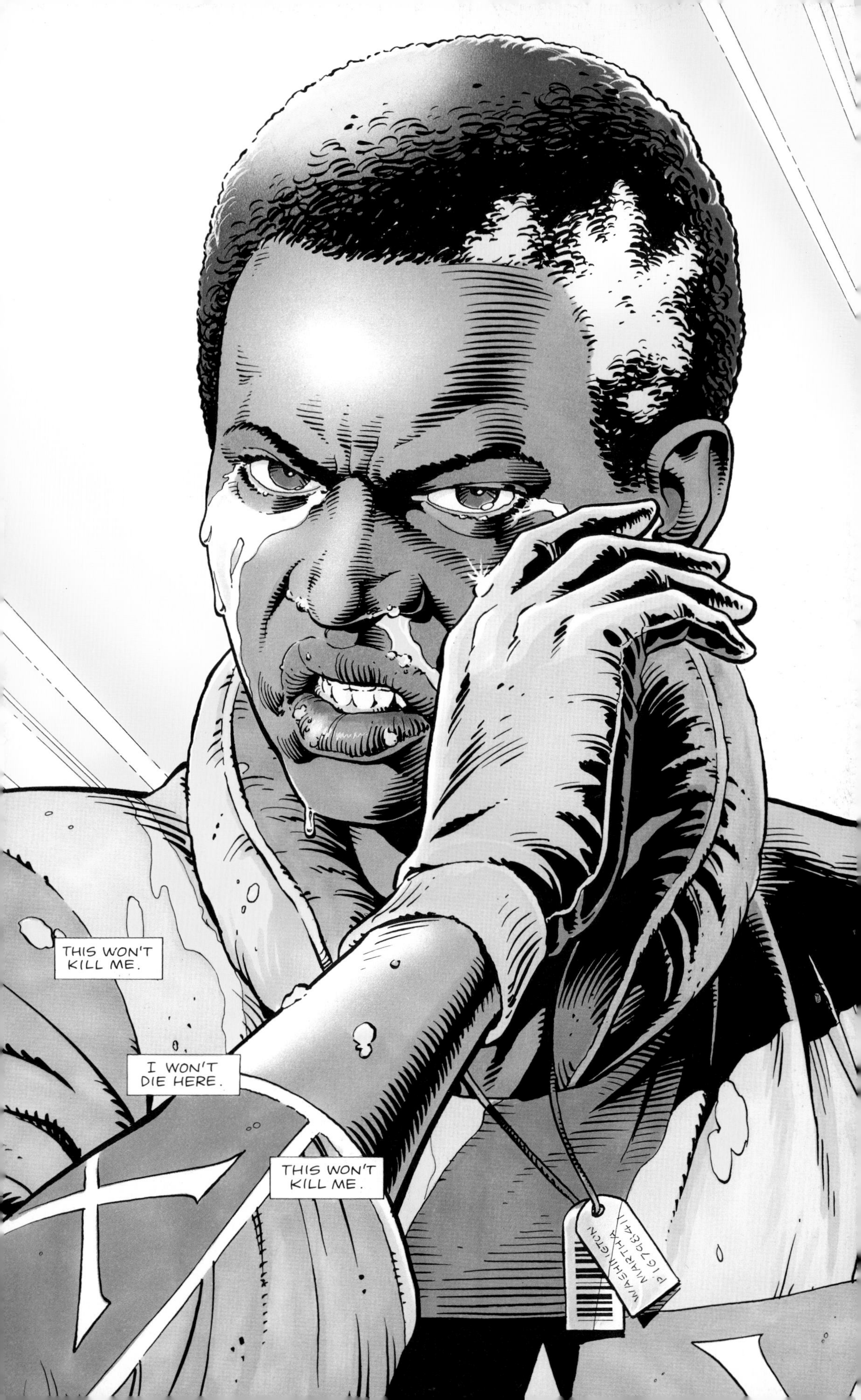
THIS WON'T KILL ME.
I WON'T DIE HERE.
THIS WON'T KILL ME.

PERSONAL CORRESPONDANCE
FROM: Sgt. Martha Washington, Amazon Base 6
TO: Mrs. John Washington, 66 Red Grove #44B,
Chicago, IL 60601
DATE: August 22, 2010

Hi, Mom! Bet you're surprised to hear from me!

Right now I'm sitting in the infirmery. Caught some
Special Sauce in the last Big Mac Attack and
suddenly they're treating me great. I didn't get
hurt too bad, but until the burns heal up a little
more I get to stay out of the fighting. They even
let me use the neatest little lap top to write this
letter. It's no bigger than a toaster but it works
fine.

I'm a sargeant now, after only six months. That
means better pay and I don't have to take orders as
much. I guess PAX is pretty happy with me.

Boy, have they kept me running! It just never lets
up here and they're pretty strict about not letting
us write home. Guess they must have their reasons.

Mom, the Rain Forest is beautiful. The mosquitoes
are all over the place and big as your fist and if
they bite you get really swollen up, though, and at
first it was really scary, in the forest. It's
bigger than anything and it's always dark, and
there's more weird animals than in a zoo. They make
tons of noise when the shelling isn't going on, and

tons of noise when the shelling isn't going on, and they sound as weird as they look. I always thought nature was supposed to be quiet like a postcard. When I'm done with work I like to take walks in it. Sometimes I run into the Reforesters but they're okay, and mostly I get to be all by myself. One time I saw a little monkie with eyes so smart you'd swear it was really a human. Half expected it to talk with me and it did click at me like I was supposed to understand. But maybe I was just imagining things.

Anyway, the big news is that I'll be coming home in a few weeks, they say before the end of the year! Commander Bracket said I could practicly count on it even though he says I'm a good soldier and he'll miss me. Maybe I'll even be home for Christmas!

Love to you and John and sorry if the letter sounds queer. Guess I should've studied harder back in school at English.

See you soon I hope!

Martha

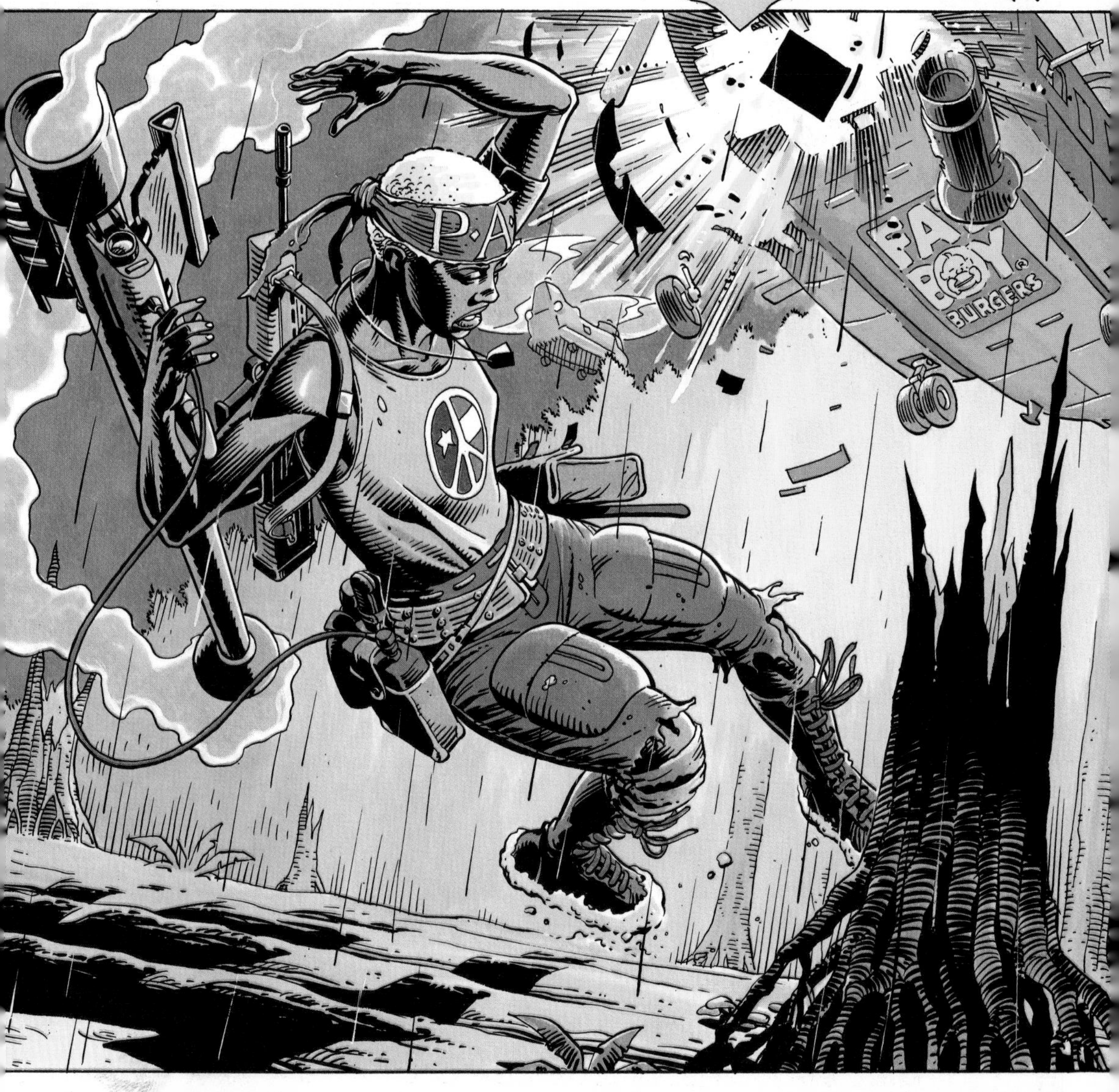
P.A
BURGERS

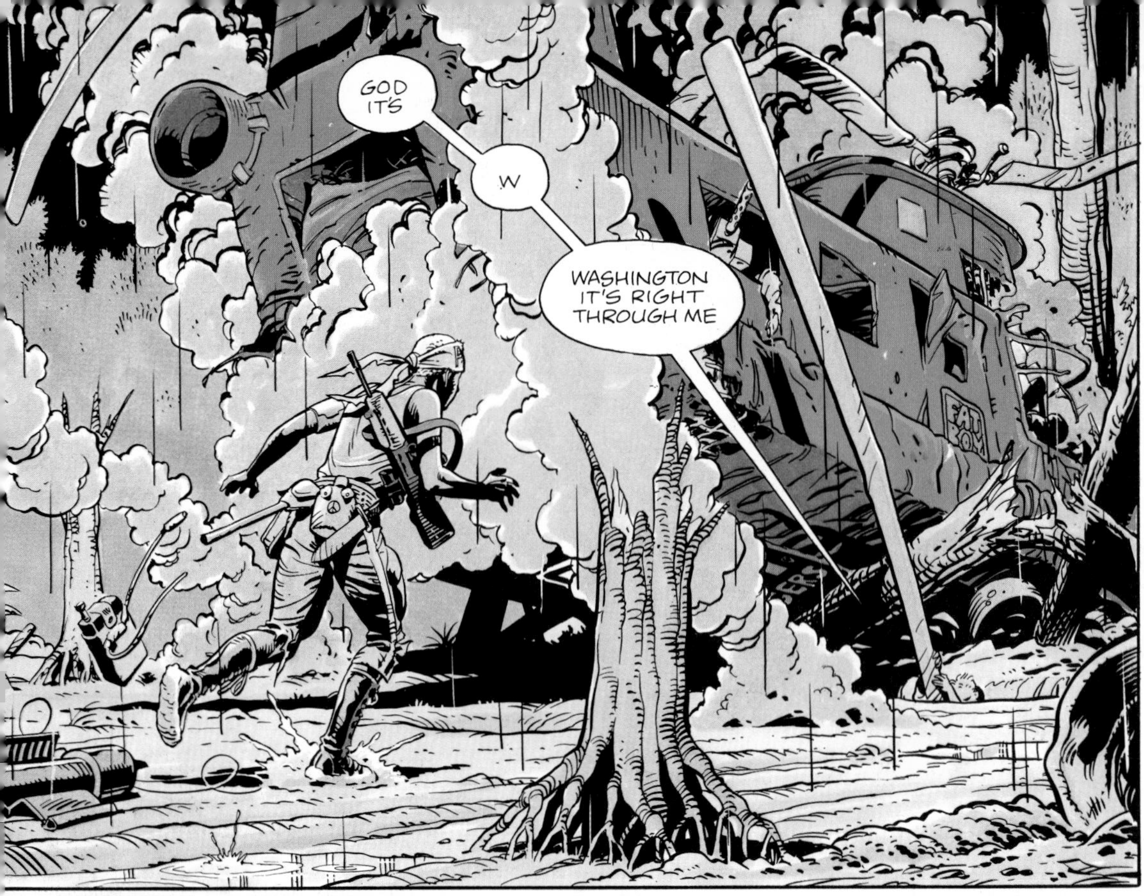
GOD IT'S
W
WASHINGTON IT'S RIGHT THROUGH ME

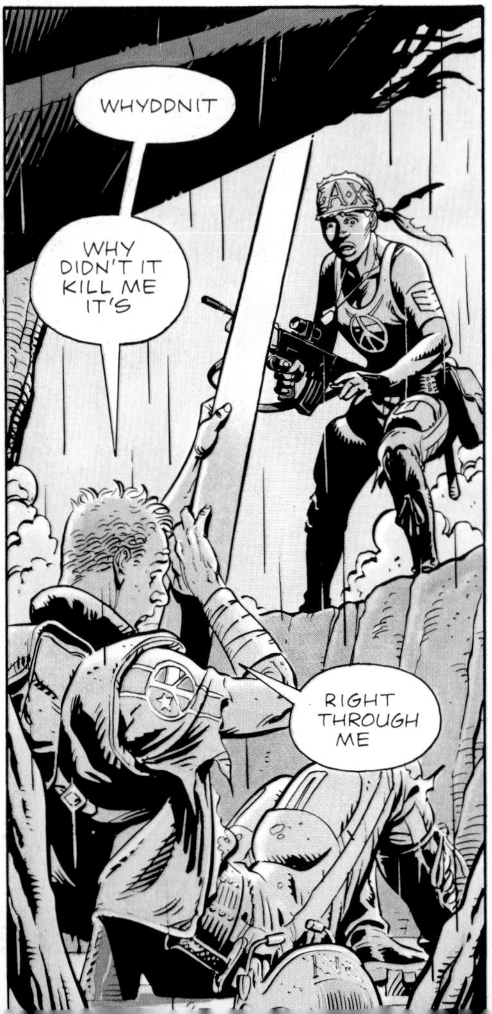
WHYDDNIT
WHY DIDN'T IT KILL ME IT'S
RIGHT THROUGH ME

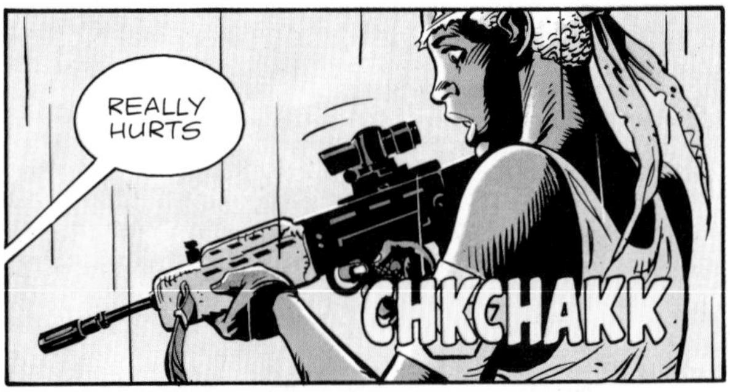
REALLY HURTS
CHKCHAKK

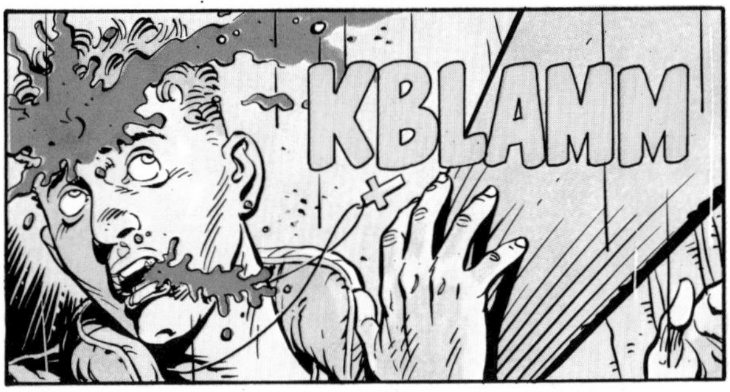
KBLAMM

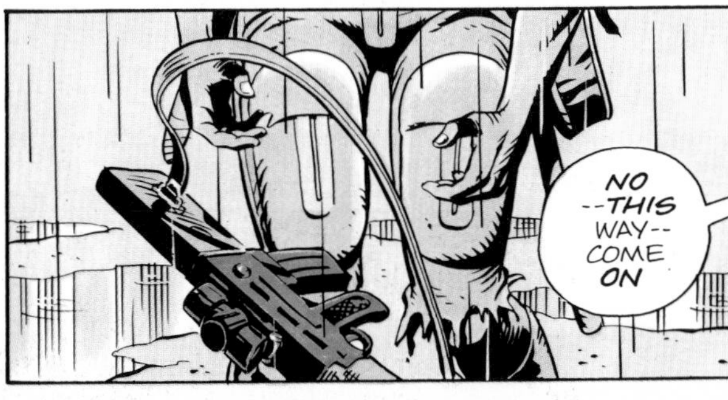
NO --THIS WAY-- COME ON

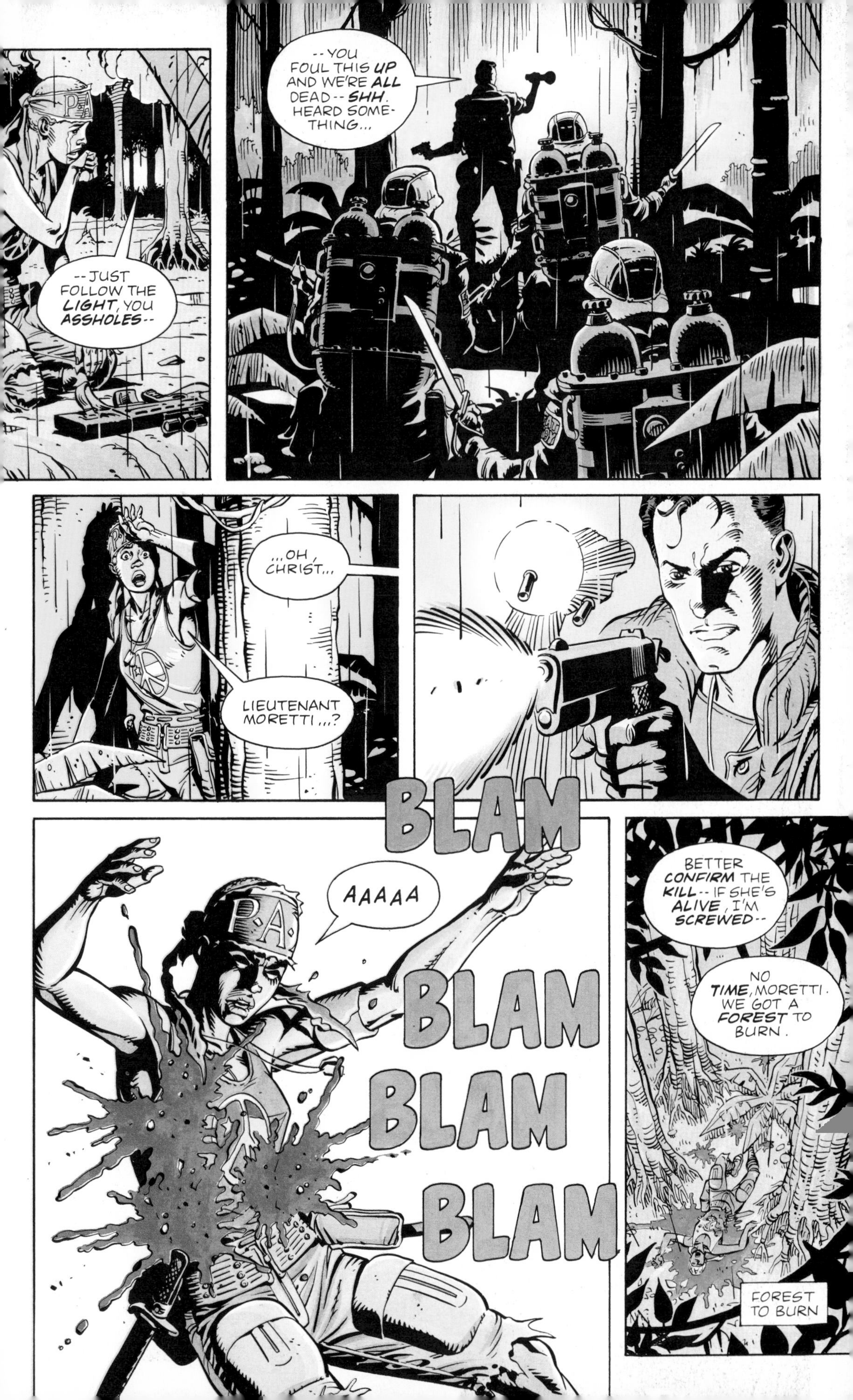
--JUST FOLLOW THE LIGHT, YOU ASSHOLES--
--YOU FOUL THIS UP AND WE'RE ALL DEAD--SHH. HEARD SOMETHING...
...OH, CHRIST...
LIEUTENANT MORETTI...?
BLAM
AAAAA
BLAM
BLAM
BLAM
BETTER CONFIRM THE KILL--IF SHE'S ALIVE, I'M SCREWED--
NO TIME, MORETTI. WE GOT A FOREST TO BURN.
FOREST TO BURN

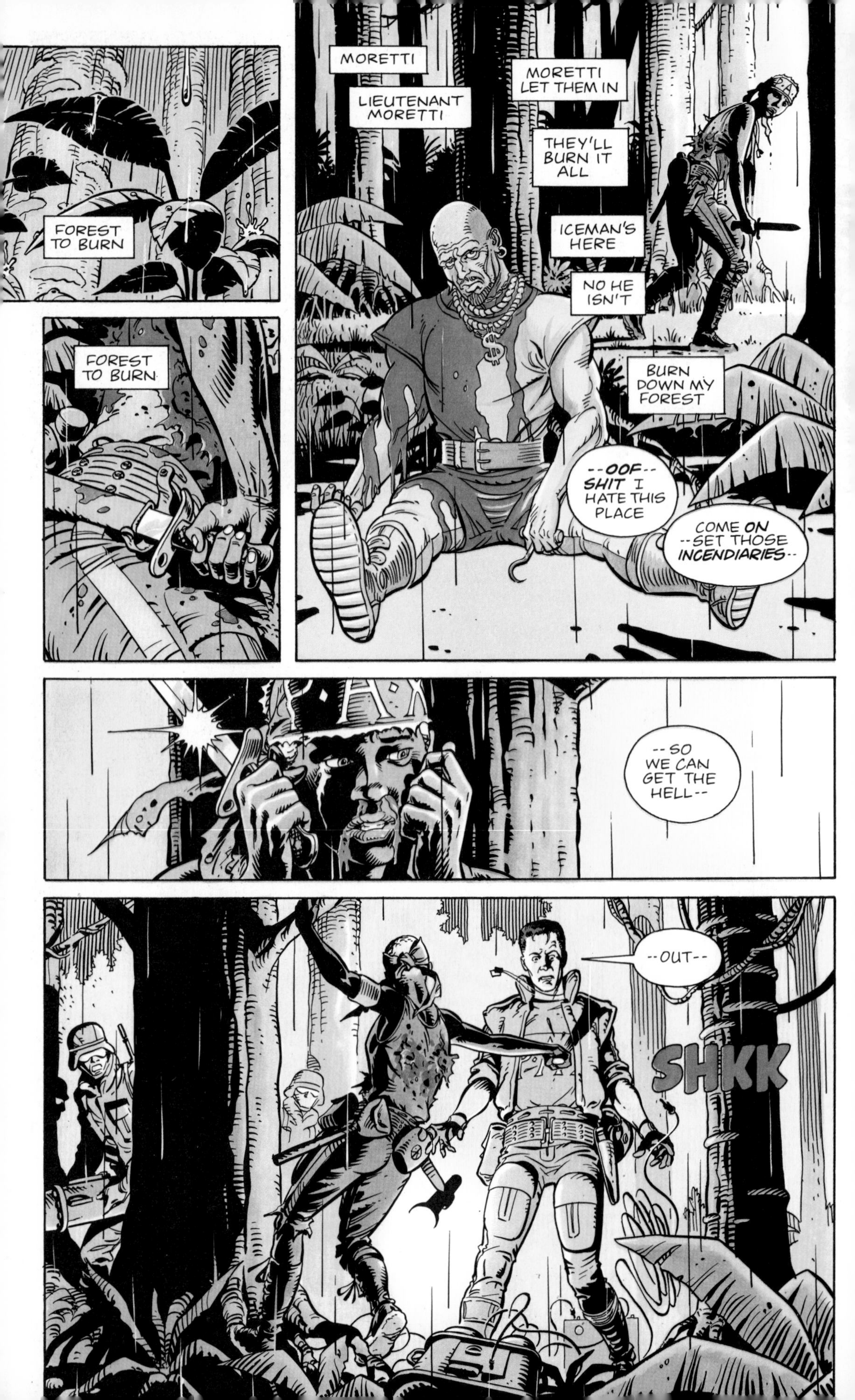
FOREST TO BURN
FOREST TO BURN
MORETTI
LIEUTENANT MORETTI
MORETTI LET THEM IN
THEY'LL BURN IT ALL
ICEMAN'S HERE
NO HE ISN'T
BURN DOWN MY FOREST
--OOF-- SHIT I HATE THIS PLACE
COME ON --SET THOSE INCENDIARIES--
--SO WE CAN GET THE HELL--
--OUT--
SHKK

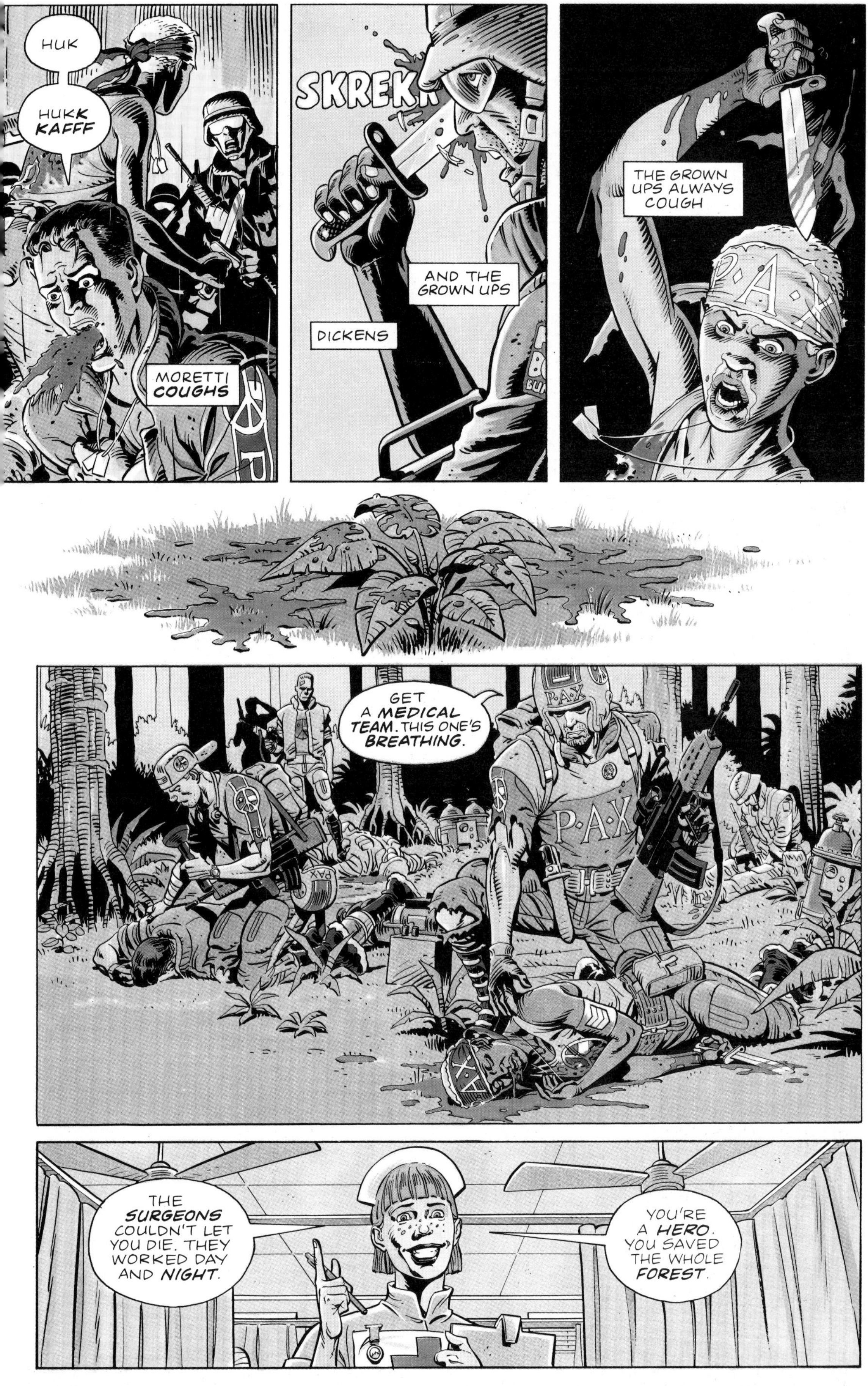
HUK
HUKK KAFFF
MORETTI COUGHS
SKREKK
DICKENS
AND THE GROWN UPS
THE GROWN UPS ALWAYS COUGH
GET A MEDICAL TEAM. THIS ONE'S BREATHING.
THE SURGEONS COULDN'T LET YOU DIE. THEY WORKED DAY AND NIGHT.
YOU'RE A HERO. YOU SAVED THE WHOLE FOREST.

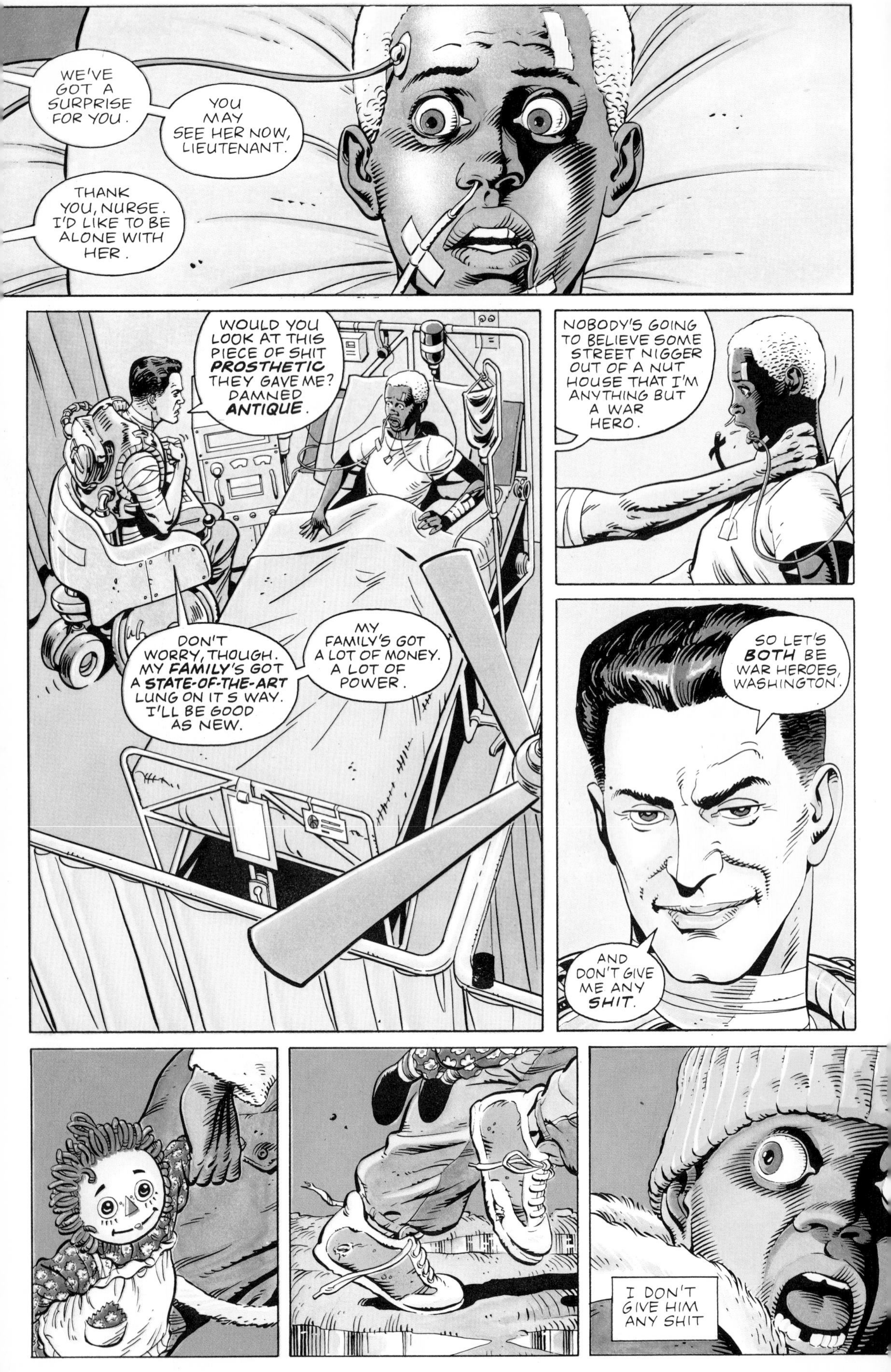
WE'VE GOT A SURPRISE FOR YOU.
YOU MAY SEE HER NOW, LIEUTENANT.
THANK YOU, NURSE. I'D LIKE TO BE ALONE WITH HER.
WOULD YOU LOOK AT THIS PIECE OF SHIT PROSTHETIC THEY GAVE ME? DAMNED ANTIQUE.
DON'T WORRY, THOUGH. MY FAMILY'S GOT A STATE-OF-THE-ART LUNG ON IT'S WAY. I'LL BE GOOD AS NEW.
MY FAMILY'S GOT A LOT OF MONEY. A LOT OF POWER.
NOBODY'S GOING TO BELIEVE SOME STREET NIGGER OUT OF A NUT HOUSE THAT I'M ANYTHING BUT A WAR HERO.
SO LET'S BOTH BE WAR HEROES, WASHINGTON.
AND DON'T GIVE ME ANY SHIT.
I DON'T GIVE HIM ANY SHIT

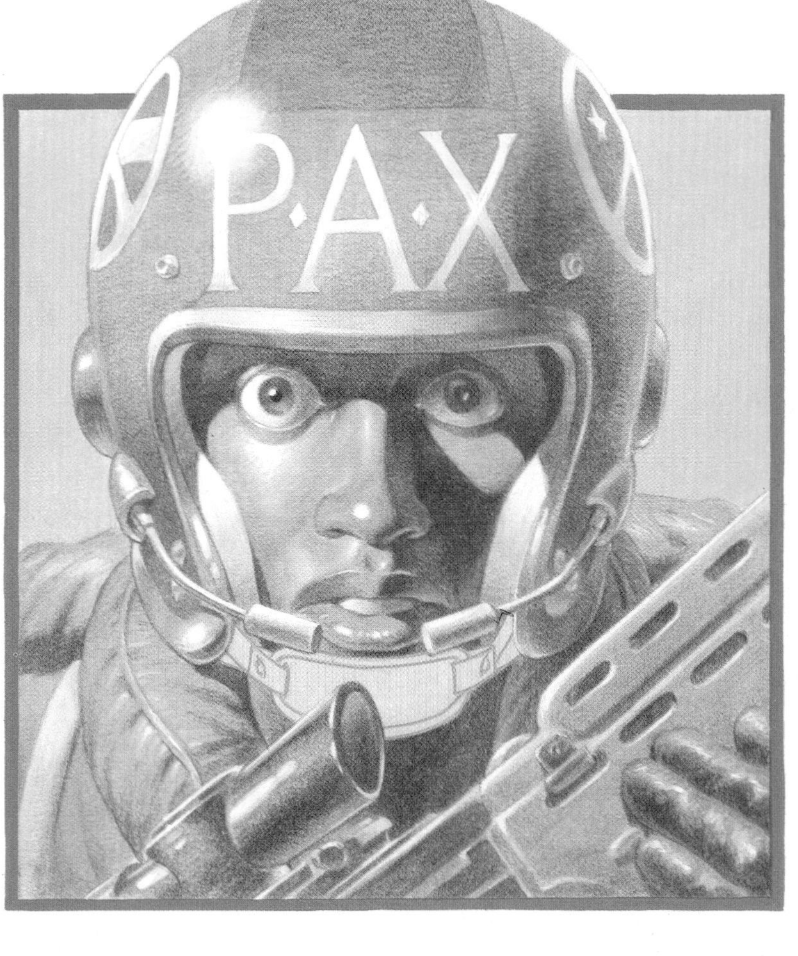
P·A·X

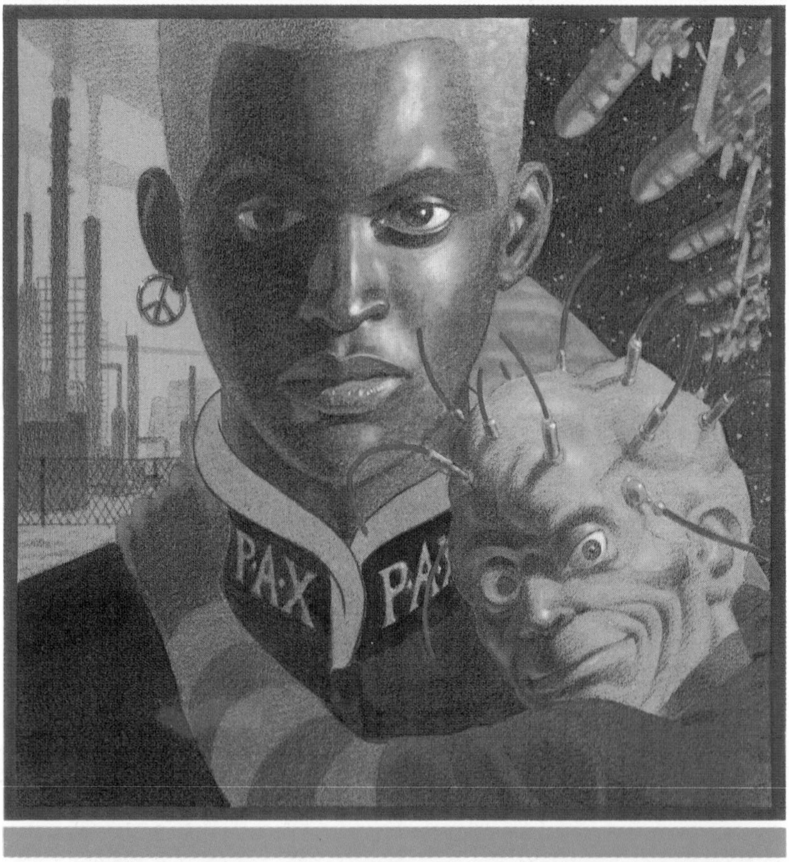
P·A·X
P·A·X

2: TRAVEL & ENTERTAINMENT

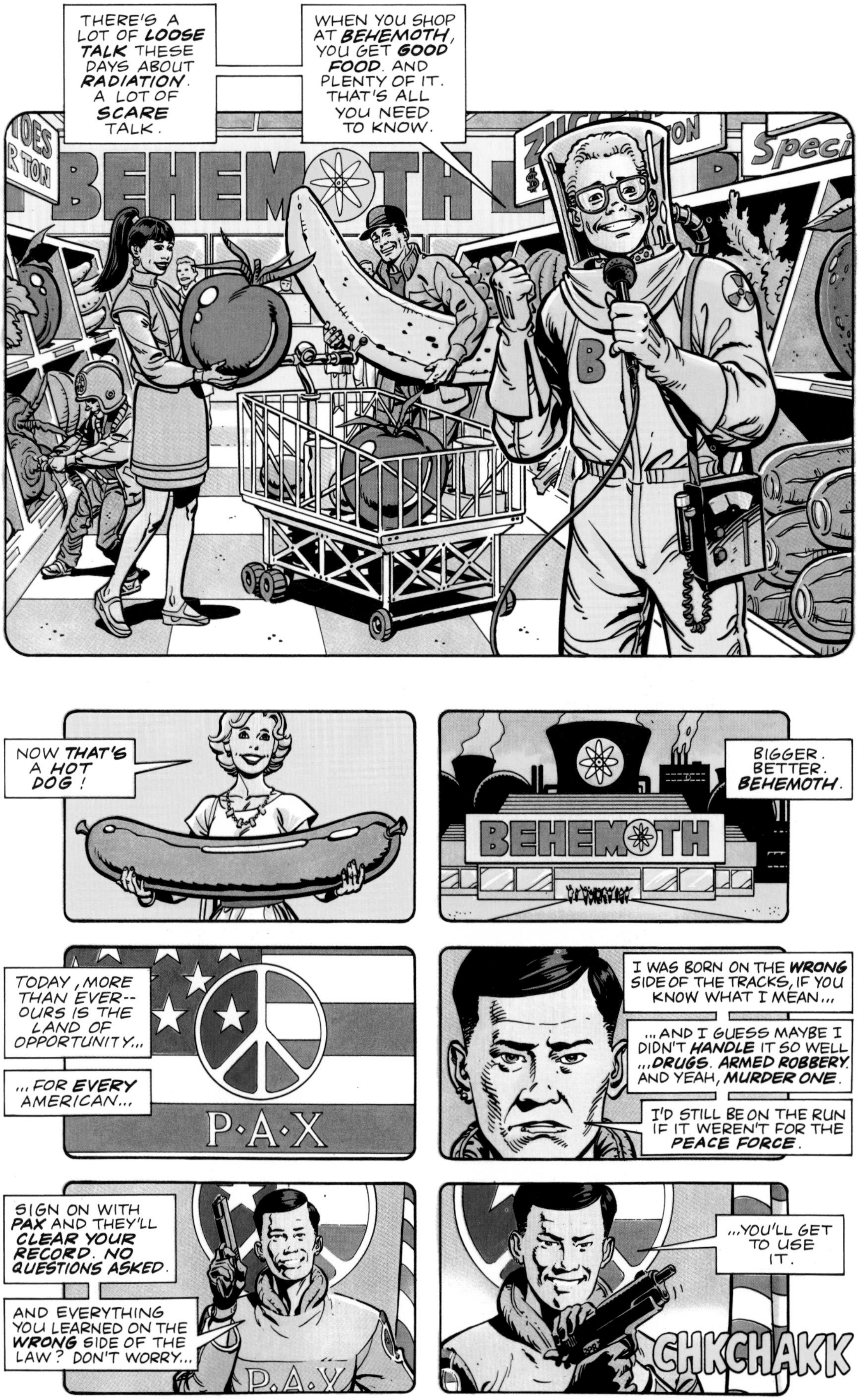
THERE'S A LOT OF **LOOSE TALK** THESE DAYS ABOUT **RADIATION**. A LOT OF **SCARE** TALK.
WHEN YOU SHOP AT **BEHEMOTH**, YOU GET **GOOD FOOD**. AND PLENTY OF IT. THAT'S ALL YOU NEED TO KNOW.
BEHEMOTH
NOW **THAT'S** A **HOT DOG**!
BEHEMOTH
BIGGER. BETTER. **BEHEMOTH**.
TODAY, MORE THAN EVER-- OURS IS THE LAND OF OPPORTUNITY...
...FOR **EVERY** AMERICAN...
P·A·X
I WAS BORN ON THE **WRONG** SIDE OF THE TRACKS, IF YOU KNOW WHAT I MEAN...
...AND I GUESS MAYBE I DIDN'T **HANDLE** IT SO WELL ...**DRUGS**. **ARMED ROBBERY**. AND YEAH, **MURDER ONE**.
I'D STILL BE ON THE RUN IF IT WEREN'T FOR THE **PEACE FORCE**.
SIGN ON WITH **PAX** AND THEY'LL **CLEAR YOUR RECORD**. **NO QUESTIONS ASKED**.
AND EVERYTHING YOU LEARNED ON THE **WRONG** SIDE OF THE LAW? DON'T WORRY...
P.A.X
...YOU'LL GET TO USE IT.
CHKCHAKK

2008: OUR COUNTRY IS AT WAR WITH FORTY FOREIGN NATIONS-- AND WITH *ITSELF.*

BUDGET CUTS FORCE AUTHORITIES TO SHUT DOWN *PRISONS* AND *MENTAL INSTITUTIONS,* BRINGING HIDEOUS *POVERTY* AND *VIOLENCE* TO CITY STREETS.

PRESIDENT *ERWIN REXALL,* FACING THE THREAT OF HIS FIRST DEFEAT IN FOUR ELECTIONS, DECLARES *MARTIAL LAW.*

CONGRESS GRANTS THE *SURGEON GENERAL* AUTHORITY TO CONDUCT HIS '*WAR ON SICKNESS!*'

CRIME IS NOT A DISEASE.

DISEASE IS A CRIME.

THE *HEALTH POLICE* JOIN THE *PEACE FORCE* IN THE *URBAN PACIFICATION* EFFORT.

FOR A TIME THE STREETS ARE SILENT.

THEN COME THE *RIOTS* -- AND THE *BATTLES.* AUTHORITIES ARE FORCED TO SURRENDER ENTIRE *NEIGHBORHOODS* TO MILITANT FACTIONS.

MAY 5, 2009: A *FIREBOMB* REDUCES THE *WHITE HOUSE* TO A BURNT SHELL.

SIXTY-SEVEN SEPARATE REVOLUTIONARY GROUPS CLAIM RESPONSIBILITY FOR THE ATROCITY.

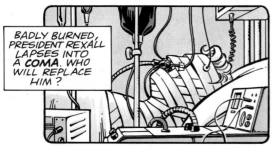

BADLY BURNED, PRESIDENT REXALL LAPSES INTO A *COMA.* WHO WILL REPLACE HIM?

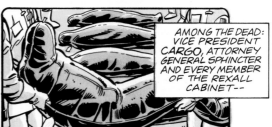

AMONG THE DEAD: VICE PRESIDENT *CARGO,* ATTORNEY GENERAL *SPHINCTER* AND EVERY MEMBER OF THE REXALL CABINET--

--EXCEPT *HOWARD NISSEN,* ACTING SECRETARY OF AGRICULTURE.

A LIBERAL DEMOCRAT MOMENTARILY BOOSTED INTO THE POSITION BY THE DEATH OF SECRETARY *PLACEBO* THREE DAYS EARLIER.

EVERYONE HAD BEEN SURE THAT HE WOULD SHORTLY BE FIRED.

IT WAS NO SECRET THAT REXALL WAS DISPLEASED WITH HIS MILITANT ENVIRONMENTALISM.

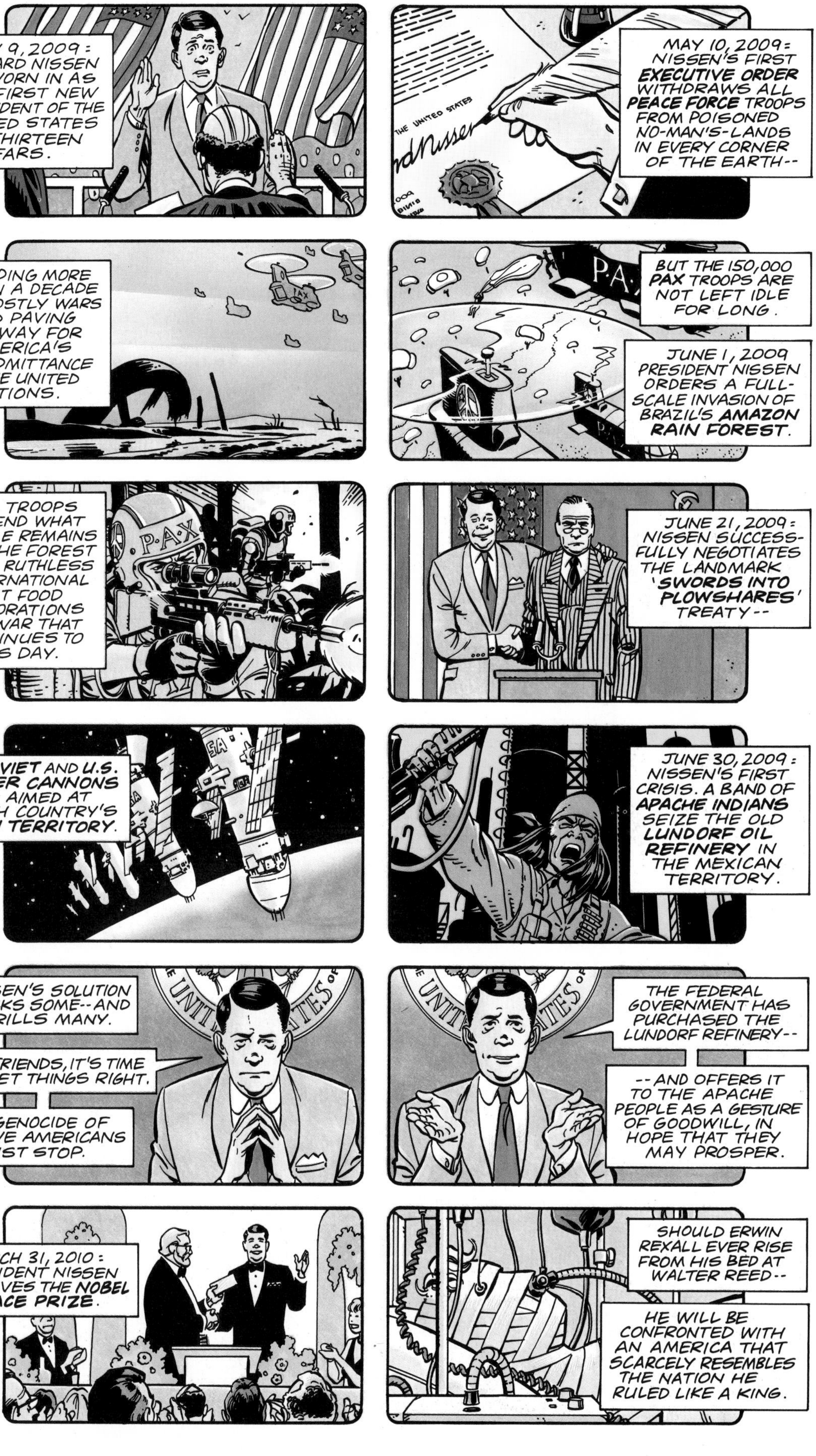
MAY 9, 2009: HOWARD NISSEN IS SWORN IN AS THE FIRST NEW PRESIDENT OF THE UNITED STATES IN THIRTEEN YEARS.
MAY 10, 2009: NISSEN'S FIRST **EXECUTIVE ORDER** WITHDRAWS ALL **PEACE FORCE** TROOPS FROM POISONED NO-MAN'S-LANDS IN EVERY CORNER OF THE EARTH--
THE UNITED STATES
--ENDING MORE THAN A DECADE OF COSTLY WARS AND PAVING THE WAY FOR AMERICA'S RE-ADMITTANCE TO THE UNITED NATIONS.
BUT THE 150,000 **PAX** TROOPS ARE NOT LEFT IDLE FOR LONG.
JUNE 1, 2009 PRESIDENT NISSEN ORDERS A FULL-SCALE INVASION OF BRAZIL'S **AMAZON RAIN FOREST**.
PAX TROOPS DEFEND WHAT LITTLE REMAINS OF THE FOREST FROM RUTHLESS INTERNATIONAL FAST FOOD CORPORATIONS IN A WAR THAT CONTINUES TO THIS DAY.
P.A.X.
JUNE 21, 2009: NISSEN SUCCESSFULLY NEGOTIATES THE LANDMARK '**SWORDS INTO PLOWSHARES**' TREATY--
--**SOVIET** AND **U.S. LASER CANNONS** ARE AIMED AT EACH COUNTRY'S **OWN TERRITORY**.
JUNE 30, 2009: NISSEN'S FIRST CRISIS. A BAND OF **APACHE INDIANS** SEIZE THE OLD **LUNDORF OIL REFINERY** IN THE MEXICAN TERRITORY.
NISSEN'S SOLUTION SHOCKS SOME--AND THRILLS MANY.
MY FRIENDS, IT'S TIME WE SET THINGS RIGHT.
THE GENOCIDE OF NATIVE AMERICANS MUST STOP.
THE FEDERAL GOVERNMENT HAS PURCHASED THE LUNDORF REFINERY--
--AND OFFERS IT TO THE APACHE PEOPLE AS A GESTURE OF GOODWILL, IN HOPE THAT THEY MAY PROSPER.
MARCH 31, 2010: PRESIDENT NISSEN RECEIVES THE **NOBEL PEACE PRIZE**.
SHOULD ERWIN REXALL EVER RISE FROM HIS BED AT WALTER REED--
HE WILL BE CONFRONTED WITH AN AMERICA THAT SCARCELY RESEMBLES THE NATION HE RULED LIKE A KING.

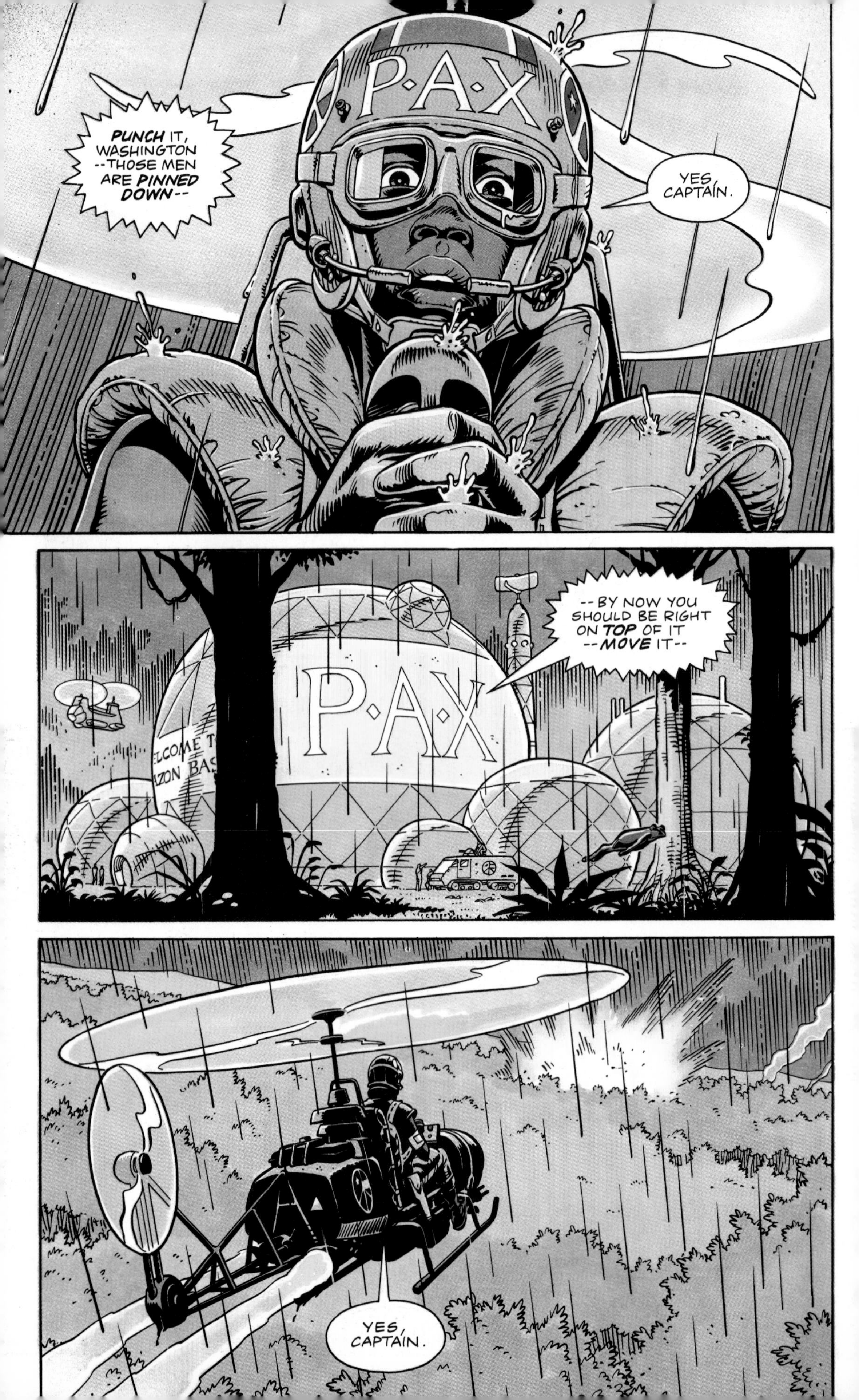
PUNCH IT, WASHINGTON --THOSE MEN ARE PINNED DOWN--
YES, CAPTAIN.
P·A·X
--BY NOW YOU SHOULD BE RIGHT ON TOP OF IT --MOVE IT--
P·A·X
YES, CAPTAIN.

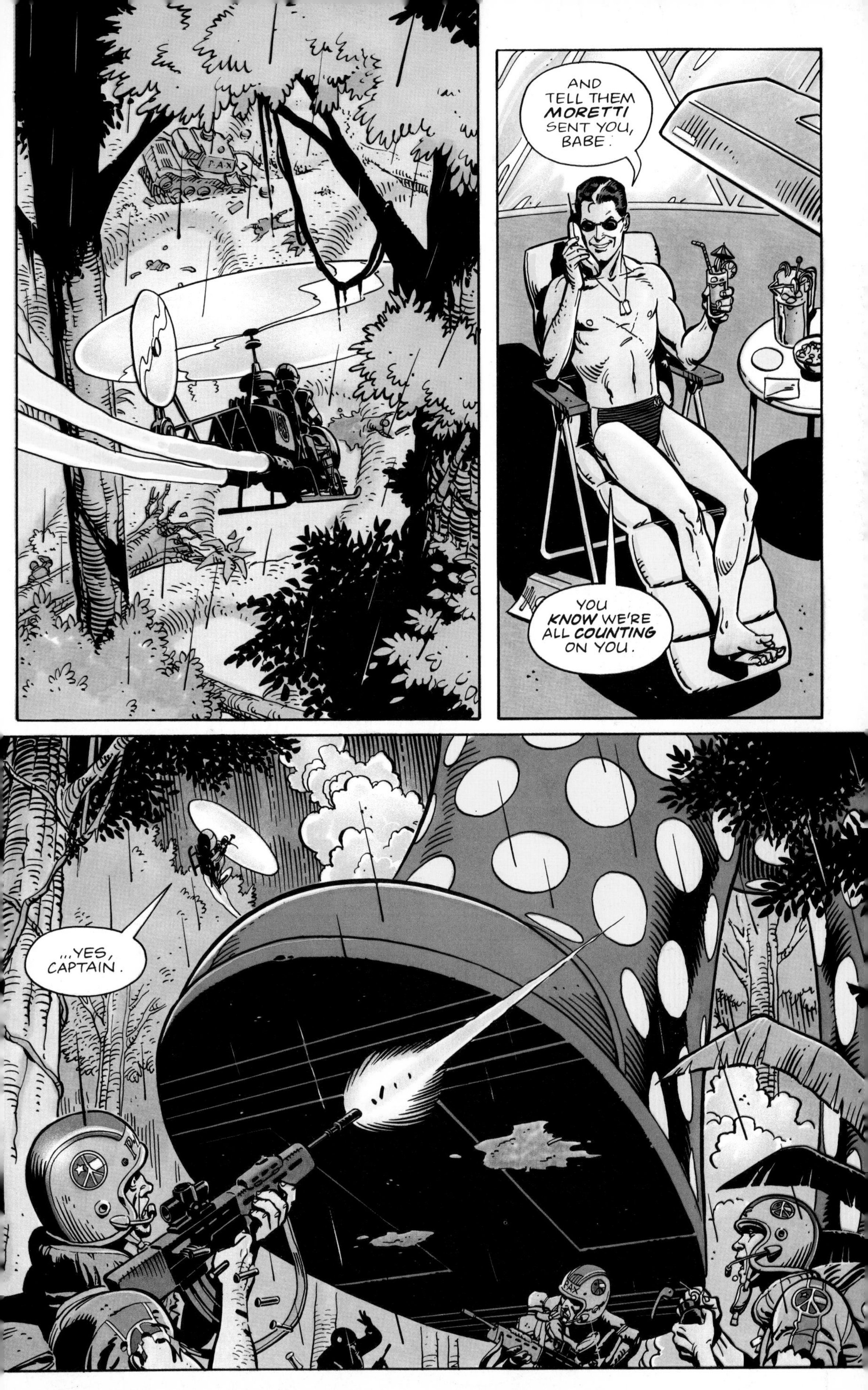
AND TELL THEM MORETTI SENT YOU, BABE.
YOU KNOW WE'RE ALL COUNTING ON YOU.
...YES, CAPTAIN.

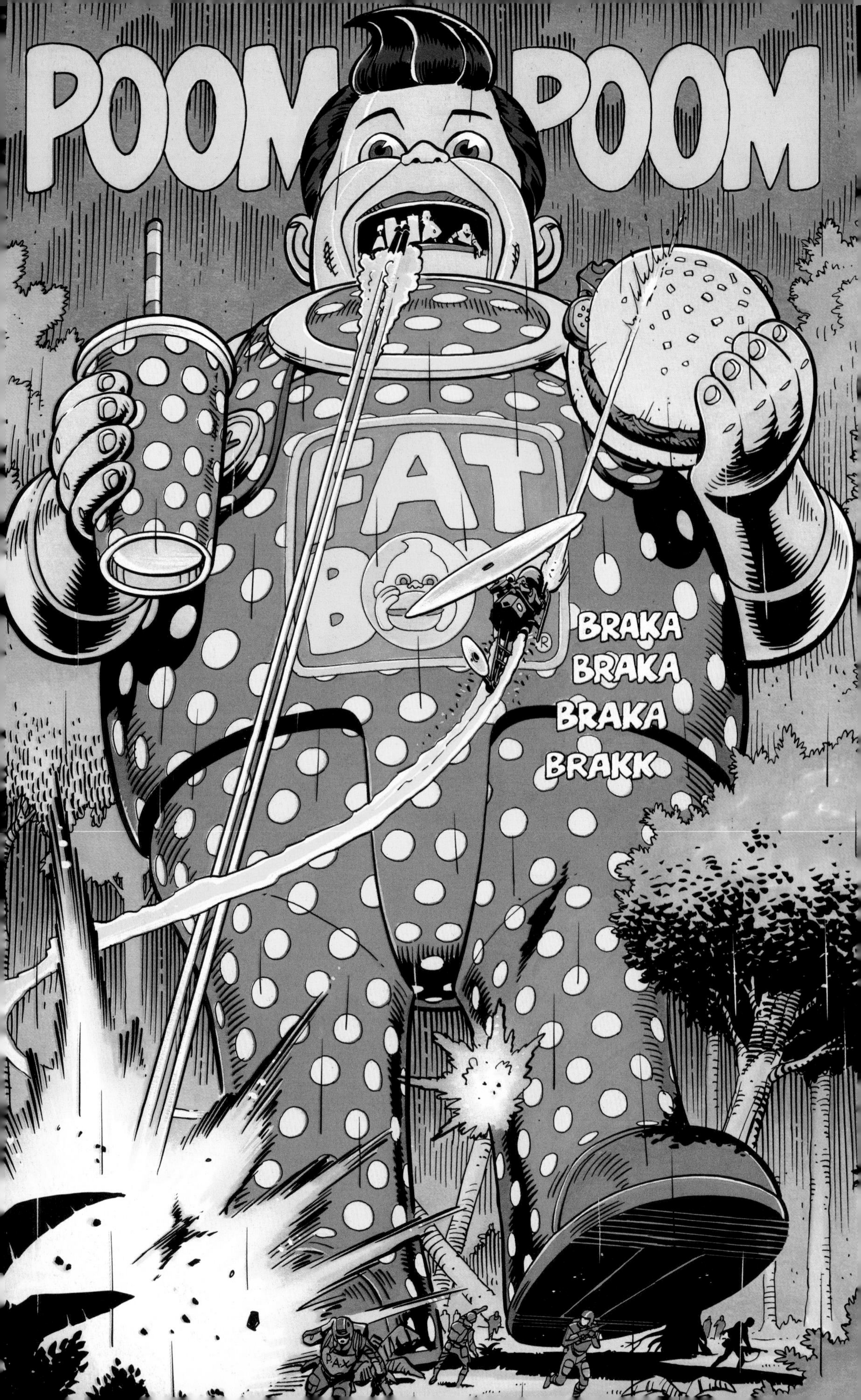
POOM POOM
FAT BOY
BRAKA
BRAKA
BRAKA
BRAKK
PAX

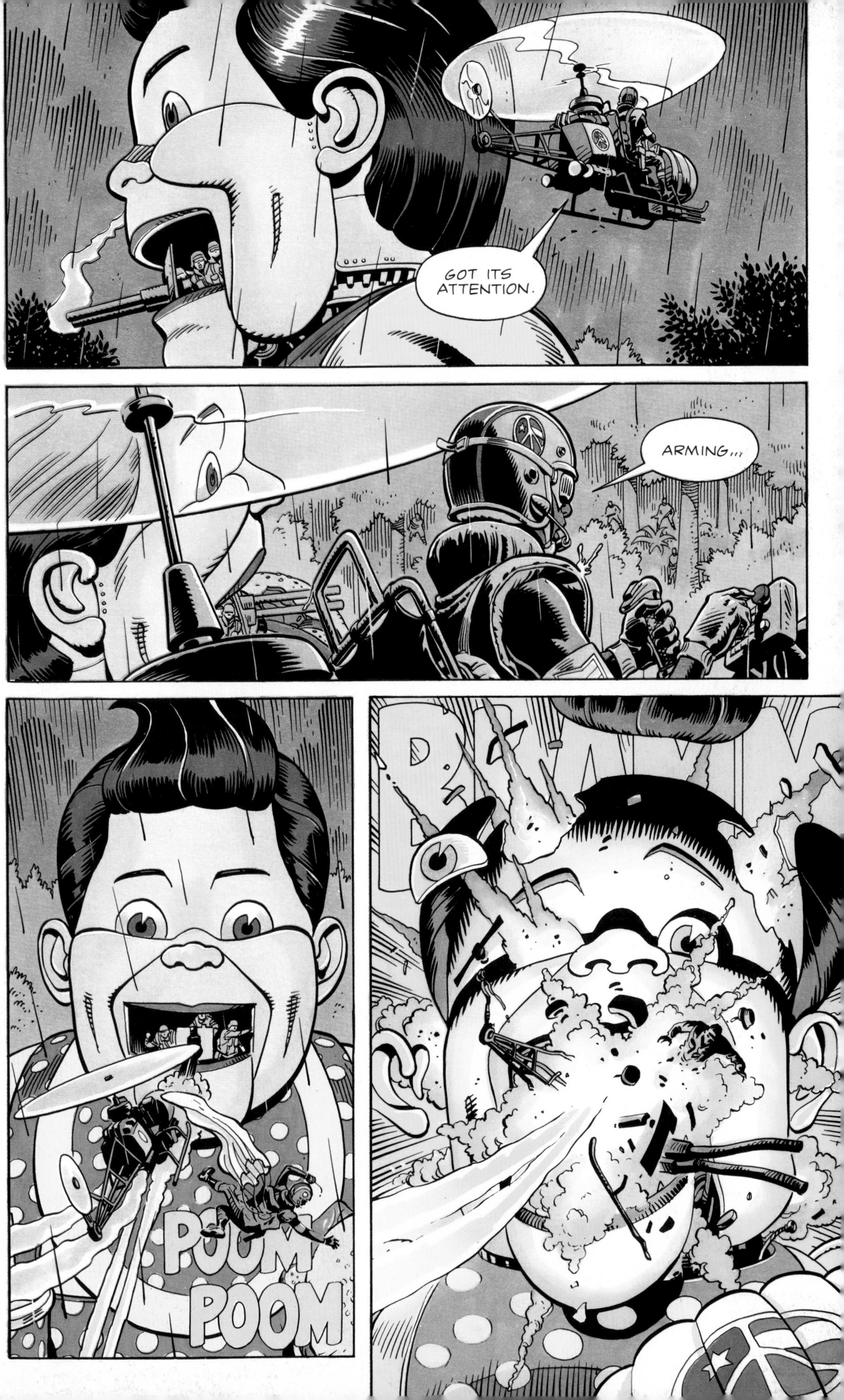
GOT ITS ATTENTION.
ARMING...
POOM
POOM

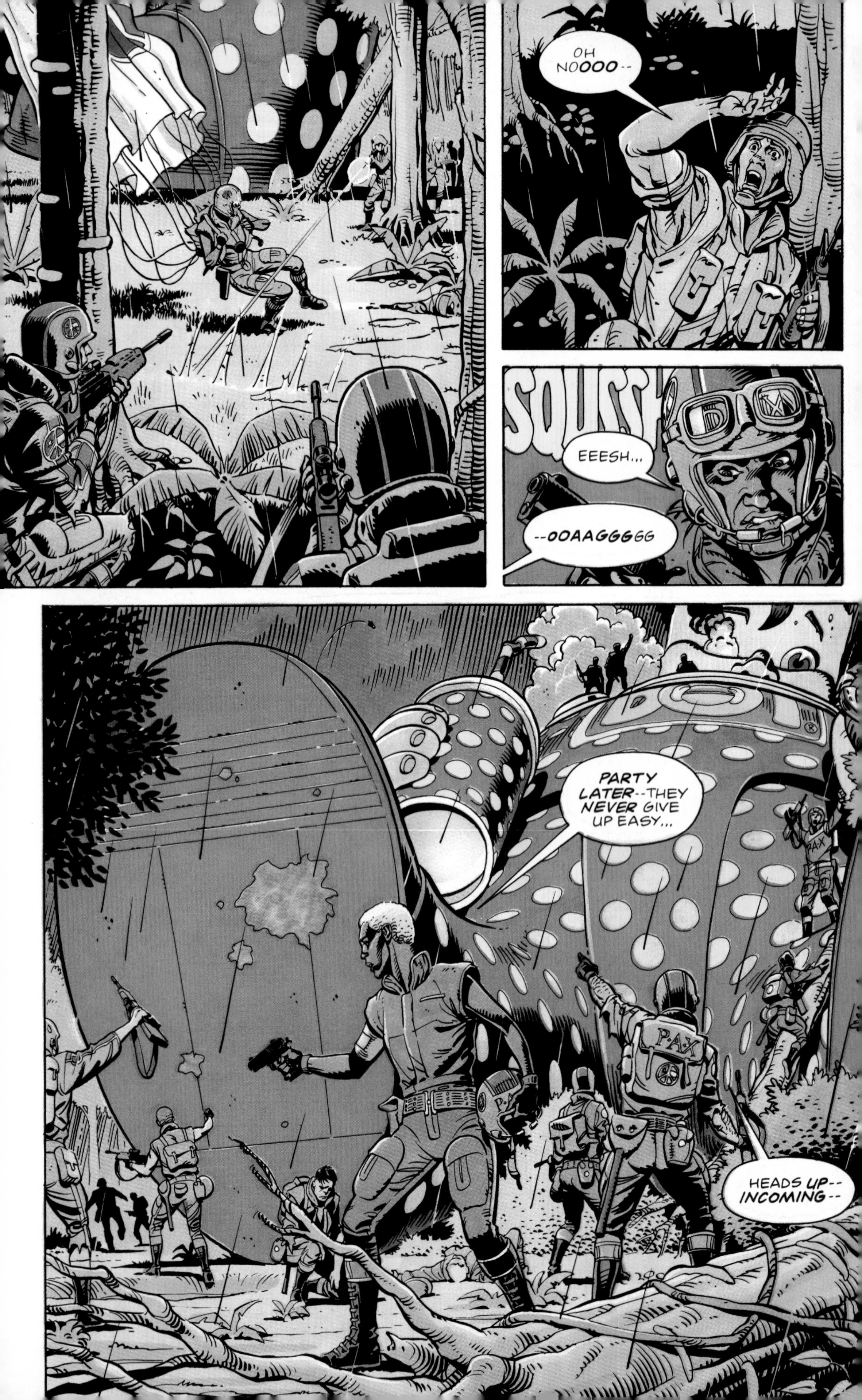
OH NOOOO--
EEESH...
--OOAAGGGGG
PARTY LATER--THEY NEVER GIVE UP EASY...
P·A·X
HEADS UP-- INCOMING--

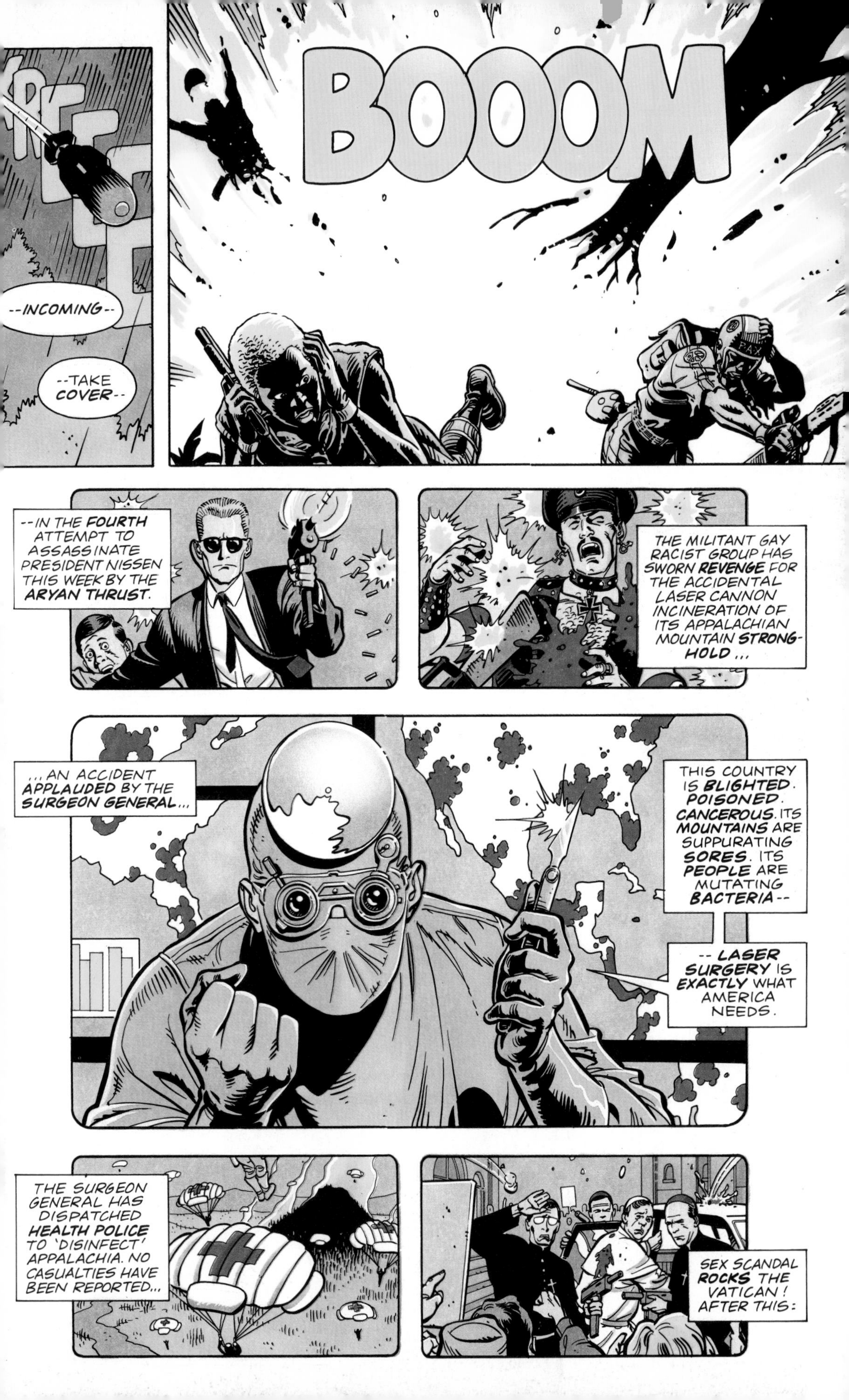
KRF
--INCOMING--
--TAKE COVER--
BOOOM
PAX
--IN THE FOURTH ATTEMPT TO ASSASSINATE PRESIDENT NISSEN THIS WEEK BY THE ARYAN THRUST.
THE MILITANT GAY RACIST GROUP HAS SWORN REVENGE FOR THE ACCIDENTAL LASER CANNON INCINERATION OF ITS APPALACHIAN MOUNTAIN STRONGHOLD ...
... AN ACCIDENT APPLAUDED BY THE SURGEON GENERAL...
THIS COUNTRY IS BLIGHTED. POISONED. CANCEROUS. ITS MOUNTAINS ARE SUPPURATING SORES. ITS PEOPLE ARE MUTATING BACTERIA--
-- LASER SURGERY IS EXACTLY WHAT AMERICA NEEDS.
THE SURGEON GENERAL HAS DISPATCHED HEALTH POLICE TO 'DISINFECT' APPALACHIA. NO CASUALTIES HAVE BEEN REPORTED...
SEX SCANDAL ROCKS THE VATICAN! AFTER THIS:

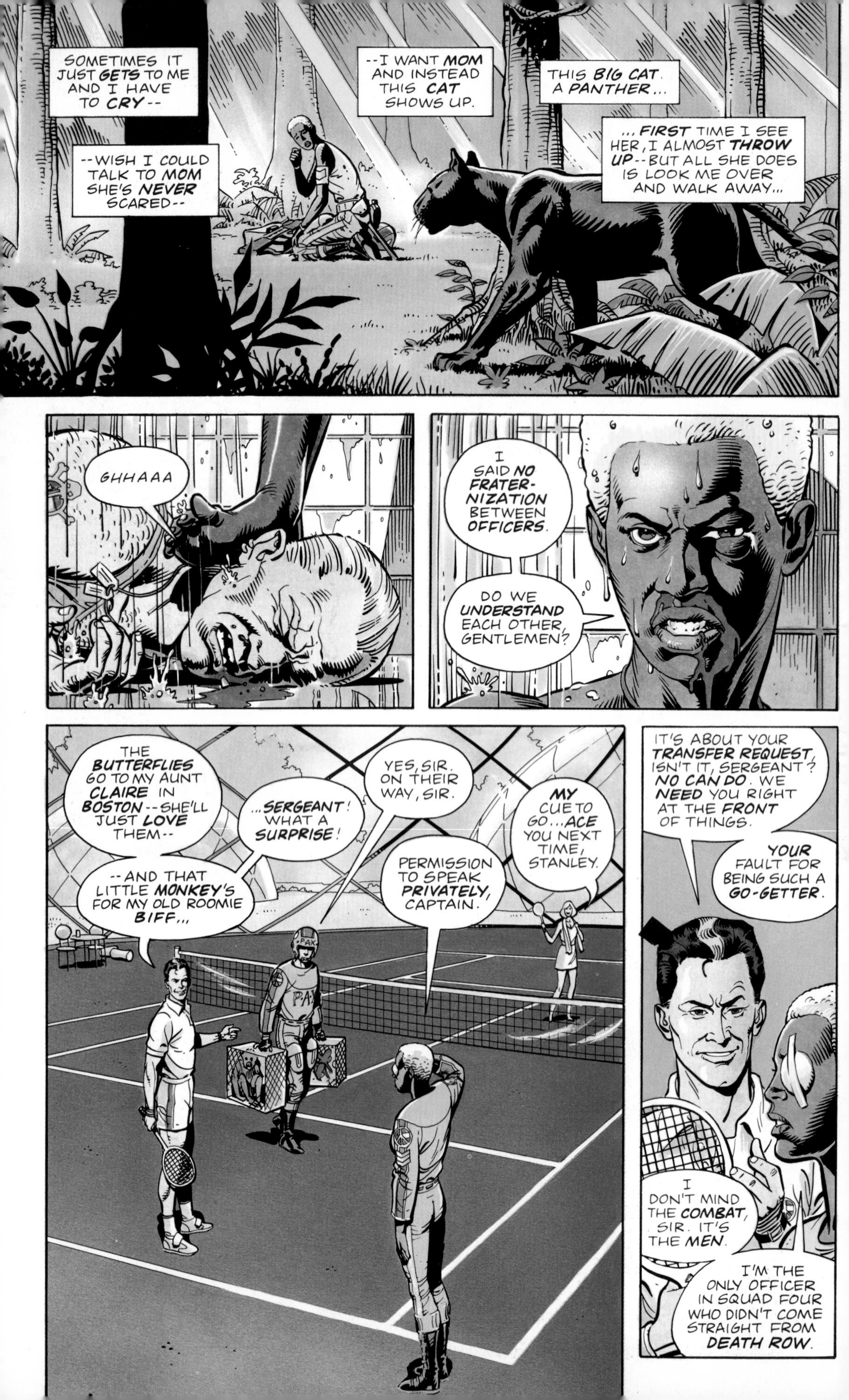
SOMETIMES IT JUST GETS TO ME AND I HAVE TO CRY--
--WISH I COULD TALK TO MOM SHE'S NEVER SCARED--
--I WANT MOM AND INSTEAD THIS CAT SHOWS UP.
THIS BIG CAT. A PANTHER...
...FIRST TIME I SEE HER, I ALMOST THROW UP--BUT ALL SHE DOES IS LOOK ME OVER AND WALK AWAY...
GHHAAA
I SAID NO FRATER-NIZATION BETWEEN OFFICERS.
DO WE UNDERSTAND EACH OTHER, GENTLEMEN?
THE BUTTERFLIES GO TO MY AUNT CLAIRE IN BOSTON--SHE'LL JUST LOVE THEM--
--AND THAT LITTLE MONKEY'S FOR MY OLD ROOMIE BIFF...
...SERGEANT! WHAT A SURPRISE!
YES, SIR. ON THEIR WAY, SIR.
PERMISSION TO SPEAK PRIVATELY, CAPTAIN.
MY CUE TO GO...ACE YOU NEXT TIME, STANLEY.
IT'S ABOUT YOUR TRANSFER REQUEST, ISN'T IT, SERGEANT? NO CAN DO. WE NEED YOU RIGHT AT THE FRONT OF THINGS.
YOUR FAULT FOR BEING SUCH A GO-GETTER.
I DON'T MIND THE COMBAT, SIR. IT'S THE MEN.
I'M THE ONLY OFFICER IN SQUAD FOUR WHO DIDN'T COME STRAIGHT FROM DEATH ROW.

GIVING YOU A ROUGH TIME, AREN'T THEY? SORRY, DOLL, BUT YOU'LL JUST HAVE TO **BUCK UP.**

PERMISSION TO SPEAK... CANDIDLY, SIR.

I'VE KEPT MY **MOUTH** SHUT. I HAVEN'T TOLD **ANYBODY** HOW YOU SOLD US **OUT.**

THWAKK

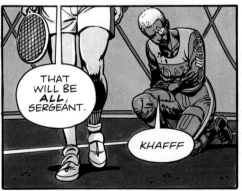

THAT WILL BE **ALL,** SERGEANT.

KHAFFF

I WANT TO **KILL** HIM.

THIS TIME SHE **SNIFFS** ME.

-- A NEWS TWELVE **DATA RAID** REVEALS THE LASER CANNON MISFIRE WAS CAUSED BY AN EXPERIMENTAL **COMMAND SYSTEM** --

-- UTILIZING **PSYCHIC SCHIZOPHRENICS** LITERALLY **WIRED IN** TO COMPUTER SOFTWARE.

COMING UP: VICTORIOUS **PAX** TROOPS PRESS THEIR ADVANTAGE -- CHARGING THE **FATBOY CATTLE- FIELDS** AT THE EDGE OF THE AMAZON...

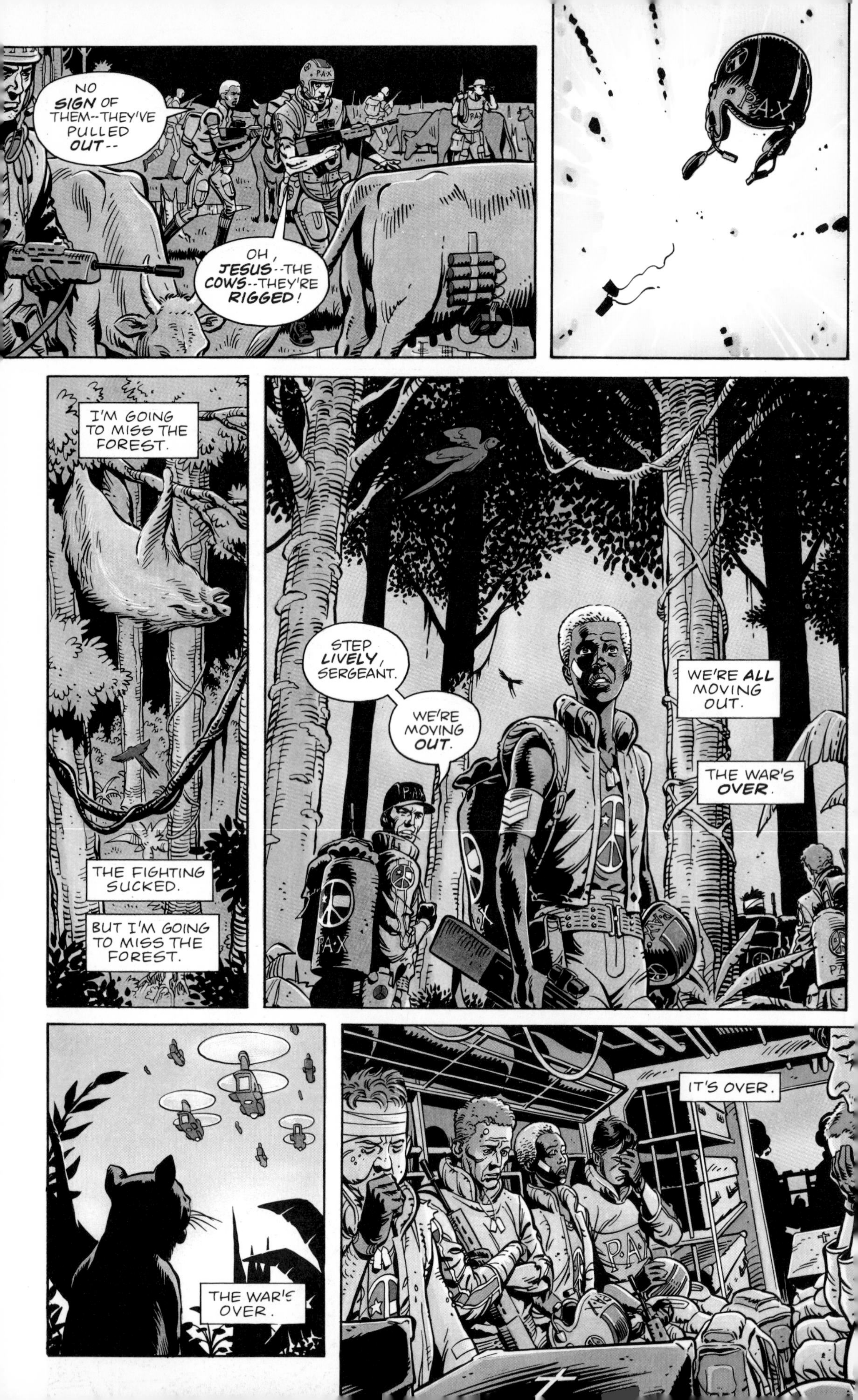
NO SIGN OF THEM--THEY'VE PULLED OUT--
OH, JESUS--THE COWS--THEY'RE RIGGED!
P·A·X
I'M GOING TO MISS THE FOREST.
THE FIGHTING SUCKED.
BUT I'M GOING TO MISS THE FOREST.
STEP LIVELY, SERGEANT.
WE'RE MOVING OUT.
WE'RE ALL MOVING OUT.
THE WAR'S OVER.
THE WAR'S OVER.
IT'S OVER.

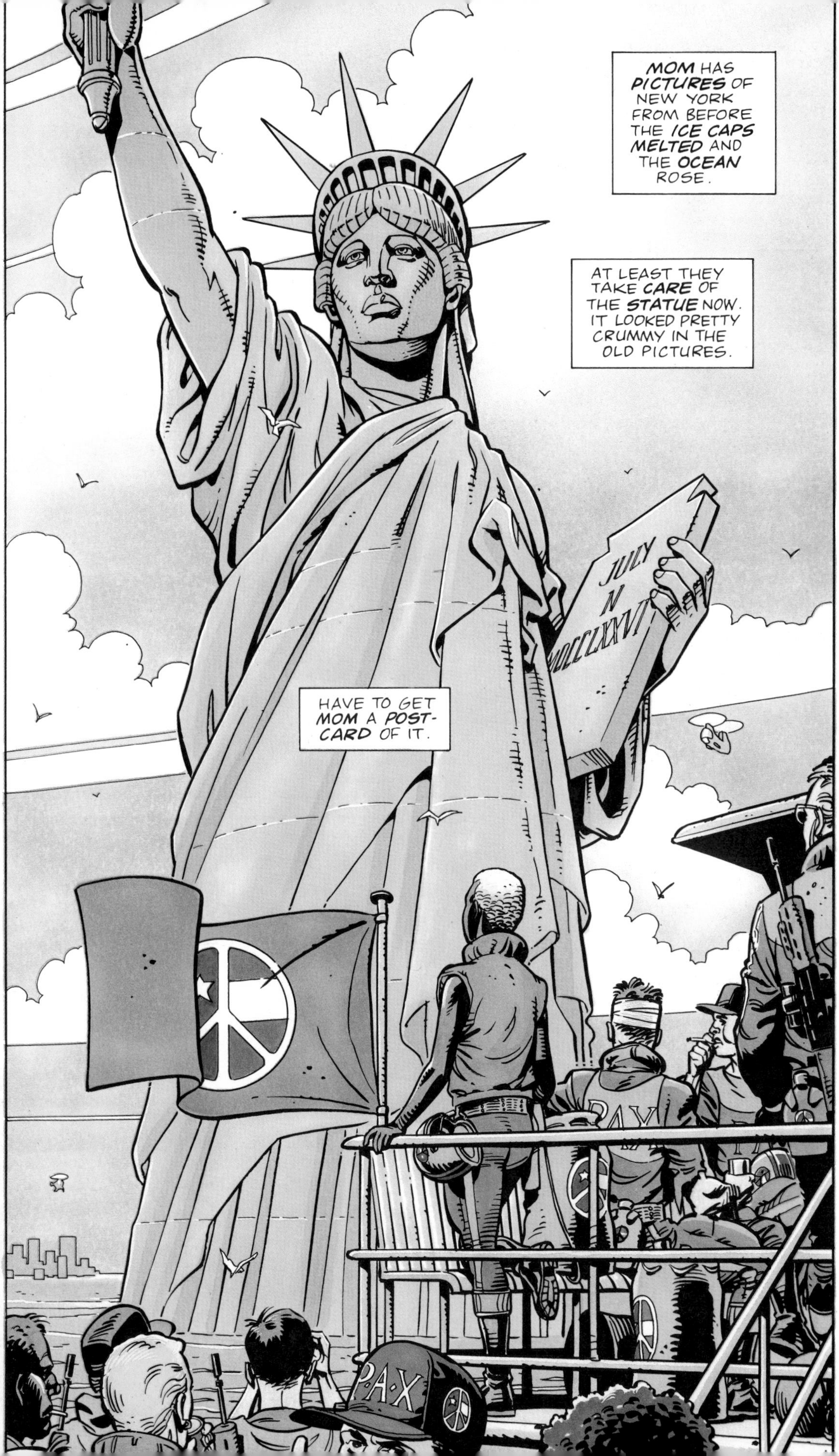
MOM HAS PICTURES OF NEW YORK FROM BEFORE THE ICE CAPS MELTED AND THE OCEAN ROSE.
AT LEAST THEY TAKE CARE OF THE STATUE NOW. IT LOOKED PRETTY CRUMMY IN THE OLD PICTURES.
HAVE TO GET MOM A POST-CARD OF IT.
P·A·X

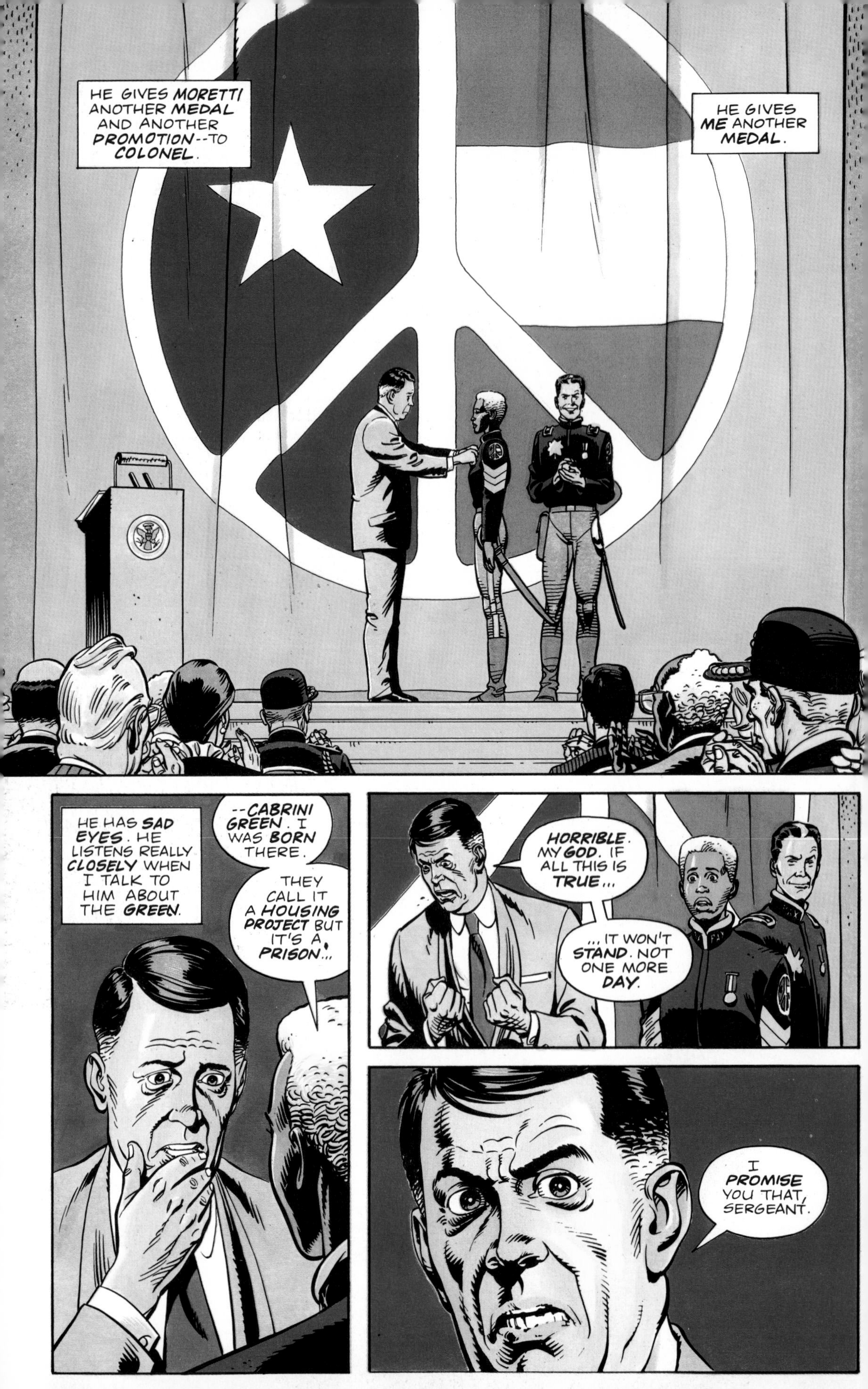
HE GIVES MORETTI ANOTHER MEDAL AND ANOTHER PROMOTION--TO COLONEL.
HE GIVES ME ANOTHER MEDAL.
HE HAS SAD EYES. HE LISTENS REALLY CLOSELY WHEN I TALK TO HIM ABOUT THE GREEN.
--CABRINI GREEN. I WAS BORN THERE.
THEY CALL IT A HOUSING PROJECT BUT IT'S A PRISON...
HORRIBLE. MY GOD. IF ALL THIS IS TRUE...
... IT WON'T STAND. NOT ONE MORE DAY.
I PROMISE YOU THAT, SERGEANT.

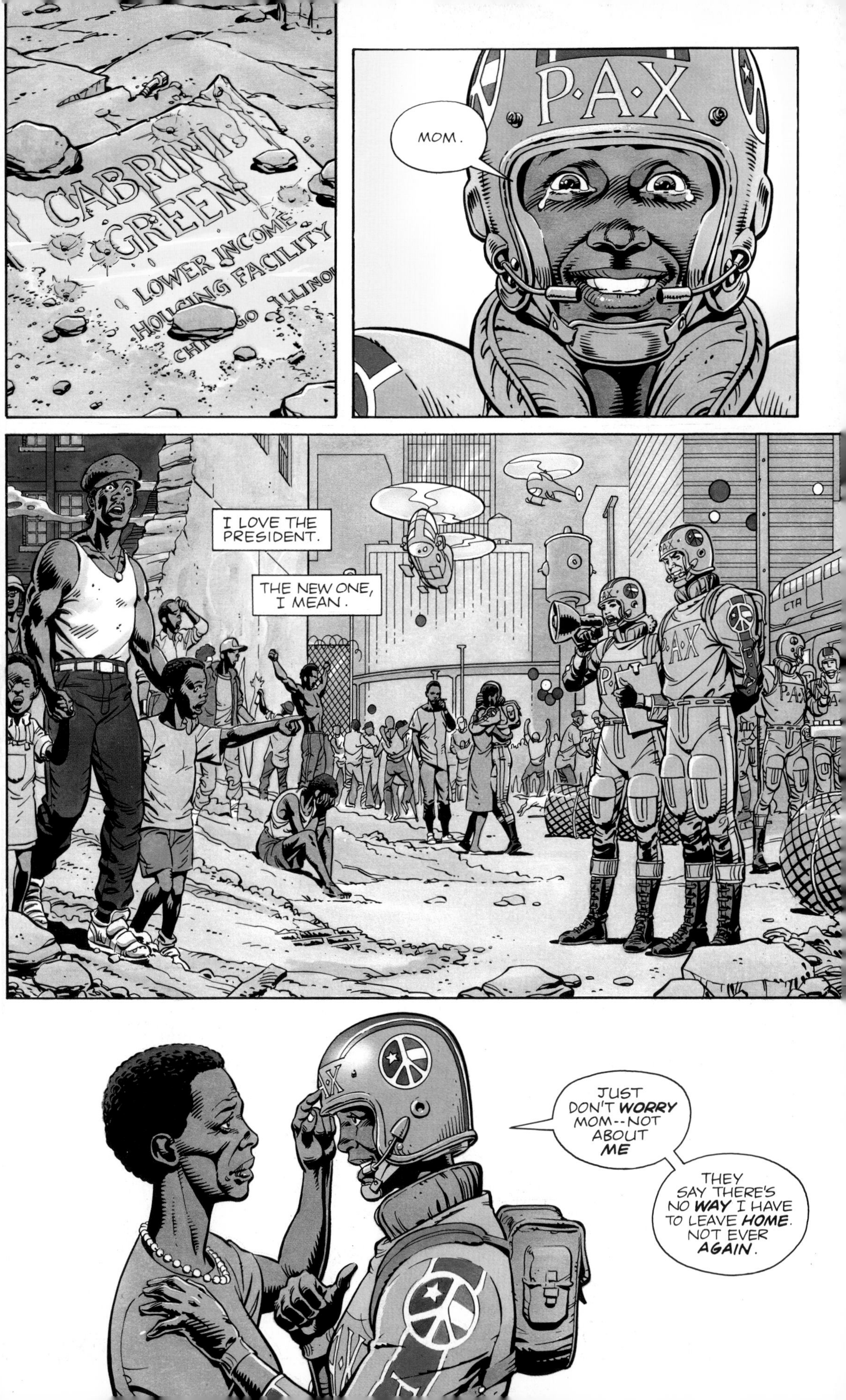
CABRINI GREEN
LOWER INCOME
HOUSING FACILITY
P·A·X
MOM.
I LOVE THE PRESIDENT.
THE NEW ONE, I MEAN.
CTA
JUST DON'T **WORRY** MOM--NOT ABOUT **ME**
THEY SAY THERE'S NO **WAY** I HAVE TO LEAVE **HOME**. NOT EVER **AGAIN**.

2011

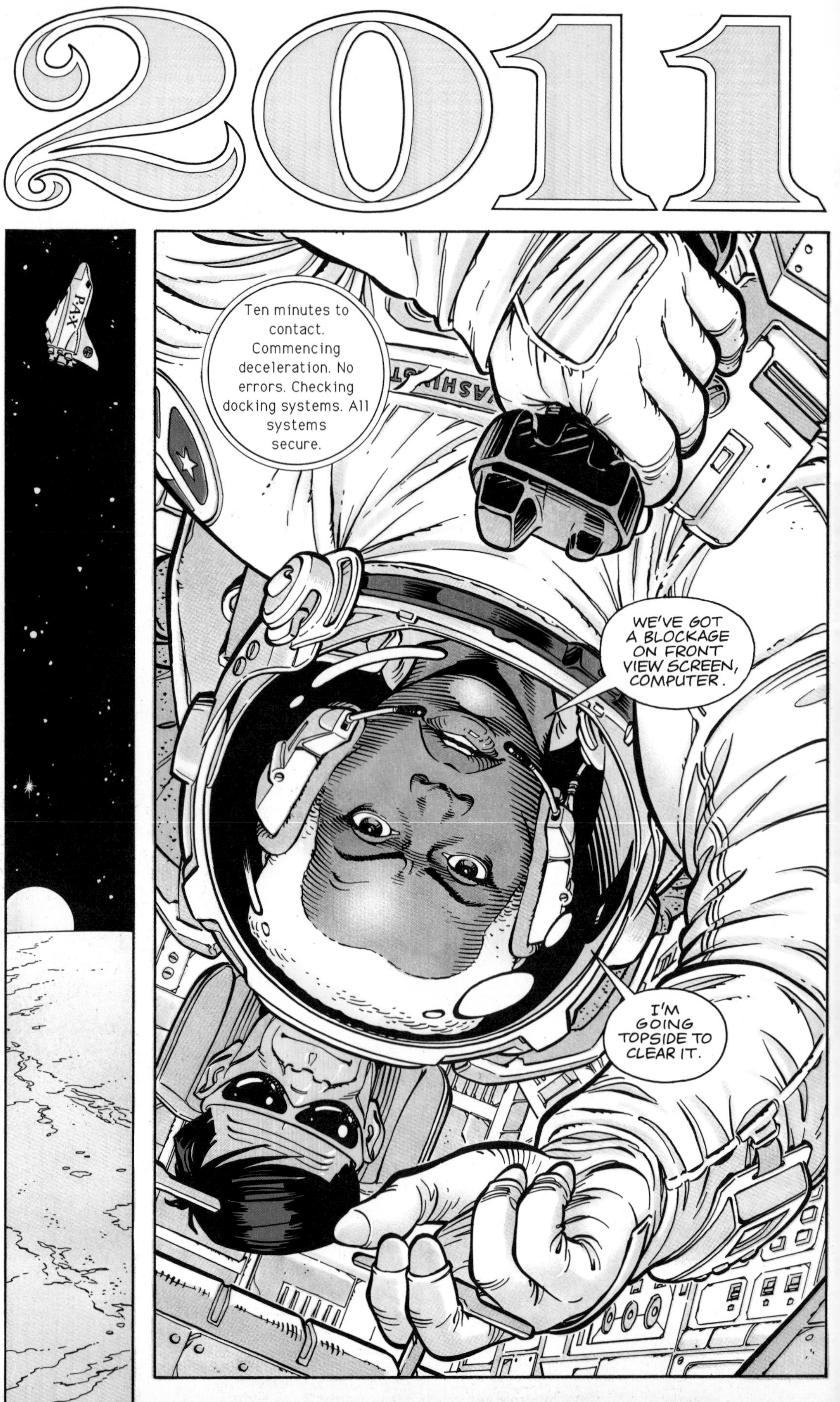
P·A·X
Ten minutes to contact. Commencing deceleration. No errors. Checking docking systems. All systems secure.
WE'VE GOT A BLOCKAGE ON FRONT VIEW SCREEN, COMPUTER.
I'M GOING TOPSIDE TO CLEAR IT.

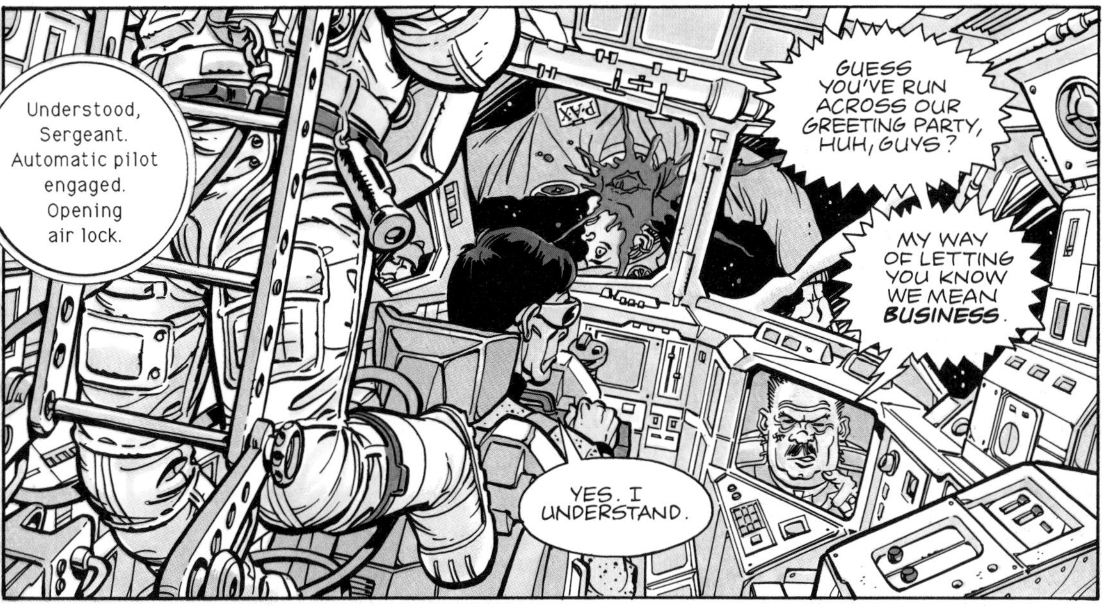

Understood, Sergeant. Automatic pilot engaged. Opening air lock.
GUESS YOU'VE RUN ACROSS OUR GREETING PARTY, HUH, GUYS?
MY WAY OF LETTING YOU KNOW WE MEAN **BUSINESS**.
YES. I UNDERSTAND.

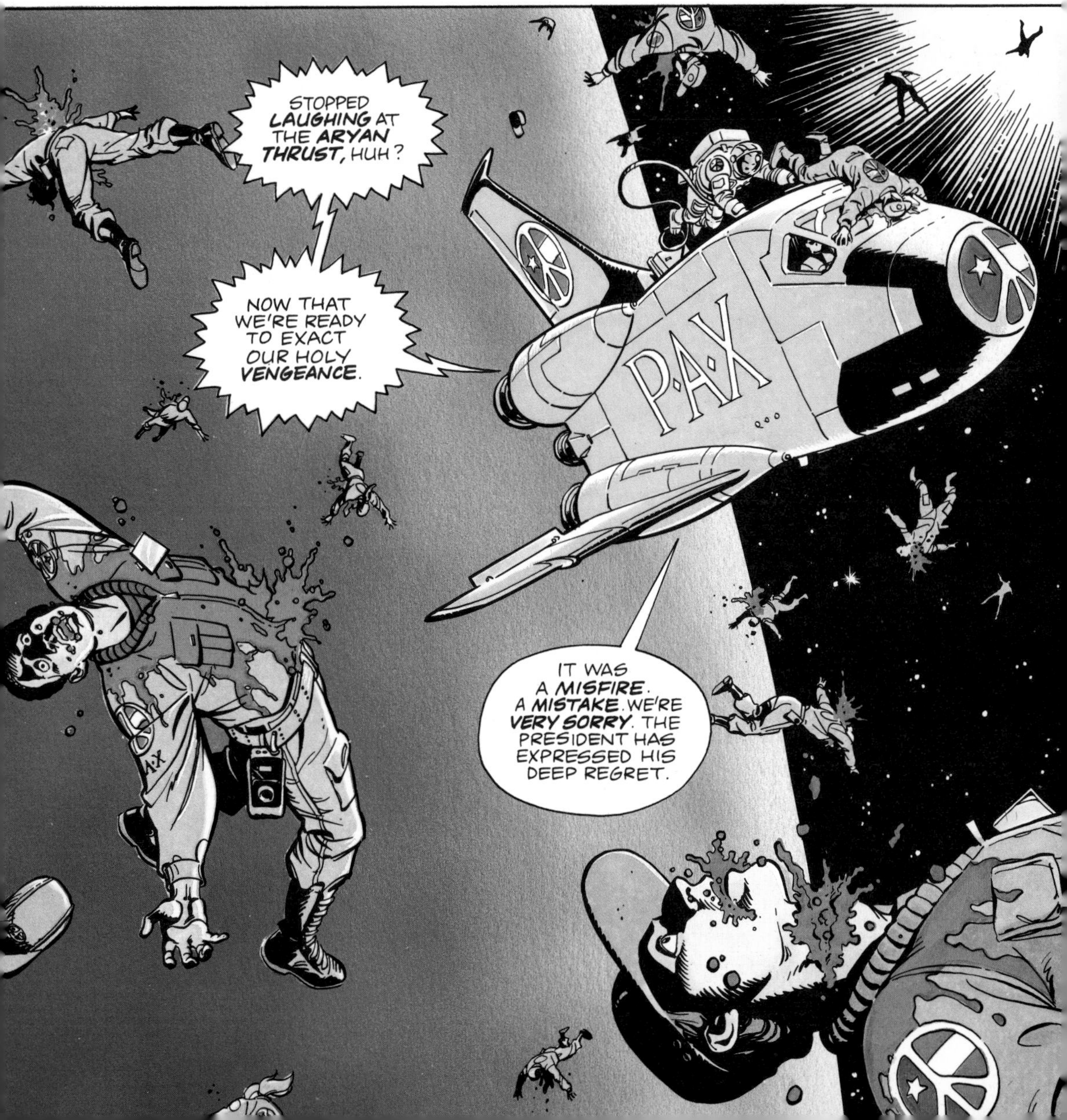

STOPPED **LAUGHING** AT THE **ARYAN THRUST,** HUH?
NOW THAT WE'RE READY TO EXACT OUR HOLY **VENGEANCE**.
IT WAS A **MISFIRE**. A **MISTAKE**. WE'RE **VERY SORRY**. THE PRESIDENT HAS EXPRESSED HIS DEEP REGRET.
P·A·X

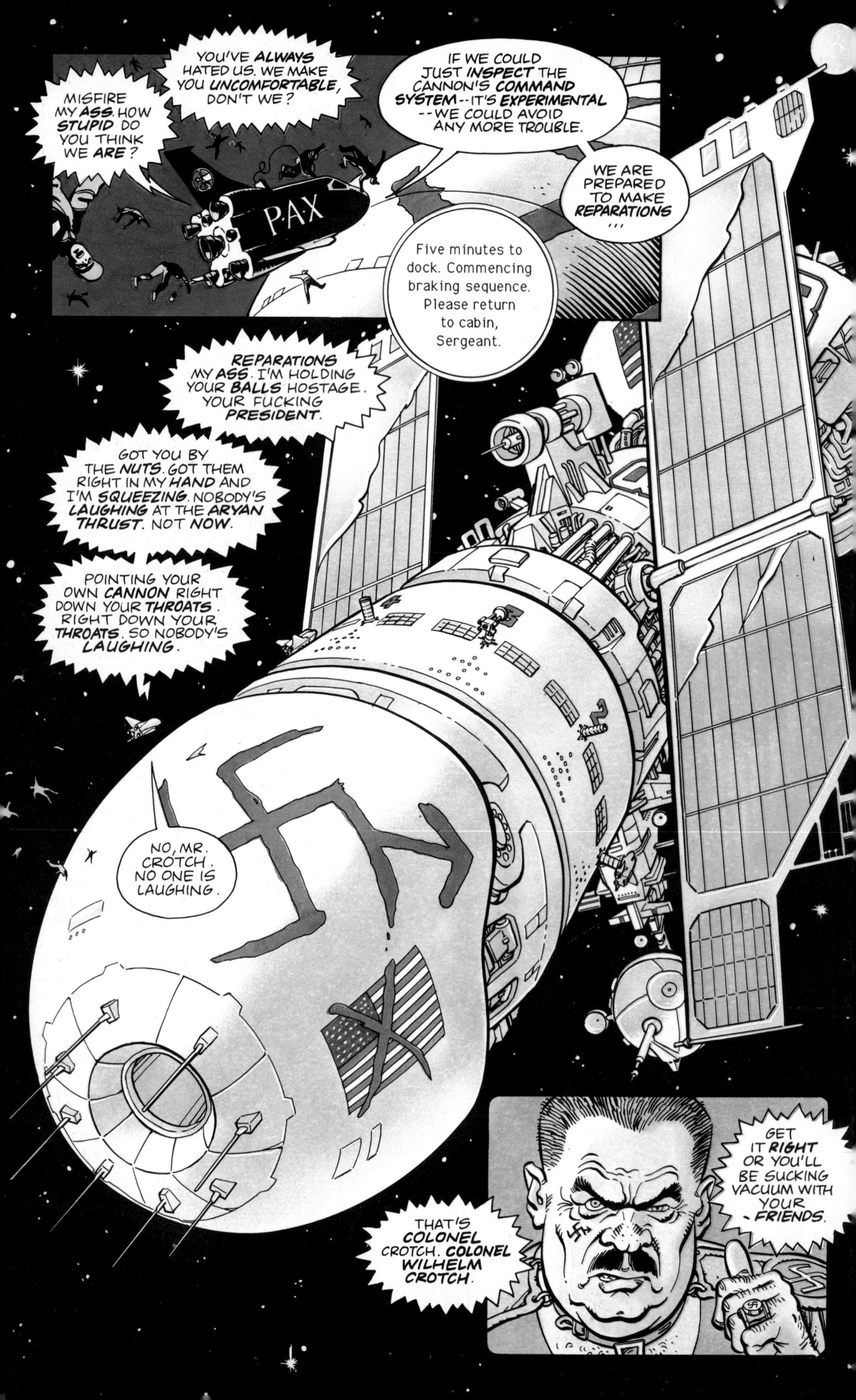
MISFIRE MY ASS. HOW STUPID DO YOU THINK WE ARE?
YOU'VE ALWAYS HATED US. WE MAKE YOU UNCOMFORTABLE, DON'T WE?
IF WE COULD JUST INSPECT THE CANNON'S COMMAND SYSTEM--IT'S EXPERIMENTAL--WE COULD AVOID ANY MORE TROUBLE.
WE ARE PREPARED TO MAKE REPARATIONS...
PAX
Five minutes to dock. Commencing braking sequence. Please return to cabin, Sergeant.
REPARATIONS MY ASS. I'M HOLDING YOUR BALLS HOSTAGE. YOUR FUCKING PRESIDENT.
GOT YOU BY THE NUTS. GOT THEM RIGHT IN MY HAND AND I'M SQUEEZING. NOBODY'S LAUGHING AT THE ARYAN THRUST. NOT NOW.
POINTING YOUR OWN CANNON RIGHT DOWN YOUR THROATS. RIGHT DOWN YOUR THROATS. SO NOBODY'S LAUGHING.
NO, MR. CROTCH. NO ONE IS LAUGHING.
GET IT RIGHT OR YOU'LL BE SUCKING VACUUM WITH YOUR FRIENDS.
THAT'S COLONEL CROTCH. COLONEL WILHELM CROTCH.

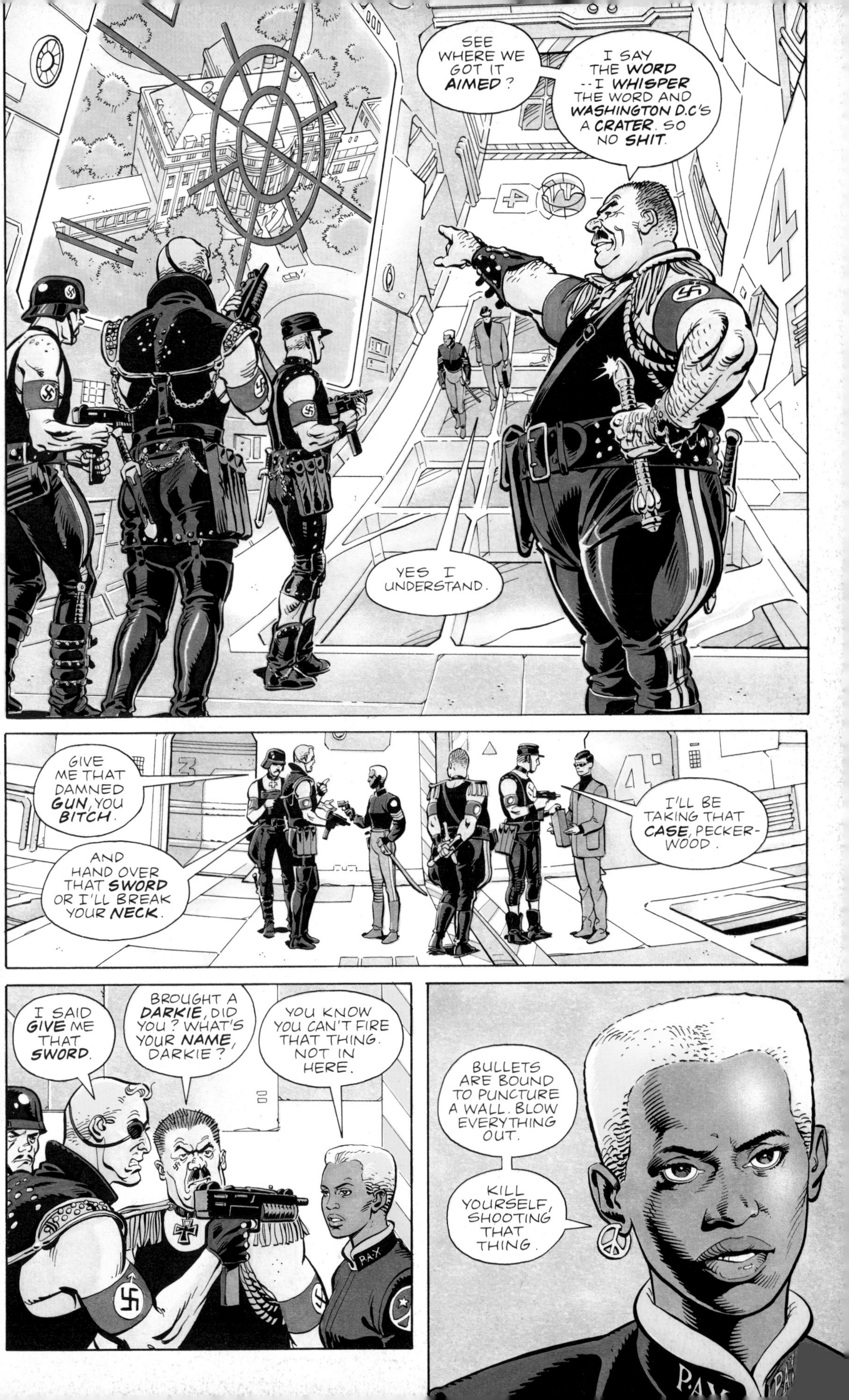
SEE WHERE WE GOT IT AIMED?
I SAY THE WORD --I WHISPER THE WORD AND WASHINGTON D.C'S A CRATER. SO NO SHIT.
YES I UNDERSTAND.
GIVE ME THAT DAMNED GUN, YOU BITCH.
AND HAND OVER THAT SWORD OR I'LL BREAK YOUR NECK.
I'LL BE TAKING THAT CASE, PECKER-WOOD.
I SAID GIVE ME THAT SWORD.
BROUGHT A DARKIE, DID YOU? WHAT'S YOUR NAME, DARKIE?
YOU KNOW YOU CAN'T FIRE THAT THING. NOT IN HERE.
BULLETS ARE BOUND TO PUNCTURE A WALL. BLOW EVERYTHING OUT.
KILL YOURSELF, SHOOTING THAT THING.

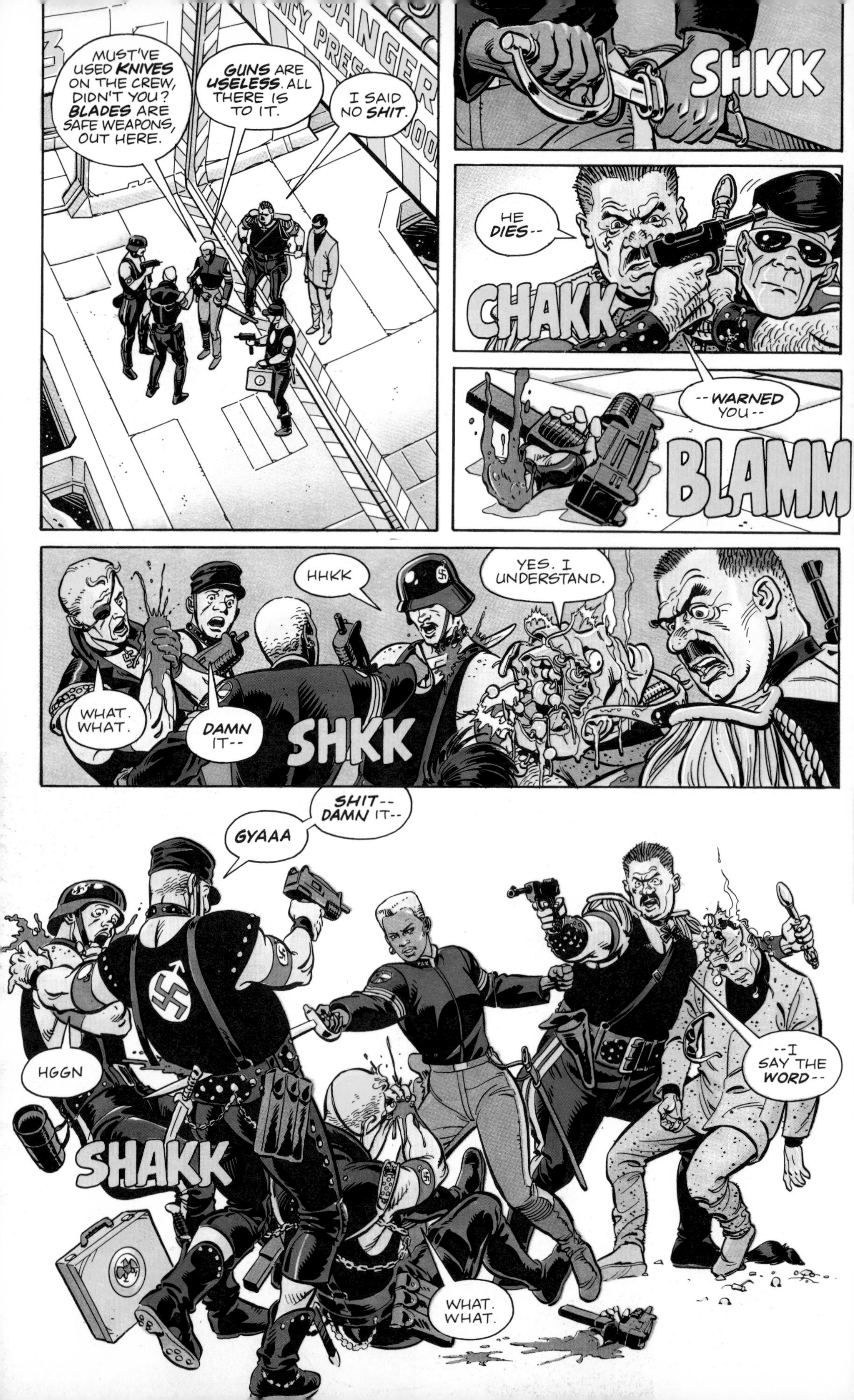
MUST'VE USED KNIVES ON THE CREW, DIDN'T YOU? BLADES ARE SAFE WEAPONS, OUT HERE.
GUNS ARE USELESS. ALL THERE IS TO IT.
I SAID NO SHIT.
SHKK
HE DIES--
CHAKK
--WARNED YOU--
BLAMM
HHKK
YES. I UNDERSTAND.
WHAT. WHAT.
DAMN IT--
SHKK
GYAAA
SHIT-- DAMN IT--
HGGN
--I SAY THE WORD--
SHAKK
WHAT. WHAT.

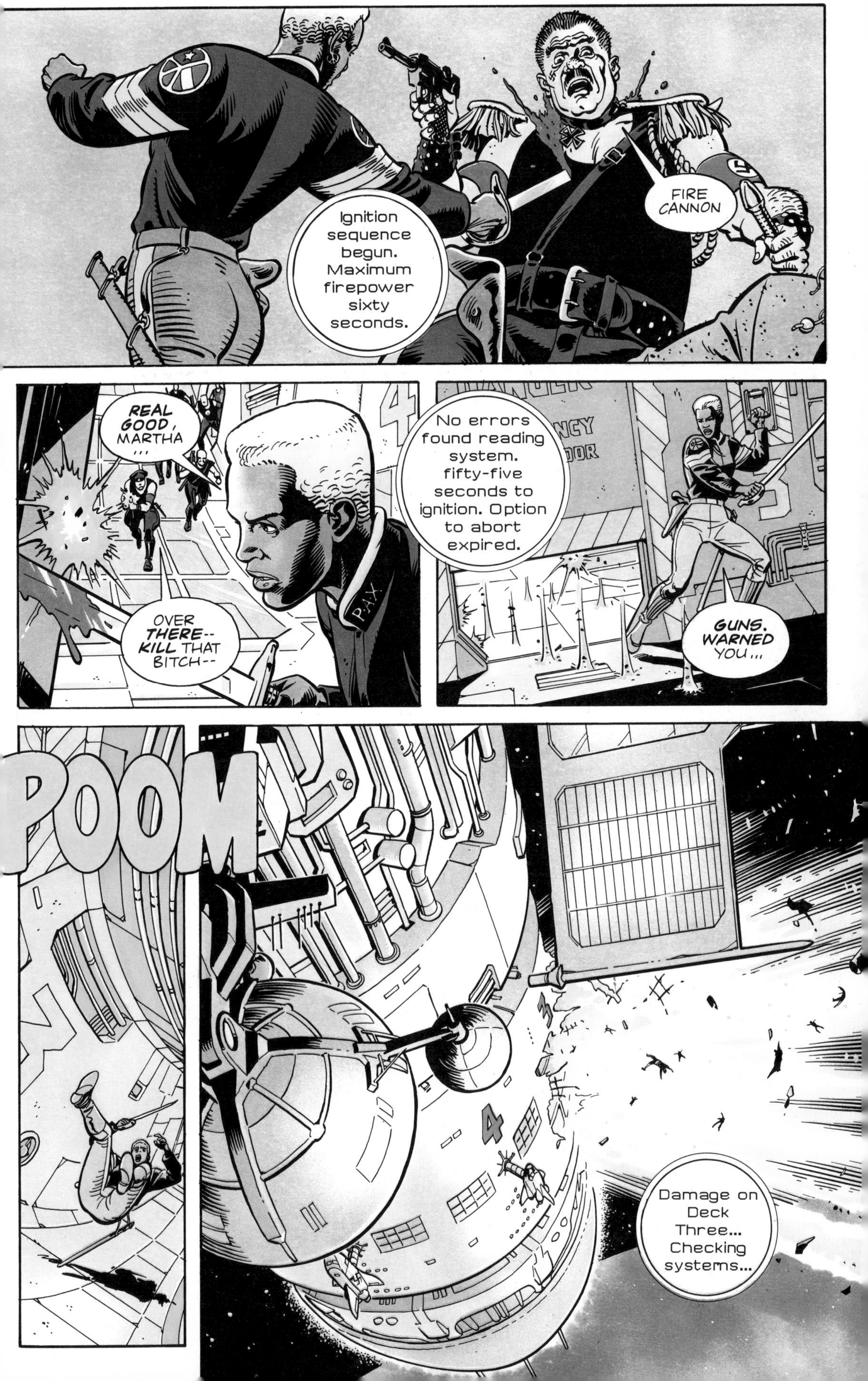
FIRE CANNON
Ignition sequence begun. Maximum firepower sixty seconds.
REAL GOOD, MARTHA ...
OVER THERE-- KILL THAT BITCH--
No errors found reading system. fifty-five seconds to ignition. Option to abort expired.
GUNS. WARNED YOU...
POOM
Damage on Deck Three... Checking systems...

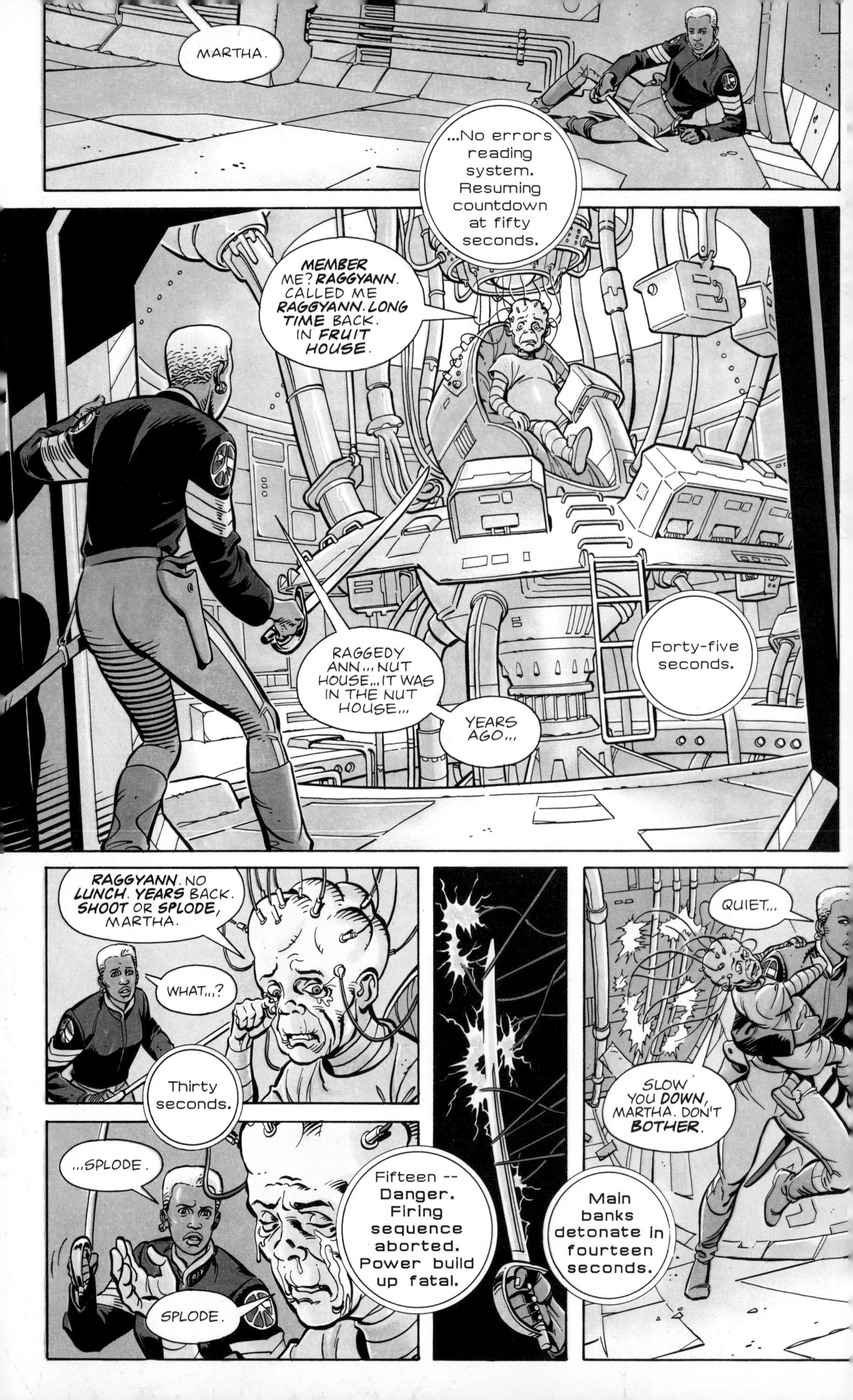

MARTHA.
...No errors reading system. Resuming countdown at fifty seconds.
MEMBER ME? RAGGYANN. CALLED ME RAGGYANN. LONG TIME BACK. IN FRUIT HOUSE.
RAGGEDY ANN... NUT HOUSE... IT WAS IN THE NUT HOUSE...
YEARS AGO...
Forty-five seconds.
RAGGYANN. NO LUNCH. YEARS BACK. SHOOT OR SPLODE, MARTHA.
WHAT...?
Thirty seconds.
...SPLODE.
SPLODE.
Fifteen -- Danger. Firing sequence aborted. Power build up fatal.
QUIET...
SLOW YOU DOWN, MARTHA. DON'T BOTHER.
Main banks detonate in fourteen seconds.

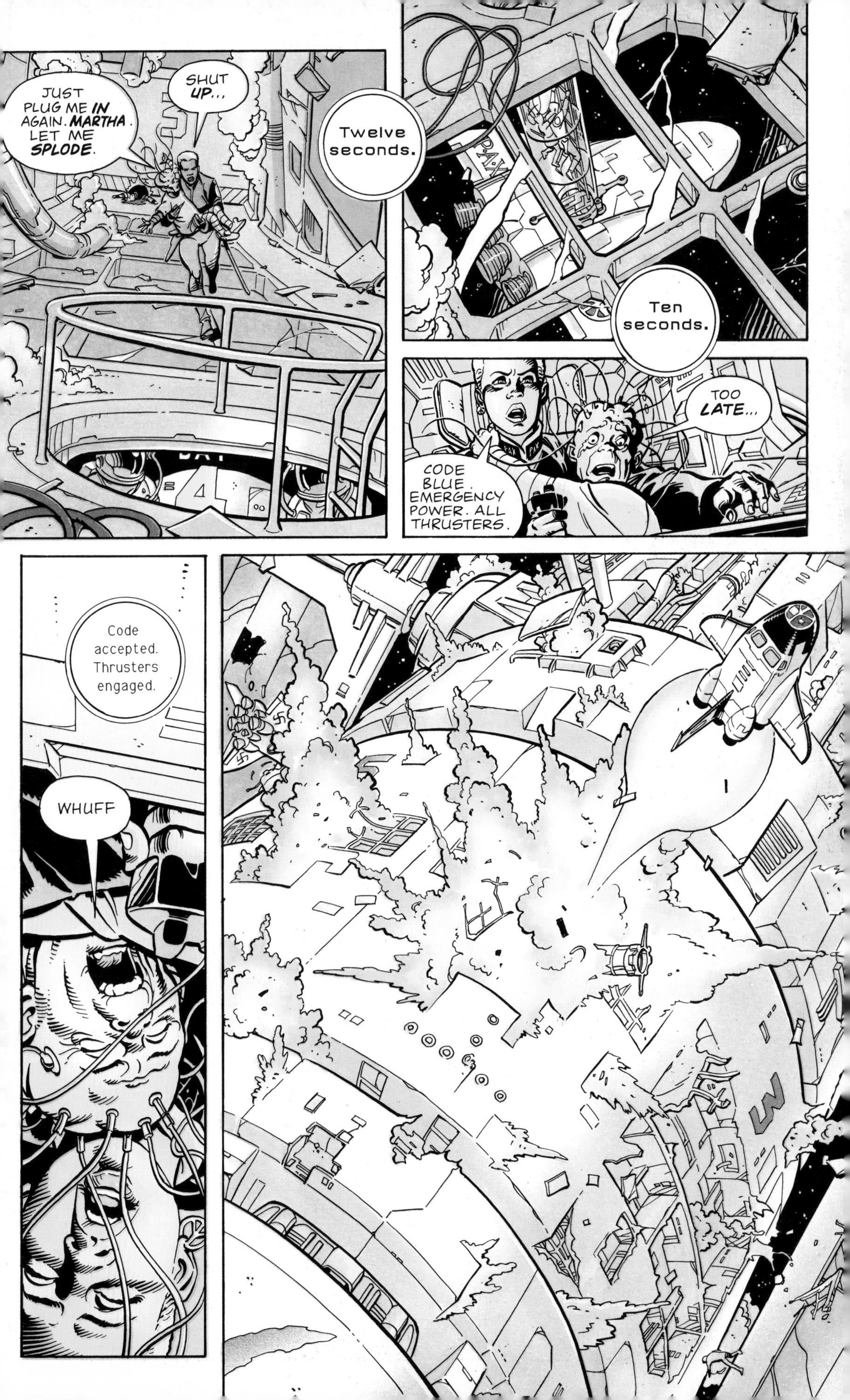
JUST PLUG ME IN AGAIN. MARTHA. LET ME SPLODE.
SHUT UP...
Twelve seconds.
Ten seconds.
TOO LATE...
CODE BLUE. EMERGENCY POWER. ALL THRUSTERS.
Code accepted. Thrusters engaged.
WHUFF

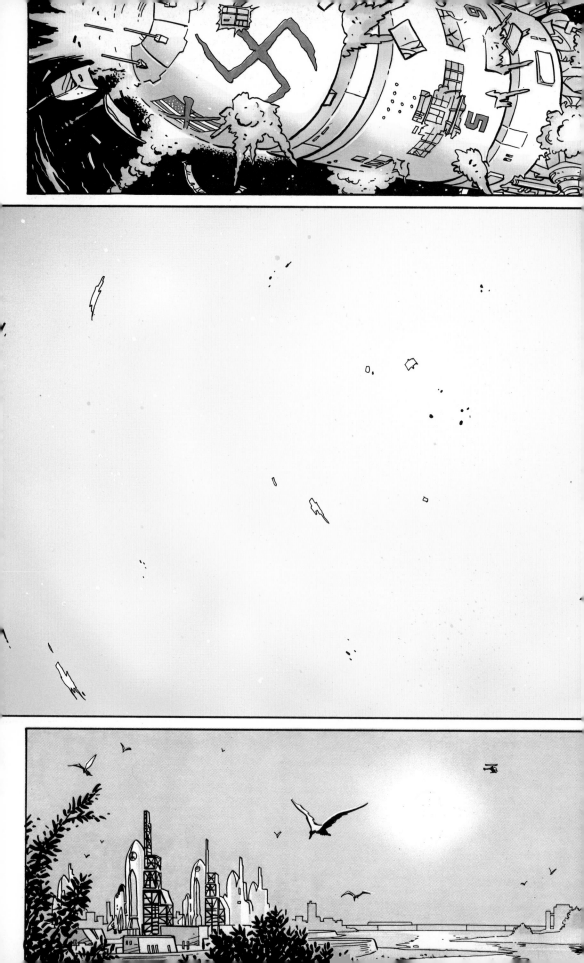

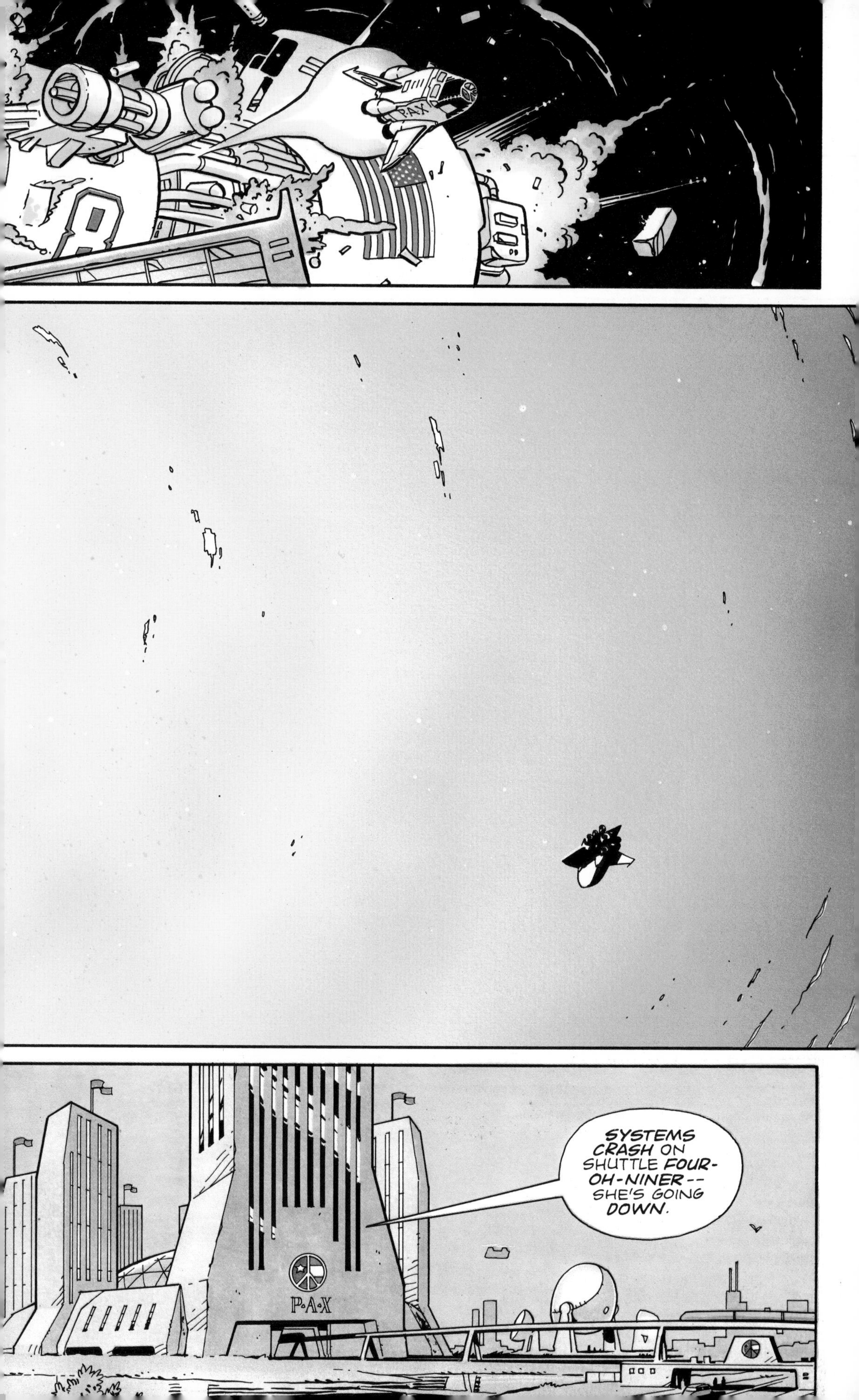
P·A·X
SYSTEMS CRASH ON SHUTTLE FOUR-OH-NINER-- SHE'S GOING DOWN.
P·A·X

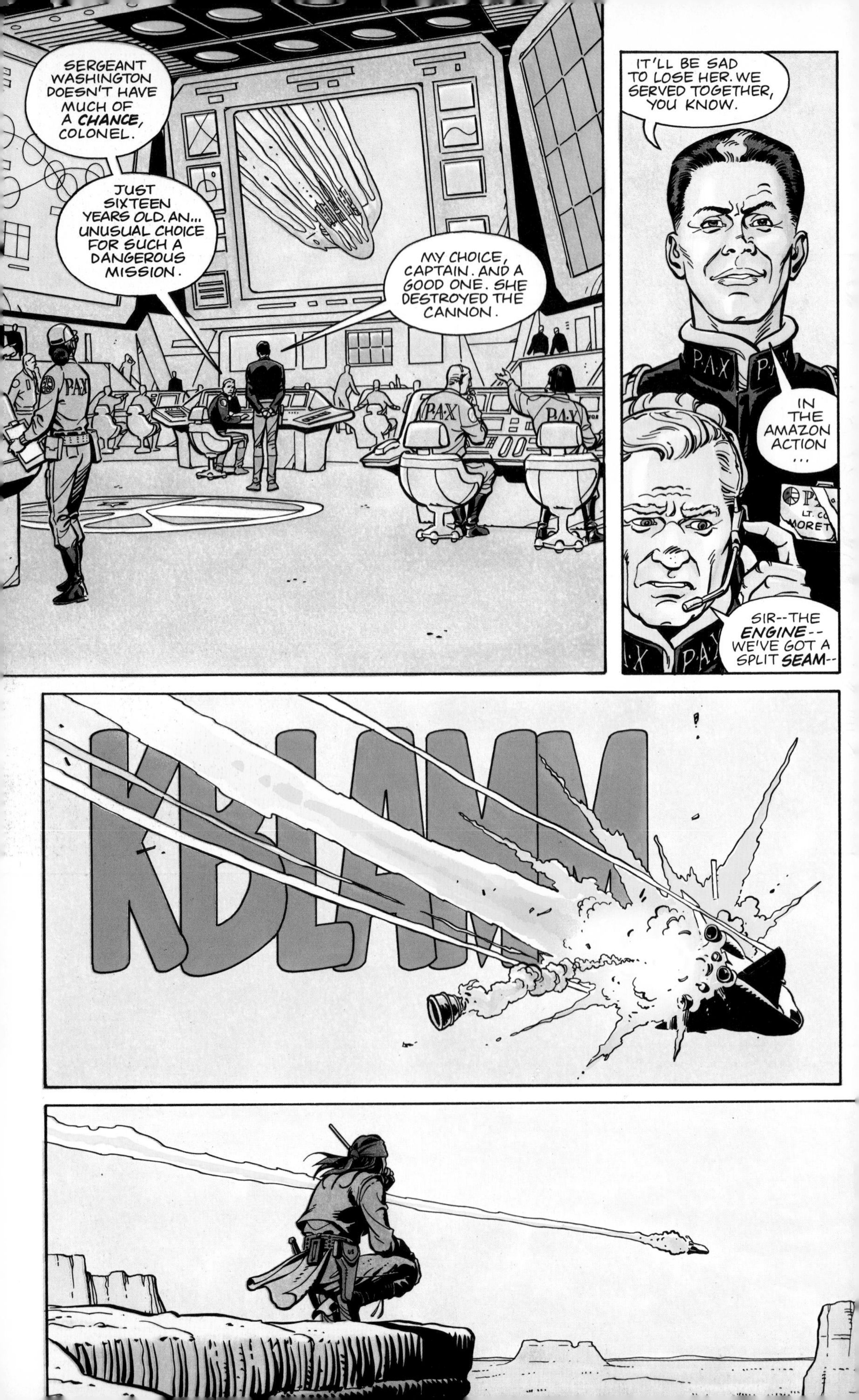
SERGEANT WASHINGTON DOESN'T HAVE MUCH OF A **CHANCE**, COLONEL.
JUST SIXTEEN YEARS OLD. AN... UNUSUAL CHOICE FOR SUCH A DANGEROUS MISSION.
MY CHOICE, CAPTAIN. AND A GOOD ONE. SHE DESTROYED THE CANNON.
IT'LL BE SAD TO LOSE HER. WE SERVED TOGETHER, YOU KNOW.
IN THE AMAZON ACTION ...
SIR--THE **ENGINE**--WE'VE GOT A SPLIT **SEAM**--

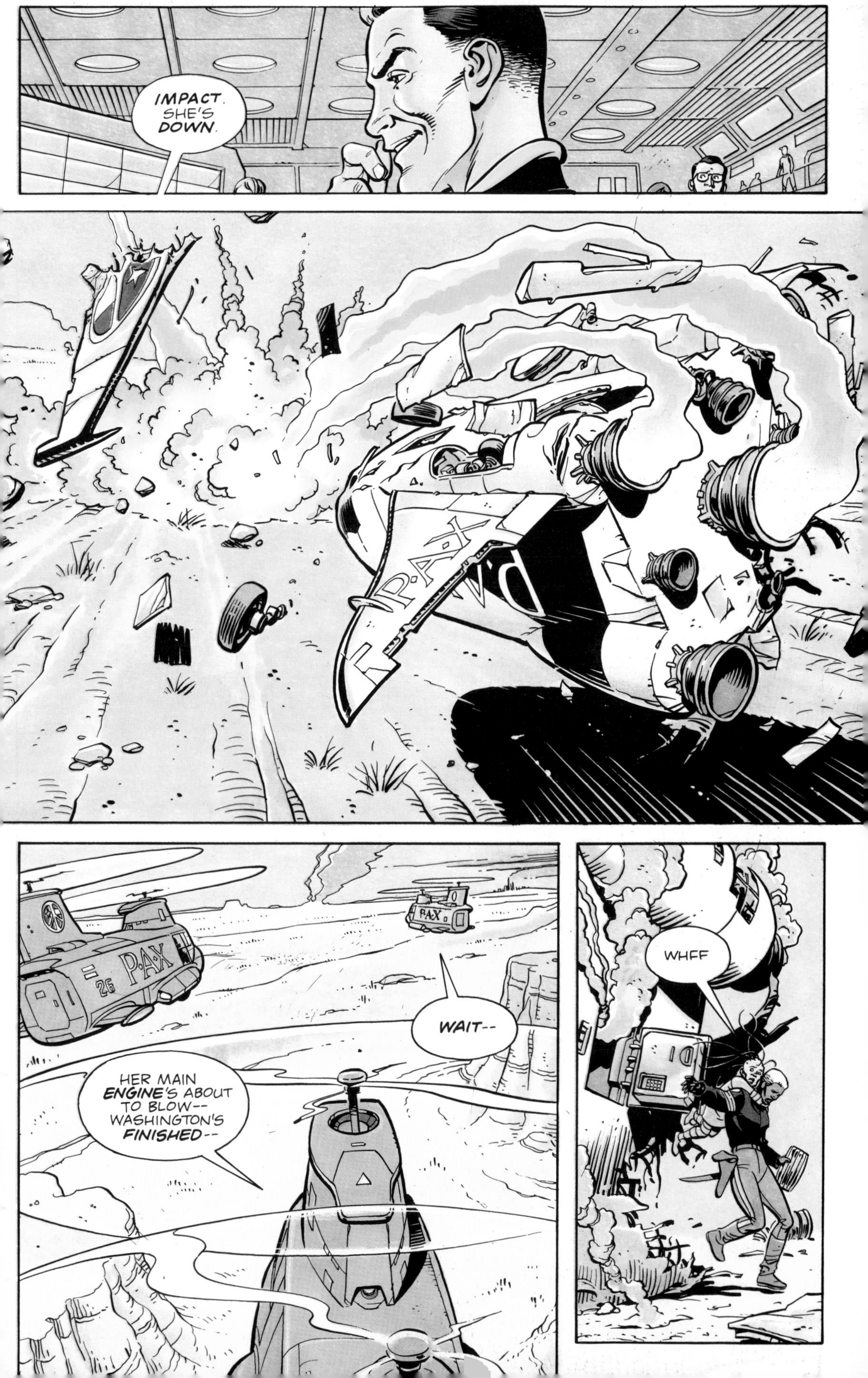
IMPACT. SHE'S DOWN.
P.A.X
P.A.X
P.A.X
WAIT--
HER MAIN ENGINE'S ABOUT TO BLOW-- WASHINGTON'S FINISHED--
WHFF

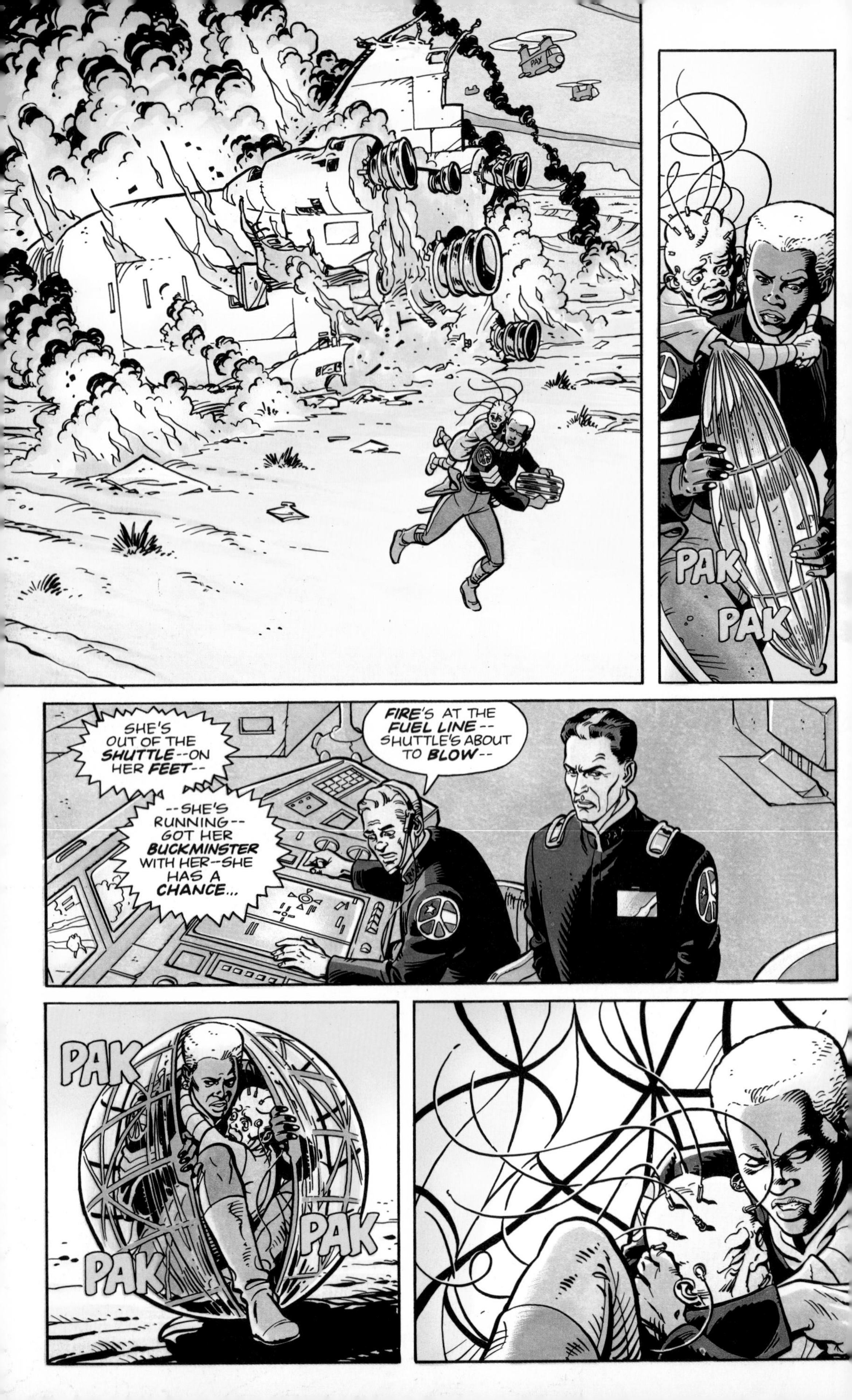

PAX
PAK
PAK
SHE'S OUT OF THE SHUTTLE--ON HER FEET--
--SHE'S RUNNING--GOT HER BUCKMINSTER WITH HER--SHE HAS A CHANCE...
FIRE'S AT THE FUEL LINE--SHUTTLE'S ABOUT TO BLOW--
PAK
PAK
PAK

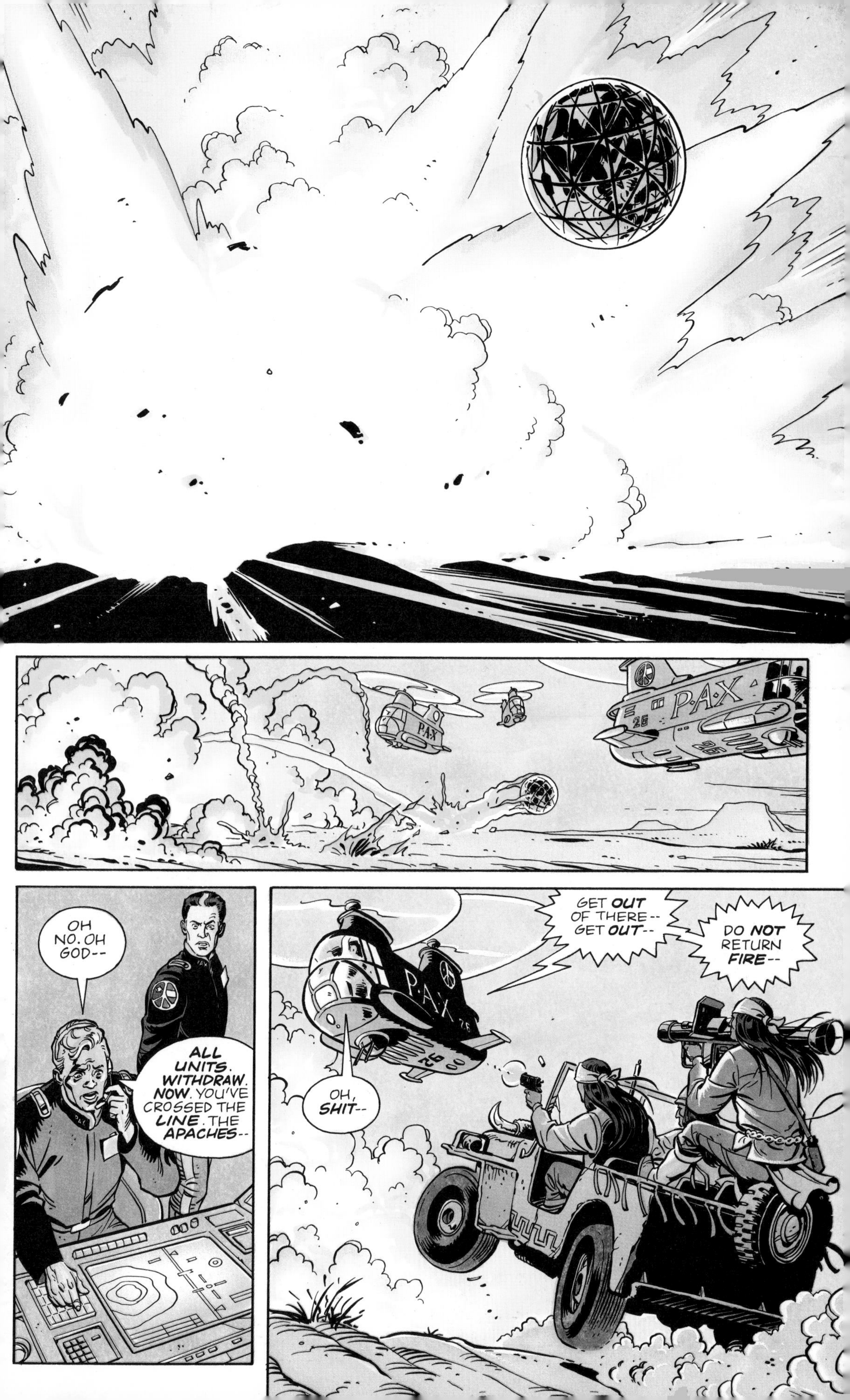
OH NO. OH GOD--
ALL UNITS. WITHDRAW. NOW. YOU'VE CROSSED THE LINE. THE APACHES--
GET OUT OF THERE-- GET OUT--
DO NOT RETURN FIRE--
OH, SHIT--

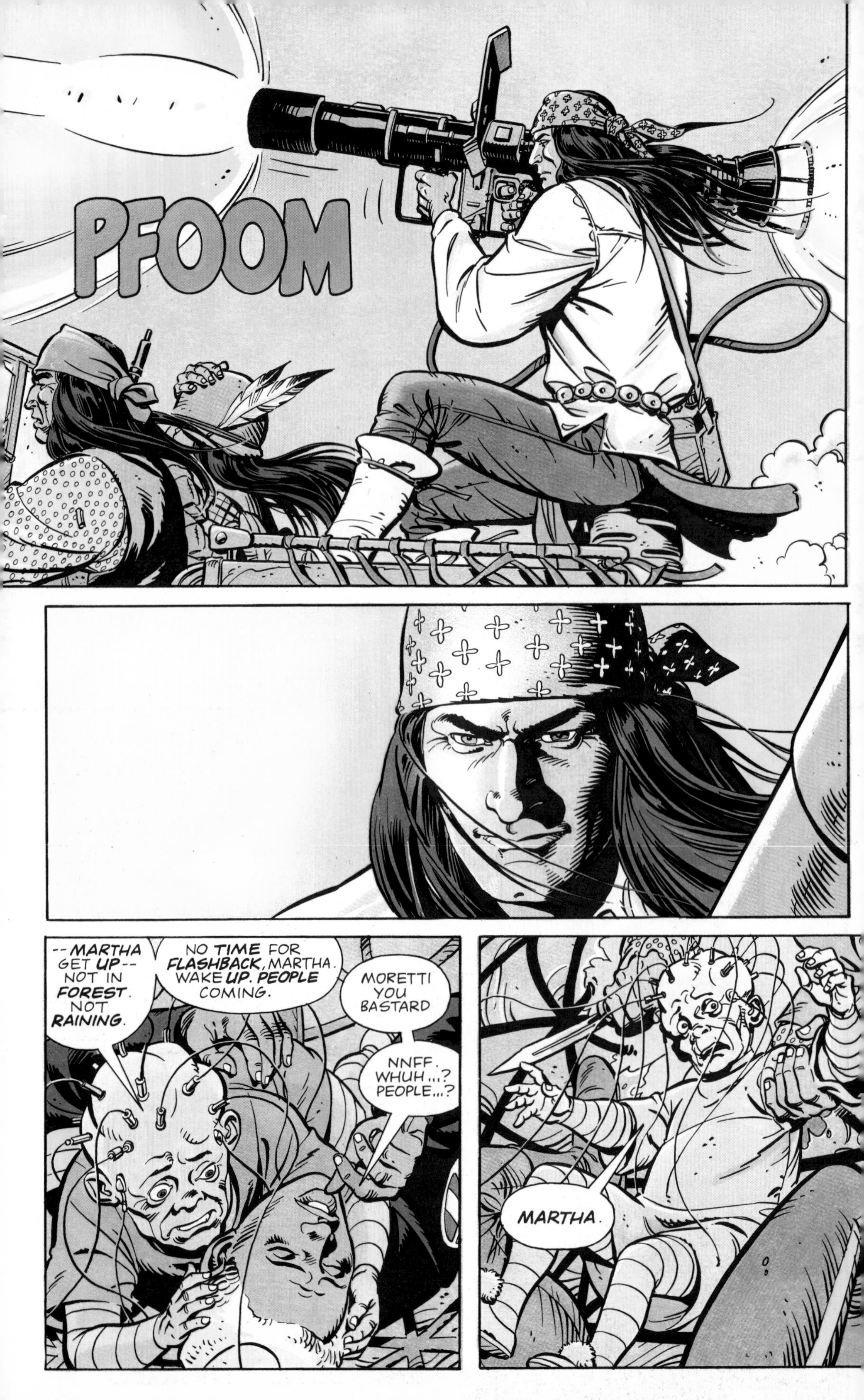
PFOOM
-- MARTHA GET UP -- NOT IN FOREST. NOT RAINING.
NO TIME FOR FLASHBACK, MARTHA. WAKE UP. PEOPLE COMING.
MORETTI YOU BASTARD
NNFF. WHUH...? PEOPLE...?
MARTHA.

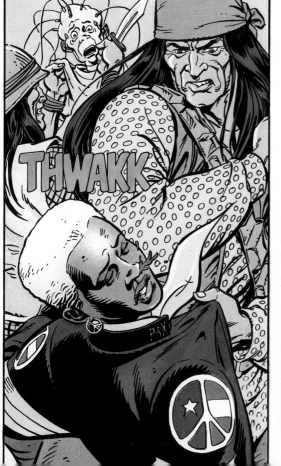

IT WAS HAILED AS HIS **CROWNING ACHIEVEMENT...**

--THE FEDERAL GOVERNMENT HAS PURCHASED THE LUNDORF REFINERY--

--AND OFFERS IT TO THE APACHE PEOPLE AS A GESTURE OF GOODWILL, IN HOPE THAT THEY MAY PROSPER.

...BUT **THIS** IS THE **LEGACY** PRESIDENT NISSEN HAS BEQUEATHED TO THE APACHE PEOPLE.

AIR SO DESPOILED THAT A SINGLE DAY'S EXPOSURE BRINGS A **HACKING COUGH** TO THE HEARTIEST...

...**SKIN** TURNED **GREY** AND **DISEASED**--

--PAINTED **RED** IN SAD PRIDE, EVERY DAY...

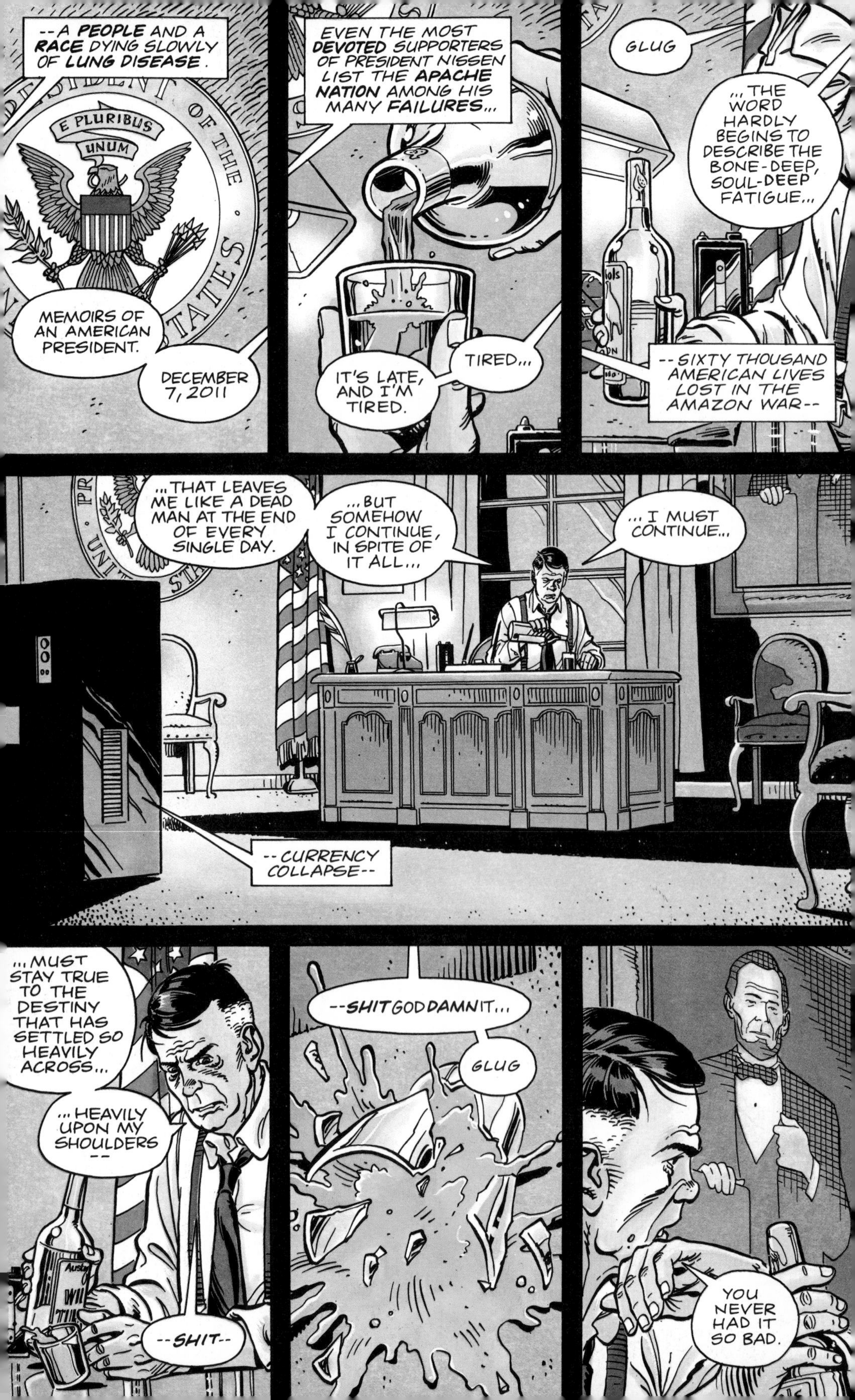
--A PEOPLE AND A RACE DYING SLOWLY OF LUNG DISEASE.
E PLURIBUS UNUM
MEMOIRS OF AN AMERICAN PRESIDENT.
DECEMBER 7, 2011
EVEN THE MOST DEVOTED SUPPORTERS OF PRESIDENT NISSEN LIST THE APACHE NATION AMONG HIS MANY FAILURES...
IT'S LATE, AND I'M TIRED.
TIRED...
GLUG
...THE WORD HARDLY BEGINS TO DESCRIBE THE BONE-DEEP, SOUL-DEEP FATIGUE...
--SIXTY THOUSAND AMERICAN LIVES LOST IN THE AMAZON WAR--
...THAT LEAVES ME LIKE A DEAD MAN AT THE END OF EVERY SINGLE DAY.
...BUT SOMEHOW I CONTINUE, IN SPITE OF IT ALL...
...I MUST CONTINUE...
--CURRENCY COLLAPSE--
...MUST STAY TRUE TO THE DESTINY THAT HAS SETTLED SO HEAVILY ACROSS...
...HEAVILY UPON MY SHOULDERS --
--SHIT--
--SHIT GOD DAMN IT...
GLUG
YOU NEVER HAD IT SO BAD.

YOU ONLY HAD ONE ENEMY-- JUST ONE--

YOU DIDN'T HAVE THE **JOB** OF SAVING THE **ENVIRON-MENT** FROM CENTURIES OF **ABUSE**--

-- AND EVERYBODY SAYING YOU CREATED ANOTHER **VIET NAM** WHEN YOU **TRIED**...

--JUST A PACK OF **RACIST CAPITALISTS** WHO NEVER HAD A CHANCE AGAINST YOU IN THE FIRST PLACE.

YOU DIDN'T HAVE MEMBERS OF YOUR OWN STAFF CALLING YOU A **TYRANT** TO THE **PRESS**...

HOUSE-KEEPING-- HIS **BOTTLE'S** EMPTY.

YOU DIDN'T FACE **THIRTY-SEVEN SEPARATIST** MOVEMENTS TEARING THE NATION TO **PIECES**...

SENATORS PLOTTING YOUR **ASSASSINATION**...

... AND THE **AFRICANS** --

I SEND **PAX** TO ABOLISH **APARTHEID** ONCE AND FOR ALL...

... AND ALL THEY SEE IS THE **WAR** AND THE **DEAD**...

..., YOU'D THINK I WAS **HITLER** THE WAY THEY...

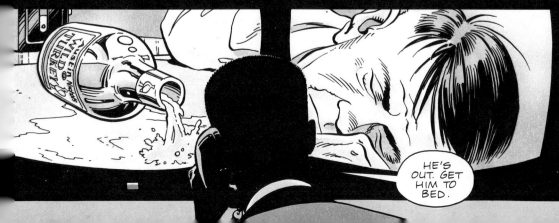

HE'S OUT. GET HIM TO BED.

Apache Sundown

Poverty and Despair in the Apache Nation

by Lisa Nordik

Nothing to lose:
Redfeather's angry army

Dancing Rabbit, four years old, stands over an oil-can filled with a bright-red mixture the texture of creosote. She dips a dirty cloth into the mix and spreads it across her acne-ridden face, her sunken chest, her swollen belly. Soon she is more or less the color of her Apache ancestors. Behind her, lined liked derelicts outside a mission, are the other coughing, grey-skinned women of her tribe.

This sad, strange ritual is repeated every morning by every member of the Apache Nation before they go to their posts at the fifty year old Lundorf Refinery. The refinery is a shameful antique, lacking even the most rudimentary of air-cleansing technology. It coughs purple-black smoke into the once beautiful sky of the Mexican Territory. The eyes sting the moment one arrives. The mouth is filled with an awful, oily taste. A single day's exposure to the

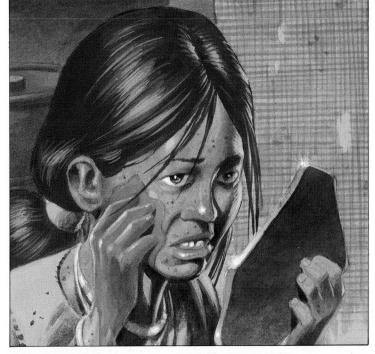

Lost pride, lost hope: *An Apache girl paints her skin*

President Nissen's signature added to the treaty last year, the tribe looked forward to cultural and economic independence. But with America's increasing use of solar power, the oil producing nations of the world have faced financial cataclysm, and with them, the lofty dream of Redfeather has turned to oil-black despair.

Starving, but armed to the teeth: A Presidential Decree protects the Apache from any assault from PAX. PAX is, in fact, forbidden even from returning fire from the warlike tribe. Nonetheless, Redfeather has formed a state of the art militia — and observers worry that Redfeather may once

A desperate, angry Chief: *On the warpath?*

poisoned air will give even the hardiest of visitors a chronic, gut-wrenching cough. A year's labor at the refinery has inflicted forty per cent of the inhabitants with a variety of undiagnosed, untreated lung diseases. There aren't many of the revered Old Ones left. Most have died coughing blood.

Redfeather's dream: The handsome young leader of the Apache Nation stirred hopes nationwide for his people and inspired an outpouring of pickets and protests when he led one hundred warriors to seize the refinery on July 20, 2009. He produced a two hundred year old treaty granting his people the land upon which the refinery was built. With

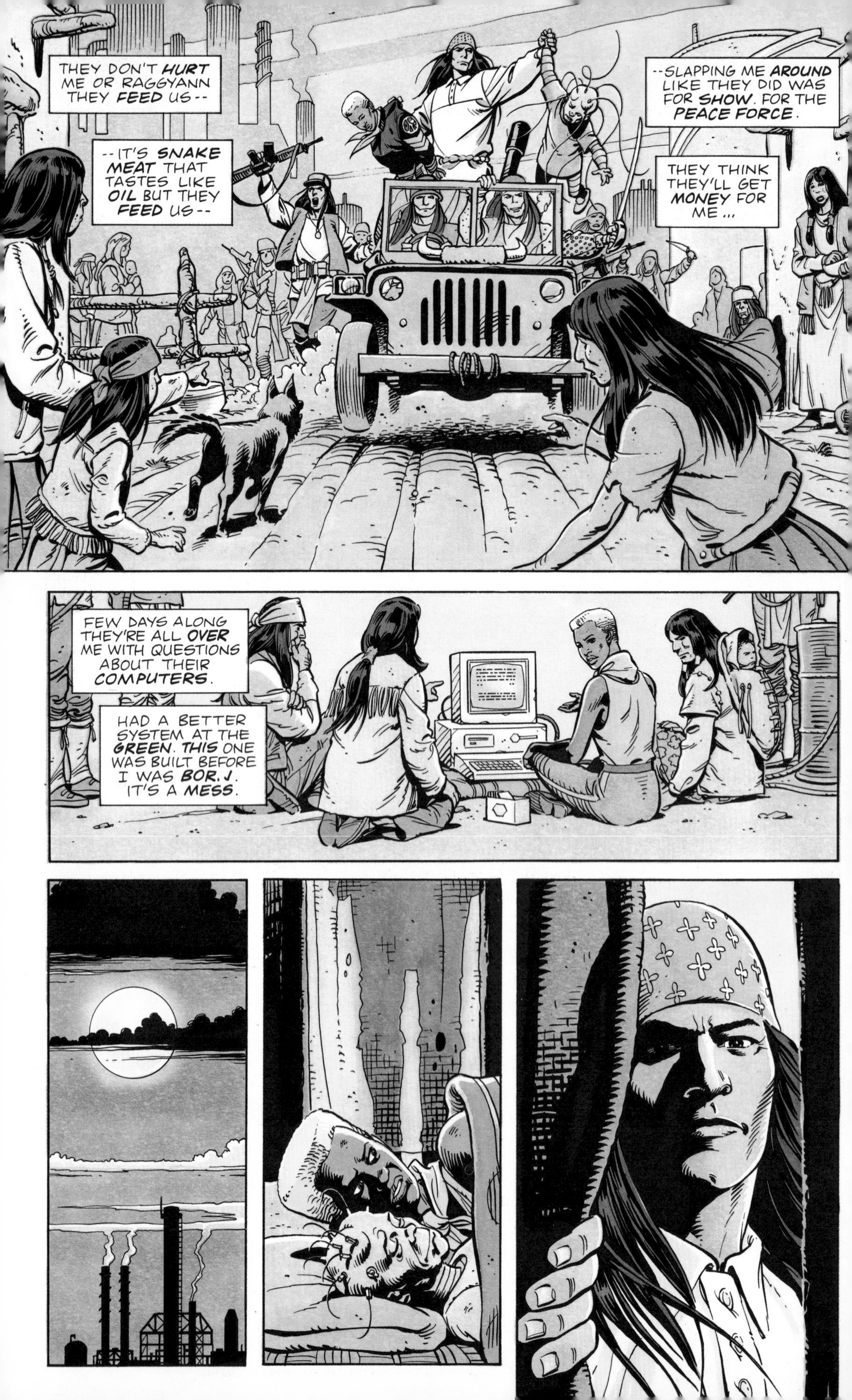
THEY DON'T HURT ME OR RAGGYANN THEY FEED US--
--IT'S SNAKE MEAT THAT TASTES LIKE OIL BUT THEY FEED US--
--SLAPPING ME AROUND LIKE THEY DID WAS FOR SHOW. FOR THE PEACE FORCE.
THEY THINK THEY'LL GET MONEY FOR ME...
FEW DAYS ALONG THEY'RE ALL OVER ME WITH QUESTIONS ABOUT THEIR COMPUTERS.
HAD A BETTER SYSTEM AT THE GREEN. THIS ONE WAS BUILT BEFORE I WAS BOR.J. IT'S A MESS.

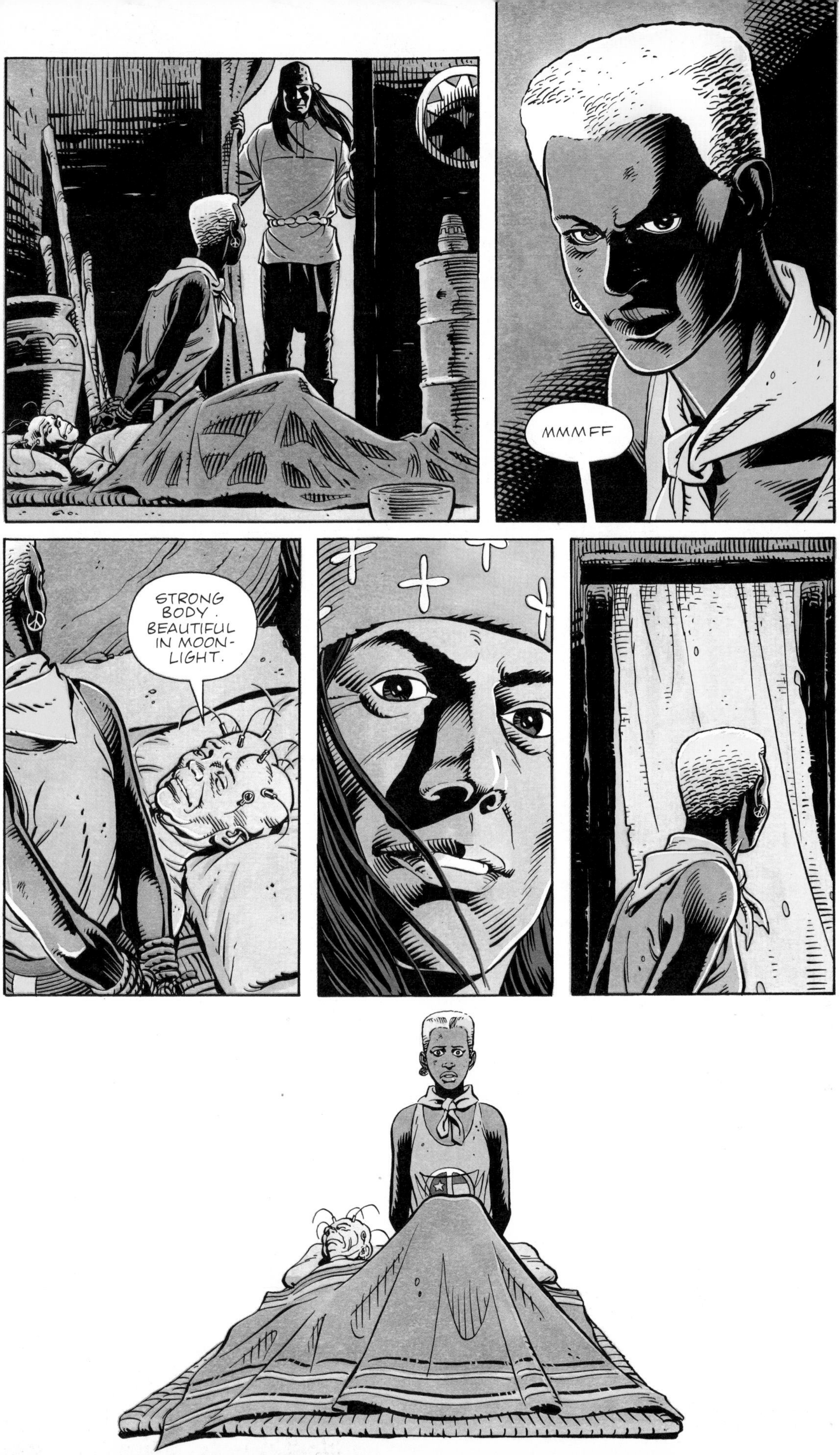
MMMFF
STRONG BODY. BEAUTIFUL IN MOON-LIGHT.

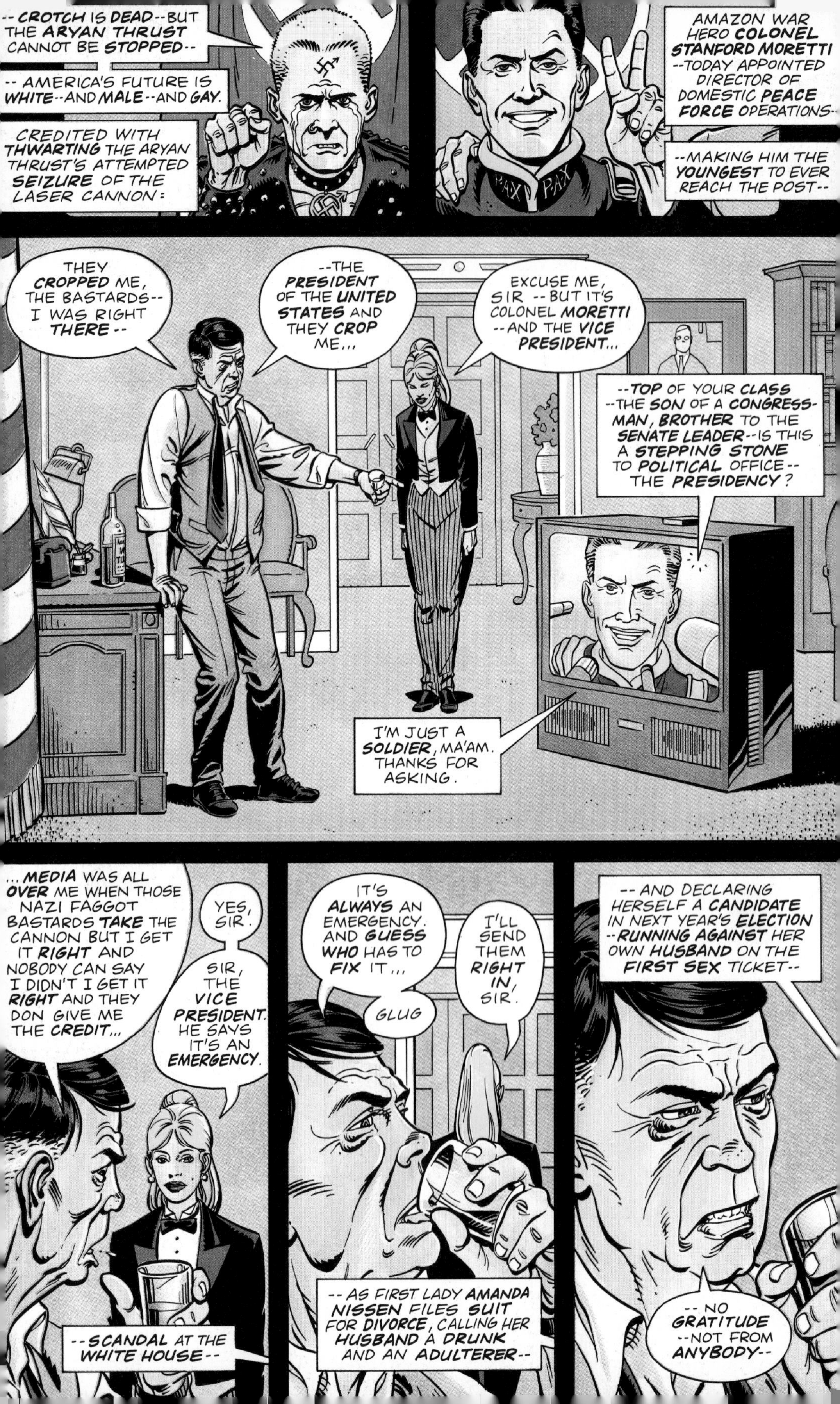
-- CROTCH IS DEAD -- BUT THE ARYAN THRUST CANNOT BE STOPPED --
-- AMERICA'S FUTURE IS WHITE -- AND MALE -- AND GAY.
CREDITED WITH THWARTING THE ARYAN THRUST'S ATTEMPTED SEIZURE OF THE LASER CANNON:
AMAZON WAR HERO COLONEL STANFORD MORETTI -- TODAY APPOINTED DIRECTOR OF DOMESTIC PEACE FORCE OPERATIONS --
-- MAKING HIM THE YOUNGEST TO EVER REACH THE POST --
PAX PAX
THEY CROPPED ME, THE BASTARDS -- I WAS RIGHT THERE --
-- THE PRESIDENT OF THE UNITED STATES AND THEY CROP ME...
EXCUSE ME, SIR -- BUT IT'S COLONEL MORETTI -- AND THE VICE PRESIDENT...
-- TOP OF YOUR CLASS -- THE SON OF A CONGRESSMAN, BROTHER TO THE SENATE LEADER -- IS THIS A STEPPING STONE TO POLITICAL OFFICE -- THE PRESIDENCY?
I'M JUST A SOLDIER, MA'AM. THANKS FOR ASKING.
... MEDIA WAS ALL OVER ME WHEN THOSE NAZI FAGGOT BASTARDS TAKE THE CANNON BUT I GET IT RIGHT AND NOBODY CAN SAY I DIDN'T I GET IT RIGHT AND THEY DON GIVE ME THE CREDIT...
YES, SIR.
SIR, THE VICE PRESIDENT. HE SAYS IT'S AN EMERGENCY.
-- SCANDAL AT THE WHITE HOUSE --
IT'S ALWAYS AN EMERGENCY. AND GUESS WHO HAS TO FIX IT...
GLUG
I'LL SEND THEM RIGHT IN, SIR.
-- AS FIRST LADY AMANDA NISSEN FILES SUIT FOR DIVORCE, CALLING HER HUSBAND A DRUNK AND AN ADULTERER --
-- AND DECLARING HERSELF A CANDIDATE IN NEXT YEAR'S ELECTION -- RUNNING AGAINST HER OWN HUSBAND ON THE FIRST SEX TICKET --
-- NO GRATITUDE -- NOT FROM ANYBODY --

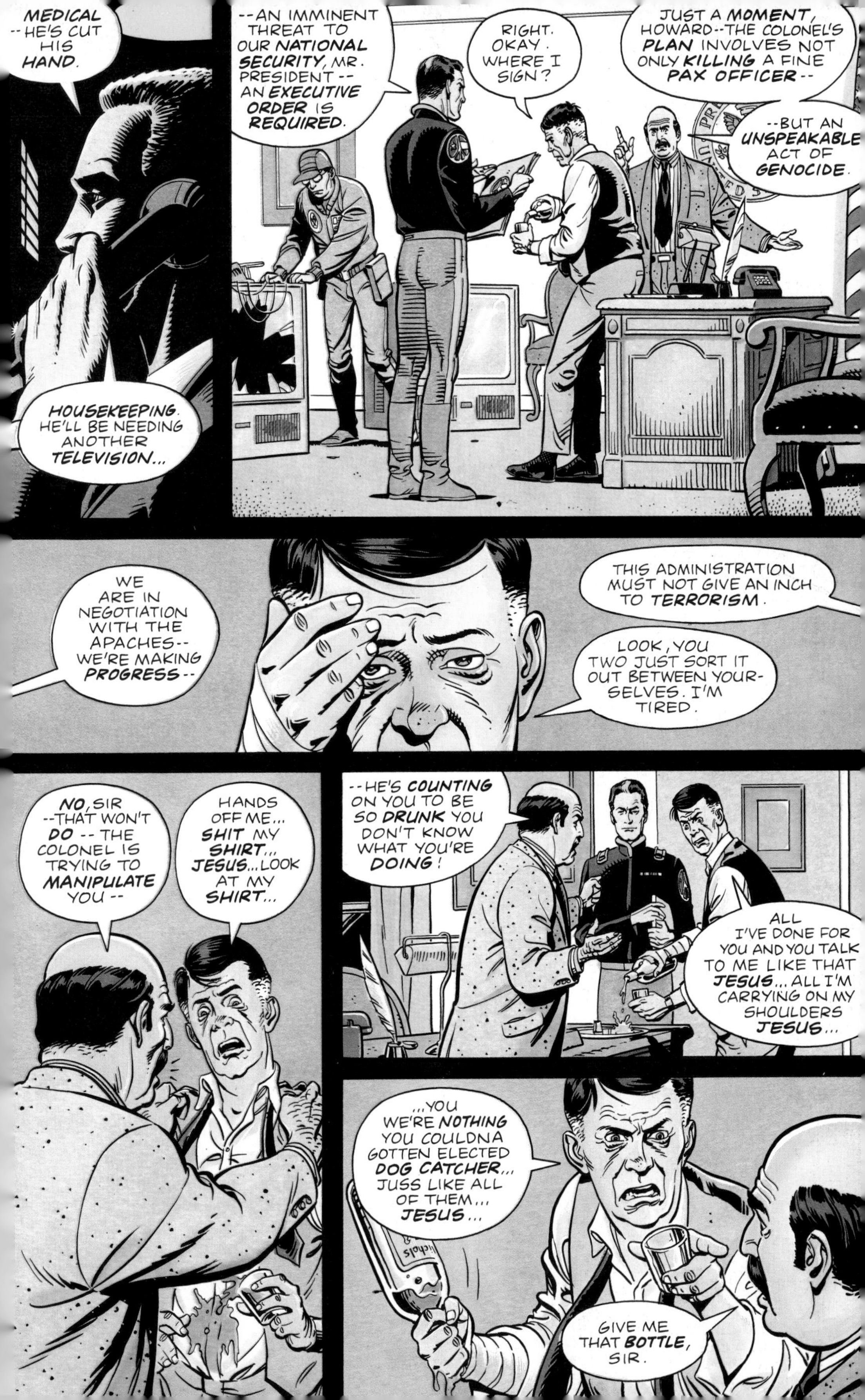
MEDICAL -- HE'S CUT HIS HAND.
HOUSEKEEPING. HE'LL BE NEEDING ANOTHER TELEVISION...
--AN IMMINENT THREAT TO OUR NATIONAL SECURITY, MR. PRESIDENT -- AN EXECUTIVE ORDER IS REQUIRED.
RIGHT. OKAY. WHERE I SIGN?
JUST A MOMENT, HOWARD--THE COLONEL'S PLAN INVOLVES NOT ONLY KILLING A FINE PAX OFFICER--
--BUT AN UNSPEAKABLE ACT OF GENOCIDE.
WE ARE IN NEGOTIATION WITH THE APACHES-- WE'RE MAKING PROGRESS--
THIS ADMINISTRATION MUST NOT GIVE AN INCH TO TERRORISM.
LOOK, YOU TWO JUST SORT IT OUT BETWEEN YOURSELVES. I'M TIRED.
NO, SIR --THAT WON'T DO -- THE COLONEL IS TRYING TO MANIPULATE YOU --
HANDS OFF ME... SHIT MY SHIRT... JESUS...LOOK AT MY SHIRT...
--HE'S COUNTING ON YOU TO BE SO DRUNK YOU DON'T KNOW WHAT YOU'RE DOING!
ALL I'VE DONE FOR YOU AND YOU TALK TO ME LIKE THAT JESUS... ALL I'M CARRYING ON MY SHOULDERS JESUS...
...YOU WE'RE NOTHING YOU COULDNA GOTTEN ELECTED DOG CATCHER... JUSS LIKE ALL OF THEM... JESUS...
GIVE ME THAT BOTTLE, SIR.

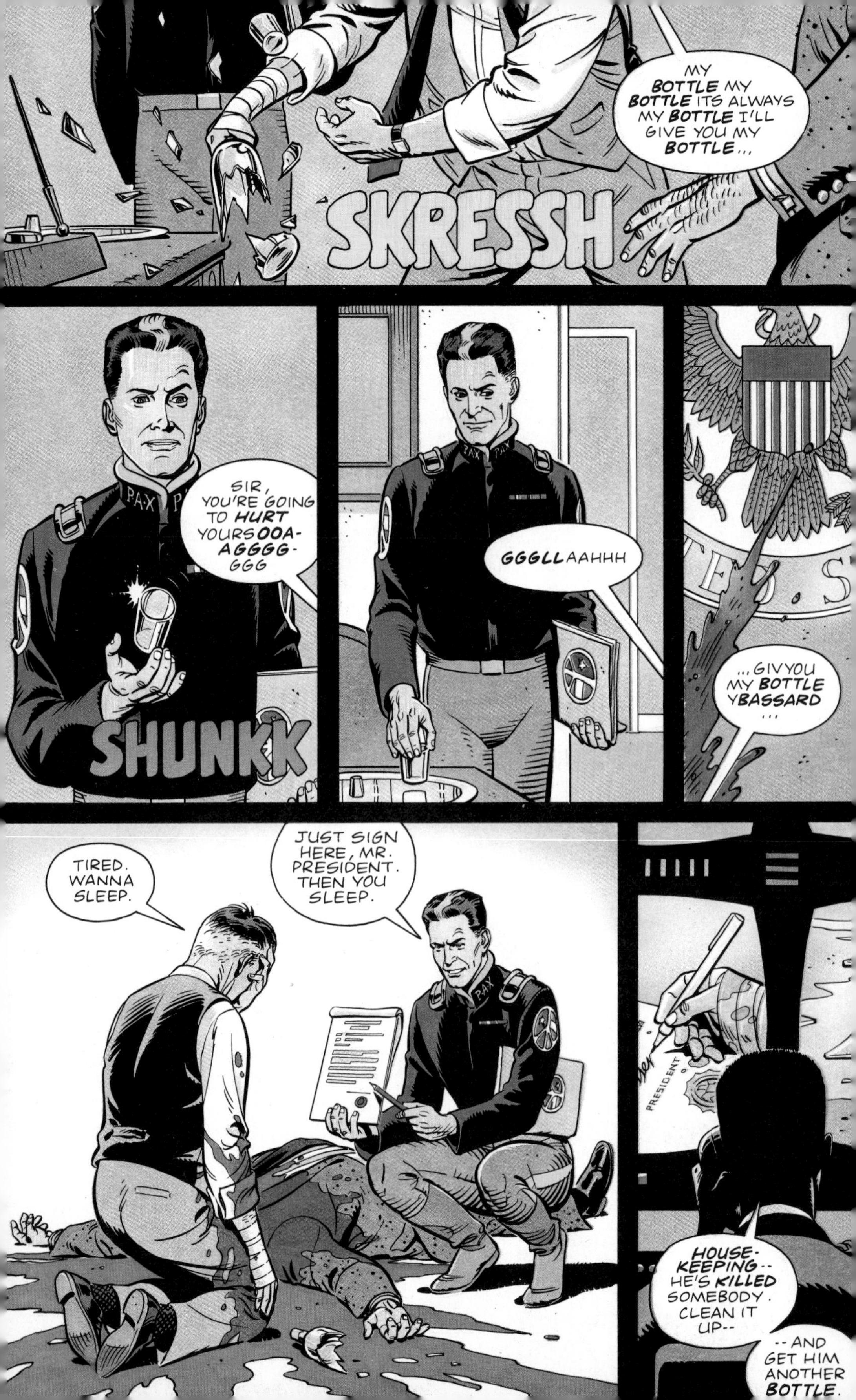
MY BOTTLE MY BOTTLE ITS ALWAYS MY BOTTLE I'LL GIVE YOU MY BOTTLE...
SKRESSH
SIR, YOU'RE GOING TO HURT YOURSOOA-AGGGG-GGG
SHUNKK
GGGLLAAHHH
...GIVYOU MY BOTTLE YBASSARD ...
TIRED. WANNA SLEEP.
JUST SIGN HERE, MR. PRESIDENT. THEN YOU SLEEP.
PRESIDENT
HOUSE-KEEPING-- HE'S KILLED SOMEBODY. CLEAN IT UP--
--AND GET HIM ANOTHER BOTTLE.

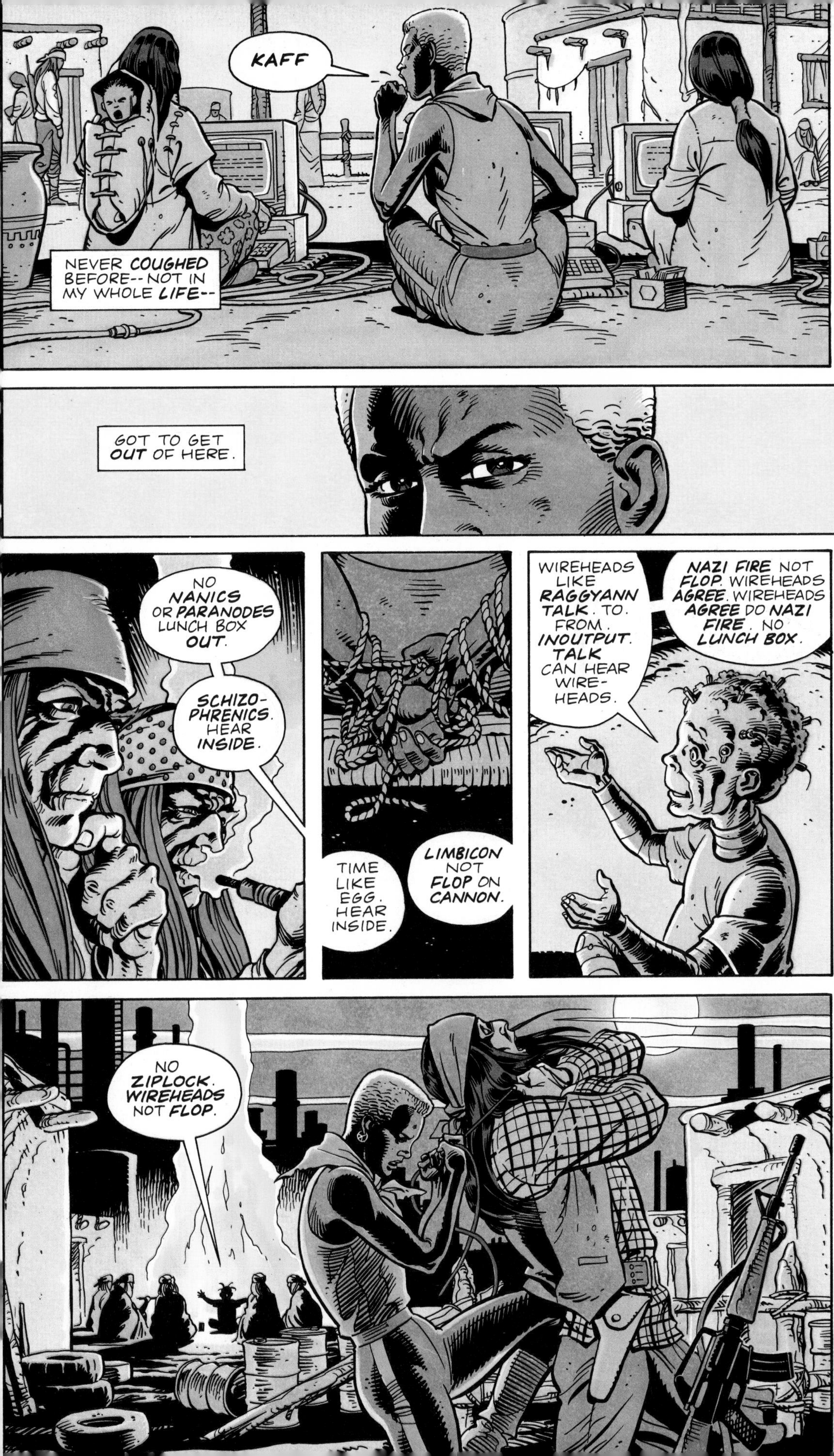
KAFF
NEVER COUGHED BEFORE--NOT IN MY WHOLE LIFE--
GOT TO GET OUT OF HERE.
NO NANICS OR PARANODES LUNCH BOX OUT.
SCHIZO-PHRENICS. HEAR INSIDE.
TIME LIKE EGG. HEAR INSIDE.
LIMBICON NOT FLOP ON CANNON.
WIREHEADS LIKE RAGGYANN TALK. TO. FROM. INOUTPUT. TALK CAN HEAR WIRE-HEADS.
NAZI FIRE NOT FLOP. WIREHEADS AGREE. WIREHEADS AGREE DO NAZI FIRE. NO LUNCH BOX.
NO ZIPLOCK. WIREHEADS NOT FLOP.

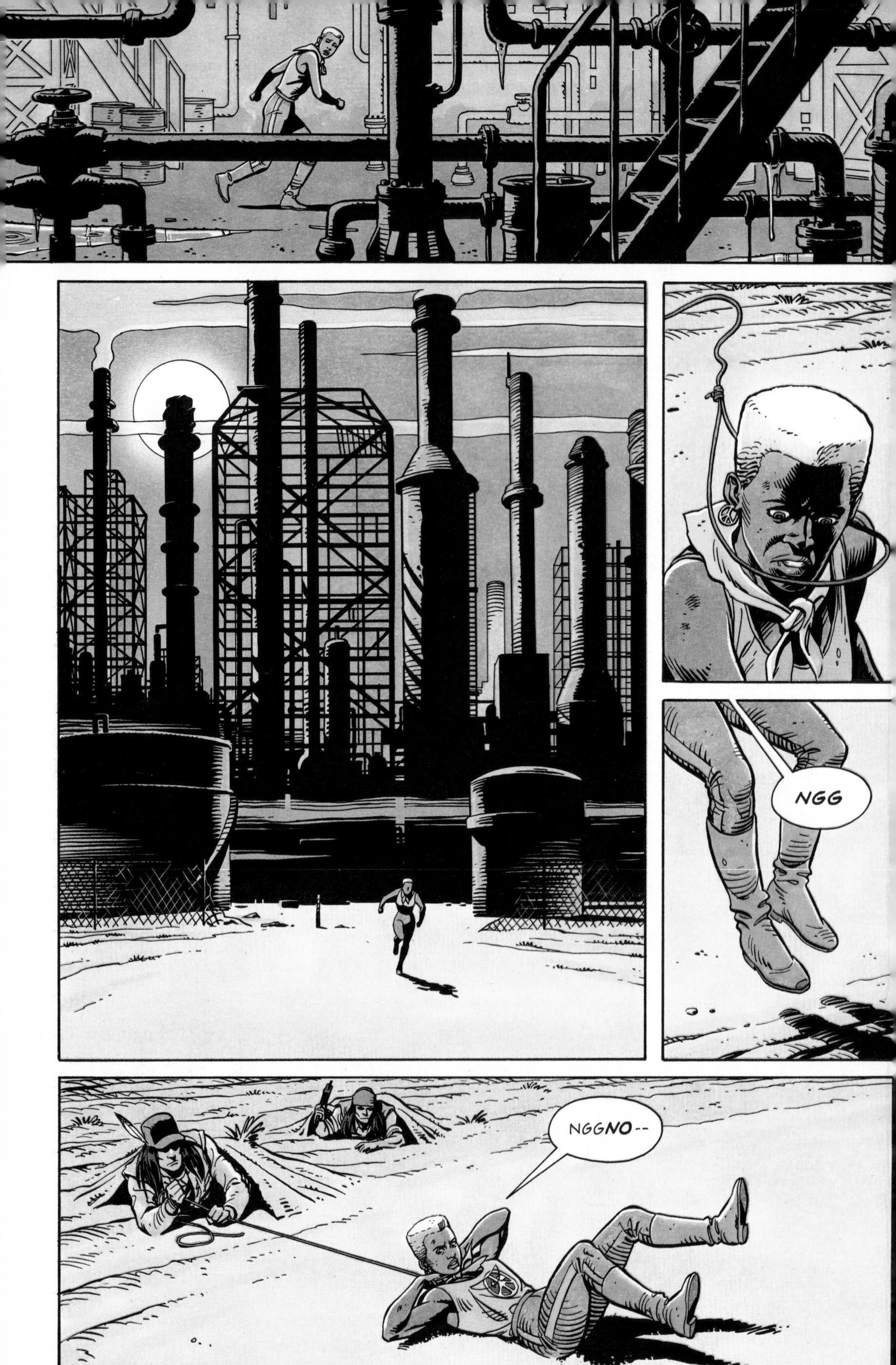
NGG
NGGNO--

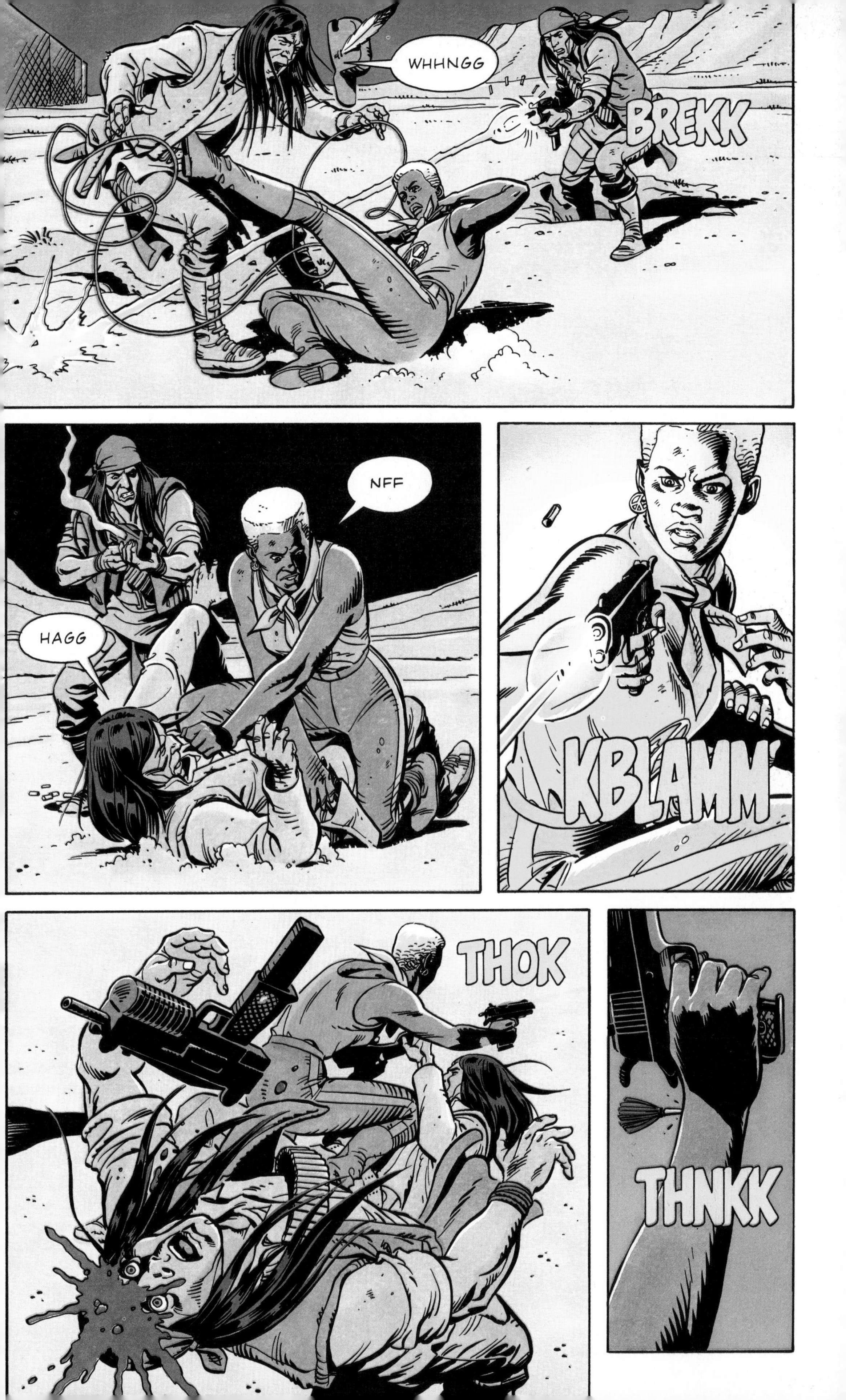
WHHNGG
BREKK
NFF
HAGG
KBLAMM
THOK
THNKK

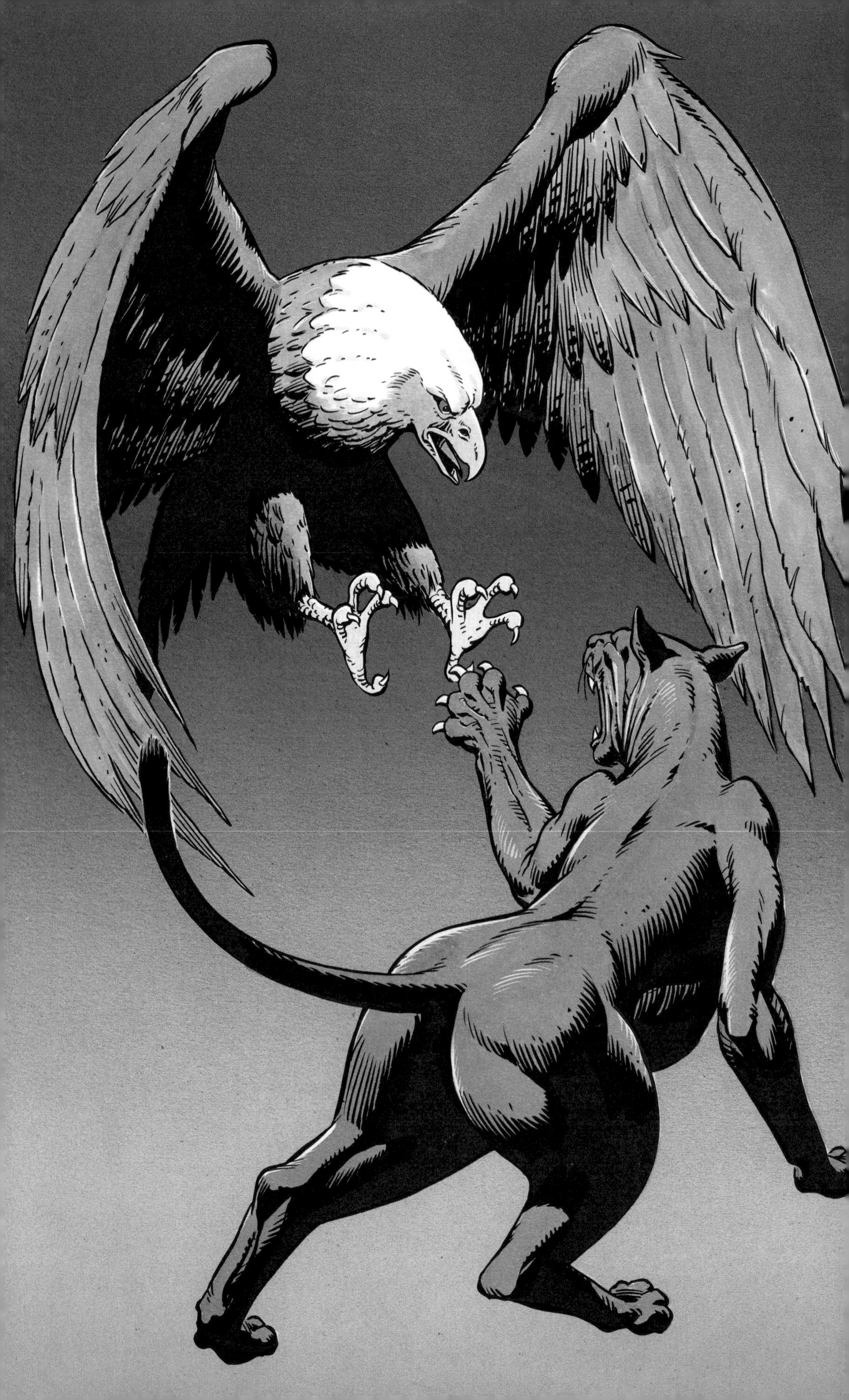

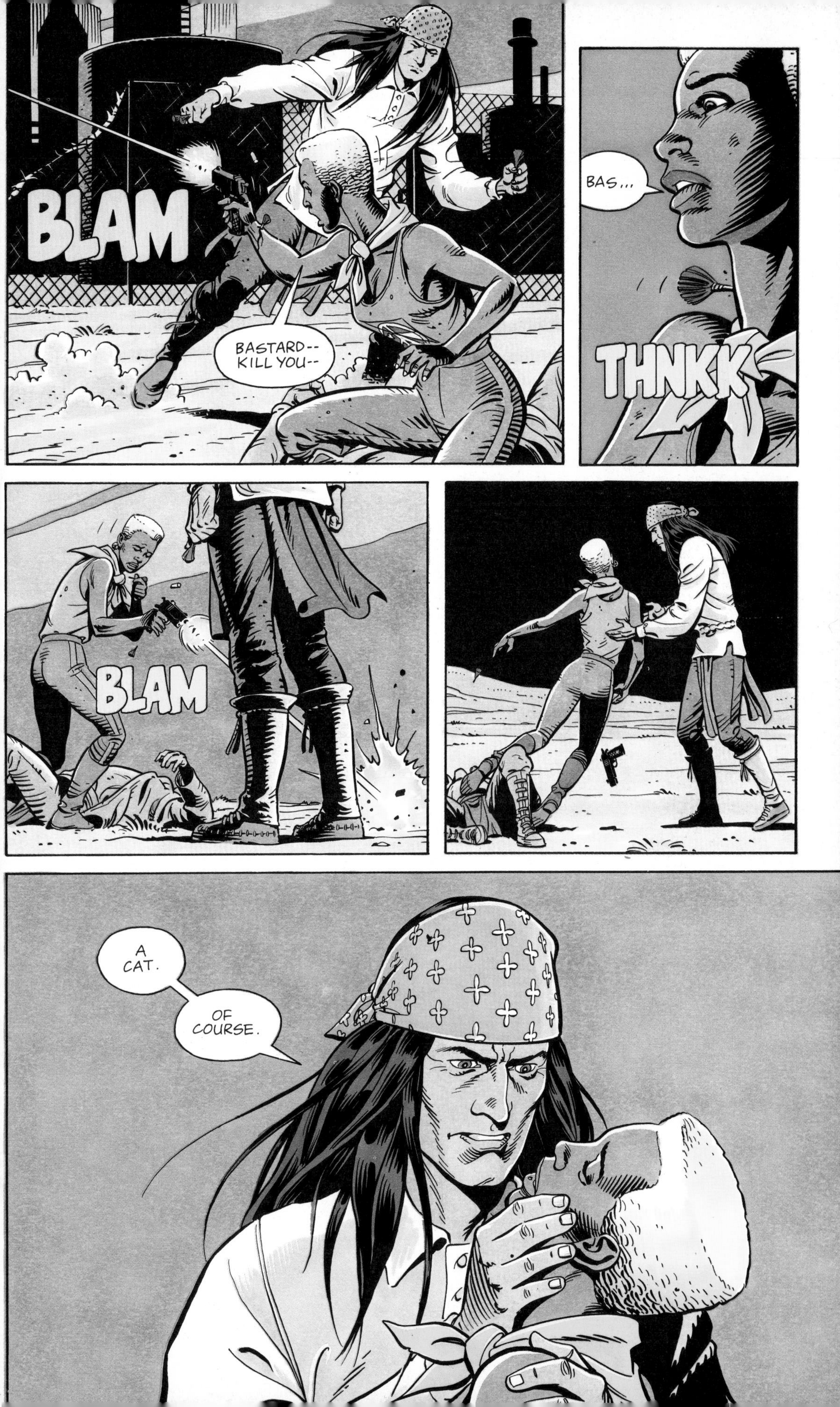
BLAM
BASTARD-- KILL YOU--
BAS...
THNKK
BLAM
A CAT.
OF COURSE.

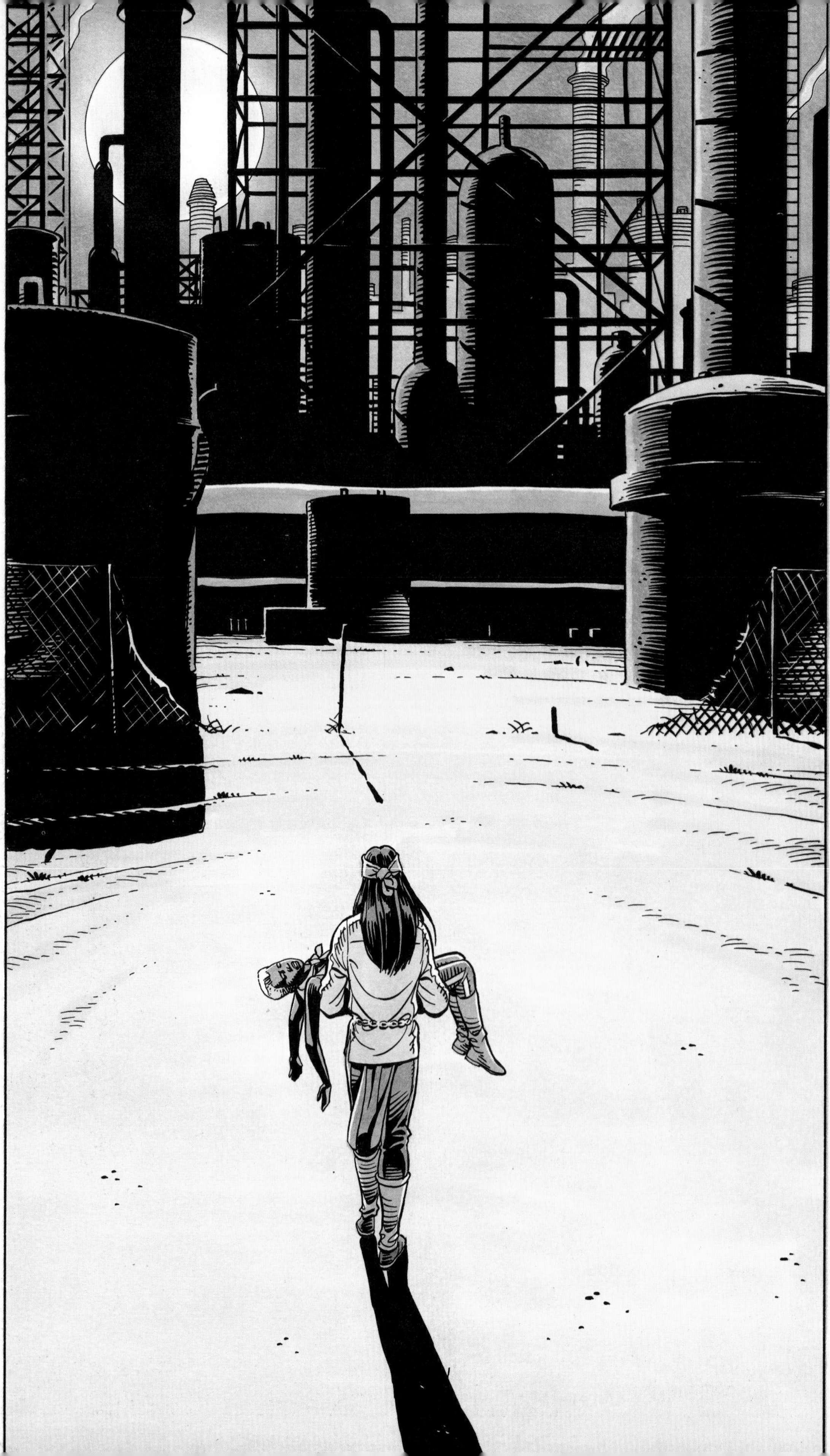

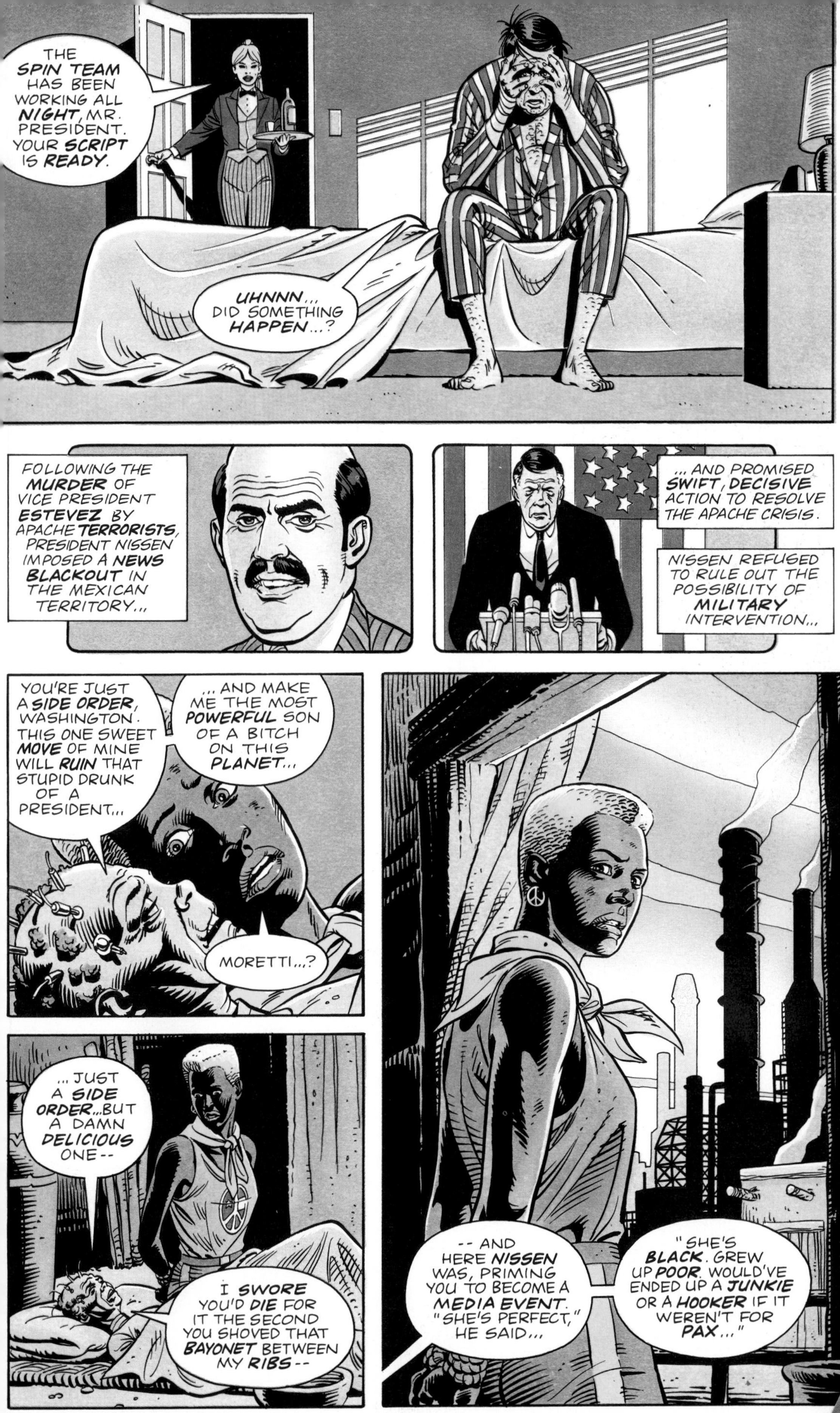
THE SPIN TEAM HAS BEEN WORKING ALL NIGHT, MR. PRESIDENT. YOUR SCRIPT IS READY.
UHNNN... DID SOMETHING HAPPEN...?
FOLLOWING THE MURDER OF VICE PRESIDENT ESTEVEZ BY APACHE TERRORISTS, PRESIDENT NISSEN IMPOSED A NEWS BLACKOUT IN THE MEXICAN TERRITORY...
... AND PROMISED SWIFT, DECISIVE ACTION TO RESOLVE THE APACHE CRISIS.
NISSEN REFUSED TO RULE OUT THE POSSIBILITY OF MILITARY INTERVENTION...
YOU'RE JUST A SIDE ORDER, WASHINGTON. THIS ONE SWEET MOVE OF MINE WILL RUIN THAT STUPID DRUNK OF A PRESIDENT...
... AND MAKE ME THE MOST POWERFUL SON OF A BITCH ON THIS PLANET...
MORETTI...?
... JUST A SIDE ORDER...BUT A DAMN DELICIOUS ONE --
I SWORE YOU'D DIE FOR IT THE SECOND YOU SHOVED THAT BAYONET BETWEEN MY RIBS --
-- AND HERE NISSEN WAS, PRIMING YOU TO BECOME A MEDIA EVENT. "SHE'S PERFECT," HE SAID...
"SHE'S BLACK. GREW UP POOR. WOULD'VE ENDED UP A JUNKIE OR A HOOKER IF IT WEREN'T FOR PAX..."

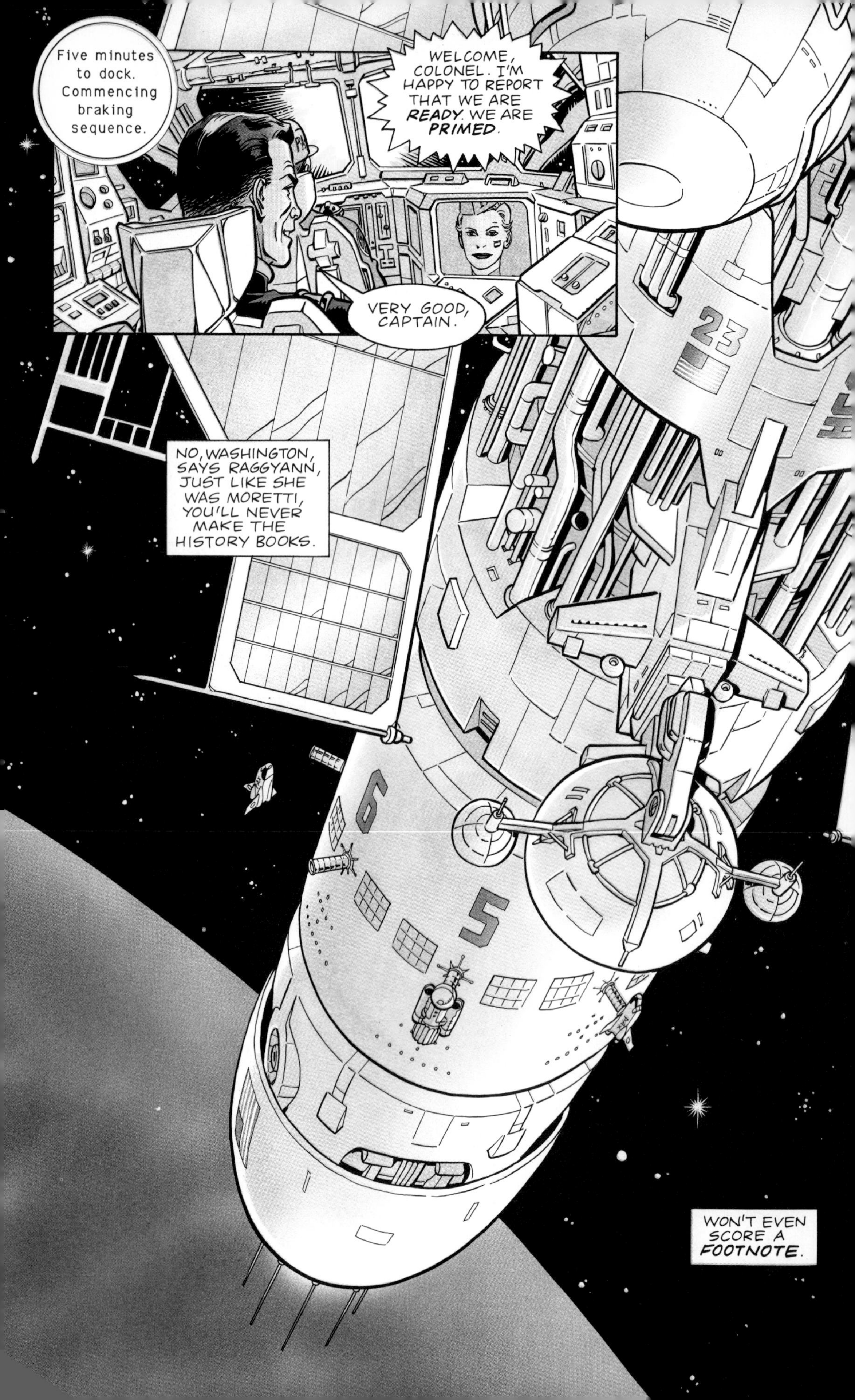
Five minutes to dock. Commencing braking sequence.
WELCOME, COLONEL. I'M HAPPY TO REPORT THAT WE ARE READY. WE ARE PRIMED.
VERY GOOD, CAPTAIN.
NO, WASHINGTON, SAYS RAGGYANN, JUST LIKE SHE WAS MORETTI, YOU'LL NEVER MAKE THE HISTORY BOOKS.
WON'T EVEN SCORE A FOOTNOTE.

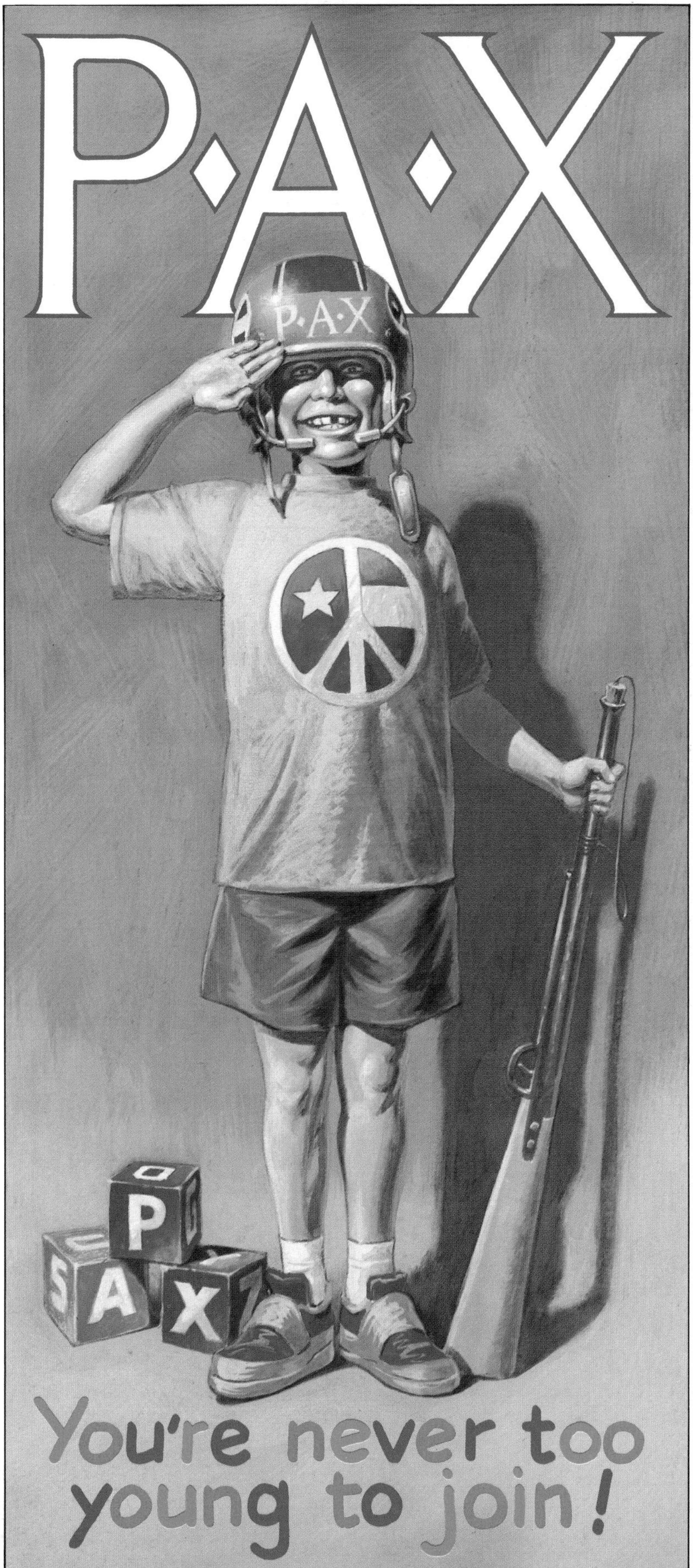
P·A·X
P·A·X
P
A
X
You're never too
young to join!

3: HEALTH & WELFARE

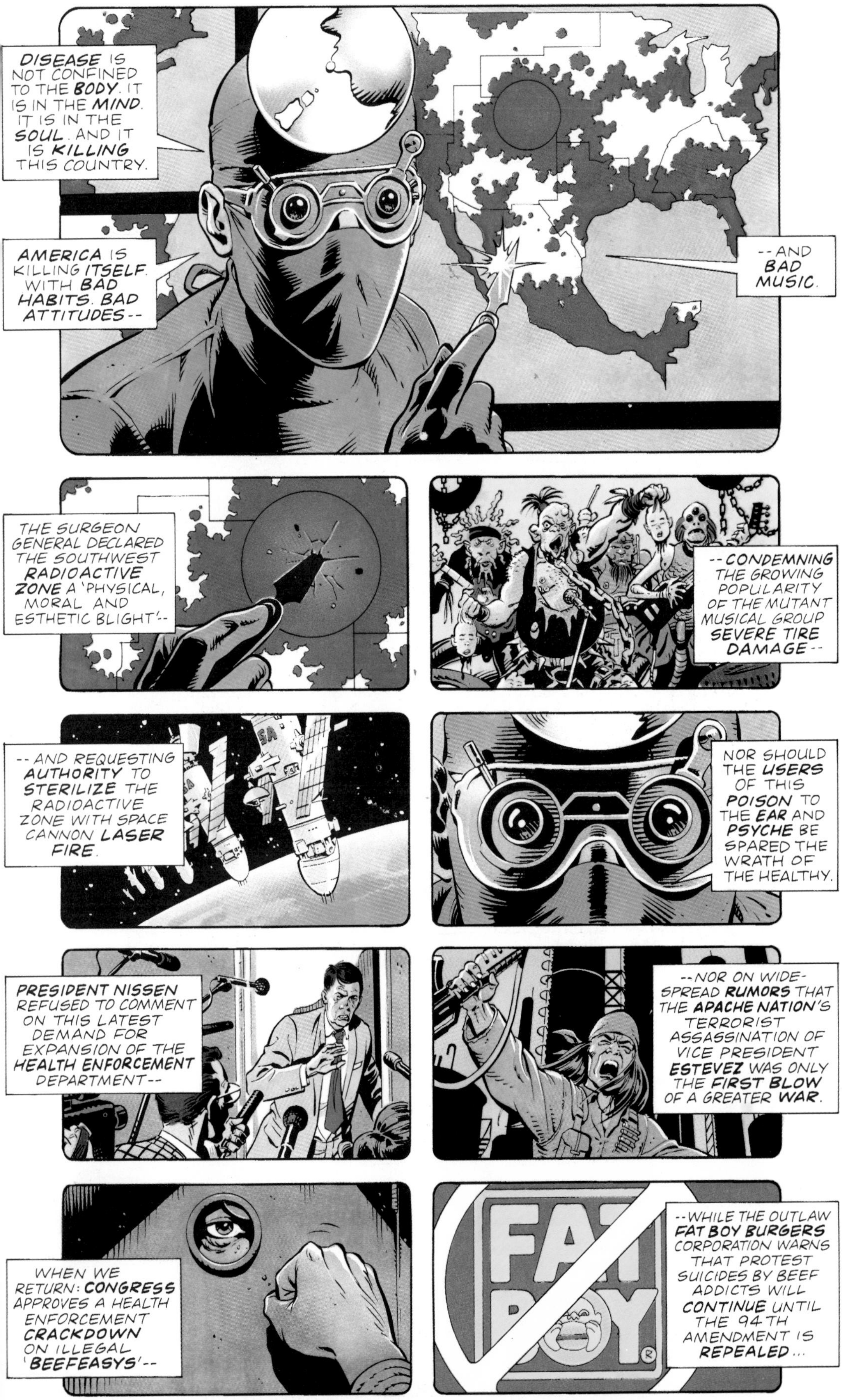
DISEASE IS NOT CONFINED TO THE BODY. IT IS IN THE MIND. IT IS IN THE SOUL. AND IT IS KILLING THIS COUNTRY.
AMERICA IS KILLING ITSELF. WITH BAD HABITS. BAD ATTITUDES--
--AND BAD MUSIC.
THE SURGEON GENERAL DECLARED THE SOUTHWEST RADIOACTIVE ZONE A 'PHYSICAL, MORAL AND ESTHETIC BLIGHT'--
--CONDEMNING THE GROWING POPULARITY OF THE MUTANT MUSICAL GROUP SEVERE TIRE DAMAGE--
--AND REQUESTING AUTHORITY TO STERILIZE THE RADIOACTIVE ZONE WITH SPACE CANNON LASER FIRE.
NOR SHOULD THE USERS OF THIS POISON TO THE EAR AND PSYCHE BE SPARED THE WRATH OF THE HEALTHY.
PRESIDENT NISSEN REFUSED TO COMMENT ON THIS LATEST DEMAND FOR EXPANSION OF THE HEALTH ENFORCEMENT DEPARTMENT--
--NOR ON WIDE-SPREAD RUMORS THAT THE APACHE NATION'S TERRORIST ASSASSINATION OF VICE PRESIDENT ESTEVEZ WAS ONLY THE FIRST BLOW OF A GREATER WAR.
WHEN WE RETURN: CONGRESS APPROVES A HEALTH ENFORCEMENT CRACKDOWN ON ILLEGAL 'BEEFEASYS'--
FAT BOY
--WHILE THE OUTLAW FAT BOY BURGERS CORPORATION WARNS THAT PROTEST SUICIDES BY BEEF ADDICTS WILL CONTINUE UNTIL THE 94TH AMENDMENT IS REPEALED...

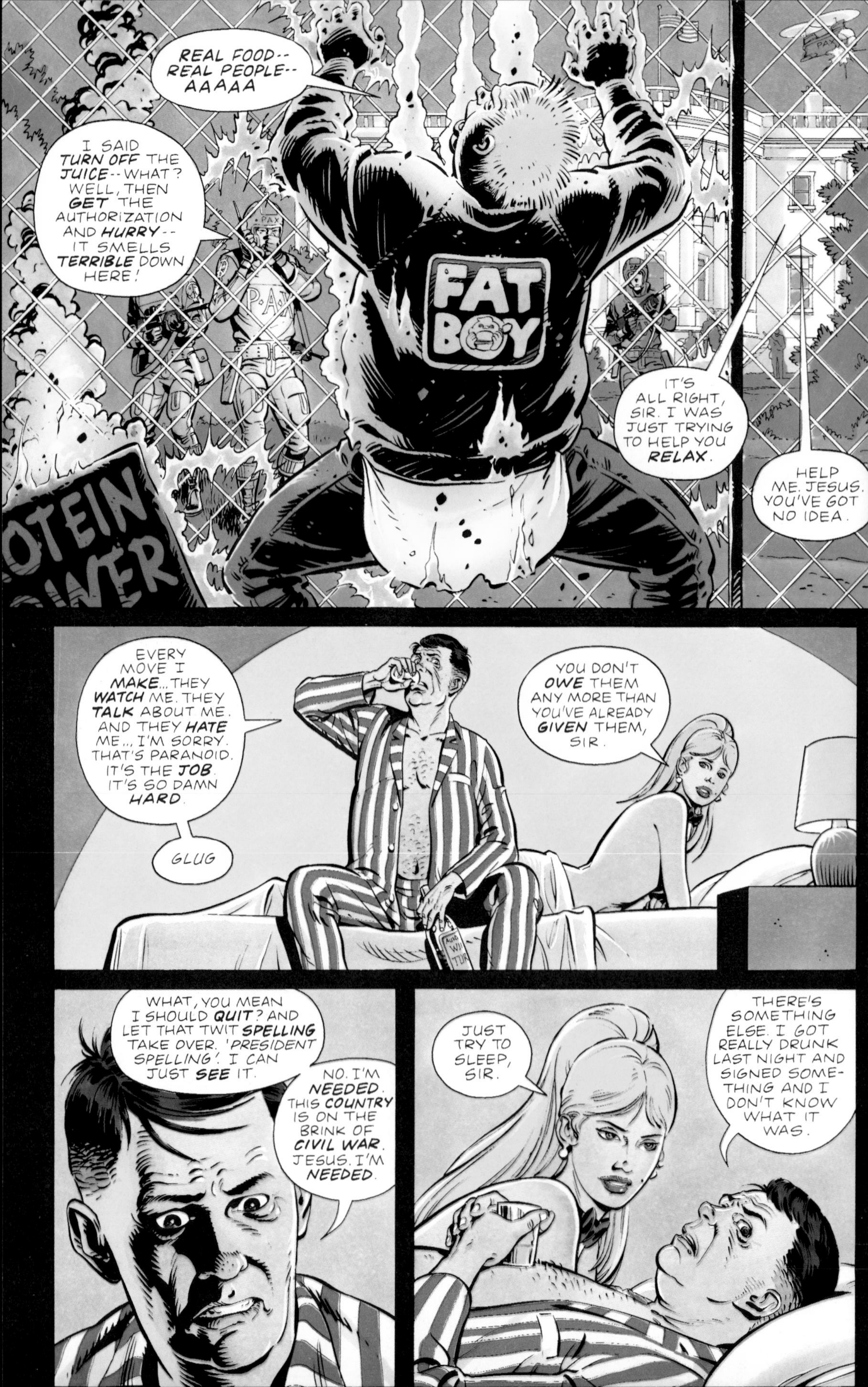

REAL FOOD-- REAL PEOPLE-- AAAAA
I SAID TURN OFF THE JUICE--WHAT? WELL, THEN GET THE AUTHORIZATION AND HURRY-- IT SMELLS TERRIBLE DOWN HERE!
FAT BOY
OTEIN
IT'S ALL RIGHT, SIR. I WAS JUST TRYING TO HELP YOU RELAX.
HELP ME. JESUS. YOU'VE GOT NO IDEA.
EVERY MOVE I MAKE... THEY WATCH ME. THEY TALK ABOUT ME. AND THEY HATE ME... I'M SORRY. THAT'S PARANOID. IT'S THE JOB. IT'S SO DAMN HARD.
GLUG
YOU DON'T OWE THEM ANY MORE THAN YOU'VE ALREADY GIVEN THEM, SIR.
WHAT, YOU MEAN I SHOULD QUIT? AND LET THAT TWIT SPELLING TAKE OVER. 'PRESIDENT SPELLING'. I CAN JUST SEE IT.
NO. I'M NEEDED. THIS COUNTRY IS ON THE BRINK OF CIVIL WAR. JESUS. I'M NEEDED.
JUST TRY TO SLEEP, SIR.
THERE'S SOMETHING ELSE. I GOT REALLY DRUNK LAST NIGHT AND SIGNED SOMETHING AND I DON'T KNOW WHAT IT WAS.

EXECUTIVE ORDER

TO: **GEN. LUCIUS SPANK,** Commander, Joint Chiefs Of Staff

FROM: **THE CHIEF**

December 11, 2011   3:04 A.M.

This order is to be destroyed immediately after you have committed its contents to memory.

Bear in mind that any discussion of this Order with anyone under any circumstances will force me to use Executive Privilege as defined in the 36th Amendment. Your summary court-martial and execution will be the price of disobedience.

You will instruct Peace Force Lt. Colonel Stanford Moretti to deploy laser fire from an orbiting laser cannon to eradicate the Apache Nation from the face of the earth.

You will falsify evidence to the effect that the Apache Nation is readying a nuclear strike on Washington, D.C..

This operation must leave no survivors and will be carried out by sunrise tomorrow morning.

Best to Helena and the kids.

nissen

PRESIDENT

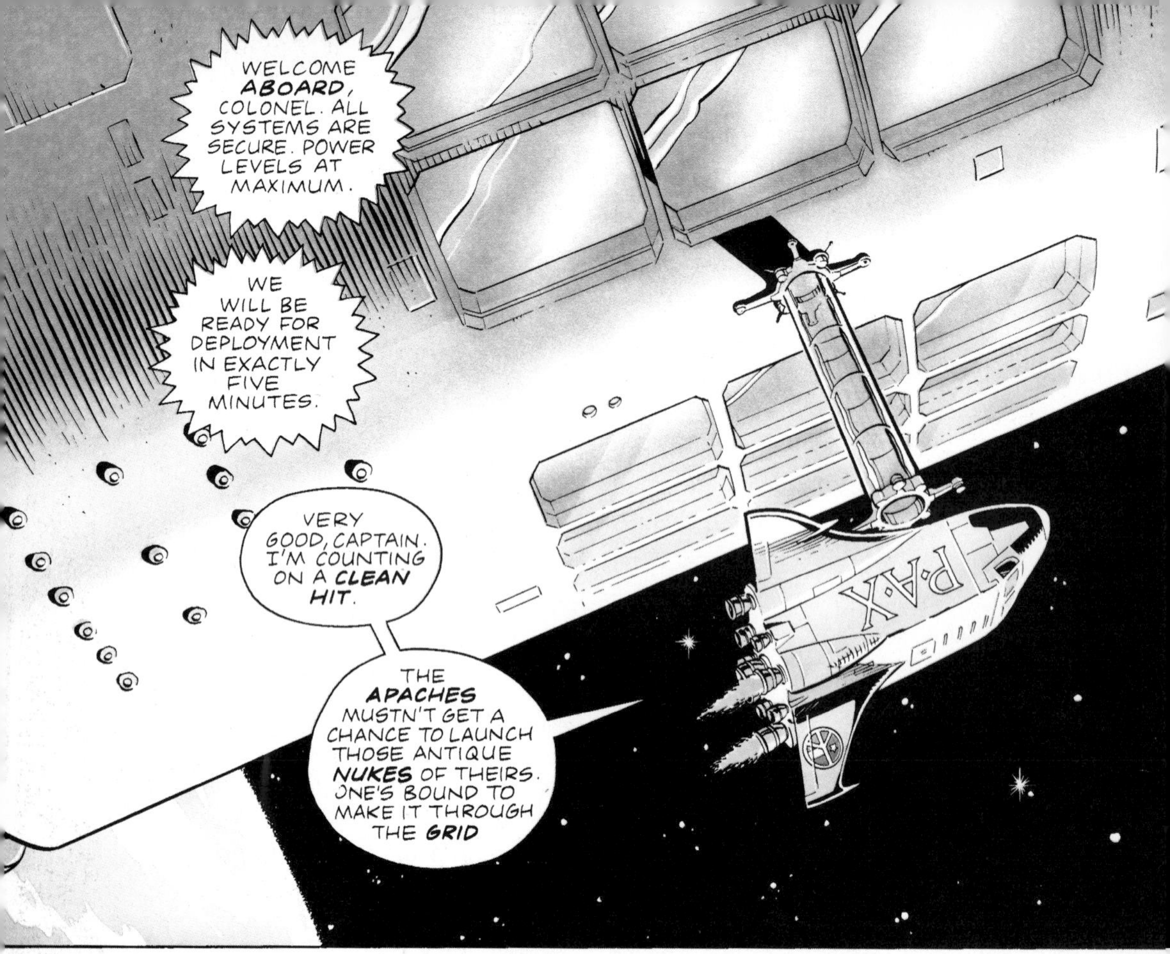
WELCOME ABOARD, COLONEL. ALL SYSTEMS ARE SECURE. POWER LEVELS AT MAXIMUM.
WE WILL BE READY FOR DEPLOYMENT IN EXACTLY FIVE MINUTES.
VERY GOOD, CAPTAIN. I'M COUNTING ON A CLEAN HIT.
THE APACHES MUSTN'T GET A CHANCE TO LAUNCH THOSE ANTIQUE NUKES OF THEIRS. ONE'S BOUND TO MAKE IT THROUGH THE GRID
P.A.X

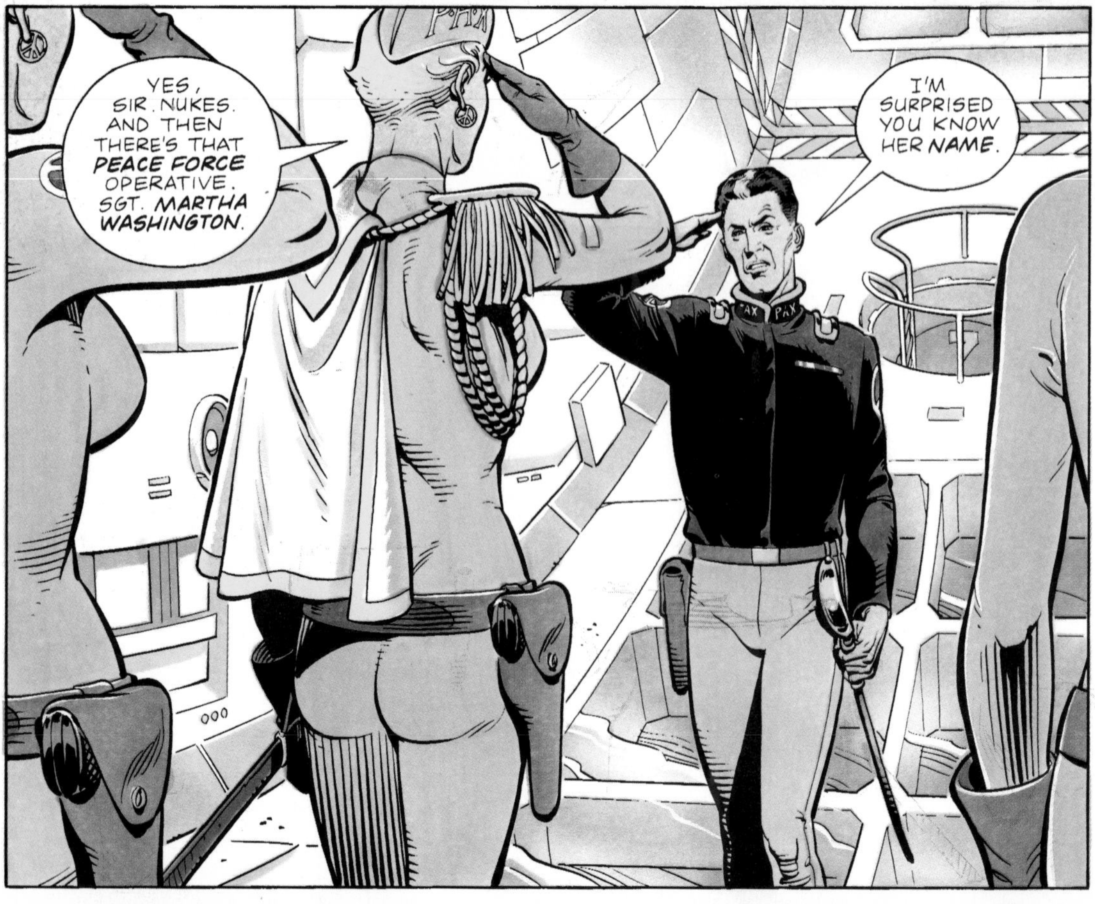
YES, SIR. NUKES. AND THEN THERE'S THAT PEACE FORCE OPERATIVE. SGT. MARTHA WASHINGTON.
I'M SURPRISED YOU KNOW HER NAME.

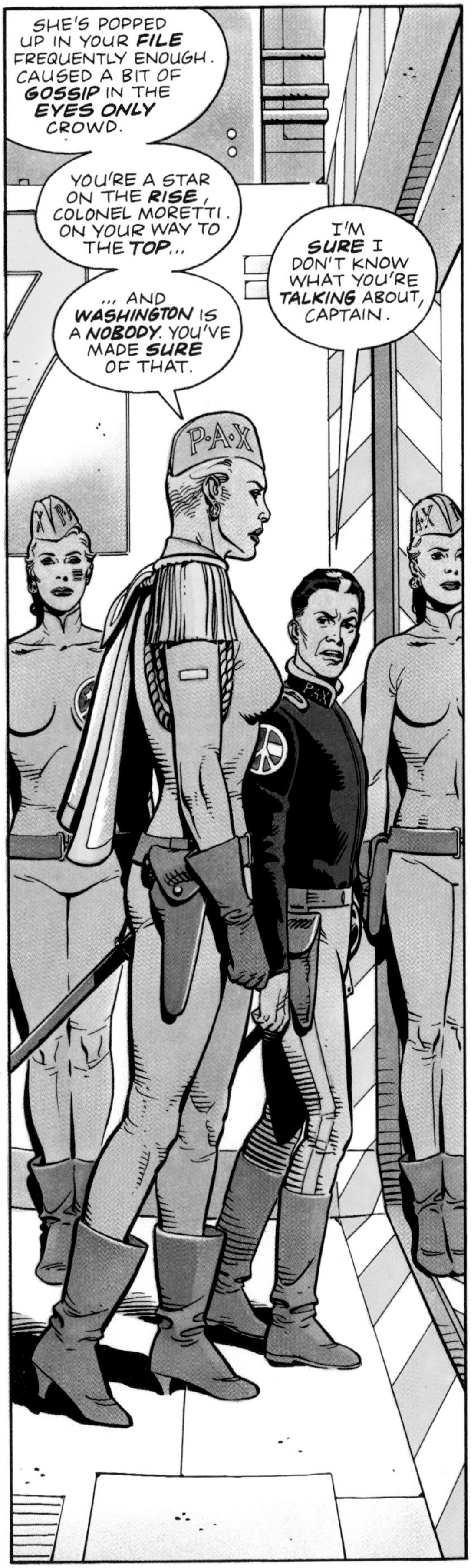
SHE'S POPPED UP IN YOUR FILE FREQUENTLY ENOUGH. CAUSED A BIT OF GOSSIP IN THE EYES ONLY CROWD.
YOU'RE A STAR ON THE RISE, COLONEL MORETTI. ON YOUR WAY TO THE TOP...
... AND WASHINGTON IS A NOBODY. YOU'VE MADE SURE OF THAT.
I'M SURE I DON'T KNOW WHAT YOU'RE TALKING ABOUT, CAPTAIN.
P·A·X

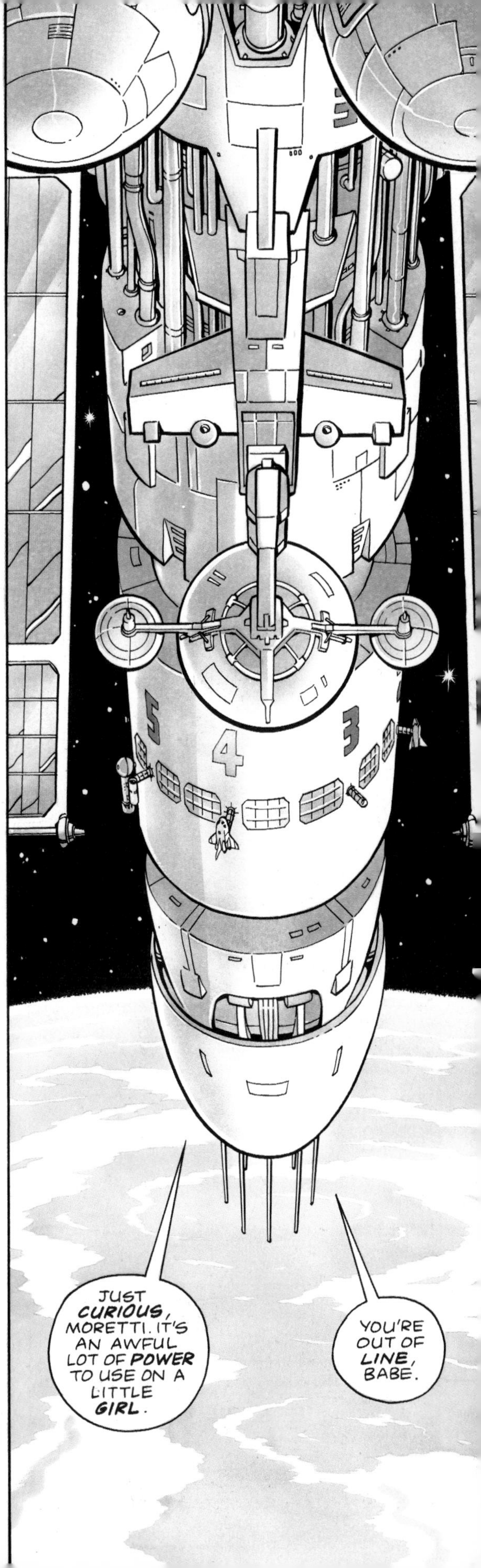
JUST CURIOUS, MORETTI. IT'S AN AWFUL LOT OF POWER TO USE ON A LITTLE GIRL.
YOU'RE OUT OF LINE, BABE.

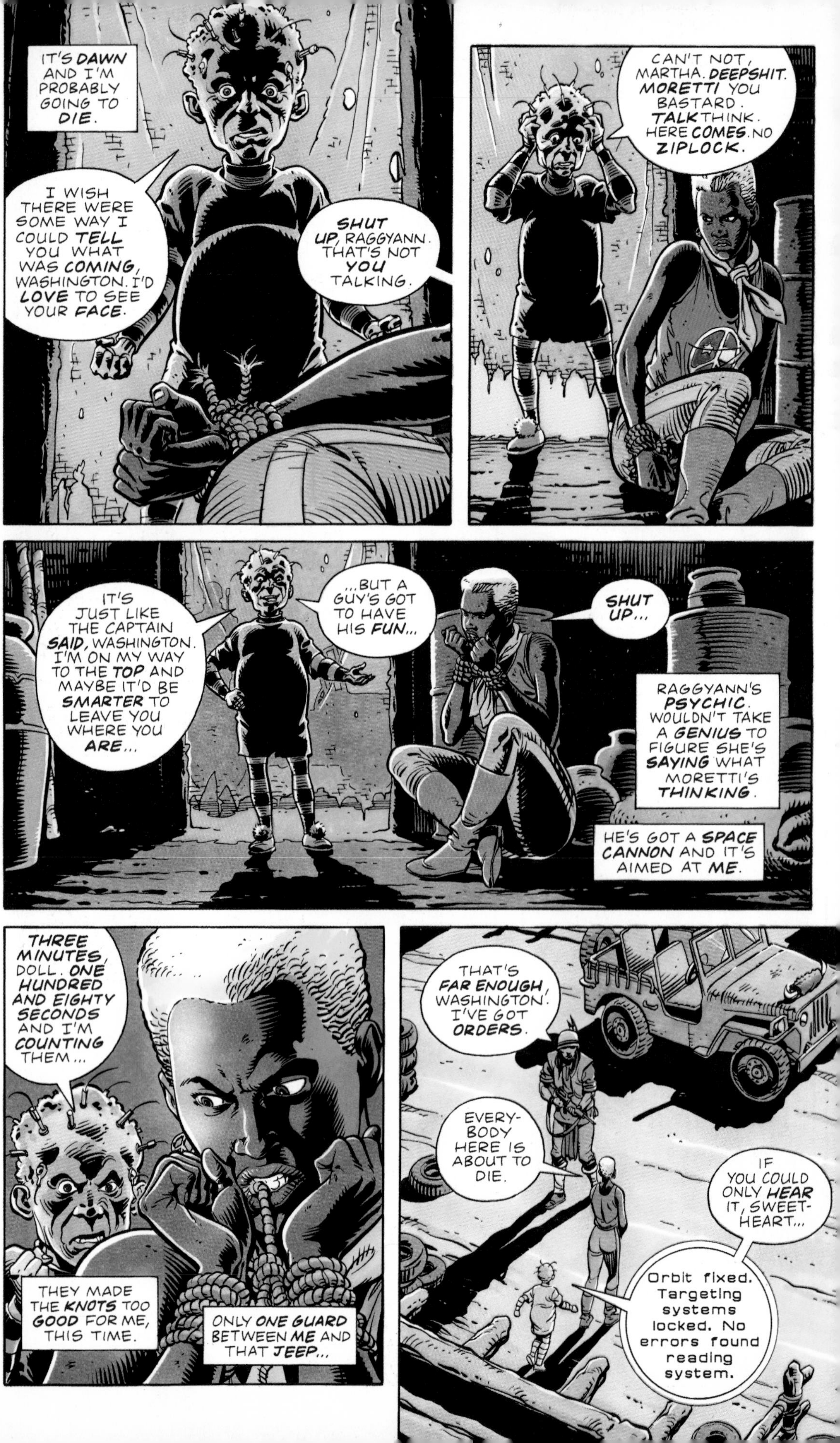
IT'S DAWN AND I'M PROBABLY GOING TO DIE.
I WISH THERE WERE SOME WAY I COULD TELL YOU WHAT WAS COMING, WASHINGTON. I'D LOVE TO SEE YOUR FACE.
SHUT UP, RAGGYANN. THAT'S NOT YOU TALKING.
CAN'T NOT, MARTHA. DEEPSHIT. MORETTI YOU BASTARD. TALK THINK. HERE COMES. NO ZIPLOCK.
IT'S JUST LIKE THE CAPTAIN SAID, WASHINGTON. I'M ON MY WAY TO THE TOP AND MAYBE IT'D BE SMARTER TO LEAVE YOU WHERE YOU ARE...
...BUT A GUY'S GOT TO HAVE HIS FUN...
SHUT UP...
RAGGYANN'S PSYCHIC. WOULDN'T TAKE A GENIUS TO FIGURE SHE'S SAYING WHAT MORETTI'S THINKING.
HE'S GOT A SPACE CANNON AND IT'S AIMED AT ME.
THREE MINUTES, DOLL. ONE HUNDRED AND EIGHTY SECONDS AND I'M COUNTING THEM...
THEY MADE THE KNOTS TOO GOOD FOR ME, THIS TIME.
ONLY ONE GUARD BETWEEN ME AND THAT JEEP...
THAT'S FAR ENOUGH, WASHINGTON. I'VE GOT ORDERS.
EVERY-BODY HERE IS ABOUT TO DIE.
IF YOU COULD ONLY HEAR IT, SWEET-HEART...
Orbit fixed. Targeting systems locked. No errors found reading system.

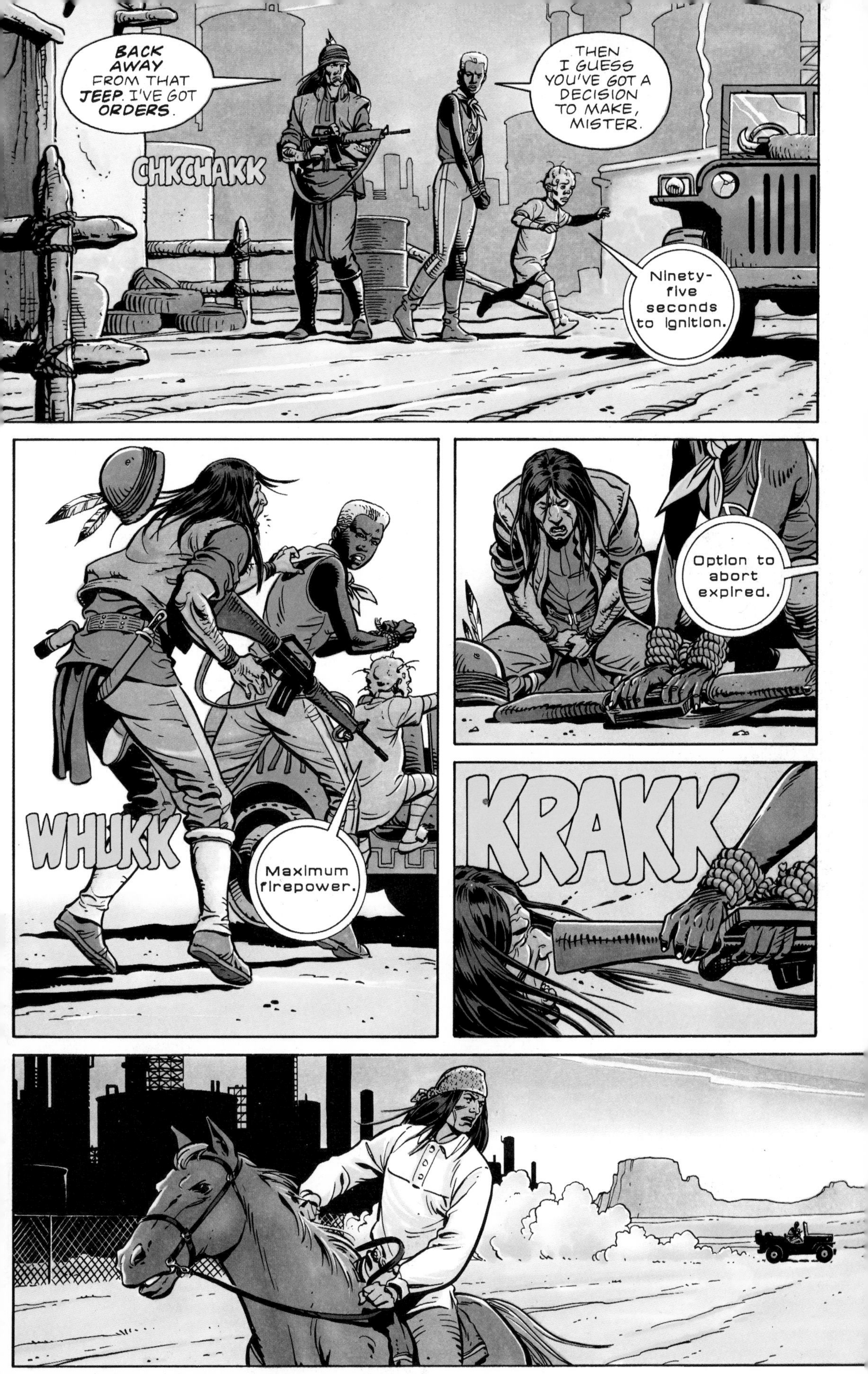
BACK AWAY FROM THAT JEEP. I'VE GOT ORDERS.
CHKCHAKK
THEN I GUESS YOU'VE GOT A DECISION TO MAKE, MISTER.
Ninety-five seconds to ignition.
WHUKK
Maximum firepower.
Option to abort expired.
KRAKK

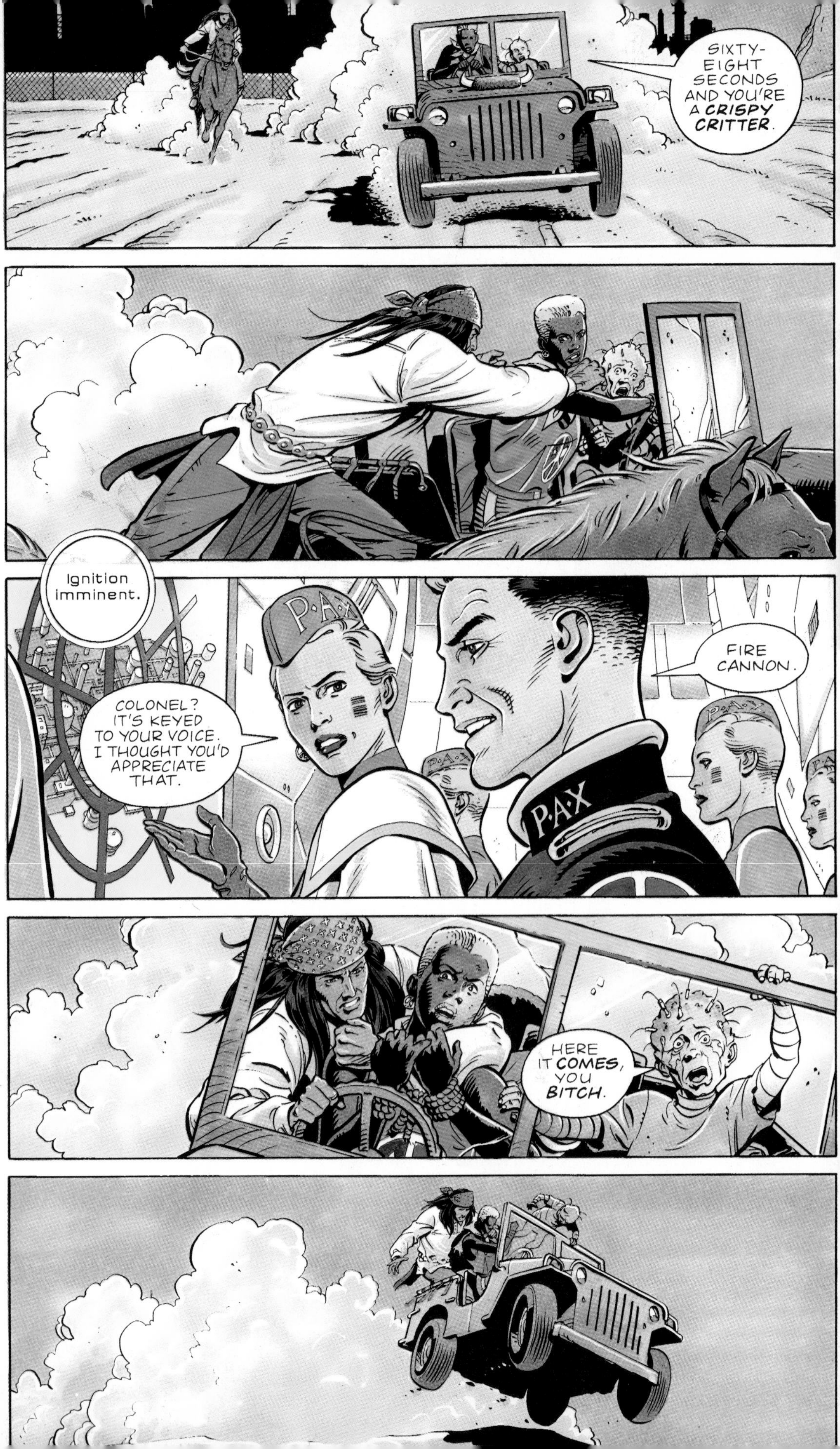
SIXTY-EIGHT SECONDS AND YOU'RE A CRISPY CRITTER.
Ignition imminent.
COLONEL? IT'S KEYED TO YOUR VOICE. I THOUGHT YOU'D APPRECIATE THAT.
FIRE CANNON.
P·A·X
HERE IT COMES, YOU BITCH.

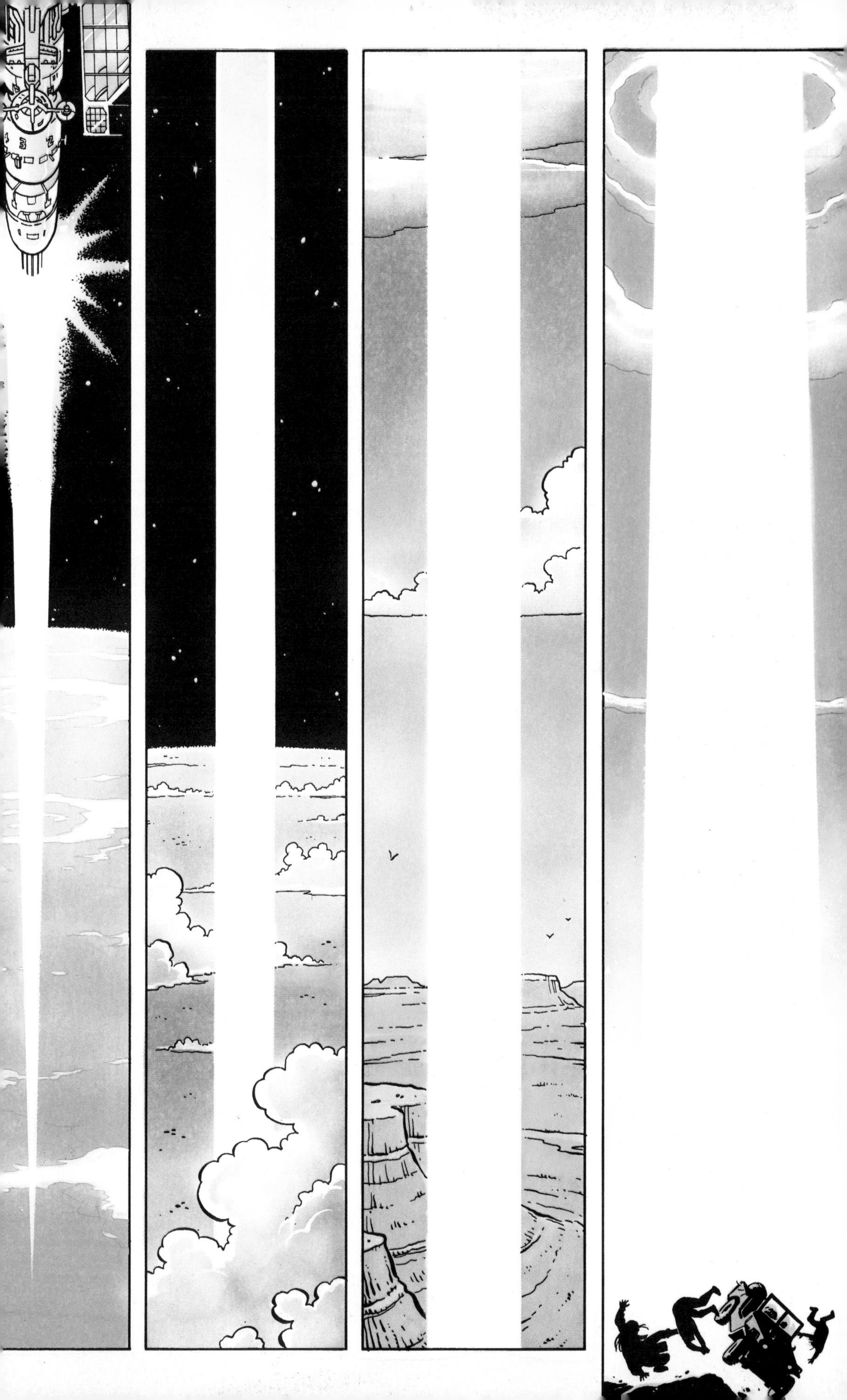

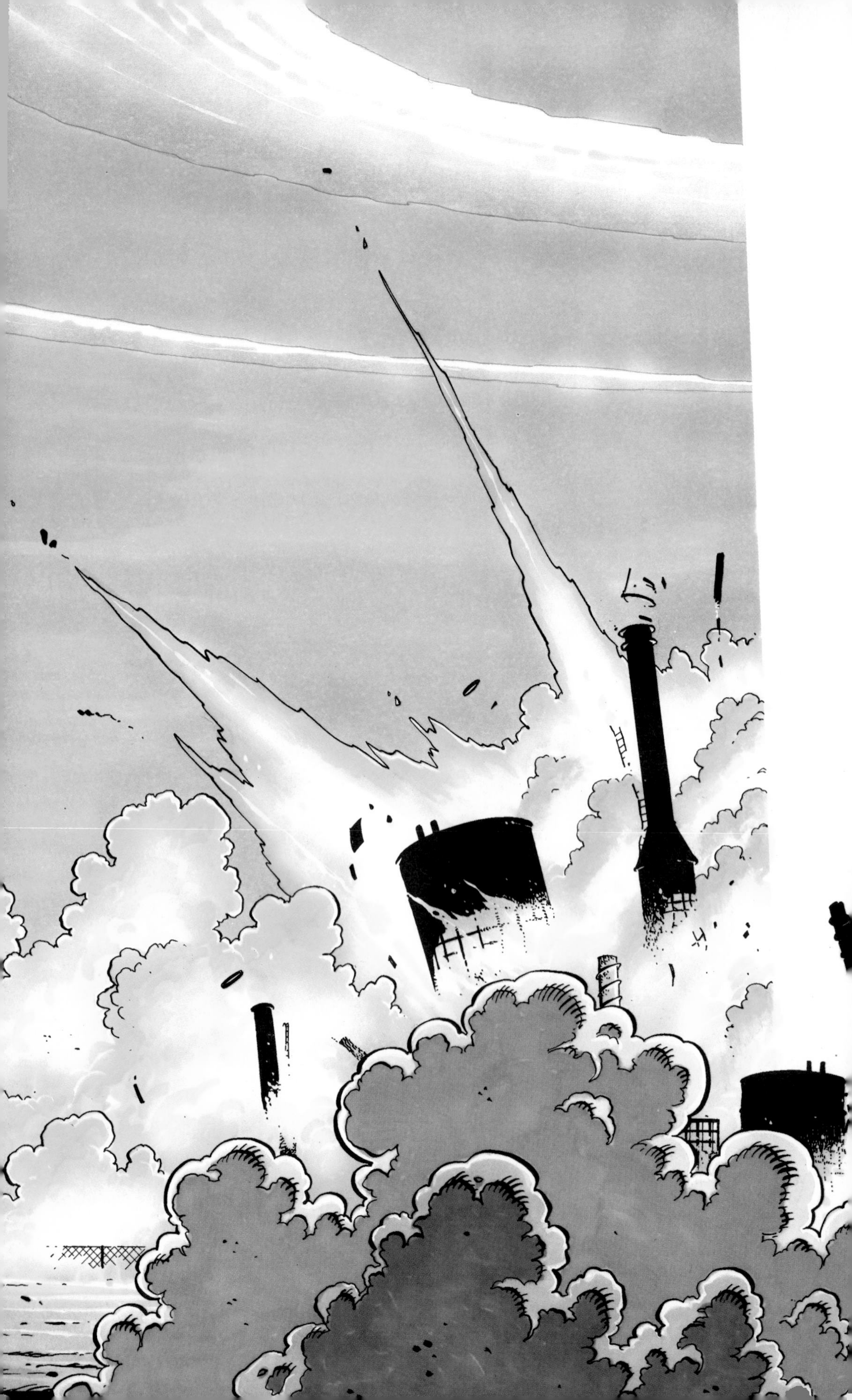

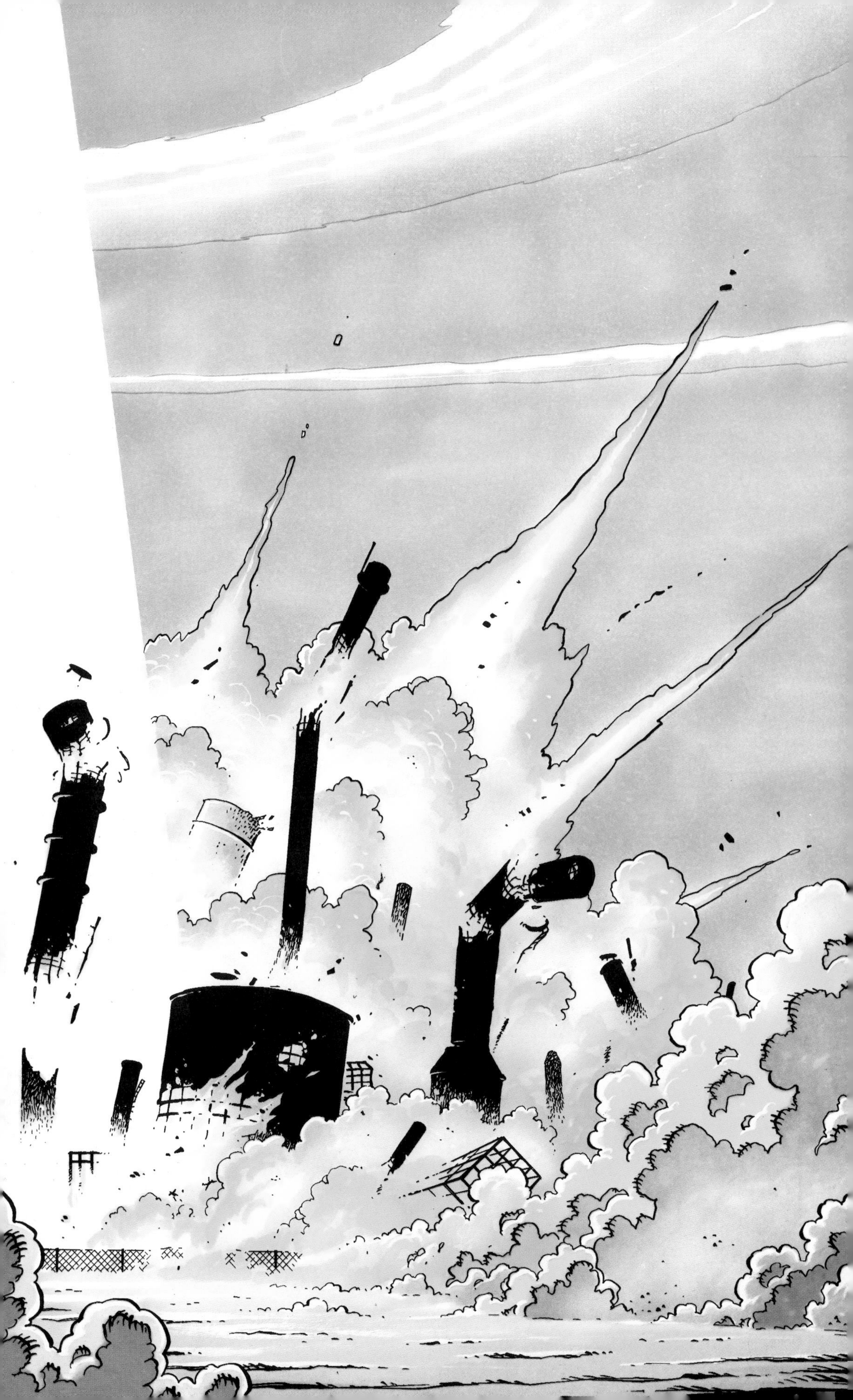

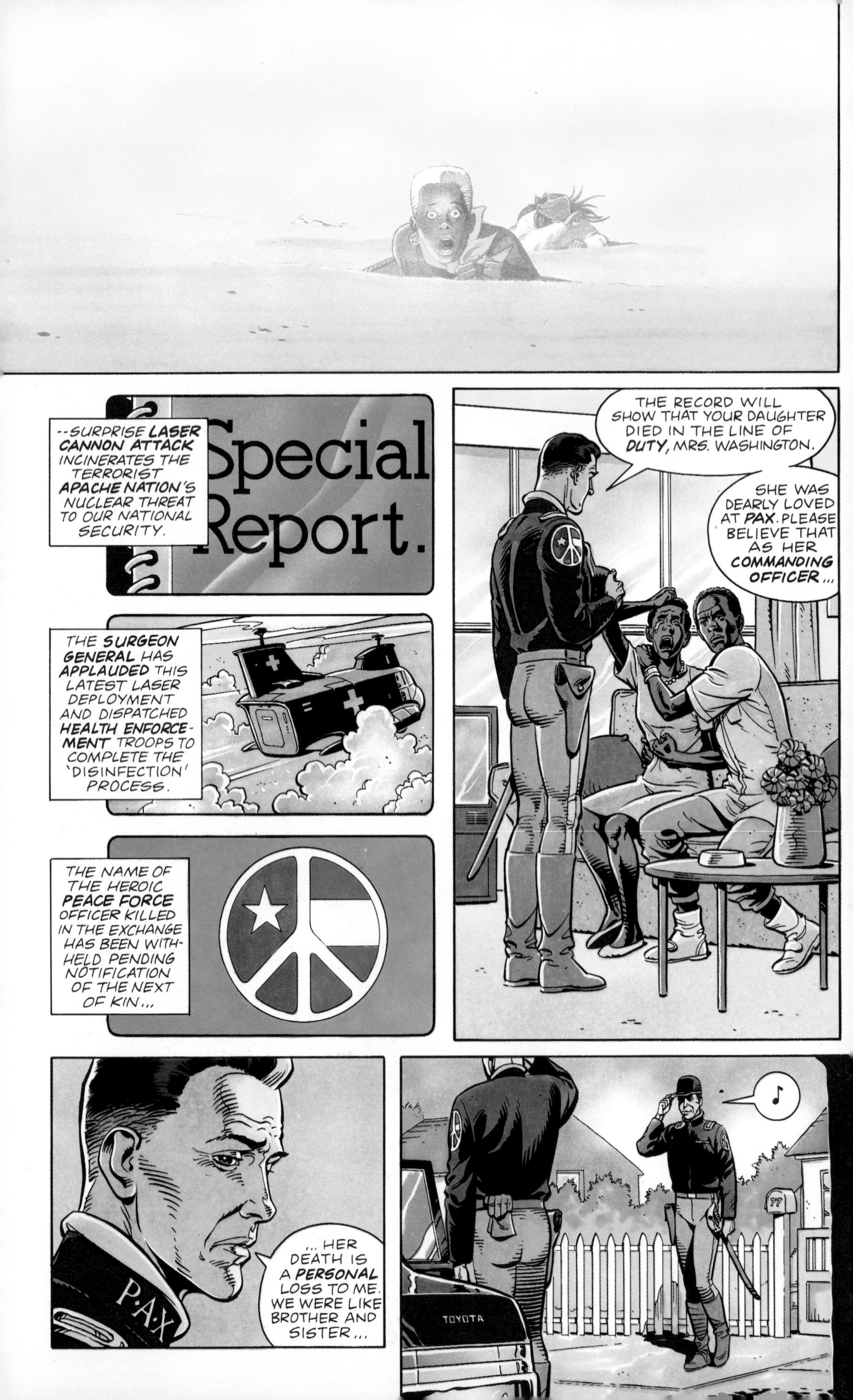

Special Report.
--SURPRISE LASER CANNON ATTACK INCINERATES THE TERRORIST APACHE NATION'S NUCLEAR THREAT TO OUR NATIONAL SECURITY.
THE SURGEON GENERAL HAS APPLAUDED THIS LATEST LASER DEPLOYMENT AND DISPATCHED HEALTH ENFORCE-MENT TROOPS TO COMPLETE THE 'DISINFECTION' PROCESS.
THE NAME OF THE HEROIC PEACE FORCE OFFICER KILLED IN THE EXCHANGE HAS BEEN WITH-HELD PENDING NOTIFICATION OF THE NEXT OF KIN...
THE RECORD WILL SHOW THAT YOUR DAUGHTER DIED IN THE LINE OF DUTY, MRS. WASHINGTON.
SHE WAS DEARLY LOVED AT PAX. PLEASE BELIEVE THAT AS HER COMMANDING OFFICER...
P·A·X
...HER DEATH IS A PERSONAL LOSS TO ME. WE WERE LIKE BROTHER AND SISTER...
♪
TOYOTA

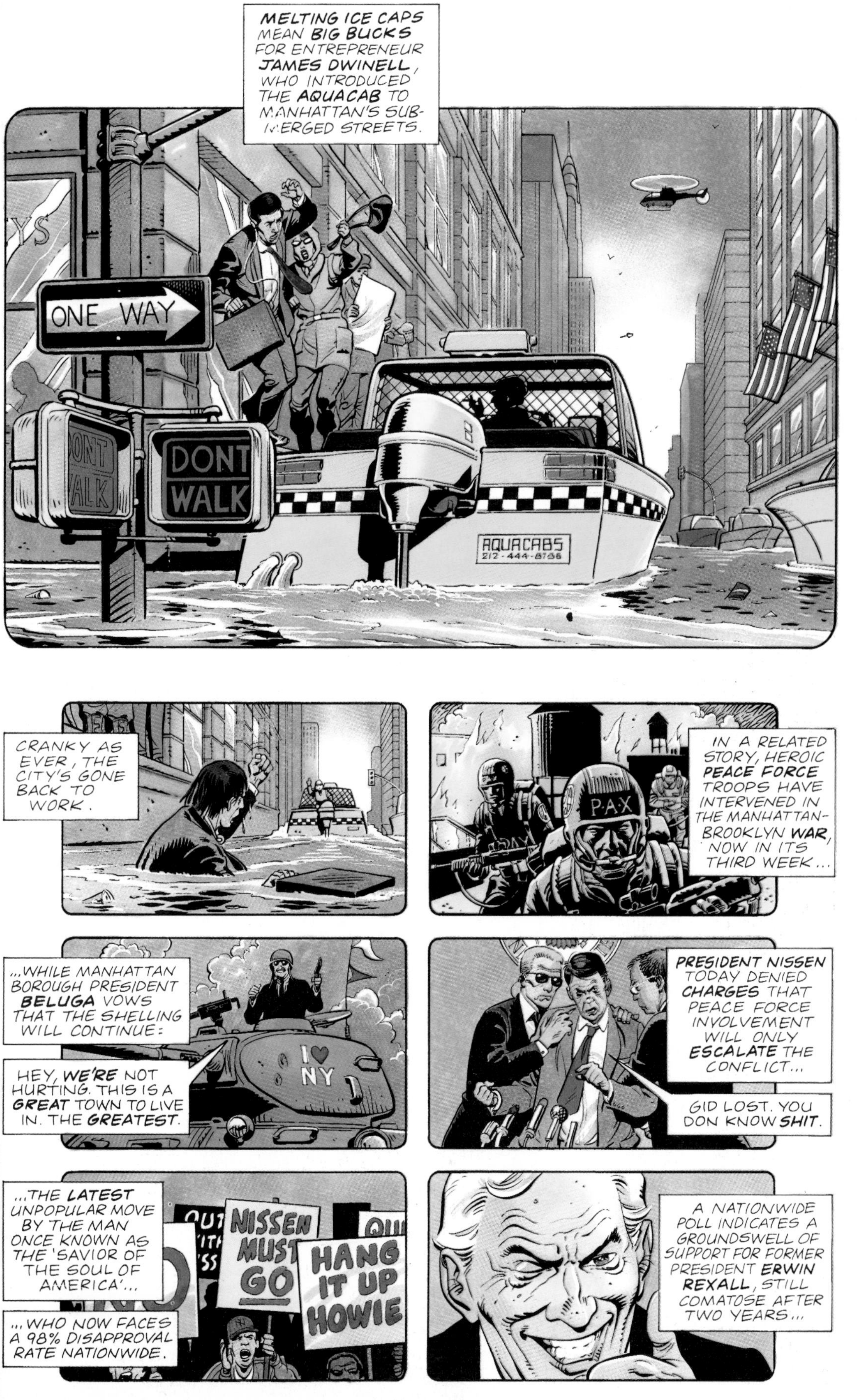

MELTING ICE CAPS MEAN BIG BUCKS FOR ENTREPRENEUR JAMES DWINELL, WHO INTRODUCED THE AQUACAB TO MANHATTAN'S SUB-MERGED STREETS.
ONE WAY
DONT WALK
DONT WALK
AQUACABS 212-444-8736
CRANKY AS EVER, THE CITY'S GONE BACK TO WORK.
IN A RELATED STORY, HEROIC PEACE FORCE TROOPS HAVE INTERVENED IN THE MANHATTAN-BROOKLYN WAR, NOW IN ITS THIRD WEEK...
P·A·X
...WHILE MANHATTAN BOROUGH PRESIDENT BELUGA VOWS THAT THE SHELLING WILL CONTINUE:
HEY, WE'RE NOT HURTING. THIS IS A GREAT TOWN TO LIVE IN. THE GREATEST.
I ♥ NY
PRESIDENT NISSEN TODAY DENIED CHARGES THAT PEACE FORCE INVOLVEMENT WILL ONLY ESCALATE THE CONFLICT...
GID LOST. YOU DON KNOW SHIT.
...THE LATEST UNPOPULAR MOVE BY THE MAN ONCE KNOWN AS THE 'SAVIOR OF THE SOUL OF AMERICA'...
...WHO NOW FACES A 98% DISAPPROVAL RATE NATIONWIDE.
NISSEN MUST GO
HANG IT UP HOWIE
A NATIONWIDE POLL INDICATES A GROUNDSWELL OF SUPPORT FOR FORMER PRESIDENT ERWIN REXALL, STILL COMATOSE AFTER TWO YEARS...

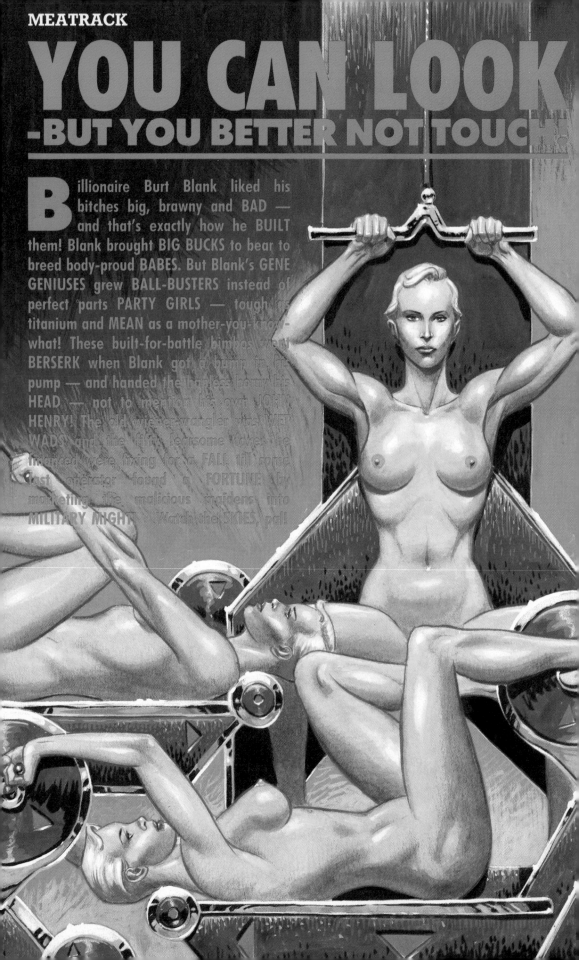

MEATRACK

YOU CAN LOOK
–BUT YOU BETTER NOT TOUCH!

Billionaire Burt Blank liked his bitches big, brawny and BAD — and that's exactly how he BUILT them! Blank brought BIG BUCKS to bear to breed body-proud BABES. But Blank's GENE GENIUSES grew BALL-BUSTERS instead of perfect parts PARTY GIRLS — tough as titanium and MEAN as a mother-you-know-what! These built-for-battle bimbos went BERSERK when Blank got a bump in his pump — and handed the hapless horny his HEAD — not to mention his own JOHN HENRY! The old wiener-wrangler shot WET WADS and the fifty fearsome foxes he financed were fixing for a FALL till some fast operator found a FORTUNE by marketing the malicious maidens into MILITARY MIGHT . . . Watch the SKIES, pal!

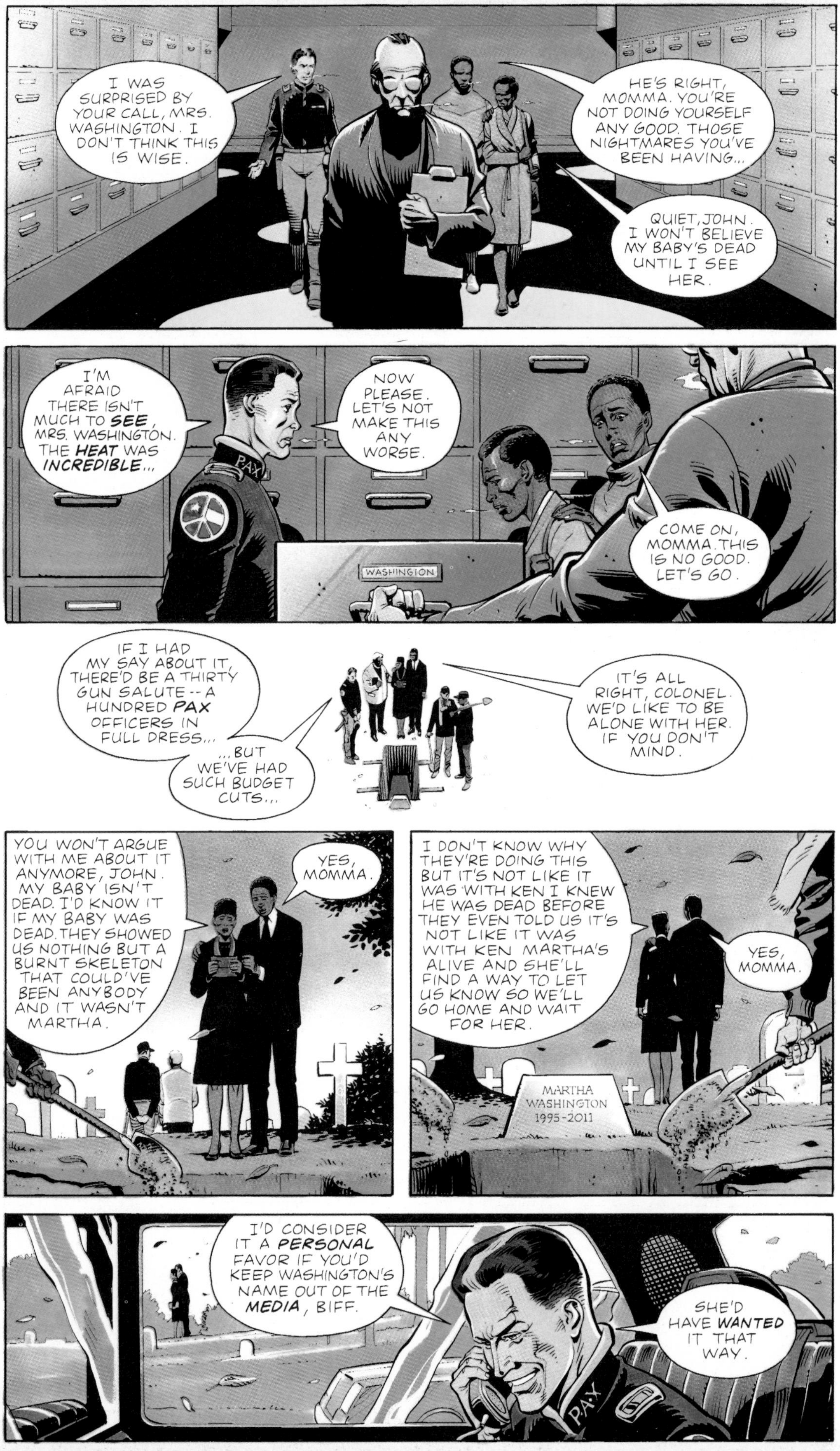
I WAS SURPRISED BY YOUR CALL, MRS. WASHINGTON. I DON'T THINK THIS IS WISE.
HE'S RIGHT, MOMMA. YOU'RE NOT DOING YOURSELF ANY GOOD. THOSE NIGHTMARES YOU'VE BEEN HAVING...
QUIET, JOHN. I WON'T BELIEVE MY BABY'S DEAD UNTIL I SEE HER.
I'M AFRAID THERE ISN'T MUCH TO SEE, MRS. WASHINGTON. THE HEAT WAS INCREDIBLE...
NOW PLEASE. LET'S NOT MAKE THIS ANY WORSE.
WASHINGTON
COME ON, MOMMA. THIS IS NO GOOD. LET'S GO.
IF I HAD MY SAY ABOUT IT, THERE'D BE A THIRTY GUN SALUTE -- A HUNDRED PAX OFFICERS IN FULL DRESS...
...BUT WE'VE HAD SUCH BUDGET CUTS...
IT'S ALL RIGHT, COLONEL. WE'D LIKE TO BE ALONE WITH HER. IF YOU DON'T MIND.
YOU WON'T ARGUE WITH ME ABOUT IT ANYMORE, JOHN. MY BABY ISN'T DEAD. I'D KNOW IT IF MY BABY WAS DEAD. THEY SHOWED US NOTHING BUT A BURNT SKELETON THAT COULD'VE BEEN ANYBODY AND IT WASN'T MARTHA.
YES, MOMMA.
I DON'T KNOW WHY THEY'RE DOING THIS BUT IT'S NOT LIKE IT WAS WITH KEN I KNEW HE WAS DEAD BEFORE THEY EVEN TOLD US IT'S NOT LIKE IT WAS WITH KEN MARTHA'S ALIVE AND SHE'LL FIND A WAY TO LET US KNOW SO WE'LL GO HOME AND WAIT FOR HER.
YES, MOMMA.
MARTHA WASHINGTON 1995-2011
I'D CONSIDER IT A PERSONAL FAVOR IF YOU'D KEEP WASHINGTON'S NAME OUT OF THE MEDIA, BIFF.
SHE'D HAVE WANTED IT THAT WAY.

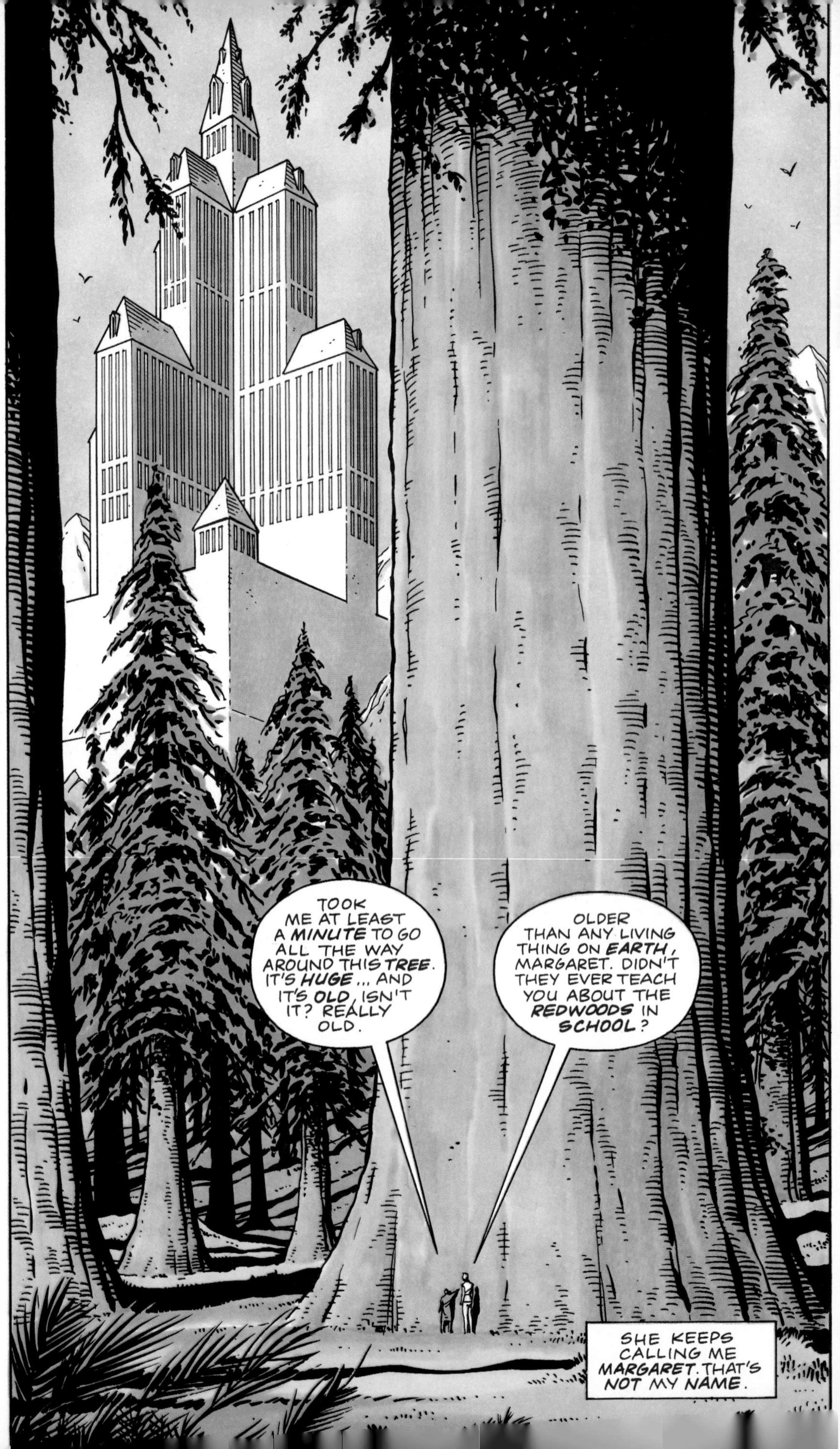
TOOK ME AT LEAST A MINUTE TO GO ALL THE WAY AROUND THIS TREE. IT'S HUGE... AND IT'S OLD, ISN'T IT? REALLY OLD.
OLDER THAN ANY LIVING THING ON EARTH, MARGARET. DIDN'T THEY EVER TEACH YOU ABOUT THE REDWOODS IN SCHOOL?
SHE KEEPS CALLING ME MARGARET. THAT'S NOT MY NAME.

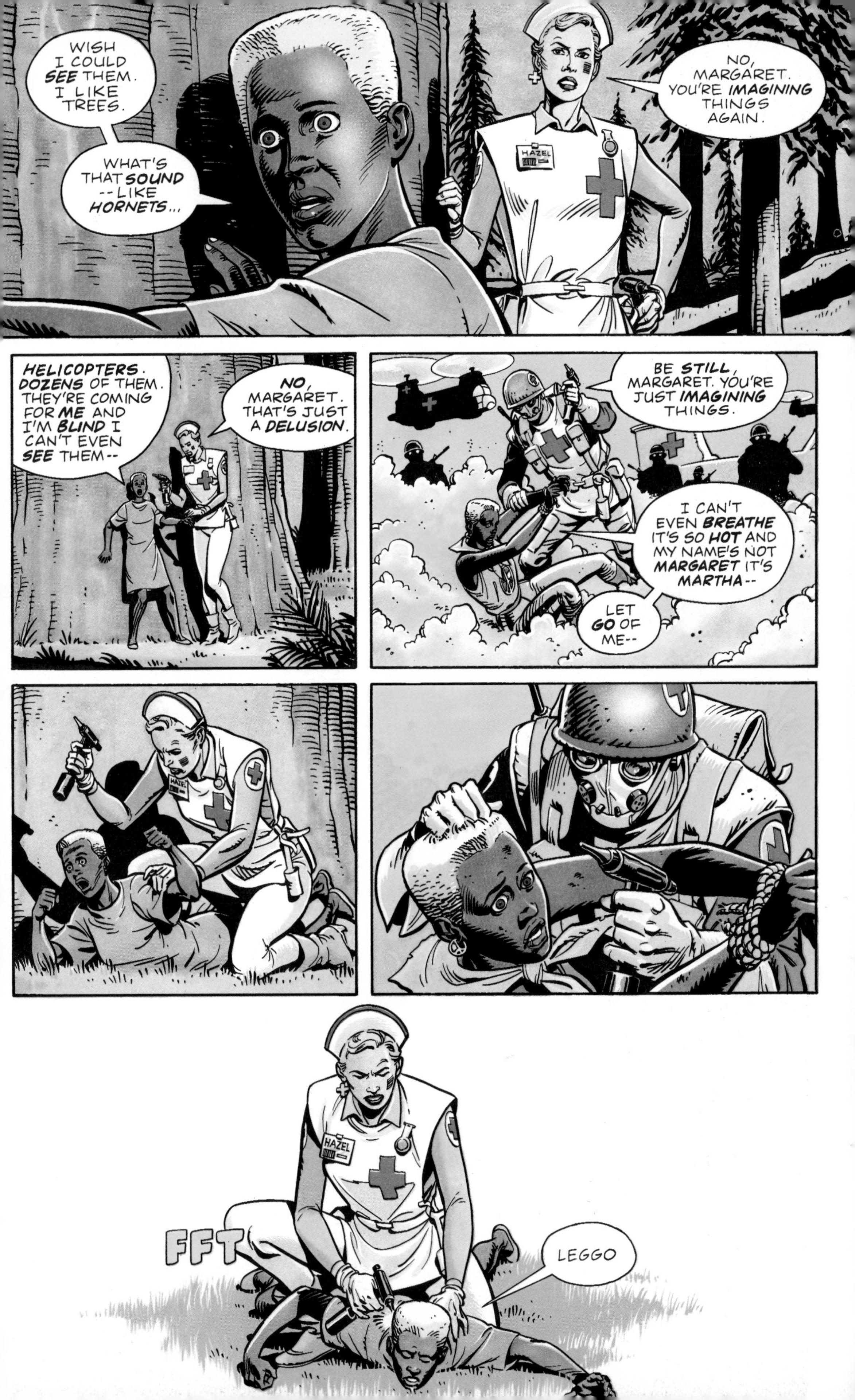
WISH I COULD SEE THEM. I LIKE TREES.
WHAT'S THAT SOUND --LIKE HORNETS...
NO, MARGARET. YOU'RE IMAGINING THINGS AGAIN.
HAZEL
HELICOPTERS. DOZENS OF THEM. THEY'RE COMING FOR ME AND I'M BLIND I CAN'T EVEN SEE THEM--
NO, MARGARET. THAT'S JUST A DELUSION.
BE STILL, MARGARET. YOU'RE JUST IMAGINING THINGS.
I CAN'T EVEN BREATHE IT'S SO HOT AND MY NAME'S NOT MARGARET IT'S MARTHA--
LET GO OF ME--
HAZEL
HAZEL
FFT
LEGGO

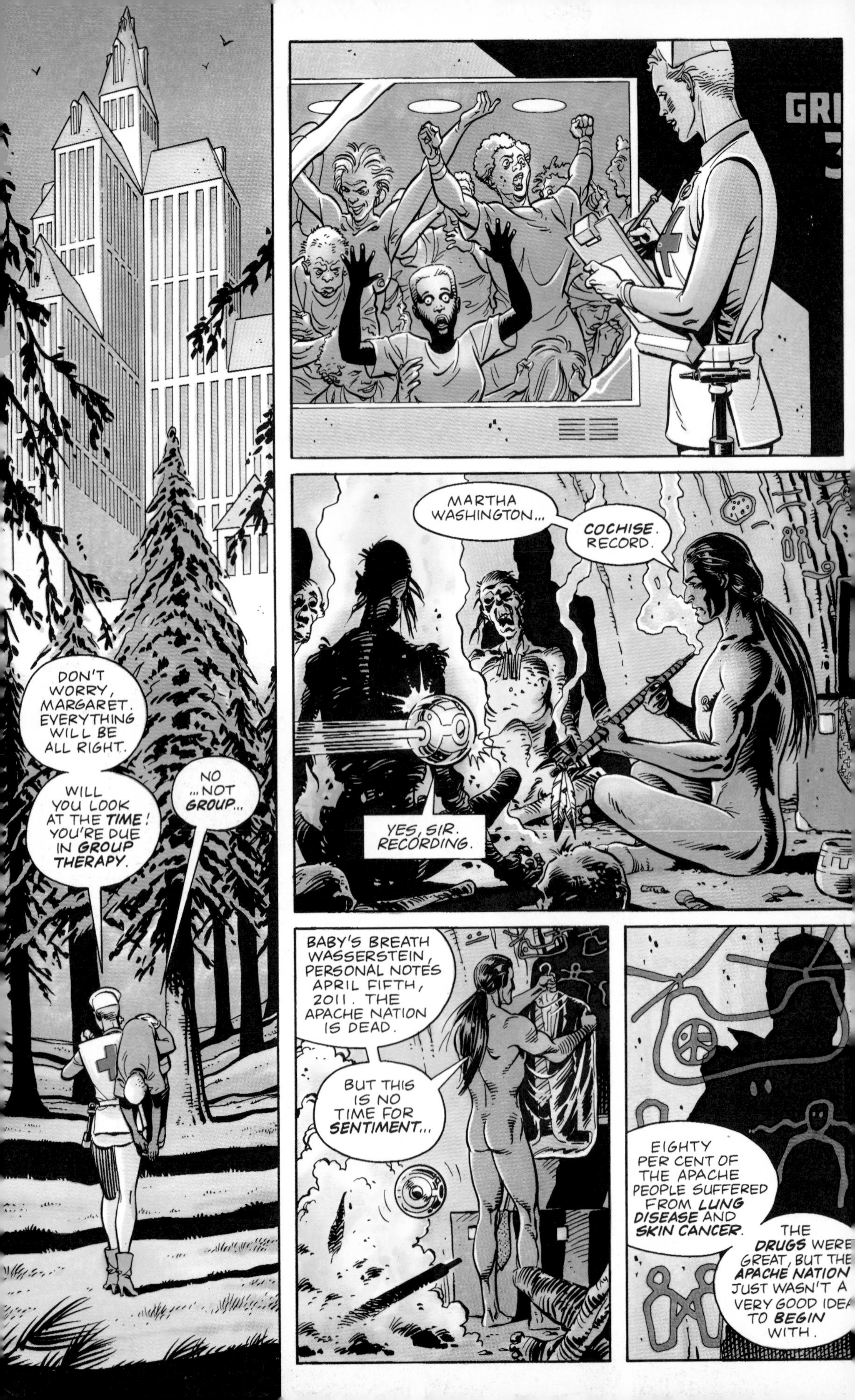
DON'T WORRY, MARGARET. EVERYTHING WILL BE ALL RIGHT.
WILL YOU LOOK AT THE TIME! YOU'RE DUE IN GROUP THERAPY.
NO ...NOT GROUP...
GRI
3
MARTHA WASHINGTON...
COCHISE. RECORD.
YES, SIR. RECORDING.
BABY'S BREATH WASSERSTEIN, PERSONAL NOTES APRIL FIFTH, 2011. THE APACHE NATION IS DEAD.
BUT THIS IS NO TIME FOR SENTIMENT...
EIGHTY PER CENT OF THE APACHE PEOPLE SUFFERED FROM LUNG DISEASE AND SKIN CANCER.
THE DRUGS WERE GREAT, BUT THE APACHE NATION JUST WASN'T A VERY GOOD IDEA TO BEGIN WITH.

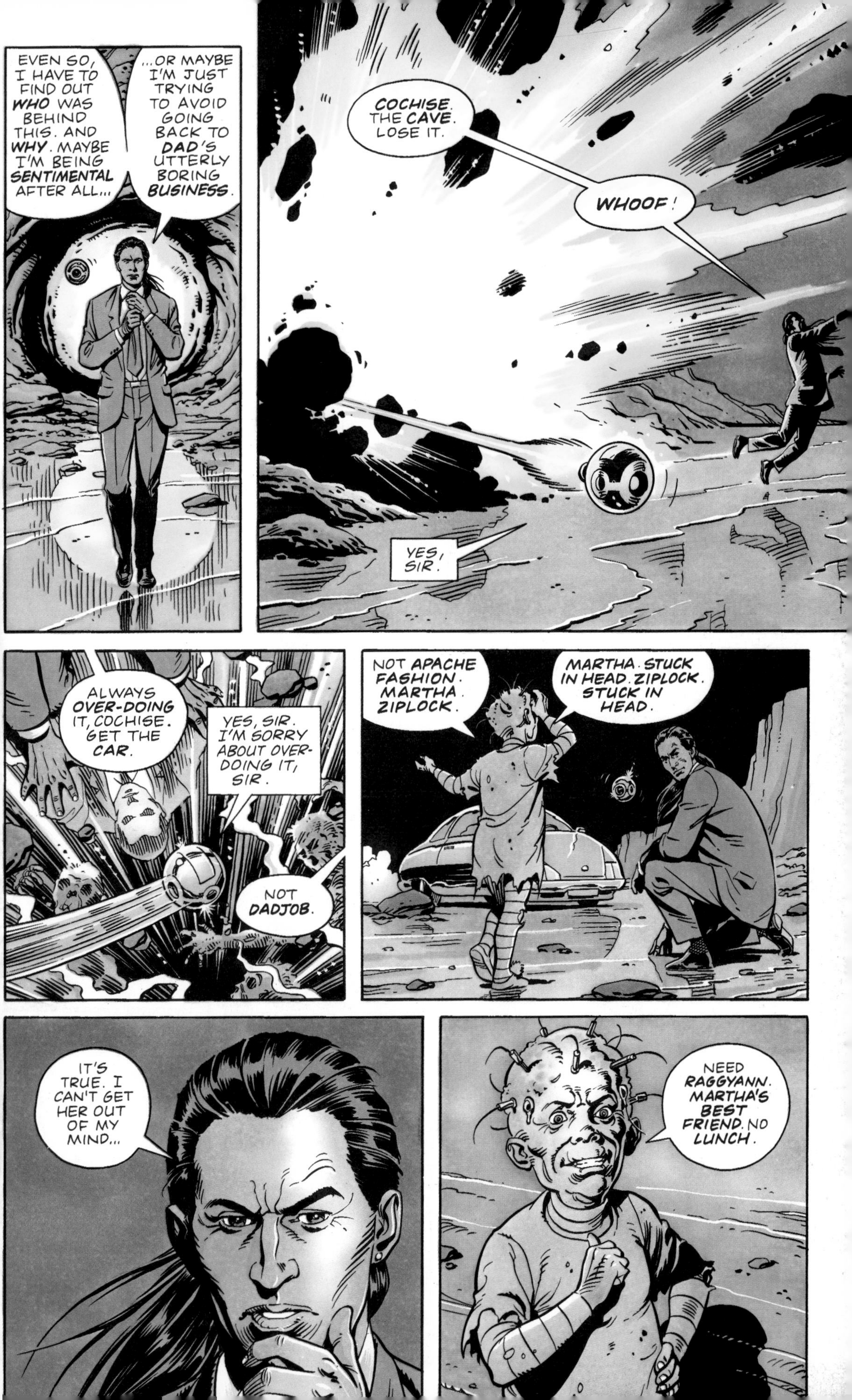
EVEN SO, I HAVE TO FIND OUT WHO WAS BEHIND THIS. AND WHY. MAYBE I'M BEING SENTIMENTAL AFTER ALL...
...OR MAYBE I'M JUST TRYING TO AVOID GOING BACK TO DAD'S UTTERLY BORING BUSINESS.
COCHISE. THE CAVE. LOSE IT.
WHOOF!
YES, SIR.
ALWAYS OVER-DOING IT, COCHISE. GET THE CAR.
YES, SIR. I'M SORRY ABOUT OVER-DOING IT, SIR.
NOT DADJOB.
NOT APACHE FASHION. MARTHA. ZIPLOCK.
MARTHA. STUCK IN HEAD. ZIPLOCK. STUCK IN HEAD.
IT'S TRUE. I CAN'T GET HER OUT OF MY MIND...
NEED RAGGYANN. MARTHA'S BEST FRIEND. NO LUNCH.

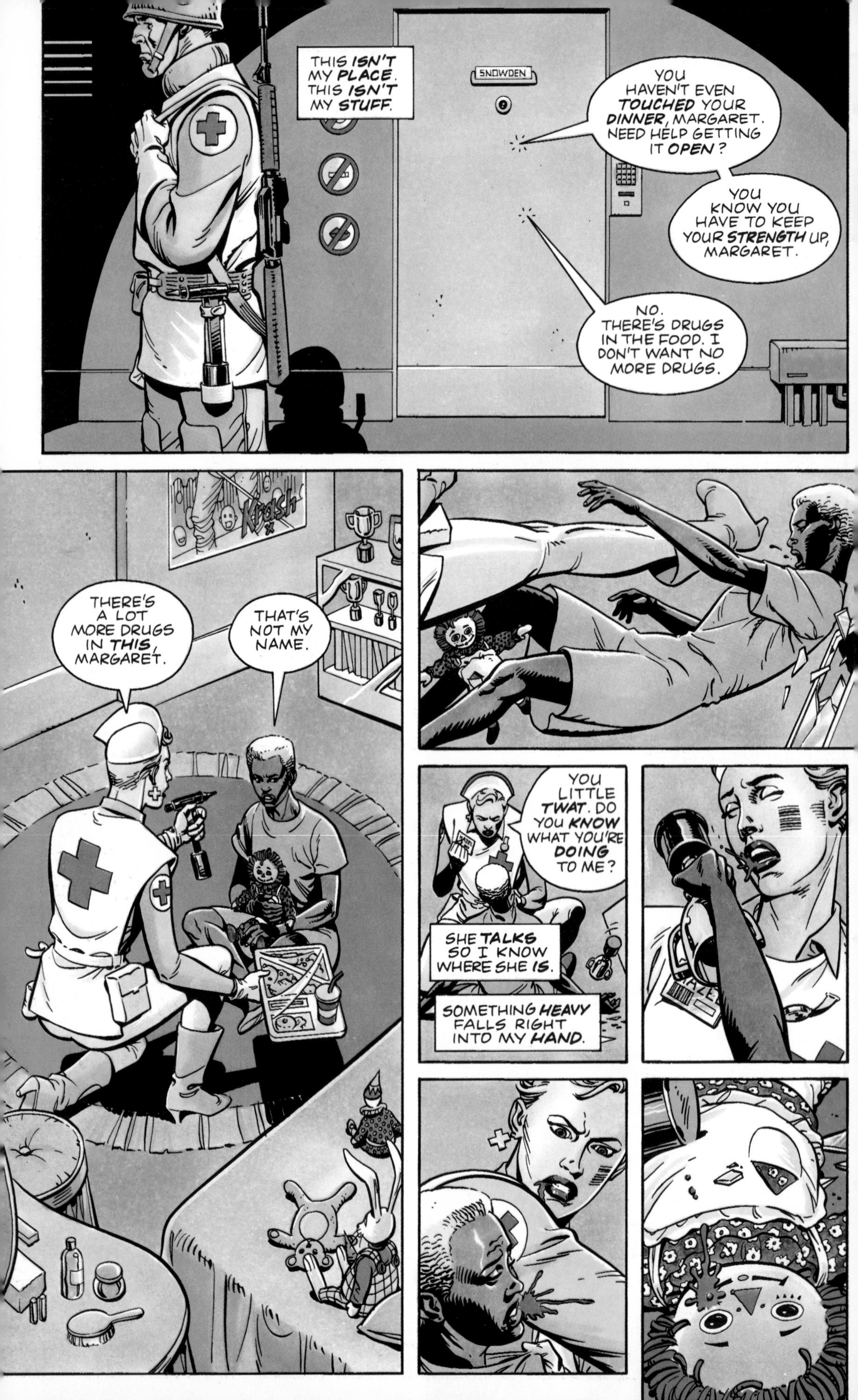

THIS ISN'T MY PLACE. THIS ISN'T MY STUFF.
SNOWDEN
YOU HAVEN'T EVEN TOUCHED YOUR DINNER, MARGARET. NEED HELP GETTING IT OPEN?
YOU KNOW YOU HAVE TO KEEP YOUR STRENGTH UP, MARGARET.
NO. THERE'S DRUGS IN THE FOOD. I DON'T WANT NO MORE DRUGS.
Krash
THERE'S A LOT MORE DRUGS IN THIS, MARGARET.
THAT'S NOT MY NAME.
YOU LITTLE TWAT. DO YOU KNOW WHAT YOU'RE DOING TO ME?
SHE TALKS SO I KNOW WHERE SHE IS.
SOMETHING HEAVY FALLS RIGHT INTO MY HAND.

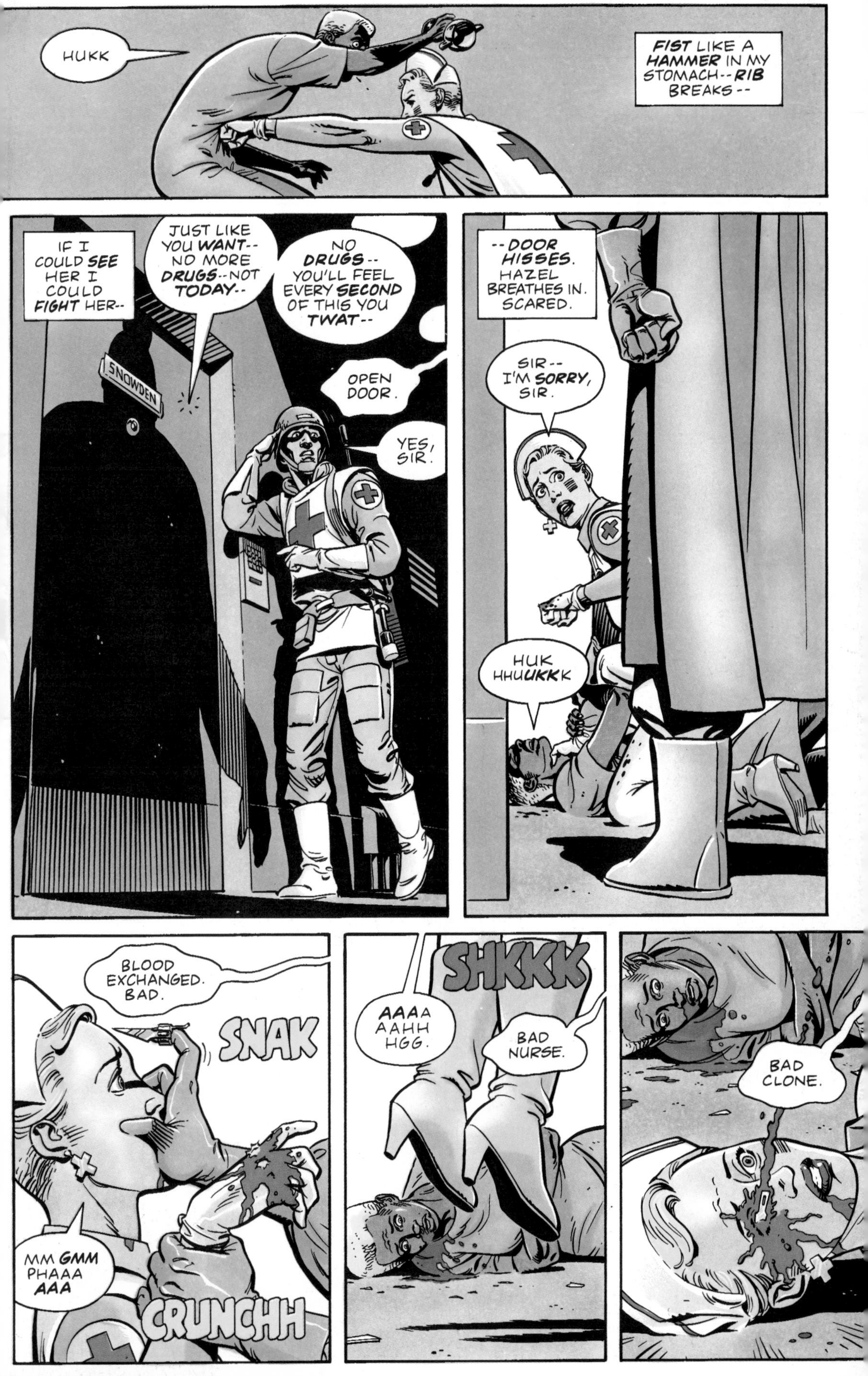
HUKK
FIST LIKE A HAMMER IN MY STOMACH--RIB BREAKS--
IF I COULD SEE HER I COULD FIGHT HER--
JUST LIKE YOU WANT--NO MORE DRUGS--NOT TODAY--
NO DRUGS--YOU'LL FEEL EVERY SECOND OF THIS YOU TWAT--
SNOWDEN
OPEN DOOR.
YES, SIR.
--DOOR HISSES. HAZEL BREATHES IN. SCARED.
SIR--I'M SORRY, SIR.
HUK HHUUKKK
BLOOD EXCHANGED. BAD.
SNAK
MM GMM PHAAA AAA
CRUNCHH
SHKKK
AAAA AAHH HGG.
BAD NURSE.
BAD CLONE.

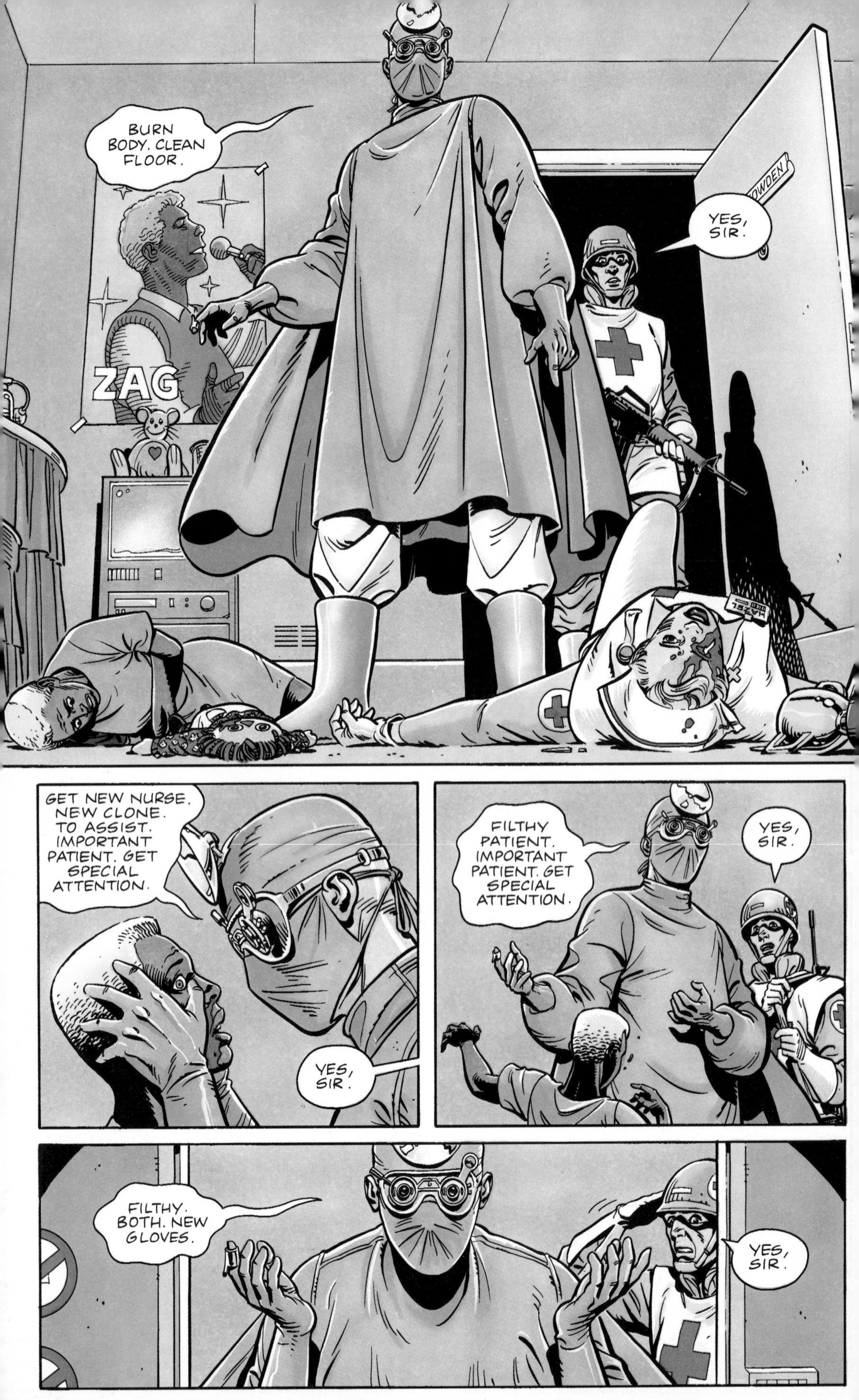
BURN BODY. CLEAN FLOOR.
ZAG
YES, SIR.
GET NEW NURSE. NEW CLONE. TO ASSIST. IMPORTANT PATIENT. GET SPECIAL ATTENTION.
YES, SIR.
FILTHY PATIENT. IMPORTANT PATIENT. GET SPECIAL ATTENTION.
YES, SIR.
FILTHY. BOTH. NEW GLOVES.
YES, SIR.

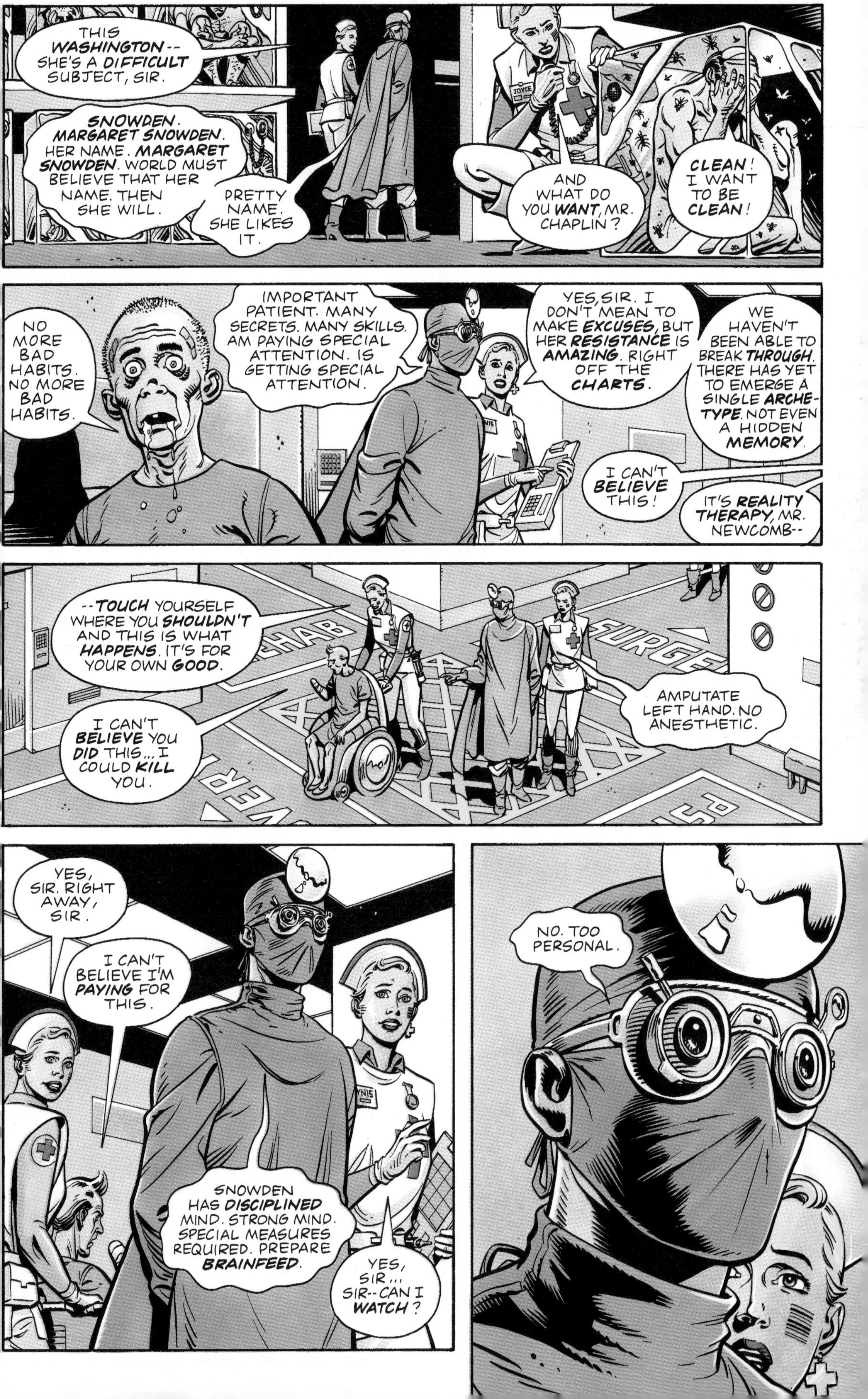
THIS WASHINGTON-- SHE'S A DIFFICULT SUBJECT, SIR.
SNOWDEN. MARGARET SNOWDEN. HER NAME. MARGARET SNOWDEN. WORLD MUST BELIEVE THAT HER NAME. THEN SHE WILL.
PRETTY NAME. SHE LIKES IT.
JOYCE
AND WHAT DO YOU WANT, MR. CHAPLIN?
CLEAN! I WANT TO BE CLEAN!
NO MORE BAD HABITS. NO MORE BAD HABITS.
IMPORTANT PATIENT. MANY SECRETS. MANY SKILLS. AM PAYING SPECIAL ATTENTION. IS GETTING SPECIAL ATTENTION.
YES, SIR. I DON'T MEAN TO MAKE EXCUSES, BUT HER RESISTANCE IS AMAZING. RIGHT OFF THE CHARTS.
WE HAVEN'T BEEN ABLE TO BREAK THROUGH. THERE HAS YET TO EMERGE A SINGLE ARCHETYPE. NOT EVEN A HIDDEN MEMORY.
I CAN'T BELIEVE THIS!
IT'S REALITY THERAPY, MR. NEWCOMB--
--TOUCH YOURSELF WHERE YOU SHOULDN'T AND THIS IS WHAT HAPPENS. IT'S FOR YOUR OWN GOOD.
I CAN'T BELIEVE YOU DID THIS... I COULD KILL YOU.
AMPUTATE LEFT HAND. NO ANESTHETIC.
YES, SIR. RIGHT AWAY, SIR.
I CAN'T BELIEVE I'M PAYING FOR THIS.
SNOWDEN HAS DISCIPLINED MIND. STRONG MIND. SPECIAL MEASURES REQUIRED. PREPARE BRAINFEED.
YES, SIR... SIR--CAN I WATCH?
NO. TOO PERSONAL.

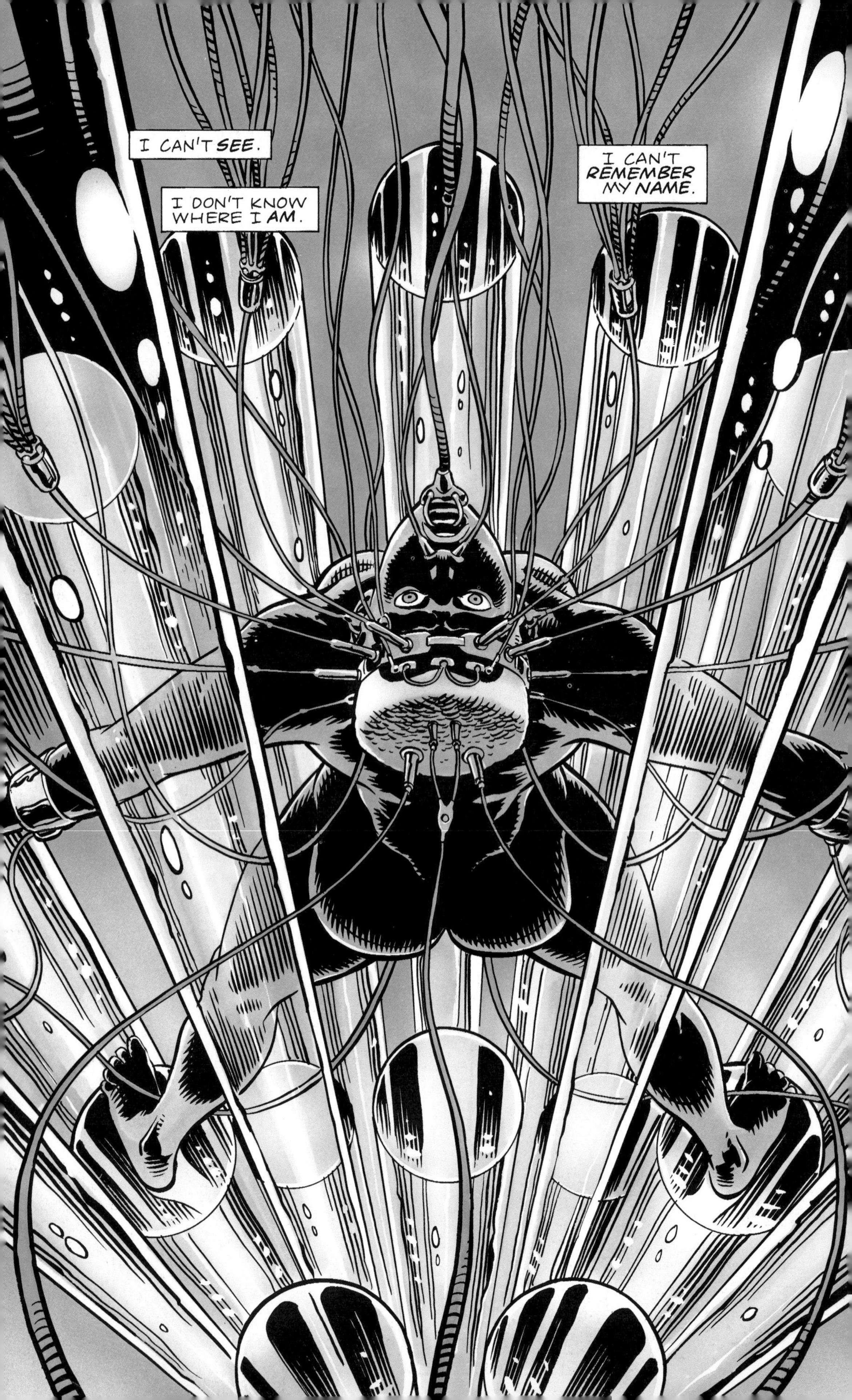

I CAN'T SEE.
I DON'T KNOW WHERE I AM.
I CAN'T REMEMBER MY NAME.

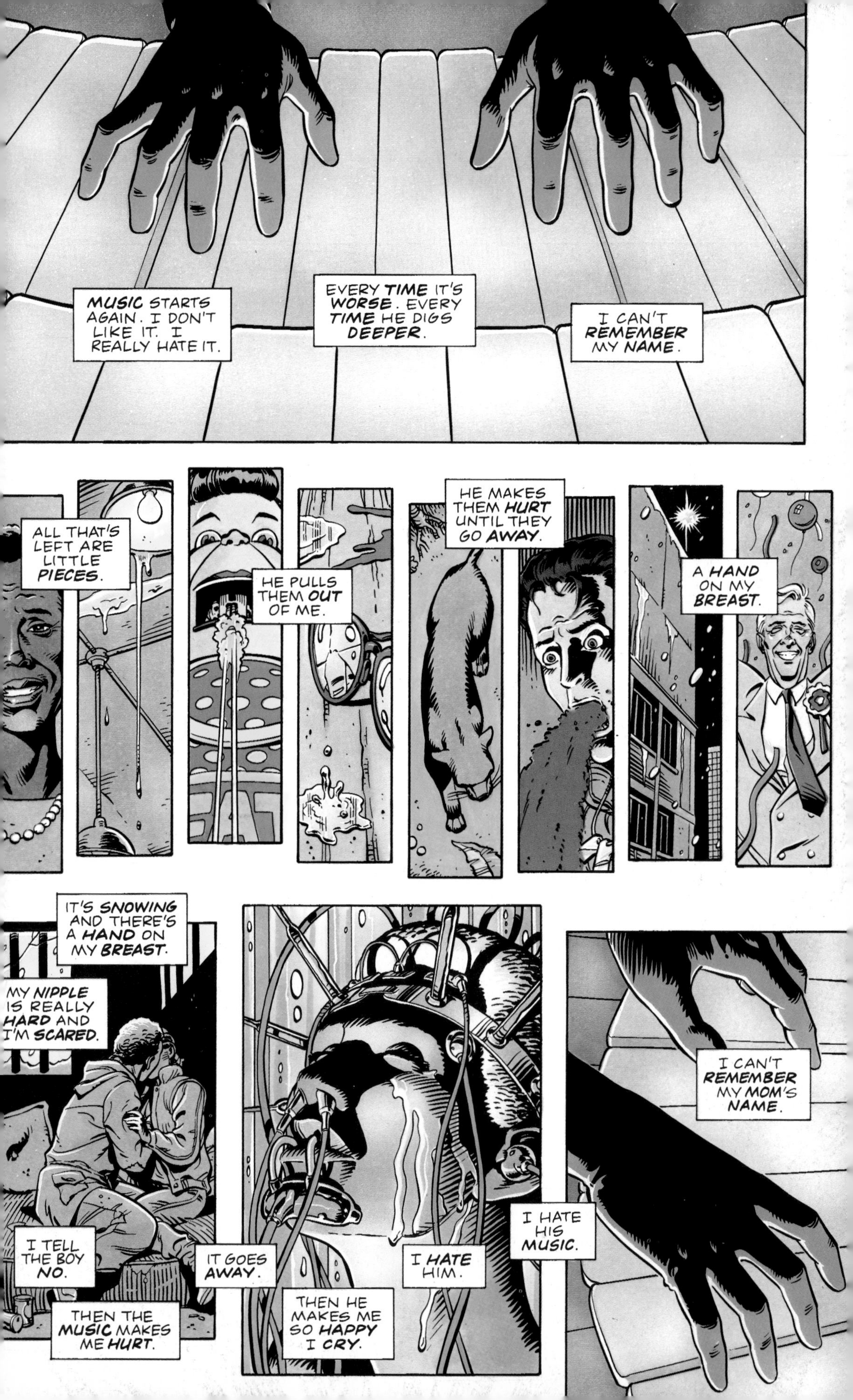

MUSIC STARTS AGAIN. I DON'T LIKE IT. I REALLY HATE IT.
EVERY TIME IT'S WORSE. EVERY TIME HE DIGS DEEPER.
I CAN'T REMEMBER MY NAME.
ALL THAT'S LEFT ARE LITTLE PIECES.
HE PULLS THEM OUT OF ME.
HE MAKES THEM HURT UNTIL THEY GO AWAY.
A HAND ON MY BREAST.
IT'S SNOWING AND THERE'S A HAND ON MY BREAST.
MY NIPPLE IS REALLY HARD AND I'M SCARED.
I TELL THE BOY NO.
THEN THE MUSIC MAKES ME HURT.
IT GOES AWAY.
THEN HE MAKES ME SO HAPPY I CRY.
I HATE HIM.
I HATE HIS MUSIC.
I CAN'T REMEMBER MY MOM'S NAME.

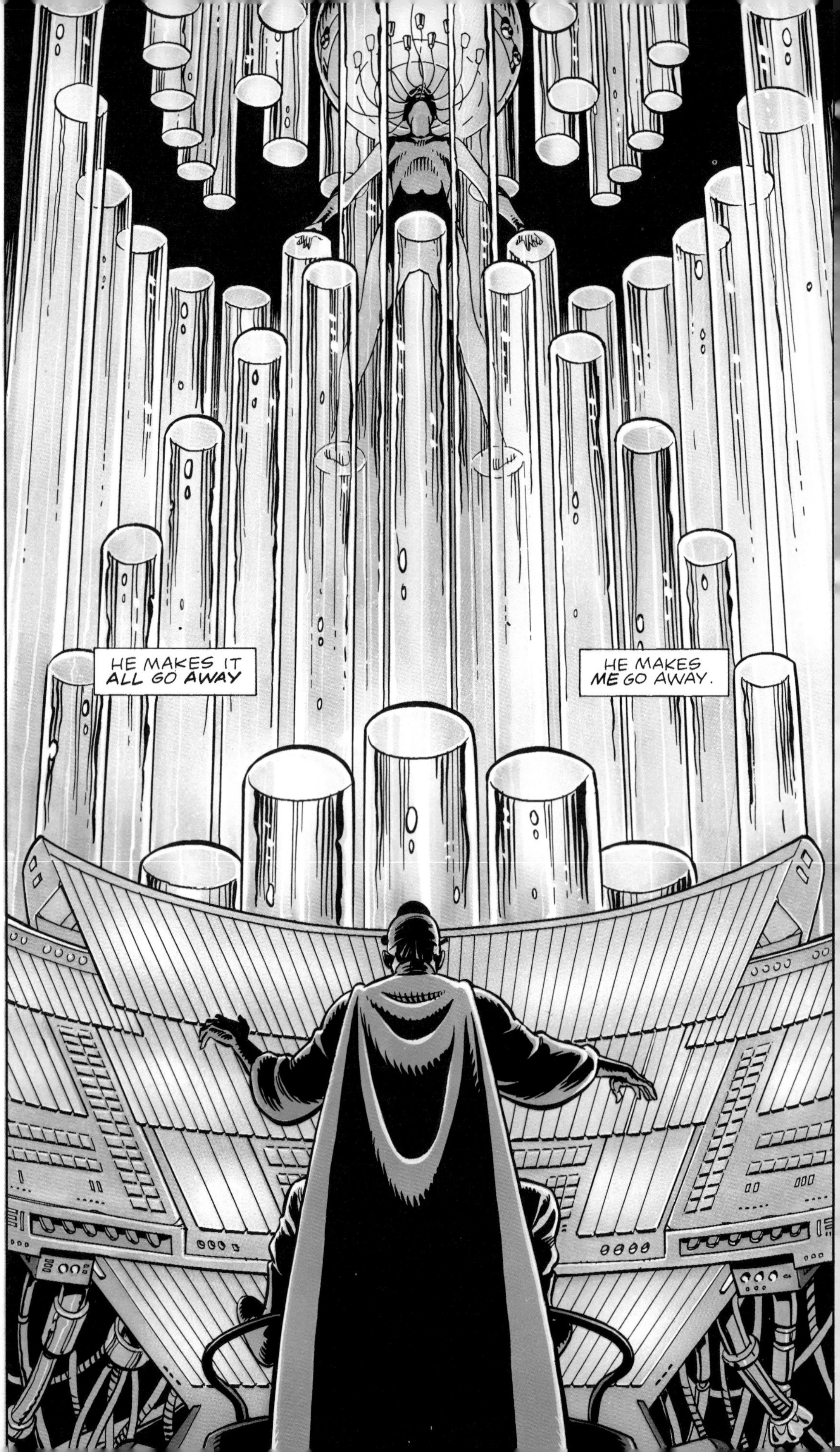
HE MAKES IT ALL GO AWAY
HE MAKES ME GO AWAY.

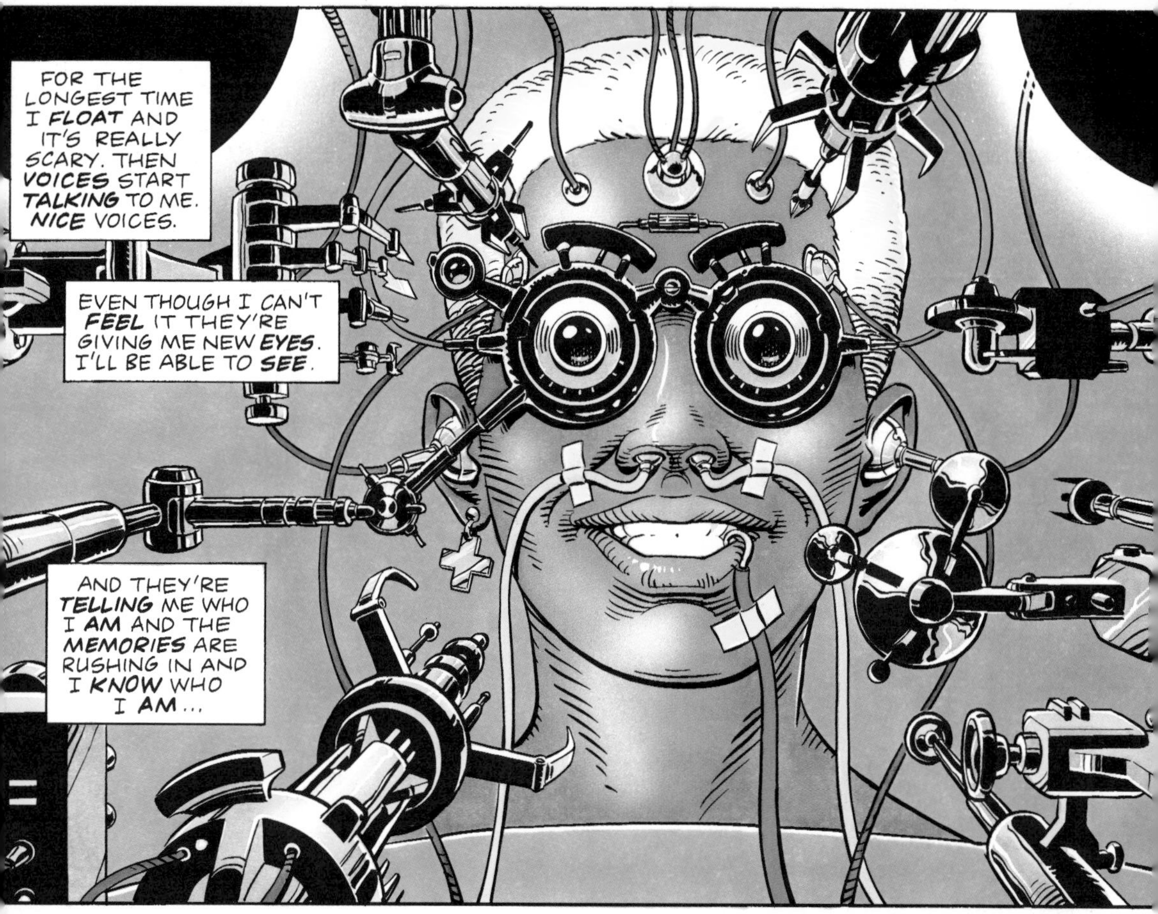
FOR THE LONGEST TIME I FLOAT AND IT'S REALLY SCARY. THEN VOICES START TALKING TO ME. NICE VOICES.
EVEN THOUGH I CAN'T FEEL IT THEY'RE GIVING ME NEW EYES. I'LL BE ABLE TO SEE.
AND THEY'RE TELLING ME WHO I AM AND THE MEMORIES ARE RUSHING IN AND I KNOW WHO I AM...

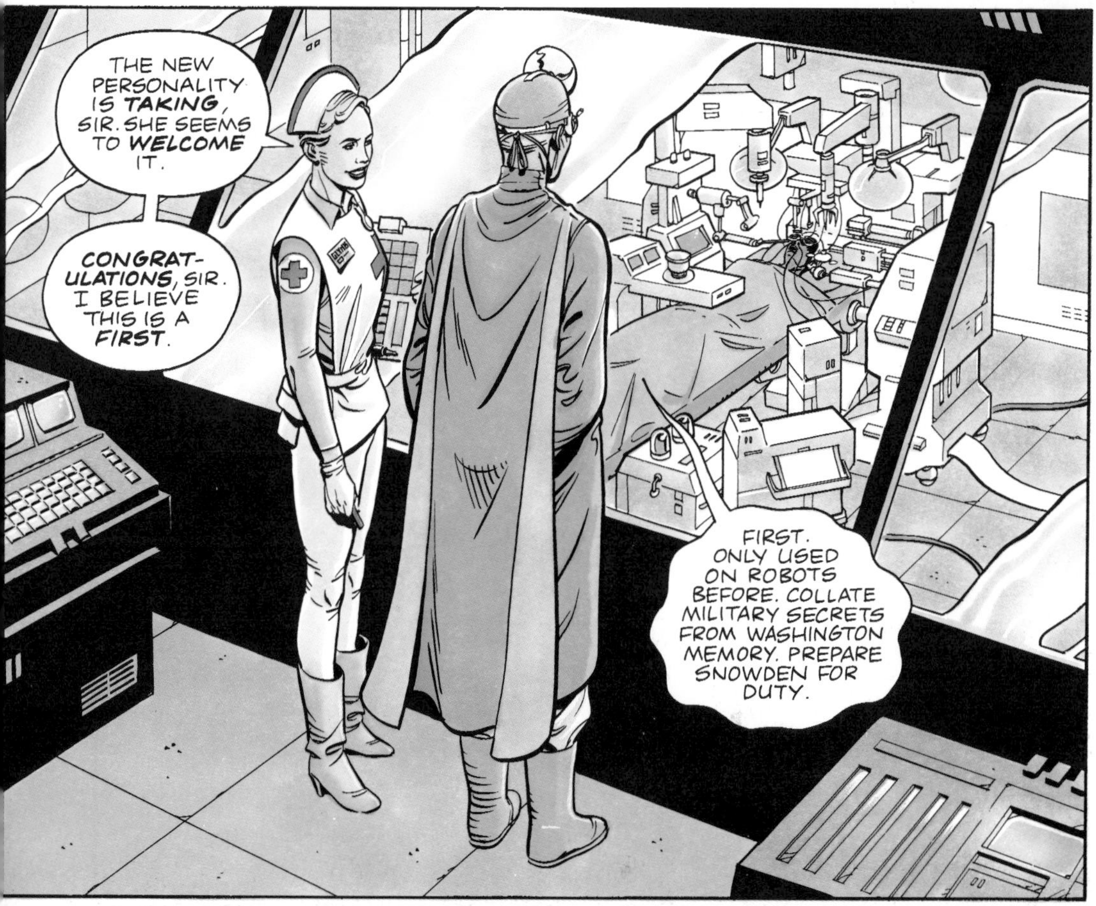
THE NEW PERSONALITY IS TAKING, SIR. SHE SEEMS TO WELCOME IT.
CONGRATULATIONS, SIR. I BELIEVE THIS IS A FIRST.
FIRST. ONLY USED ON ROBOTS BEFORE. COLLATE MILITARY SECRETS FROM WASHINGTON MEMORY. PREPARE SNOWDEN FOR DUTY.

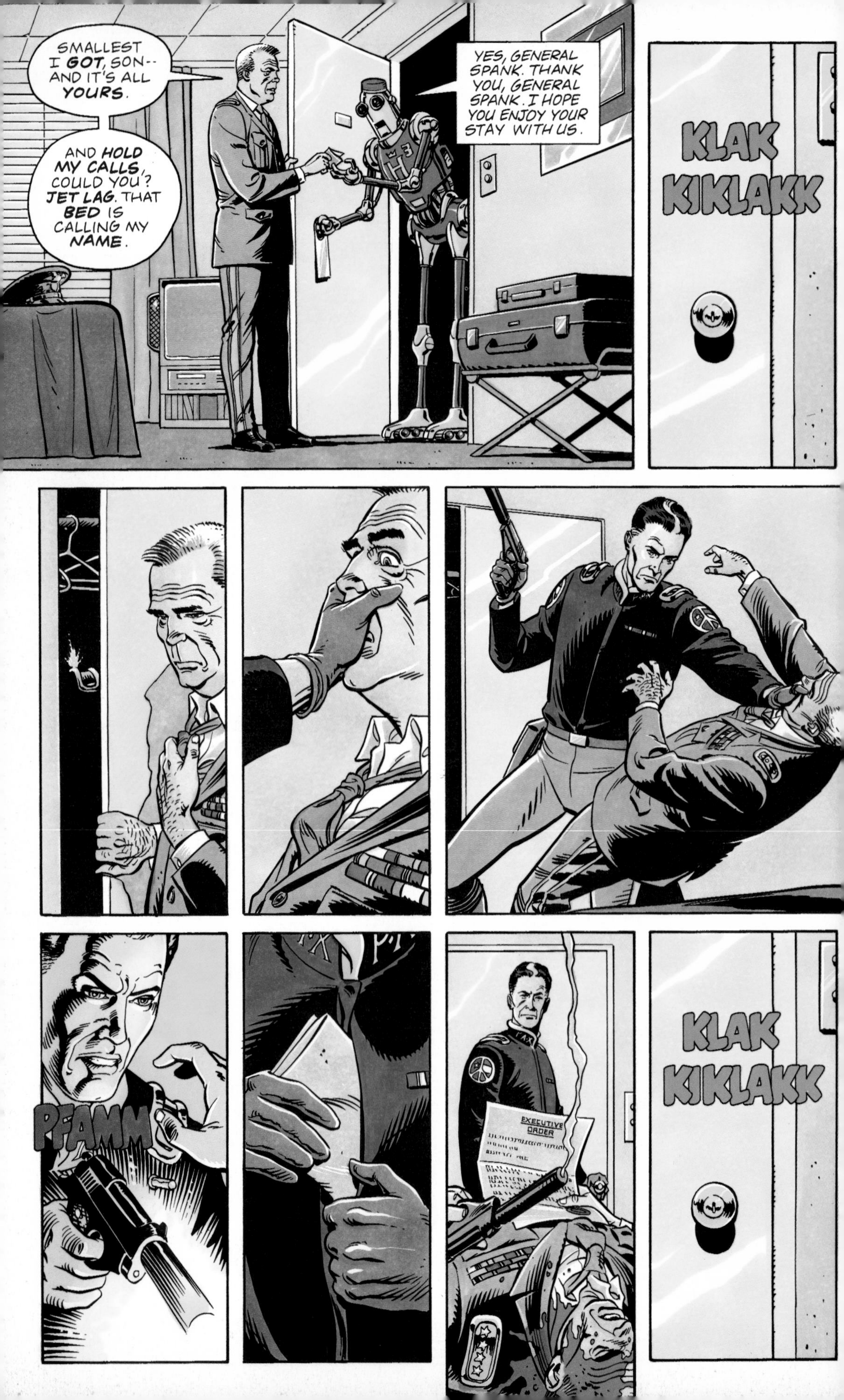
SMALLEST I GOT, SON-- AND IT'S ALL YOURS.
AND HOLD MY CALLS, COULD YOU? JET LAG. THAT BED IS CALLING MY NAME.
YES, GENERAL SPANK. THANK YOU, GENERAL SPANK. I HOPE YOU ENJOY YOUR STAY WITH US.
KLAK KIKLAKK
PFAMM
EXECUTIVE ORDER
KLAK KIKLAKK

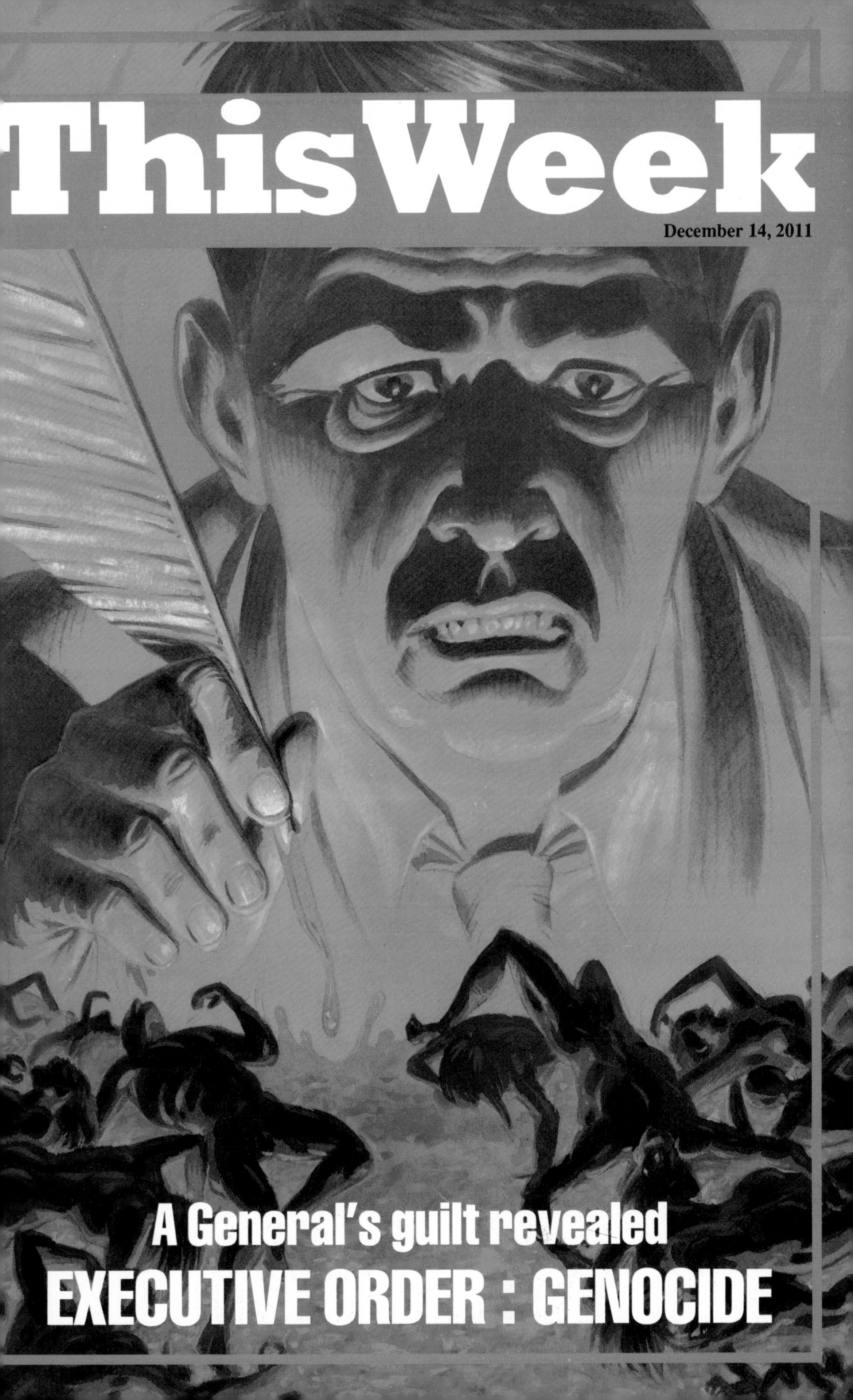
ThisWeek
December 14, 2011
A General's guilt revealed
EXECUTIVE ORDER : GENOCIDE

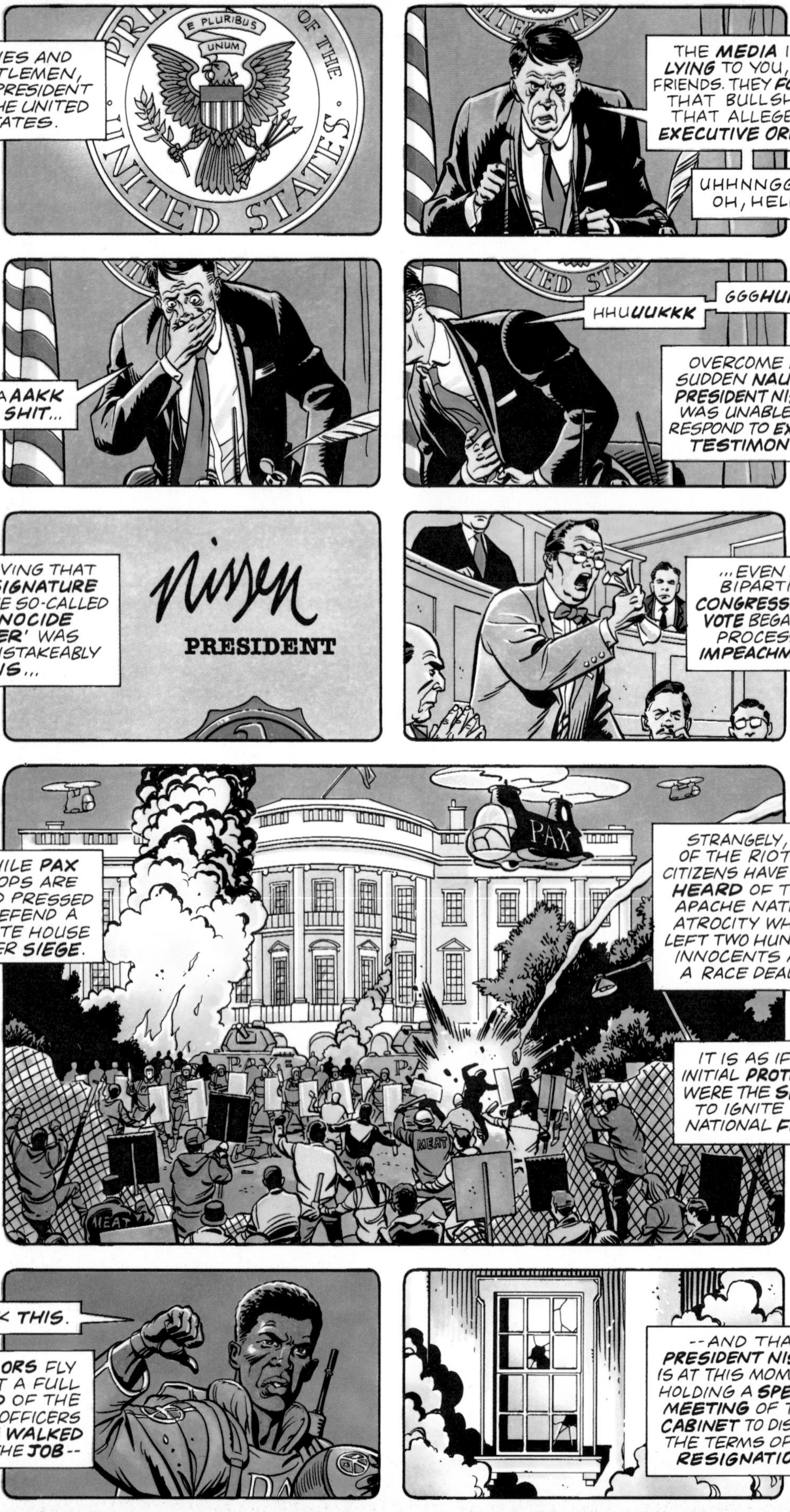
E PLURIBUS UNUM
LADIES AND GENTLEMEN, THE PRESIDENT OF THE UNITED STATES.
THE MEDIA IS LYING TO YOU, MY FRIENDS. THEY FORGED THAT BULLSH-- THAT ALLEGED EXECUTIVE ORDER...
UHHNNGGG... OH, HELL...
GHHAAAKK ...OH SHIT...
GGGHUKKK
HHUUUKKK
OVERCOME BY SUDDEN NAUSEA, PRESIDENT NISSEN WAS UNABLE TO RESPOND TO EXPERT TESTIMONY--
--PROVING THAT THE SIGNATURE ON THE SO-CALLED 'GENOCIDE ORDER' WAS UNMISTAKEABLY HIS...
Nissen
PRESIDENT
...EVEN AS A BIPARTISAN CONGRESSIONAL VOTE BEGAN THE PROCESS OF IMPEACHMENT...
...WHILE PAX TROOPS ARE HARD PRESSED TO DEFEND A WHITE HOUSE UNDER SIEGE.
PAX
STRANGELY, FEW OF THE RIOTING CITIZENS HAVE EVEN HEARD OF THE APACHE NATION ATROCITY WHICH LEFT TWO HUNDRED INNOCENTS AND A RACE DEAD...
IT IS AS IF THE INITIAL PROTESTS WERE THE SPARK TO IGNITE A NATIONAL FURY.
MEAT
FUCK THIS.
RUMORS FLY --THAT A FULL THIRD OF THE PAX OFFICERS HAVE WALKED OFF THE JOB--
--AND THAT PRESIDENT NISSEN IS AT THIS MOMENT HOLDING A SPECIAL MEETING OF THE CABINET TO DISCUSS THE TERMS OF HIS RESIGNATION...

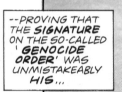

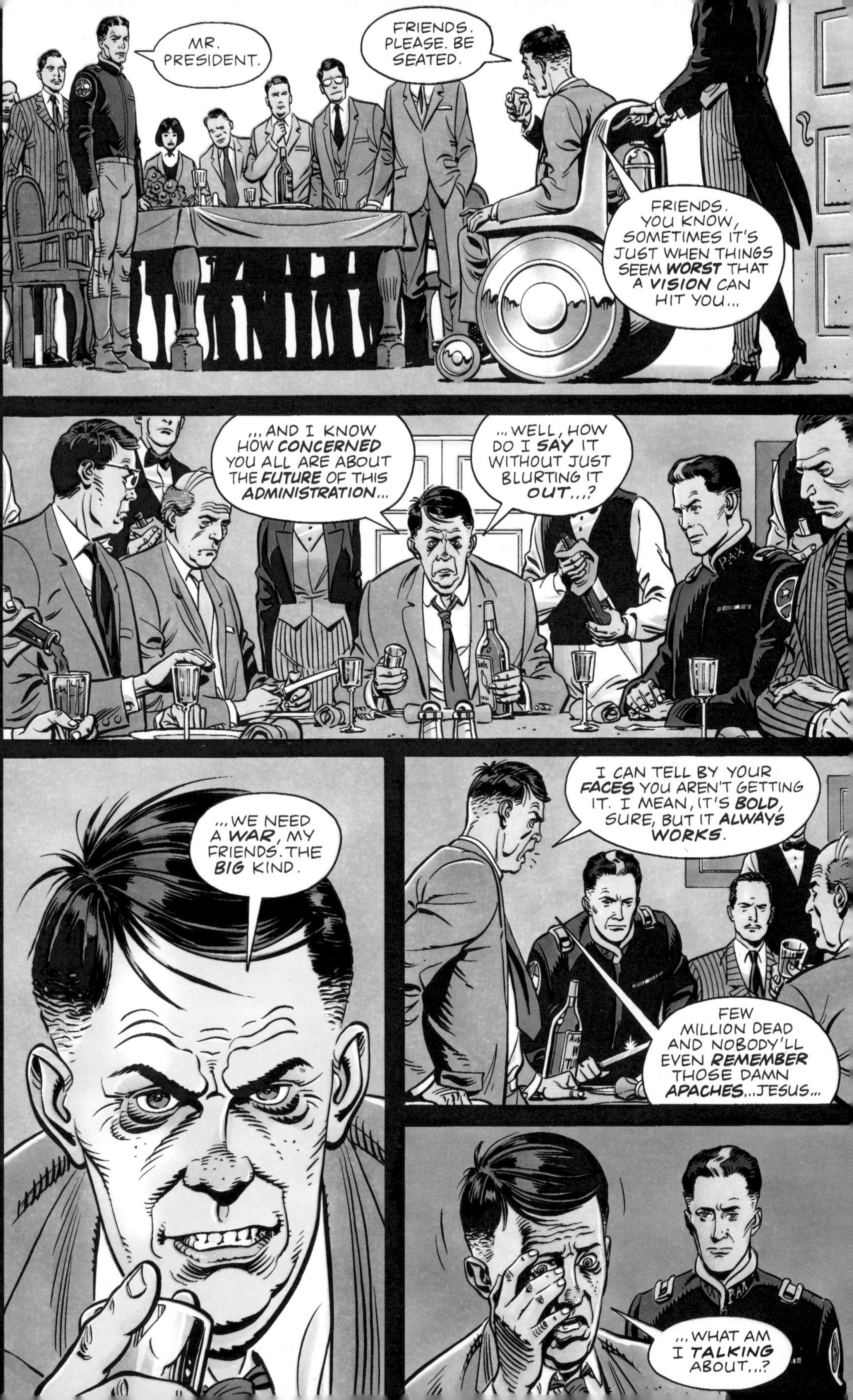
MR. PRESIDENT.
FRIENDS. PLEASE. BE SEATED.
FRIENDS. YOU KNOW, SOMETIMES IT'S JUST WHEN THINGS SEEM WORST THAT A VISION CAN HIT YOU...
...AND I KNOW HOW CONCERNED YOU ALL ARE ABOUT THE FUTURE OF THIS ADMINISTRATION...
...WELL, HOW DO I SAY IT WITHOUT JUST BLURTING IT OUT...?
...WE NEED A WAR, MY FRIENDS. THE BIG KIND.
I CAN TELL BY YOUR FACES YOU AREN'T GETTING IT. I MEAN, IT'S BOLD, SURE, BUT IT ALWAYS WORKS.
FEW MILLION DEAD AND NOBODY'LL EVEN REMEMBER THOSE DAMN APACHES...JESUS...
...WHAT AM I TALKING ABOUT...?

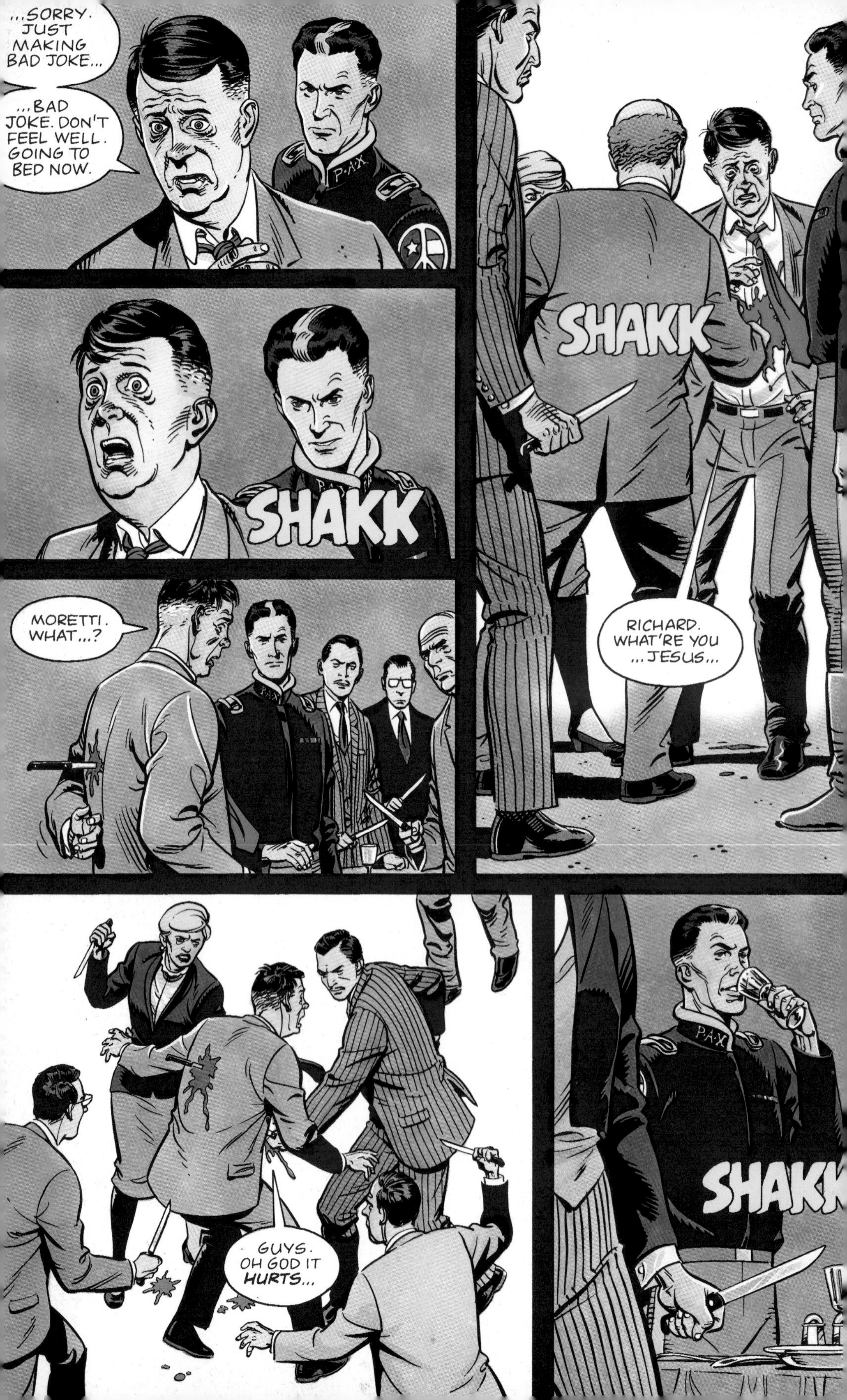
...SORRY. JUST MAKING BAD JOKE...
...BAD JOKE. DON'T FEEL WELL. GOING TO BED NOW.
P·A·X
SHAKK
MORETTI. WHAT...?
SHAKK
RICHARD. WHAT'RE YOU ...JESUS...
GUYS. OH GOD IT HURTS...
P·A·X
SHAKK

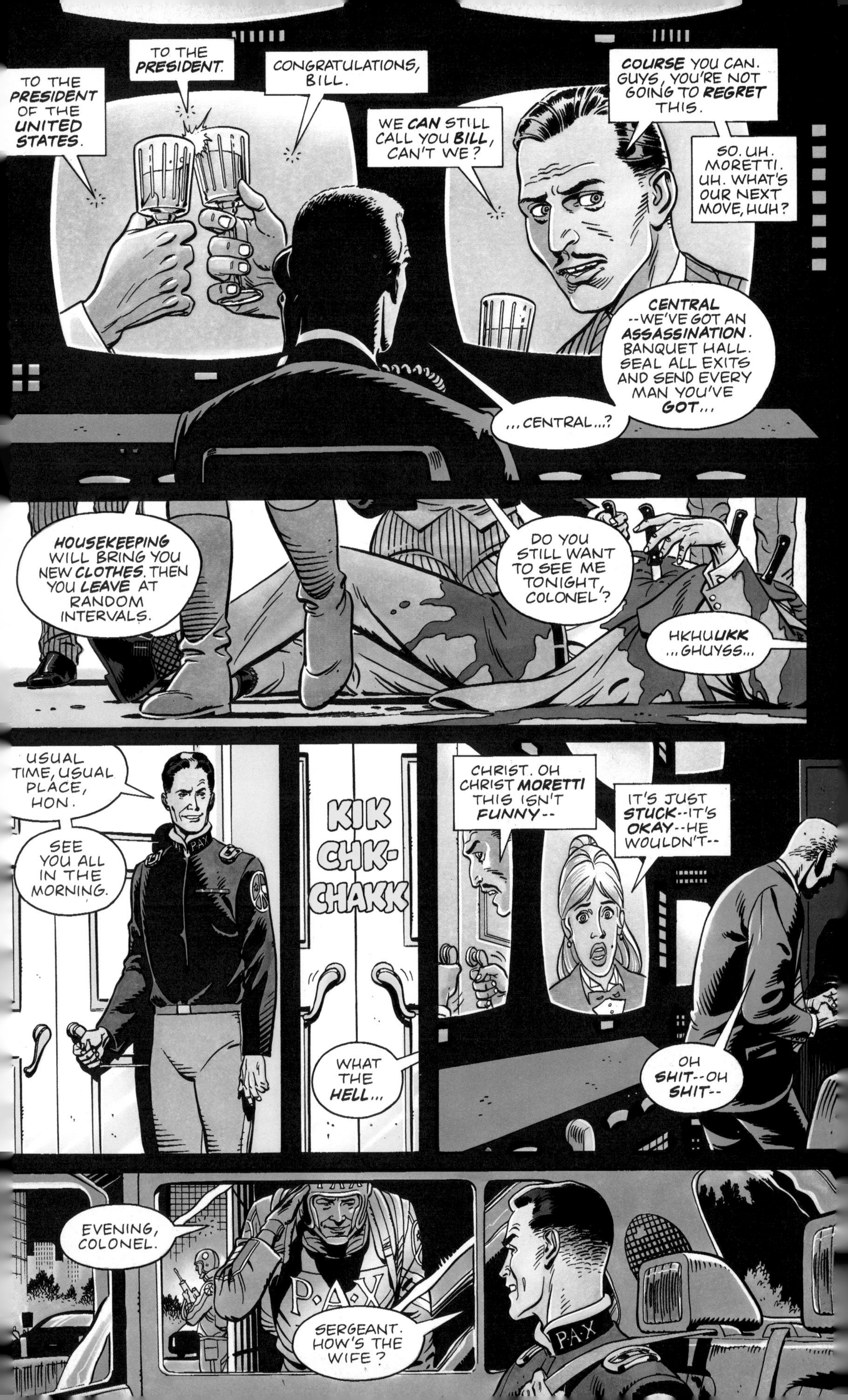
TO THE PRESIDENT OF THE UNITED STATES.
TO THE PRESIDENT.
CONGRATULATIONS, BILL.
WE CAN STILL CALL YOU BILL, CAN'T WE?
COURSE YOU CAN. GUYS, YOU'RE NOT GOING TO REGRET THIS.
SO. UH. MORETTI. UH. WHAT'S OUR NEXT MOVE, HUH?
CENTRAL --WE'VE GOT AN ASSASSINATION. BANQUET HALL. SEAL ALL EXITS AND SEND EVERY MAN YOU'VE GOT...
...CENTRAL...?
HOUSEKEEPING WILL BRING YOU NEW CLOTHES. THEN YOU LEAVE AT RANDOM INTERVALS.
DO YOU STILL WANT TO SEE ME TONIGHT, COLONEL?
HKHUUKK ...GHUYSS...
USUAL TIME, USUAL PLACE, HON.
SEE YOU ALL IN THE MORNING.
KIK CHK-CHAKK
WHAT THE HELL...
CHRIST. OH CHRIST MORETTI THIS ISN'T FUNNY--
IT'S JUST STUCK--IT'S OKAY--HE WOULDN'T--
OH SHIT--OH SHIT--
EVENING, COLONEL.
SERGEANT. HOW'S THE WIFE?

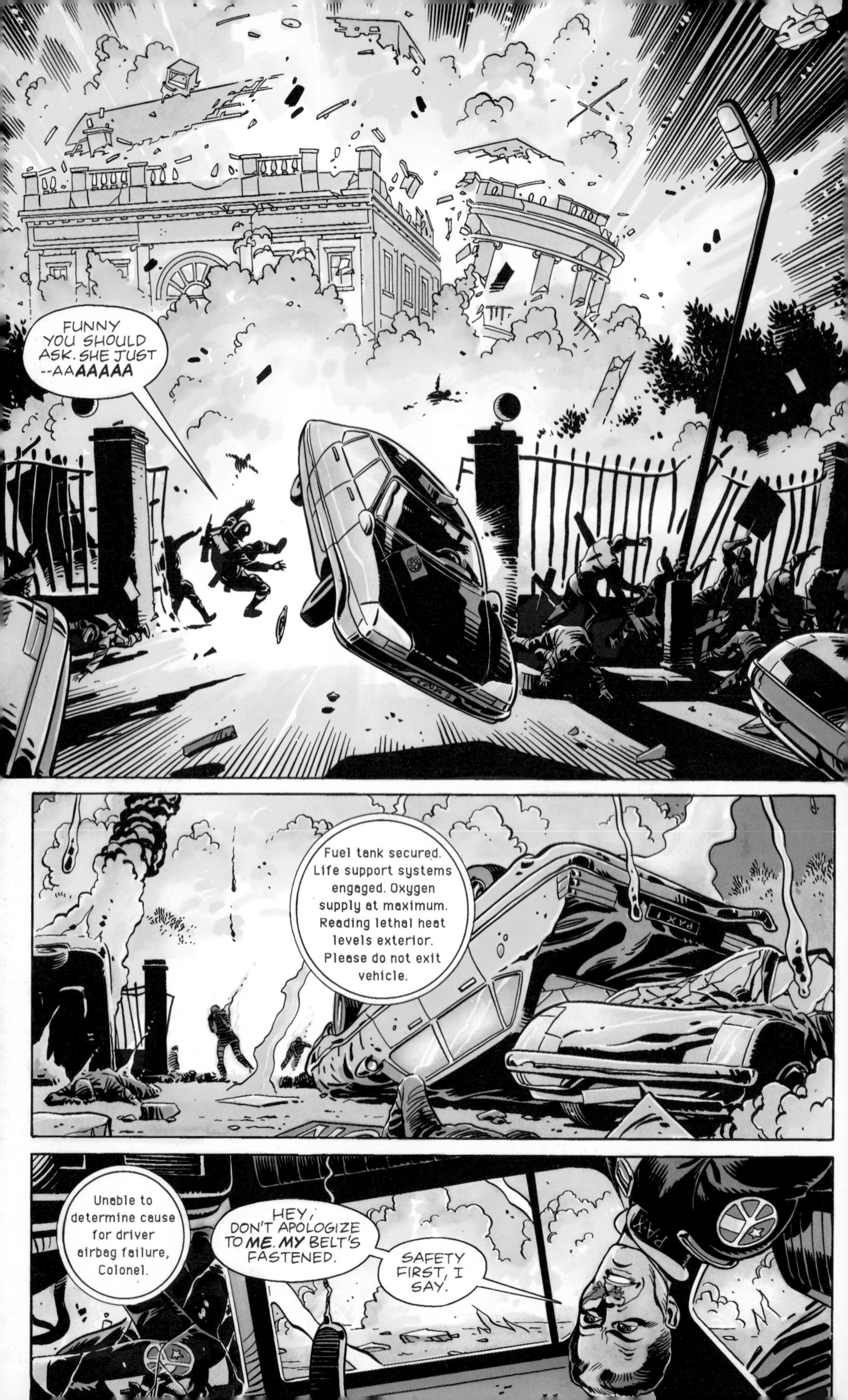
FUNNY YOU SHOULD ASK. SHE JUST --AAAAAAA
Fuel tank secured. Life support systems engaged. Oxygen supply at maximum. Reading lethal heat levels exterior. Please do not exit vehicle.
Unable to determine cause for driver airbag failure, Colonel.
HEY, DON'T APOLOGIZE TO ME. MY BELT'S FASTENED.
SAFETY FIRST, I SAY.

WE ARE AS YET UNABLE TO CONFIRM REPORTS THAT **PRESIDENT NISSEN** AND HIS ENTIRE **CABINET** HAVE BEEN KILLED.

THIS MARKS A BIZARRE AND HORRIBLE CASE OF HISTORY REPEATING ITSELF--

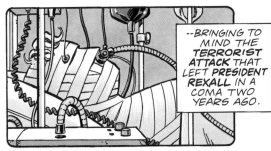

--BRINGING TO MIND THE **TERRORIST ATTACK** THAT LEFT **PRESIDENT REXALL** IN A COMA TWO YEARS AGO.

NUKE DEEP. NO **LUNCH**.

QUIET, RAGGYANN.

WE SHOULD BE GETTING **CLOSE**, COCHISE.

THREE HUNDRED YARDS TO SECURITY PERIMETER. I READ A **COPTER** COMING, SIR. BETTER FIND **COVER**.

BOTTLEBRAIN. EGG BEATER- BOTTLEBRAIN

QUIET, RAGGYANN.

HERE WE ARE, SWEETIE. **FORTRESS HEALTH**. THEY'LL FIX YOU UP **GOOD** HERE.

WHATEVER YOU SAY, BLOSSOM. I GUESS I JUST FEEL A LITTLE SORRY FOR MY **OLD** DOCTORS...

...I'M SURE THEY COULD USE THE **WORK** AND THEY WERE REAL **NICE**...

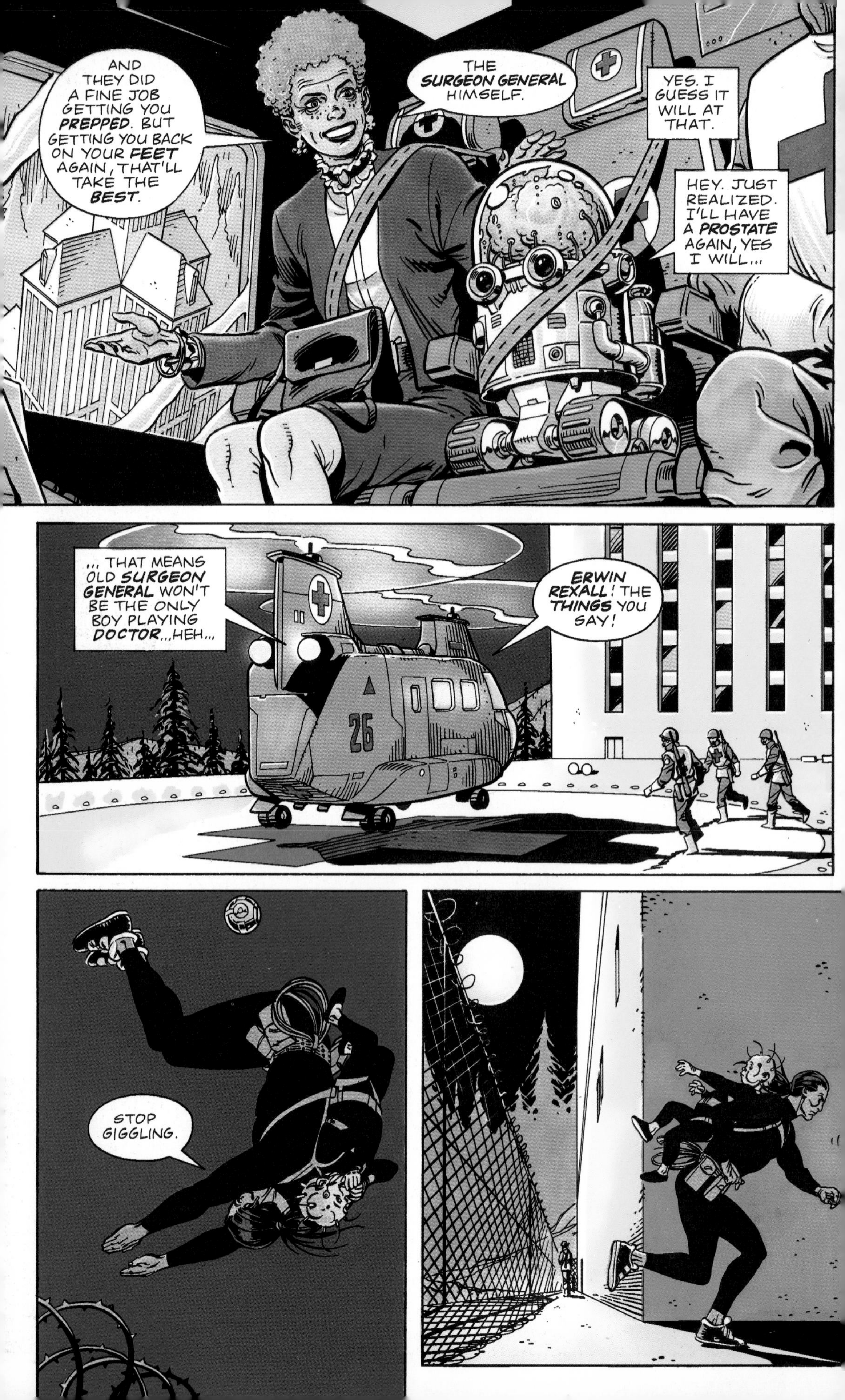
AND THEY DID A FINE JOB GETTING YOU PREPPED. BUT GETTING YOU BACK ON YOUR FEET AGAIN, THAT'LL TAKE THE BEST.
THE SURGEON GENERAL HIMSELF.
YES. I GUESS IT WILL AT THAT.
HEY. JUST REALIZED. I'LL HAVE A PROSTATE AGAIN, YES I WILL...
... THAT MEANS OLD SURGEON GENERAL WON'T BE THE ONLY BOY PLAYING DOCTOR...HEH...
ERWIN REXALL! THE THINGS YOU SAY!
26
STOP GIGGLING.

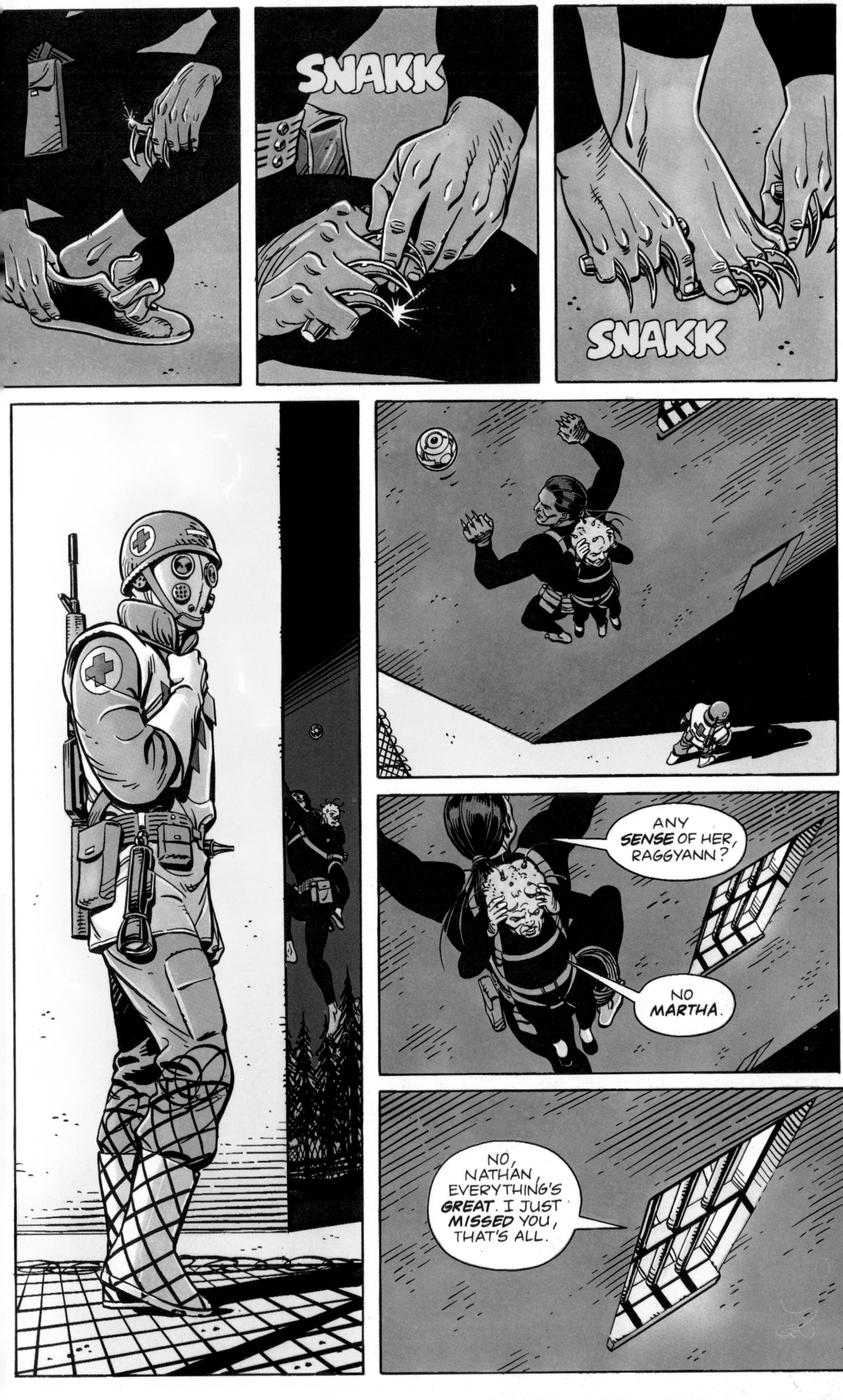

SNAKK
SNAKK
ANY SENSE OF HER, RAGGYANN?
NO MARTHA.
NO, NATHAN, EVERYTHING'S GREAT. I JUST MISSED YOU, THAT'S ALL.

NATHAN'S MY BOYFRIEND. STATIONED IN *APPALACHIA*.

WE'RE *ENGAGED*. WE'RE GOING TO GET *MARRIED*.

IT'S SO GREAT TO HEAR YOUR *VOICE*, HONEY. I'M COUNTING THE *DAYS*, YOU KNOW. TILL WE CAN BE *TOGETHER* ALL THE *TIME*.

TELL ME --WHAT ARE YOU *DOING*, RIGHT NOW? WHAT EXACTLY?

IT'S MY DAY *OFF* BUT ALL I FELT LIKE DOING WAS TAKING A *SHOWER* AND TALKING TO *YOU*.

ACTUALLY, I TOOK *THREE* SHOWERS. SILLY, HUH? ALL I'M *WEARING* IS A *TOWEL*...

...TAKE IT OFF.

WHAT...?

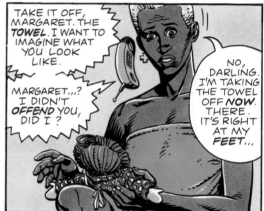

TAKE IT OFF, MARGARET. THE *TOWEL*. I WANT TO IMAGINE WHAT YOU LOOK LIKE.

MARGARET...? I DIDN'T *OFFEND* YOU, DID I?

NO, DARLING. I'M TAKING THE TOWEL OFF *NOW*. THERE. IT'S RIGHT AT MY *FEET*...

WHAT THE HELL...

WHOOM

COCHISE...

I KNOW, SIR. OVER-DOING IT AGAIN. I'M SORRY, SIR.

IT WON'T COME OUT.
IT WON'T COME OUT.
IT'S BLOOD.
I'LL CALL HOUSEKEEPING.
IT'S BLOOD.
I'LL CALL HOUSEKEEPING.
NO REASON TO CRY.
THERE'S NO REASON AT ALL.
BEEP BEEP BEEP BEEP
Sergeant Snowden. Red alert. Security breach on level thirty-one.
SEAL LEVELS TWENTY UP. OPEN ME A PATH ON TUBE ELEVEN.
Yes, Sergeant.
HOW MANY?
Reading two human heartbeats, one robot device.
FIRE-POWER?
Formidable. Includes NAPE-G63 capability.
BUT ONLY TWO PEOPLE...
...RIGHT TOOL FOR THE JOB...

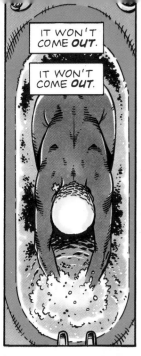

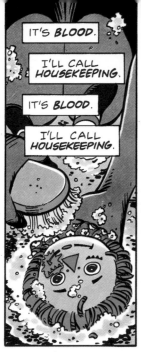

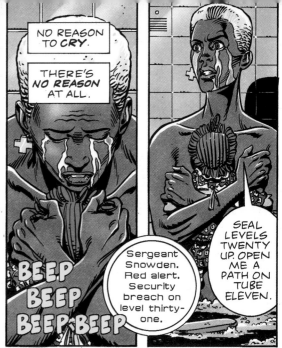

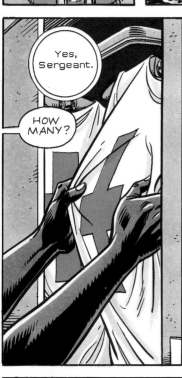

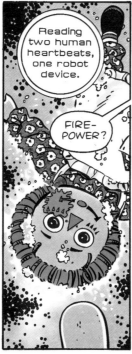

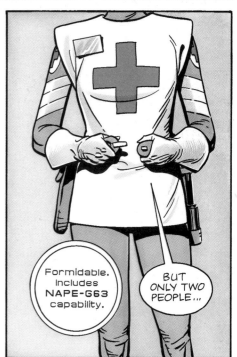

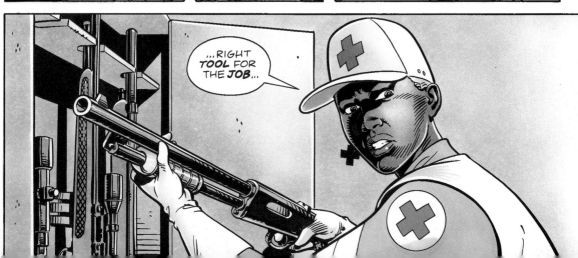

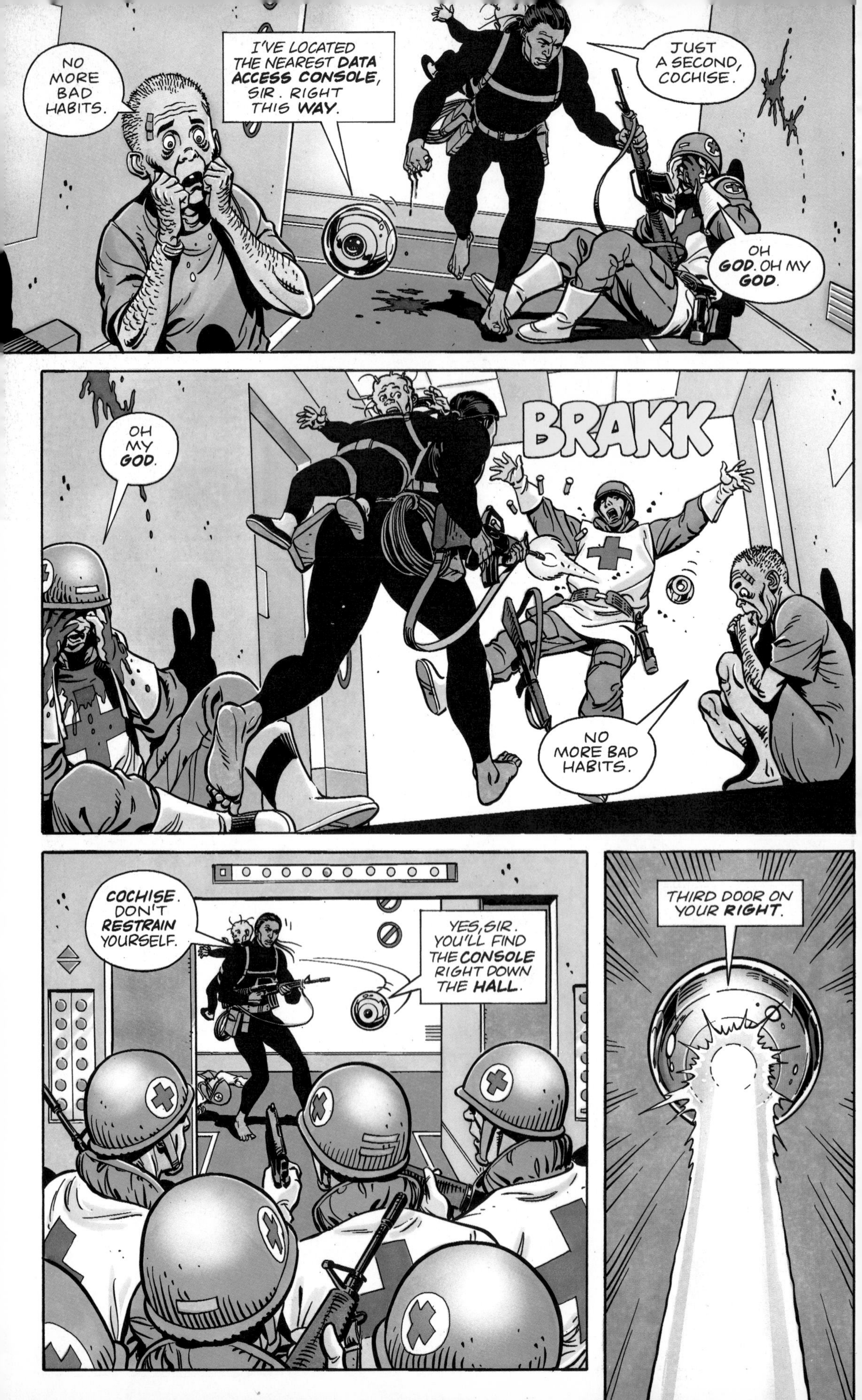
NO MORE BAD HABITS.
I'VE LOCATED THE NEAREST DATA ACCESS CONSOLE, SIR. RIGHT THIS WAY.
JUST A SECOND, COCHISE.
OH GOD. OH MY GOD.
OH MY GOD.
BRAKK
NO MORE BAD HABITS.
COCHISE. DON'T RESTRAIN YOURSELF.
YES, SIR. YOU'LL FIND THE CONSOLE RIGHT DOWN THE HALL.
THIRD DOOR ON YOUR RIGHT.

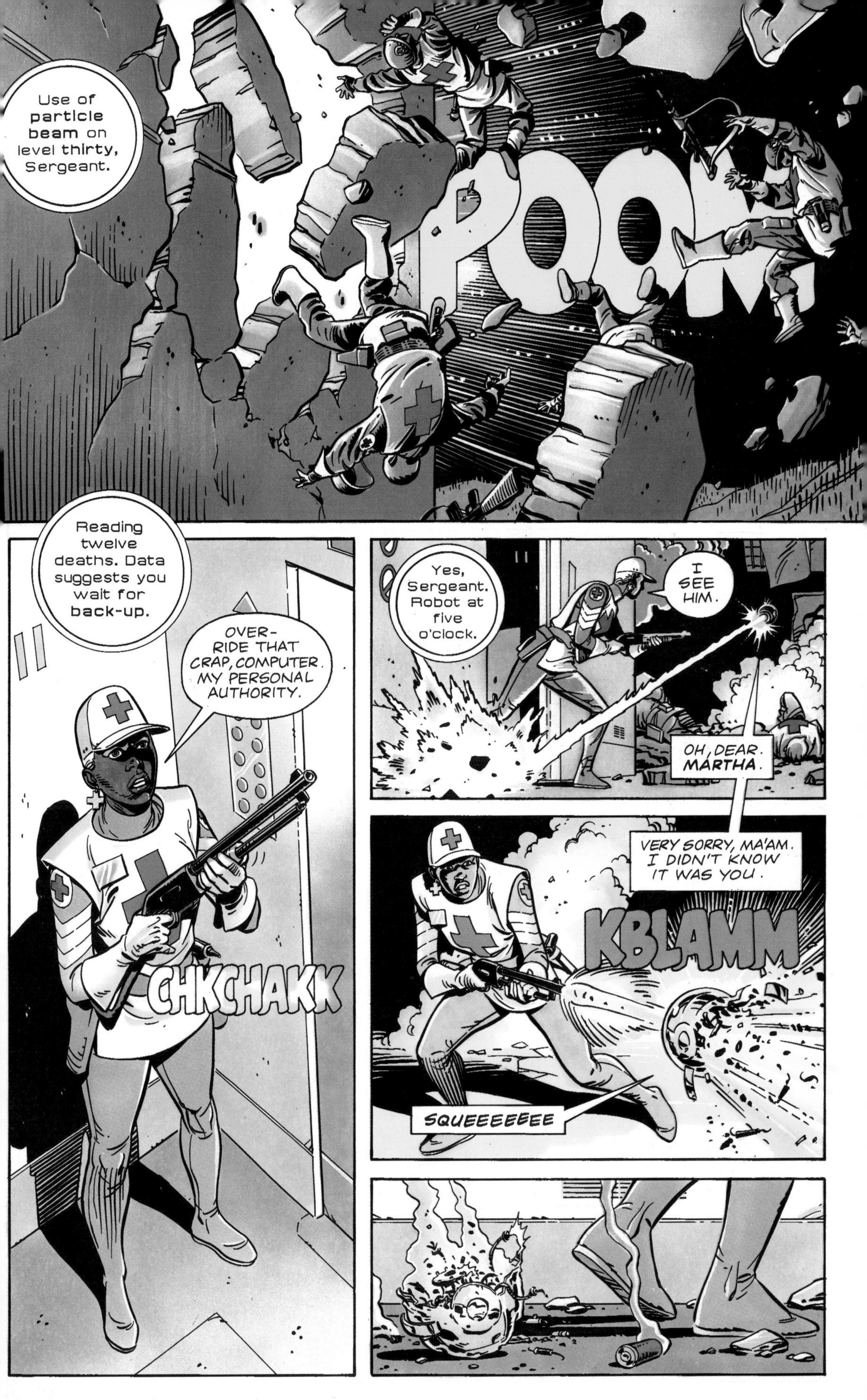
Use of particle beam on level thirty, Sergeant.
POOM
Reading twelve deaths. Data suggests you wait for back-up.
OVER-RIDE THAT CRAP, COMPUTER. MY PERSONAL AUTHORITY.
CHKCHAKK
Yes, Sergeant. Robot at five o'clock.
I SEE HIM.
OH, DEAR. MARTHA.
VERY SORRY, MA'AM. I DIDN'T KNOW IT WAS YOU.
KBLAMM
SQUEEEEEEEE

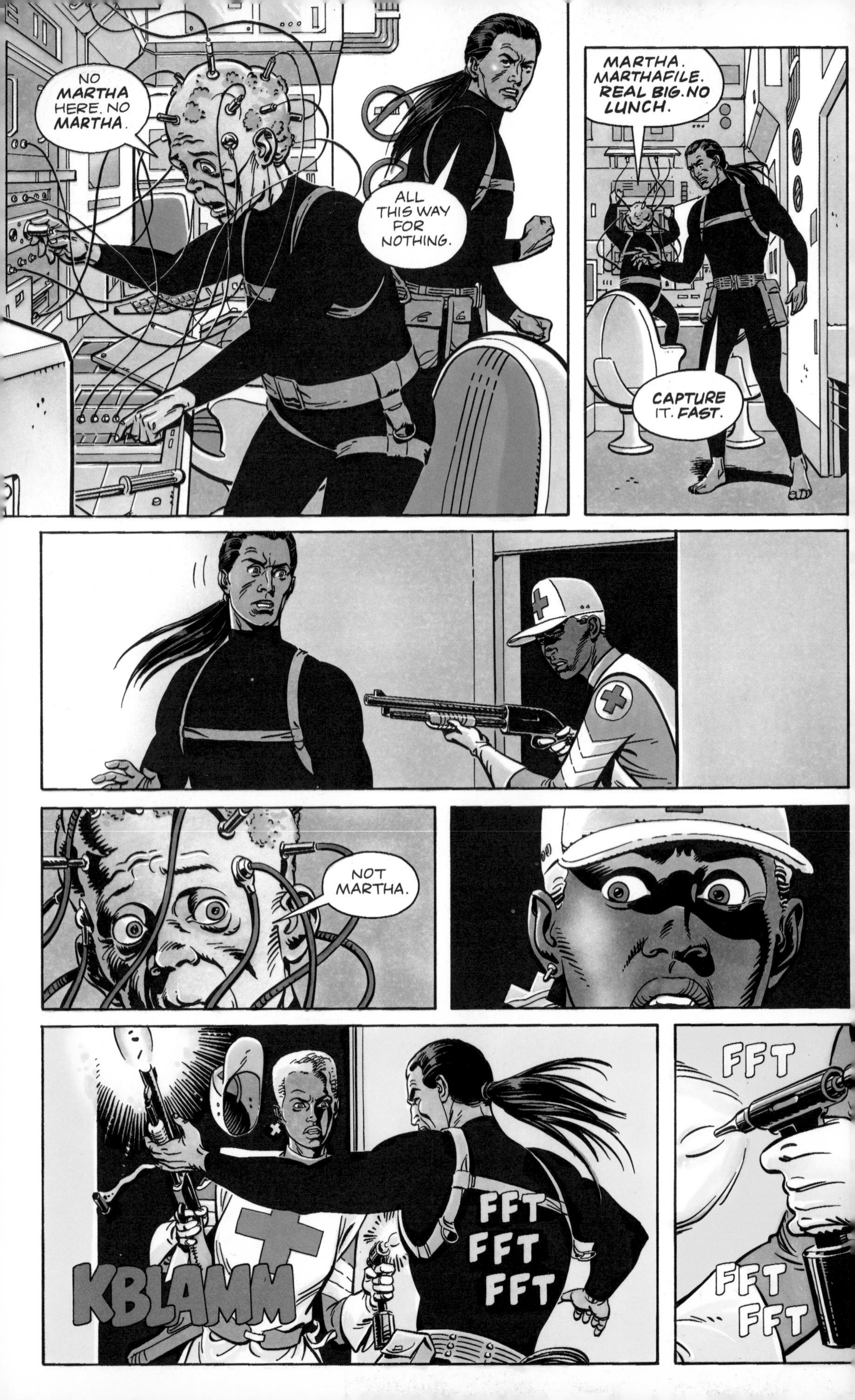
NO MARTHA HERE. NO MARTHA.
ALL THIS WAY FOR NOTHING.
MARTHA. MARTHAFILE. REAL BIG. NO LUNCH.
CAPTURE IT. FAST.
NOT MARTHA.
KBLAMM
FFT FFT FFT
FFT
FFT FFT

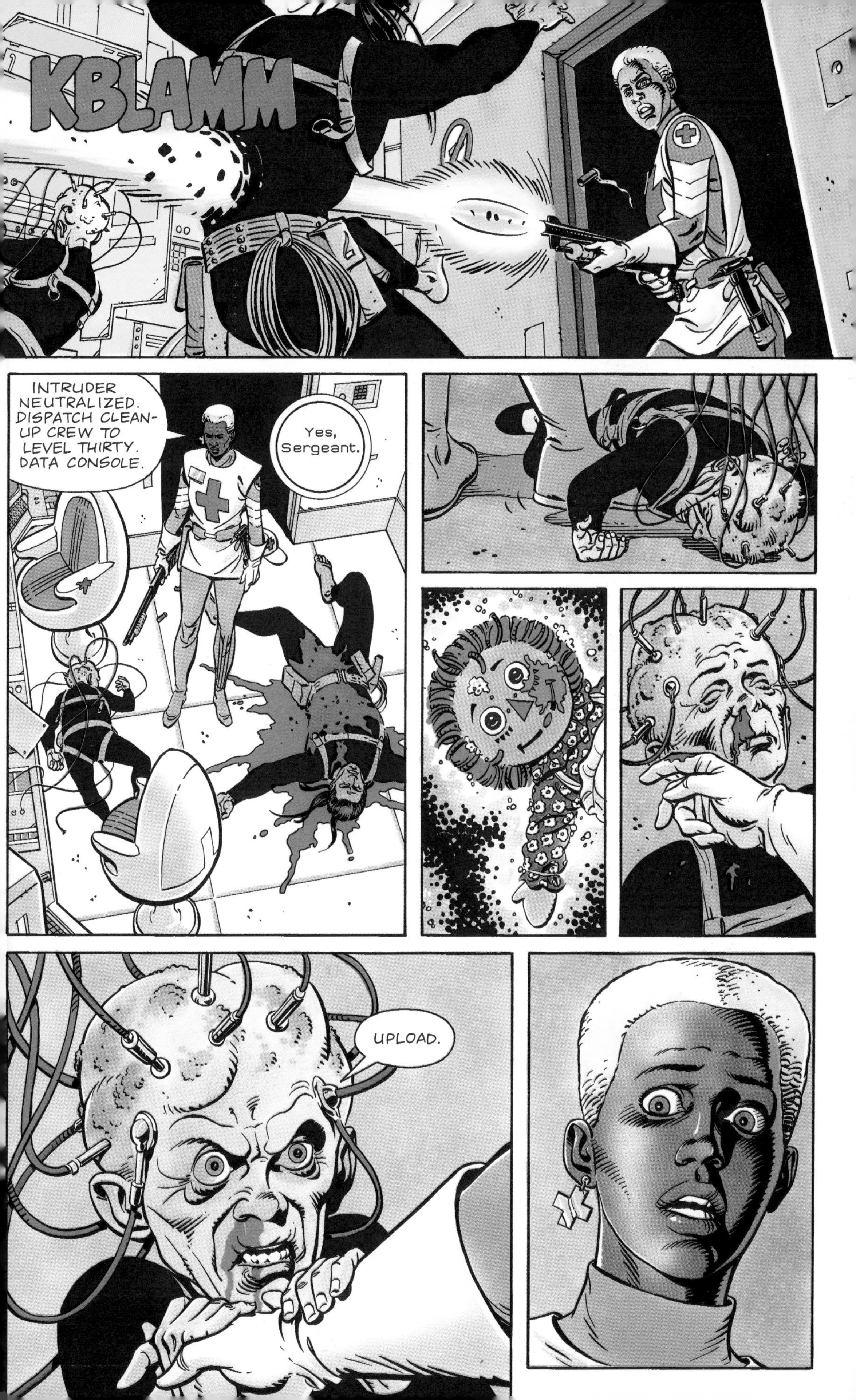
KBLAMM
INTRUDER NEUTRALIZED. DISPATCH CLEAN-UP CREW TO LEVEL THIRTY. DATA CONSOLE.
Yes, Sergeant.
UPLOAD.

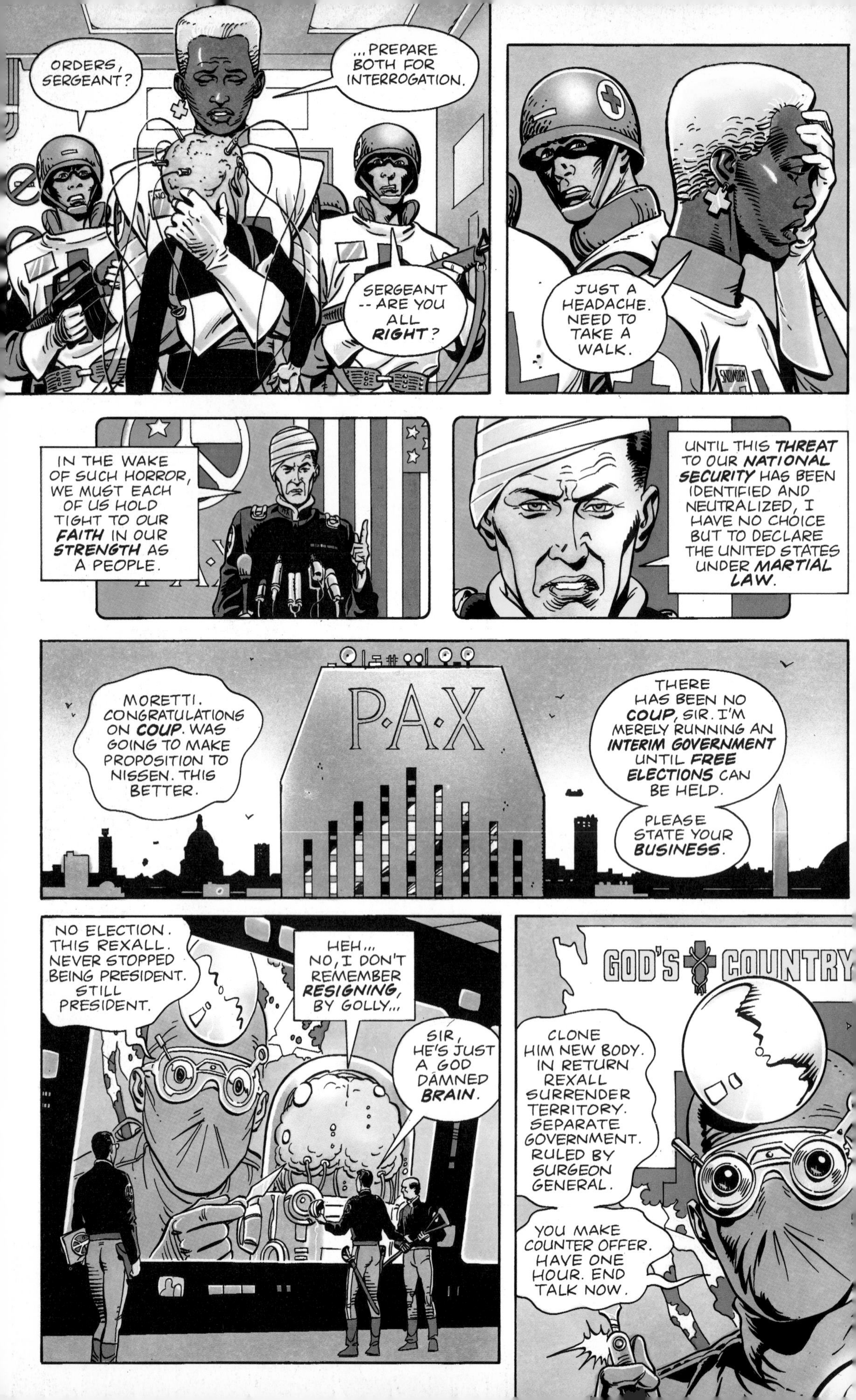
ORDERS, SERGEANT?
...PREPARE BOTH FOR INTERROGATION.
SERGEANT -- ARE YOU ALL RIGHT?
JUST A HEADACHE. NEED TO TAKE A WALK.
IN THE WAKE OF SUCH HORROR, WE MUST EACH OF US HOLD TIGHT TO OUR FAITH IN OUR STRENGTH AS A PEOPLE.
UNTIL THIS THREAT TO OUR NATIONAL SECURITY HAS BEEN IDENTIFIED AND NEUTRALIZED, I HAVE NO CHOICE BUT TO DECLARE THE UNITED STATES UNDER MARTIAL LAW.
P·A·X
MORETTI. CONGRATULATIONS ON COUP. WAS GOING TO MAKE PROPOSITION TO NISSEN. THIS BETTER.
THERE HAS BEEN NO COUP, SIR. I'M MERELY RUNNING AN INTERIM GOVERNMENT UNTIL FREE ELECTIONS CAN BE HELD.
PLEASE STATE YOUR BUSINESS.
NO ELECTION. THIS REXALL. NEVER STOPPED BEING PRESIDENT. STILL PRESIDENT.
HEH... NO, I DON'T REMEMBER RESIGNING, BY GOLLY...
SIR, HE'S JUST A GOD DAMNED BRAIN.
GOD'S COUNTRY
CLONE HIM NEW BODY. IN RETURN REXALL SURRENDER TERRITORY. SEPARATE GOVERNMENT. RULED BY SURGEON GENERAL.
YOU MAKE COUNTER OFFER. HAVE ONE HOUR. END TALK NOW.

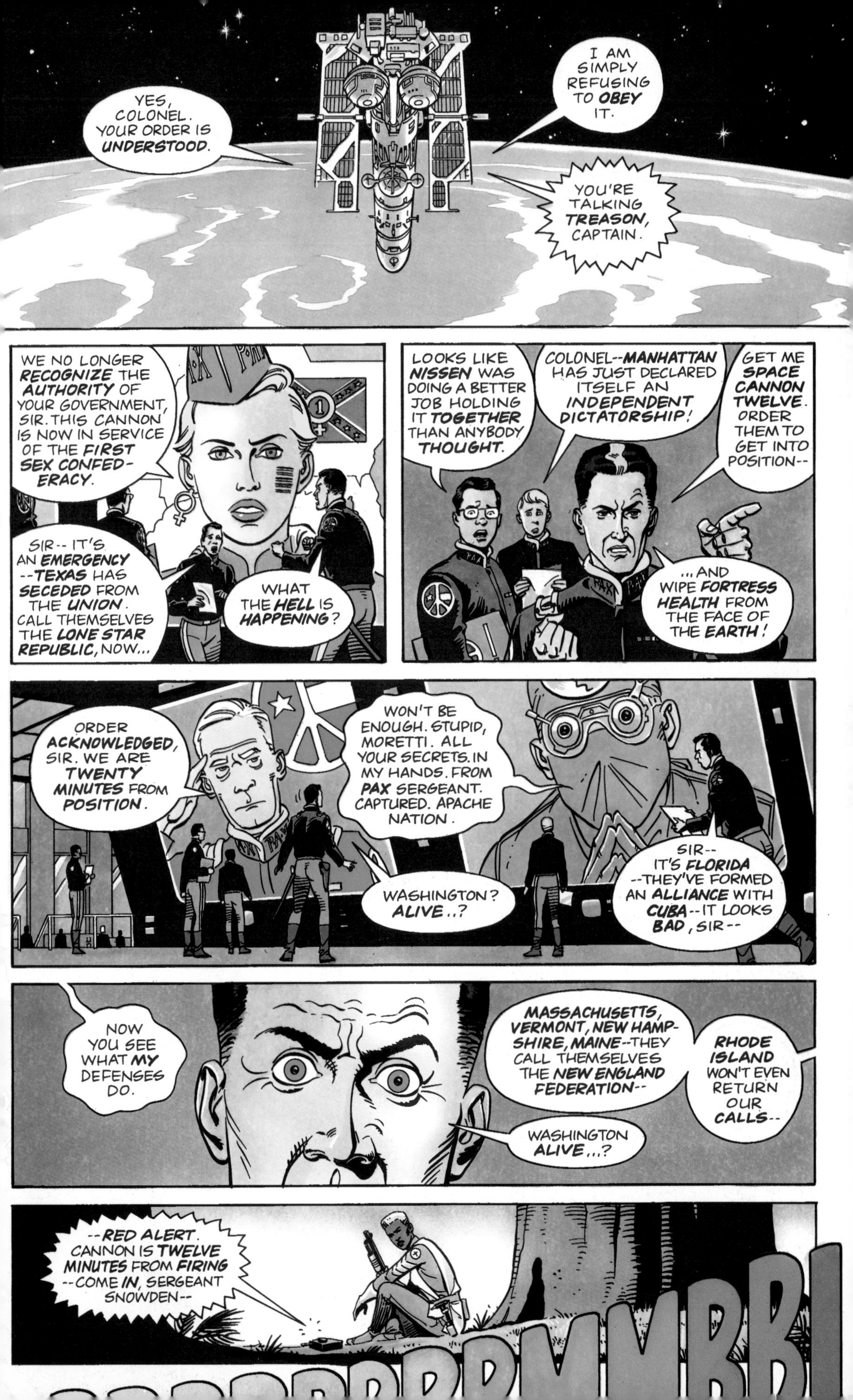
YES, COLONEL. YOUR ORDER IS UNDERSTOOD.
I AM SIMPLY REFUSING TO OBEY IT.
YOU'RE TALKING TREASON, CAPTAIN.
WE NO LONGER RECOGNIZE THE AUTHORITY OF YOUR GOVERNMENT, SIR. THIS CANNON IS NOW IN SERVICE OF THE FIRST SEX CONFED-ERACY.
SIR-- IT'S AN EMERGENCY --TEXAS HAS SECEDED FROM THE UNION. CALL THEMSELVES THE LONE STAR REPUBLIC, NOW...
WHAT THE HELL IS HAPPENING?
LOOKS LIKE NISSEN WAS DOING A BETTER JOB HOLDING IT TOGETHER THAN ANYBODY THOUGHT.
COLONEL--MANHATTAN HAS JUST DECLARED ITSELF AN INDEPENDENT DICTATORSHIP!
GET ME SPACE CANNON TWELVE. ORDER THEM TO GET INTO POSITION--
...AND WIPE FORTRESS HEALTH FROM THE FACE OF THE EARTH!
ORDER ACKNOWLEDGED, SIR. WE ARE TWENTY MINUTES FROM POSITION.
WON'T BE ENOUGH. STUPID, MORETTI. ALL YOUR SECRETS. IN MY HANDS. FROM PAX SERGEANT. CAPTURED. APACHE NATION.
WASHINGTON? ALIVE..?
SIR-- IT'S FLORIDA --THEY'VE FORMED AN ALLIANCE WITH CUBA--IT LOOKS BAD, SIR--
NOW YOU SEE WHAT MY DEFENSES DO.
MASSACHUSETTS, VERMONT, NEW HAMP-SHIRE, MAINE--THEY CALL THEMSELVES THE NEW ENGLAND FEDERATION--
RHODE ISLAND WON'T EVEN RETURN OUR CALLS--
WASHINGTON ALIVE...?
--RED ALERT. CANNON IS TWELVE MINUTES FROM FIRING --COME IN, SERGEANT SNOWDEN--
RRRRRMMBBI

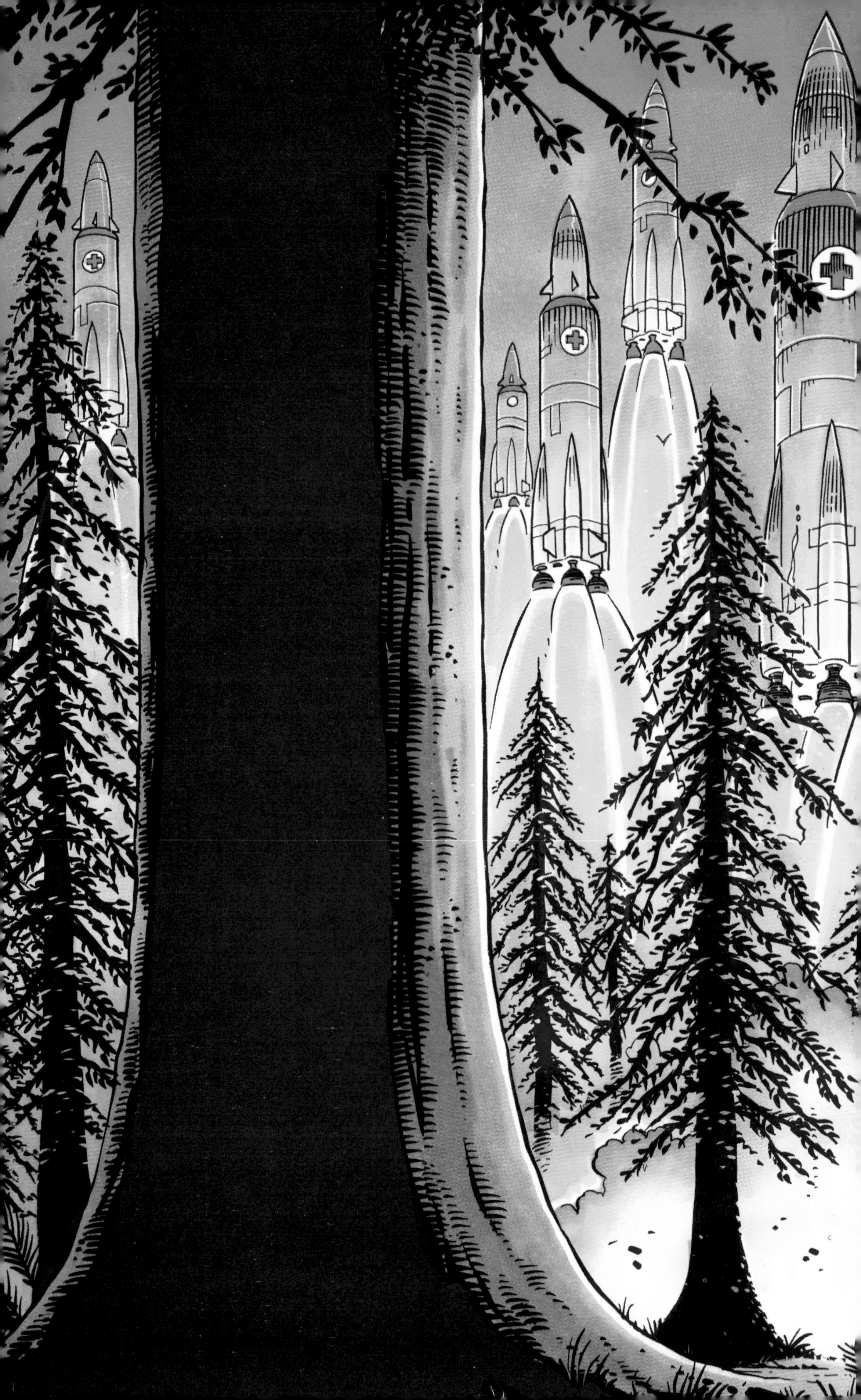

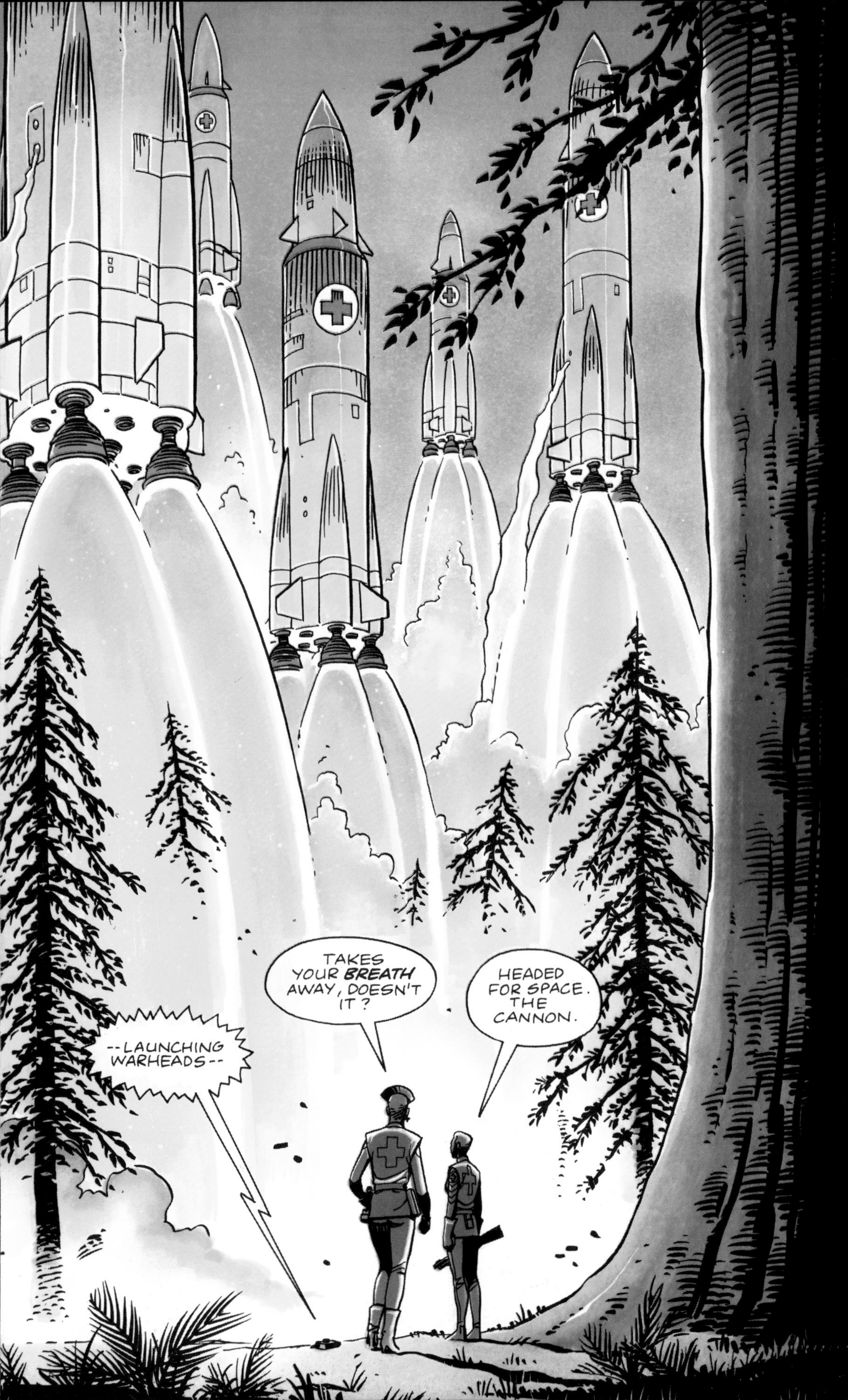
--LAUNCHING WARHEADS--
TAKES YOUR BREATH AWAY, DOESN'T IT?
HEADED FOR SPACE. THE CANNON.

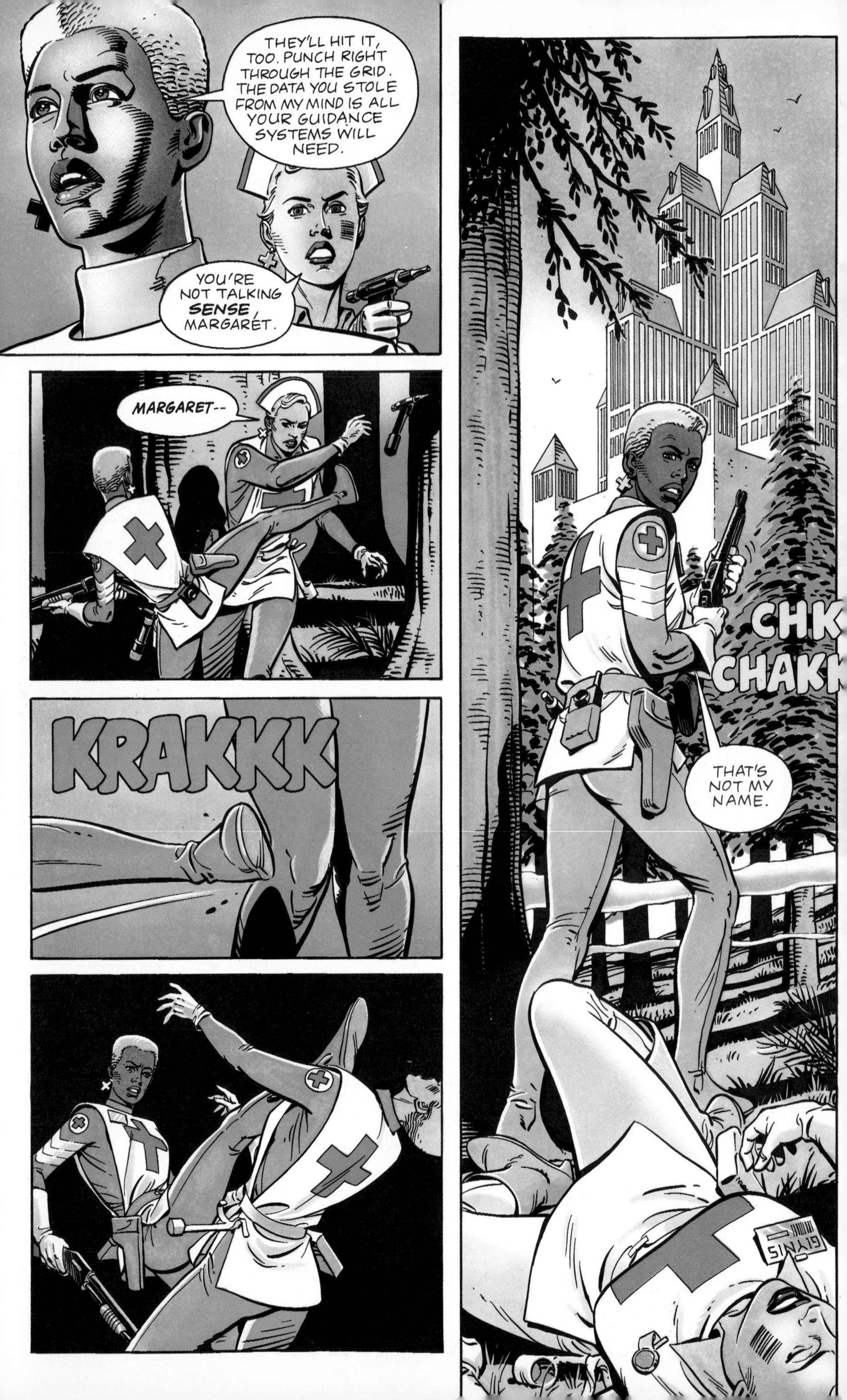

THEY'LL HIT IT, TOO. PUNCH RIGHT THROUGH THE GRID. THE DATA YOU STOLE FROM MY MIND IS ALL YOUR GUIDANCE SYSTEMS WILL NEED.
YOU'RE NOT TALKING **SENSE**, MARGARET.
MARGARET--
KRAKKK
CHK
CHAK
THAT'S NOT MY NAME.

Washington. Jefferson. Lincoln. Roosevelt. Quayle. Rexall. These are names eternally etched in the heart of every true American.

But our hearts are proving more durable than our mountains. Acid rain. Gulf stream fallout. You've heard the terms. You know what's happening to this most precious monument. It's up to you to eat a little less. To work a little harder. To live a little cheaper. To go a little further into debt. So you can give. No contribution is too small. Help us save our Legacy. Help us save Mount Rushmore.

4: DEATH & TAXES

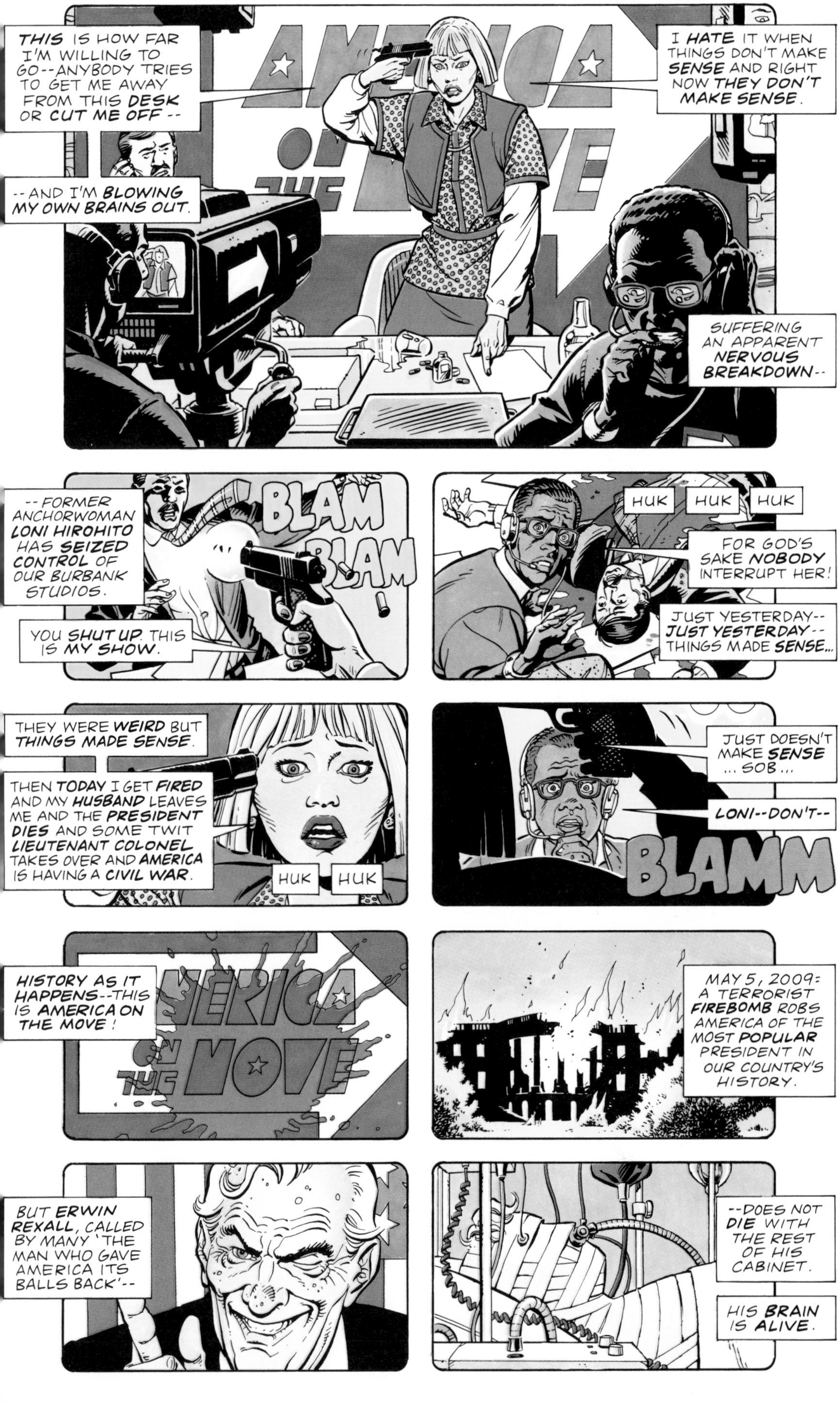
THIS IS HOW FAR I'M WILLING TO GO--ANYBODY TRIES TO GET ME AWAY FROM THIS DESK OR CUT ME OFF--
I HATE IT WHEN THINGS DON'T MAKE SENSE AND RIGHT NOW THEY DON'T MAKE SENSE.
--AND I'M BLOWING MY OWN BRAINS OUT.
SUFFERING AN APPARENT NERVOUS BREAKDOWN--
--FORMER ANCHORWOMAN LONI HIROHITO HAS SEIZED CONTROL OF OUR BURBANK STUDIOS.
BLAM
BLAM
YOU SHUT UP. THIS IS MY SHOW.
HUK
HUK
HUK
FOR GOD'S SAKE NOBODY INTERRUPT HER!
JUST YESTERDAY--JUST YESTERDAY--THINGS MADE SENSE...
THEY WERE WEIRD BUT THINGS MADE SENSE.
THEN TODAY I GET FIRED AND MY HUSBAND LEAVES ME AND THE PRESIDENT DIES AND SOME TWIT LIEUTENANT COLONEL TAKES OVER AND AMERICA IS HAVING A CIVIL WAR.
HUK
HUK
JUST DOESN'T MAKE SENSE ... SOB ...
LONI--DON'T--
BLAMM
HISTORY AS IT HAPPENS--THIS IS AMERICA ON THE MOVE!
MAY 5, 2009: A TERRORIST FIREBOMB ROBS AMERICA OF THE MOST POPULAR PRESIDENT IN OUR COUNTRY'S HISTORY.
BUT ERWIN REXALL, CALLED BY MANY 'THE MAN WHO GAVE AMERICA ITS BALLS BACK'--
--DOES NOT DIE WITH THE REST OF HIS CABINET.
HIS BRAIN IS ALIVE.

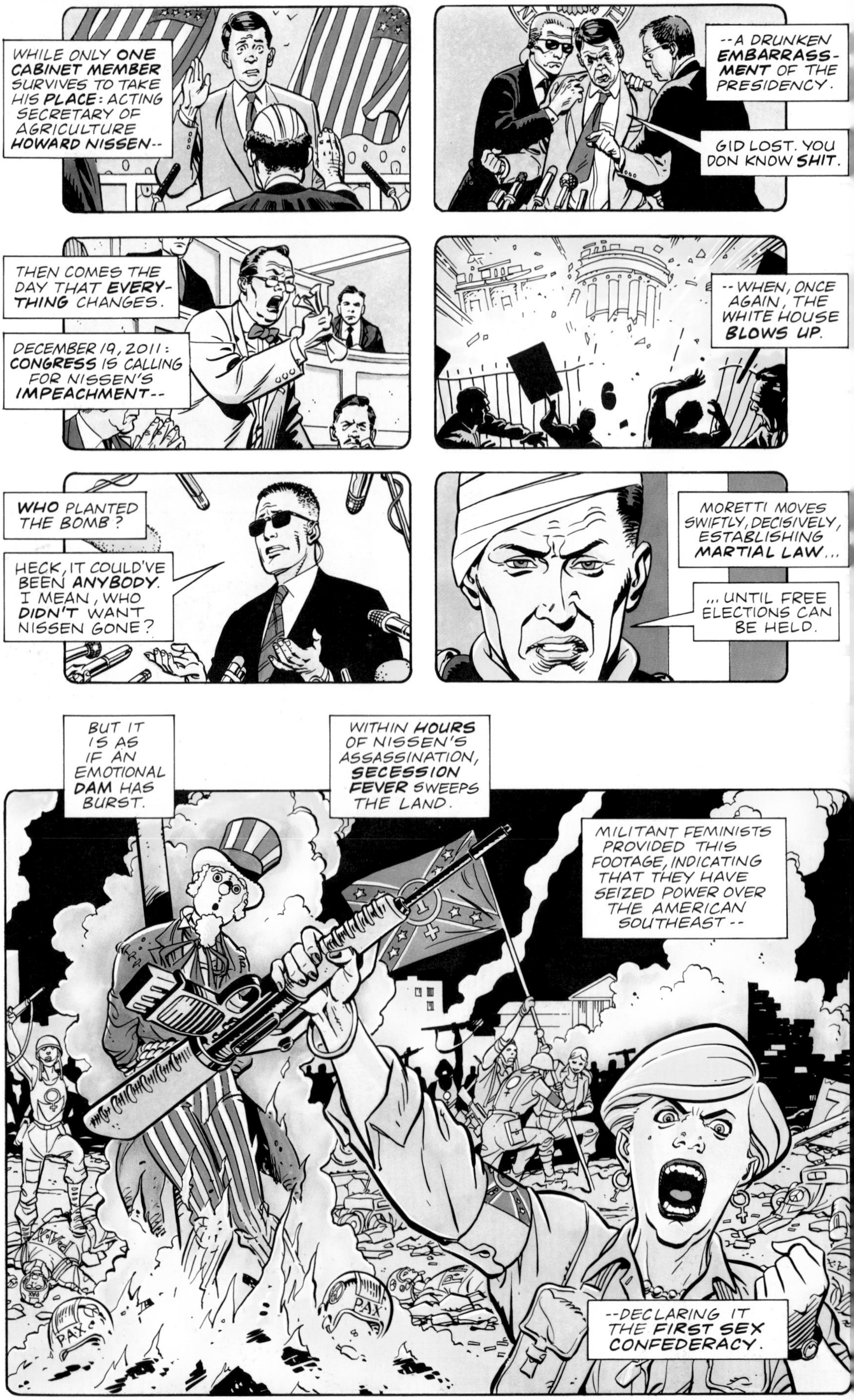
WHILE ONLY ONE CABINET MEMBER SURVIVES TO TAKE HIS PLACE: ACTING SECRETARY OF AGRICULTURE HOWARD NISSEN--
--A DRUNKEN EMBARRASSMENT OF THE PRESIDENCY.
GID LOST. YOU DON KNOW SHIT.
THEN COMES THE DAY THAT EVERYTHING CHANGES.
DECEMBER 19, 2011: CONGRESS IS CALLING FOR NISSEN'S IMPEACHMENT--
--WHEN, ONCE AGAIN, THE WHITE HOUSE BLOWS UP.
WHO PLANTED THE BOMB?
HECK, IT COULD'VE BEEN ANYBODY. I MEAN, WHO DIDN'T WANT NISSEN GONE?
MORETTI MOVES SWIFTLY, DECISIVELY, ESTABLISHING MARTIAL LAW...
...UNTIL FREE ELECTIONS CAN BE HELD.
BUT IT IS AS IF AN EMOTIONAL DAM HAS BURST.
WITHIN HOURS OF NISSEN'S ASSASSINATION, SECESSION FEVER SWEEPS THE LAND.
MILITANT FEMINISTS PROVIDED THIS FOOTAGE, INDICATING THAT THEY HAVE SEIZED POWER OVER THE AMERICAN SOUTHEAST--
--DECLARING IT THE FIRST SEX CONFEDERACY.
PAX
PAX

THE VERY **BIRTH-PLACE** OF THE UNION --**NEW ENGLAND**--

--DEMANDS UNITED NATIONS REPRESENTATION AS AN INDEPENDENT FEDERATION.

MANHATTAN BOROUGH PRESIDENT **BELUGA** DECLARES **VICTORY** OVER **BROOKLYN**--

--ANNEXING IT AND FORMING THE **EAST COAST CAPITALIST DICTATORSHIP.**

BELUGA **DENIES** THE WIDESPREAD BELIEF THAT HE FACES AS MANY AS FORTY WARRING SEPERATIST MOVEMENTS WITHIN MANHATTAN.

THERE ARE SCATTERED REPORTS OF **SHELLING** ON THE BORDER OF THE **MEXICAN TERRITORY**--

-- AND THE SELF-PROCLAIMED **LONE STAR REPUBLIC.**

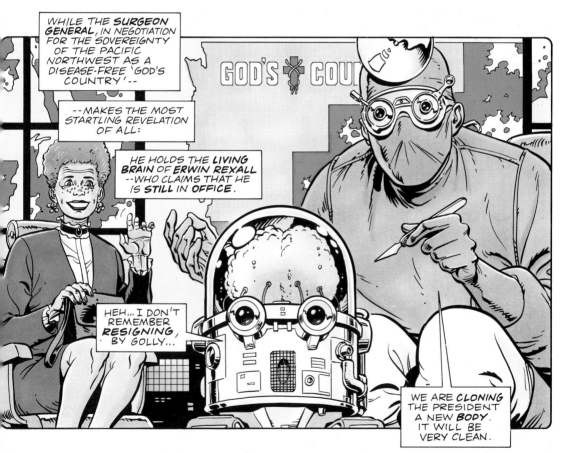

WHILE THE **SURGEON GENERAL,** IN NEGOTIATION FOR THE SOVEREIGNTY OF THE PACIFIC NORTHWEST AS A DISEASE-FREE 'GOD'S COUNTRY'--

--MAKES THE MOST STARTLING REVELATION OF ALL:

HE HOLDS THE **LIVING BRAIN** OF ERWIN REXALL --WHO CLAIMS THAT HE IS **STILL** IN **OFFICE.**

GOD'S ✟ COUN

HEH... I DON'T REMEMBER **RESIGNING,** BY GOLLY...

WE ARE **CLONING** THE PRESIDENT A NEW **BODY.** IT WILL BE VERY CLEAN.

IRONICALLY, IT WAS REXALL HIMSELF WHO DRAFTED THE '**NO HOLDS BARRED**' AMENDMENT--

--COMMITTING **MILITARY FORCE** AGAINST ANY ENEMY WHO HOLDS AN AMERICAN CITIZEN **HOSTAGE** ...

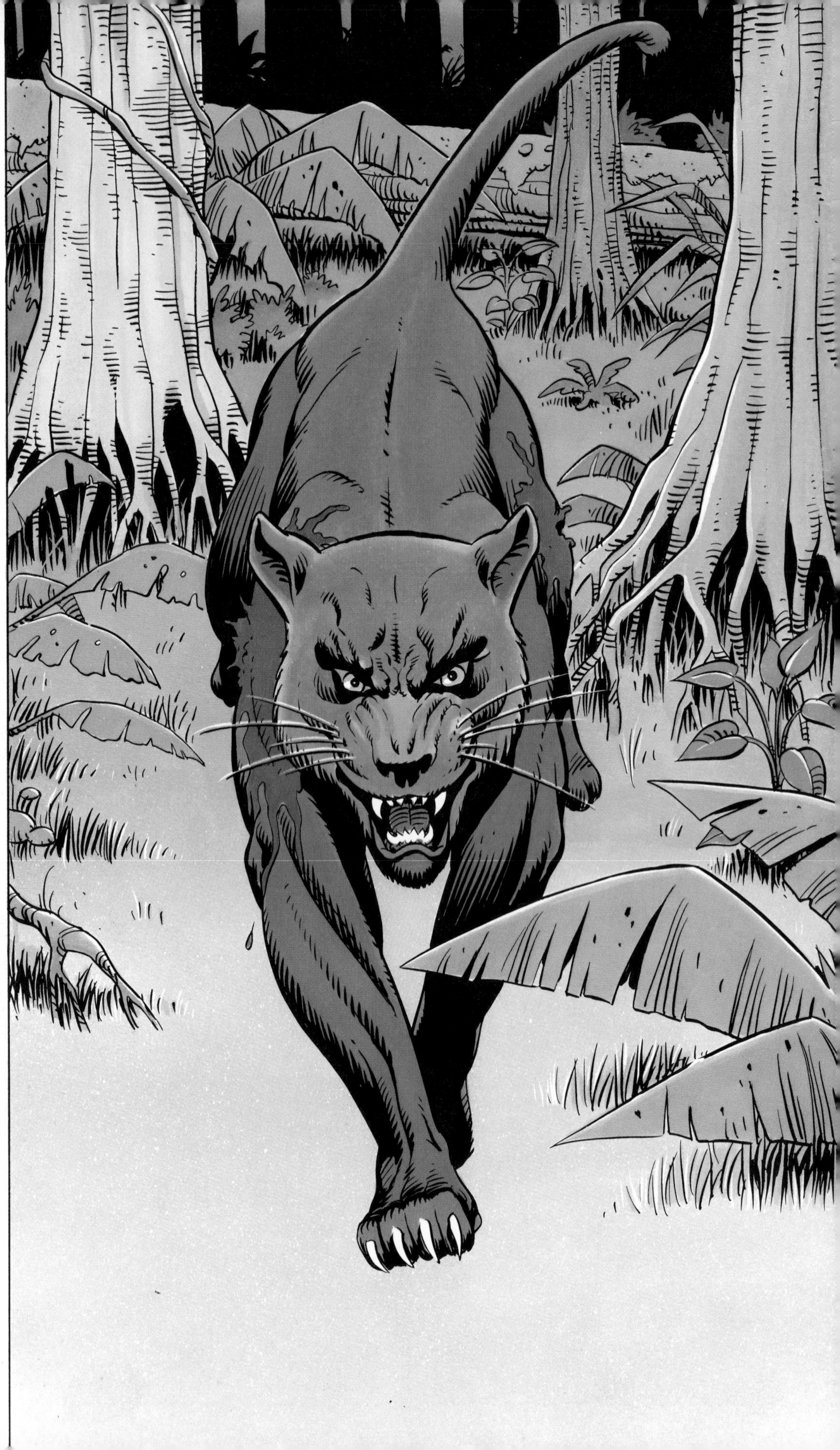

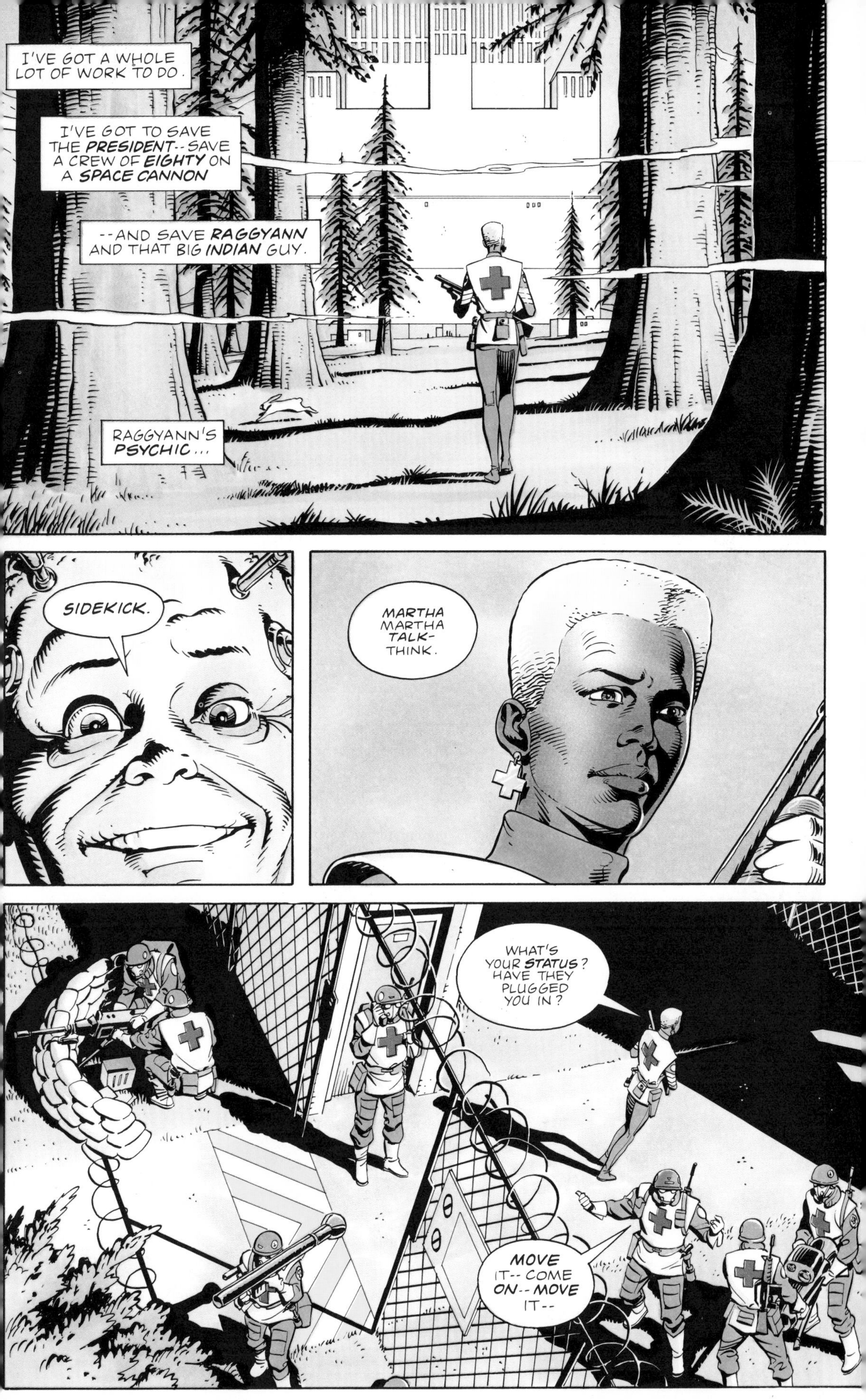

I'VE GOT A WHOLE LOT OF WORK TO DO.
I'VE GOT TO SAVE THE PRESIDENT-- SAVE A CREW OF EIGHTY ON A SPACE CANNON
--AND SAVE RAGGYANN AND THAT BIG INDIAN GUY.
RAGGYANN'S PSYCHIC...
SIDEKICK.
MARTHA MARTHA TALK-THINK.
WHAT'S YOUR STATUS? HAVE THEY PLUGGED YOU IN?
MOVE IT-- COME ON-- MOVE IT--

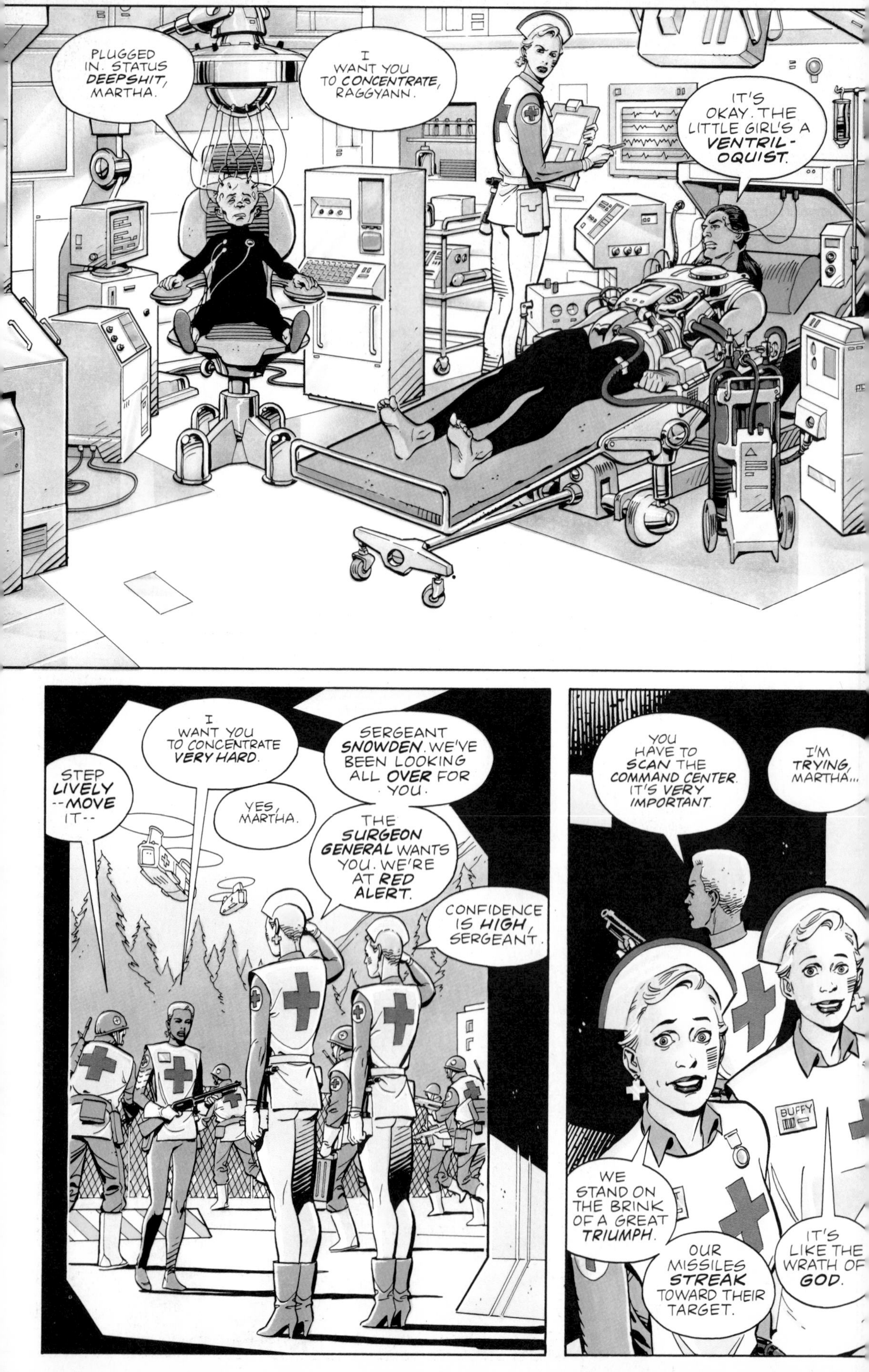
PLUGGED IN. STATUS DEEPSHIT, MARTHA.
I WANT YOU TO CONCENTRATE, RAGGYANN.
IT'S OKAY. THE LITTLE GIRL'S A VENTRIL-OQUIST.
STEP LIVELY --MOVE IT--
I WANT YOU TO CONCENTRATE VERY HARD.
YES, MARTHA.
SERGEANT SNOWDEN. WE'VE BEEN LOOKING ALL OVER FOR YOU.
THE SURGEON GENERAL WANTS YOU. WE'RE AT RED ALERT.
CONFIDENCE IS HIGH, SERGEANT.
YOU HAVE TO SCAN THE COMMAND CENTER. IT'S VERY IMPORTANT.
I'M TRYING, MARTHA...
BUFFY
WE STAND ON THE BRINK OF A GREAT TRIUMPH.
OUR MISSILES STREAK TOWARD THEIR TARGET.
IT'S LIKE THE WRATH OF GOD.

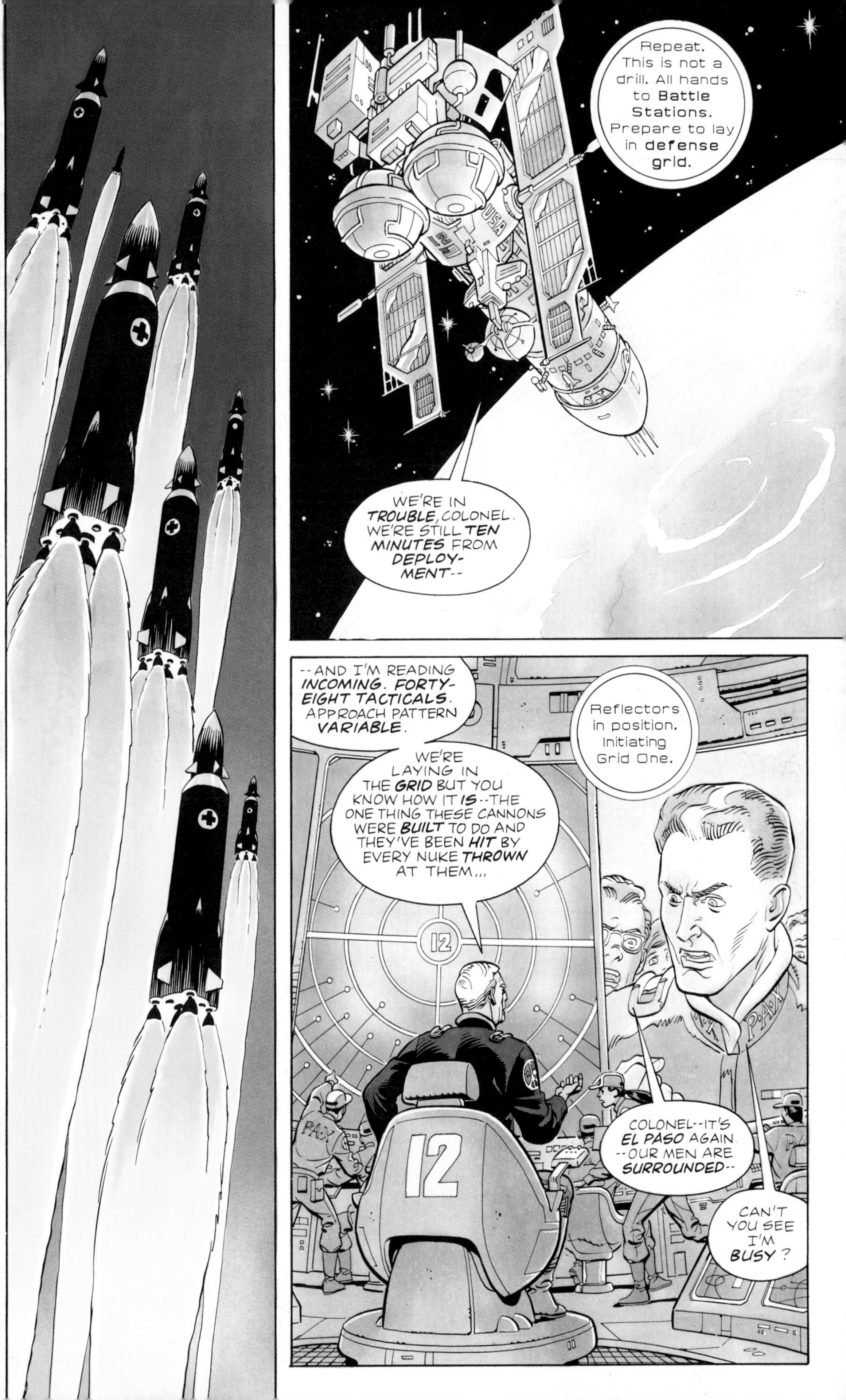
Repeat. This is not a drill. All hands to Battle Stations. Prepare to lay in defense grid.
WE'RE IN TROUBLE, COLONEL. WE'RE STILL TEN MINUTES FROM DEPLOY-MENT--
USA
12
--AND I'M READING INCOMING. FORTY-EIGHT TACTICALS. APPROACH PATTERN VARIABLE.
Reflectors in position. Initiating Grid One.
WE'RE LAYING IN THE GRID BUT YOU KNOW HOW IT IS--THE ONE THING THESE CANNONS WERE BUILT TO DO AND THEY'VE BEEN HIT BY EVERY NUKE THROWN AT THEM...
12
COLONEL--IT'S EL PASO AGAIN --OUR MEN ARE SURROUNDED--
CAN'T YOU SEE I'M BUSY?
12

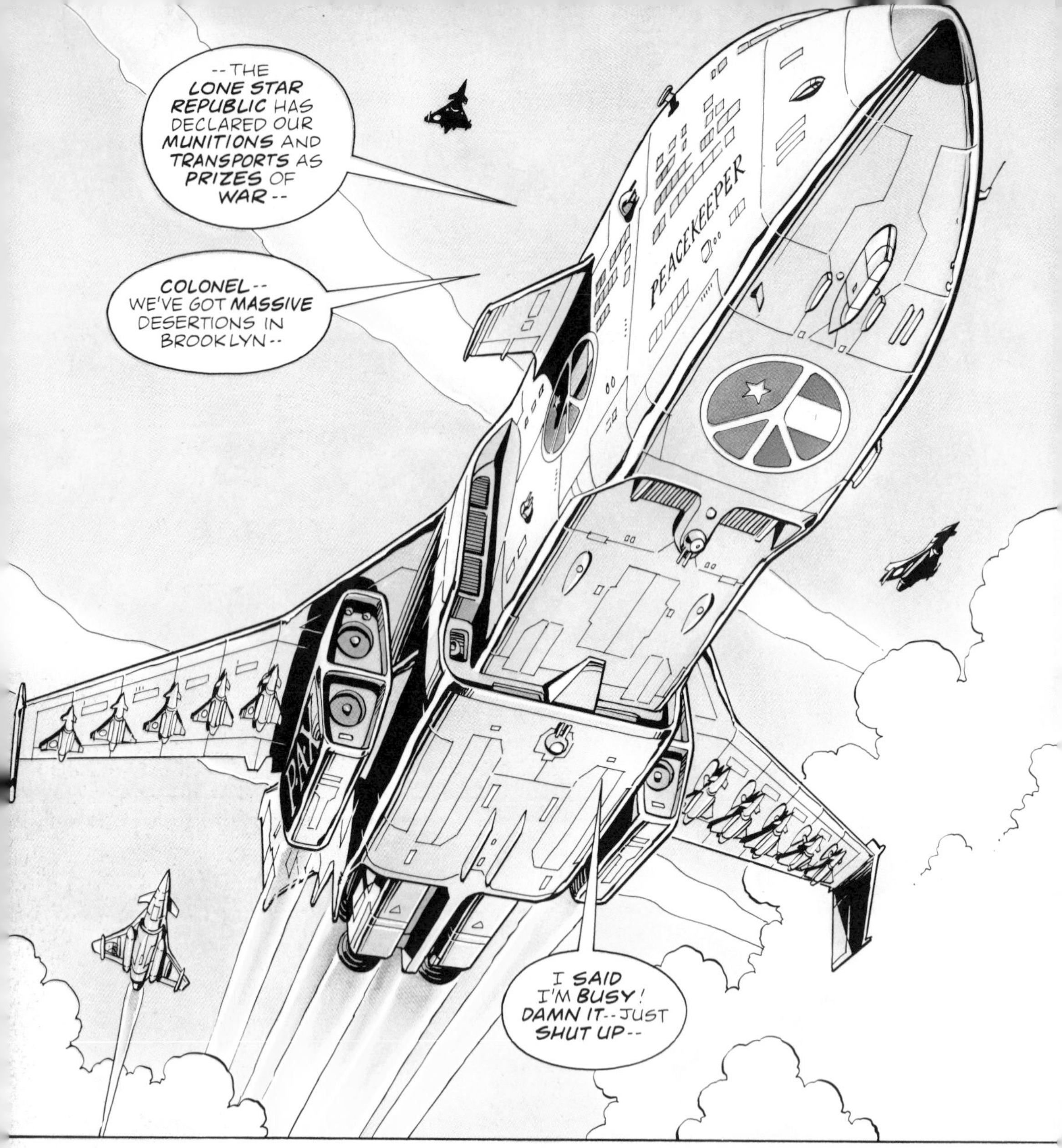
--THE LONE STAR REPUBLIC HAS DECLARED OUR MUNITIONS AND TRANSPORTS AS PRIZES OF WAR--
COLONEL-- WE'VE GOT MASSIVE DESERTIONS IN BROOKLYN--
PEACEKEEPER
PAX
I SAID I'M BUSY! DAMN IT--JUST SHUT UP--

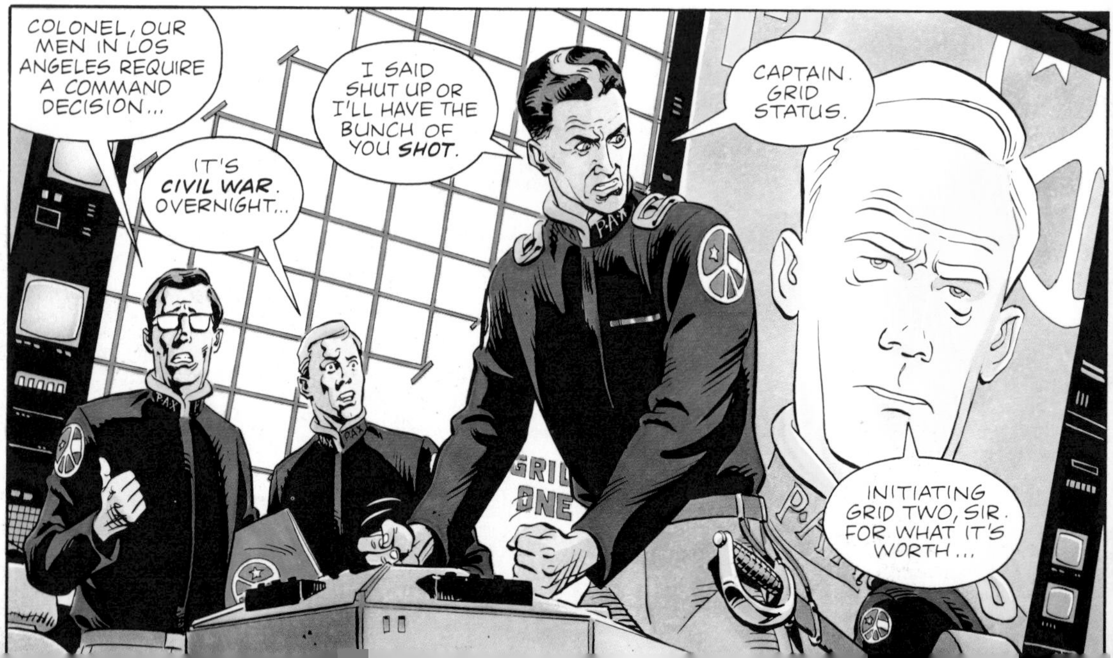
COLONEL, OUR MEN IN LOS ANGELES REQUIRE A COMMAND DECISION...
IT'S CIVIL WAR. OVERNIGHT...
I SAID SHUT UP OR I'LL HAVE THE BUNCH OF YOU SHOT.
CAPTAIN. GRID STATUS.
INITIATING GRID TWO, SIR. FOR WHAT IT'S WORTH...

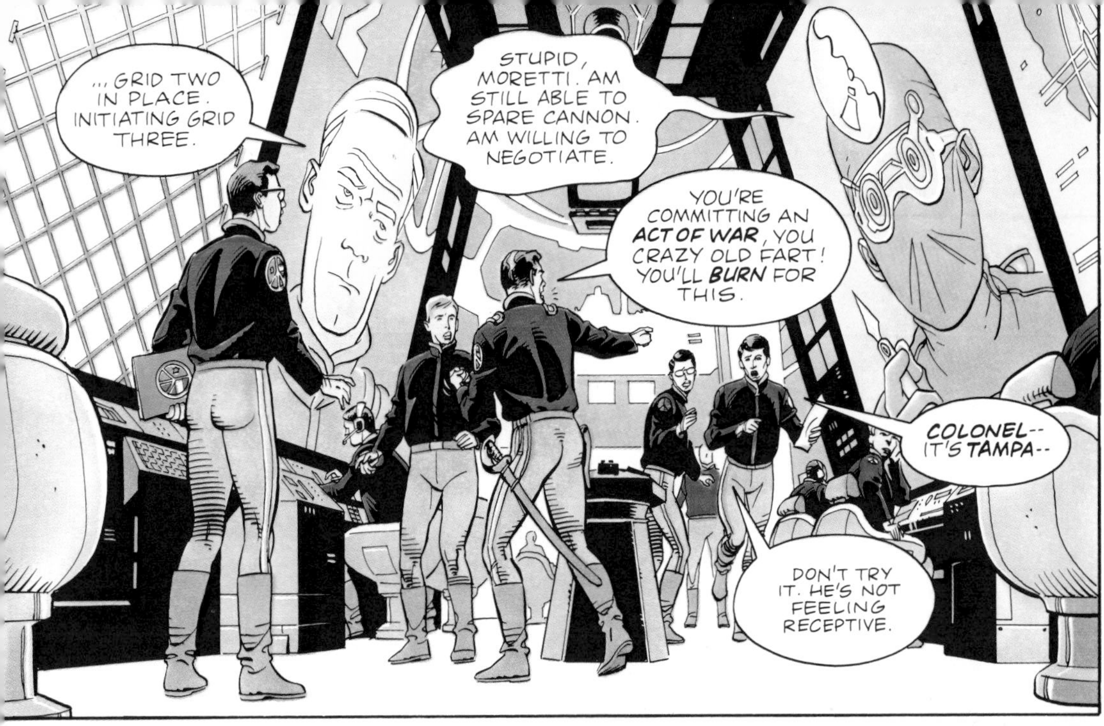
...GRID TWO IN PLACE. INITIATING GRID THREE.
STUPID, MORETTI. AM STILL ABLE TO SPARE CANNON. AM WILLING TO NEGOTIATE.
YOU'RE COMMITTING AN **ACT OF WAR**, YOU CRAZY OLD FART! YOU'LL **BURN** FOR THIS.
COLONEL-- IT'S **TAMPA**--
DON'T TRY IT. HE'S NOT FEELING RECEPTIVE.

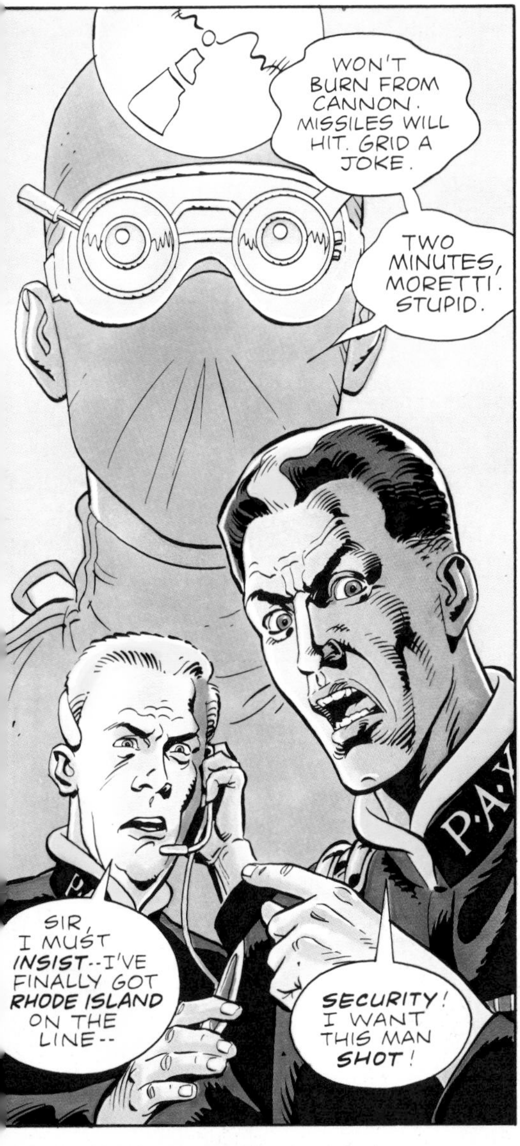
WON'T BURN FROM CANNON. MISSILES WILL HIT. GRID A JOKE.
TWO MINUTES, MORETTI. STUPID.
SIR, I MUST **INSIST**--I'VE FINALLY GOT **RHODE ISLAND** ON THE LINE--
SECURITY! I WANT THIS MAN **SHOT**!

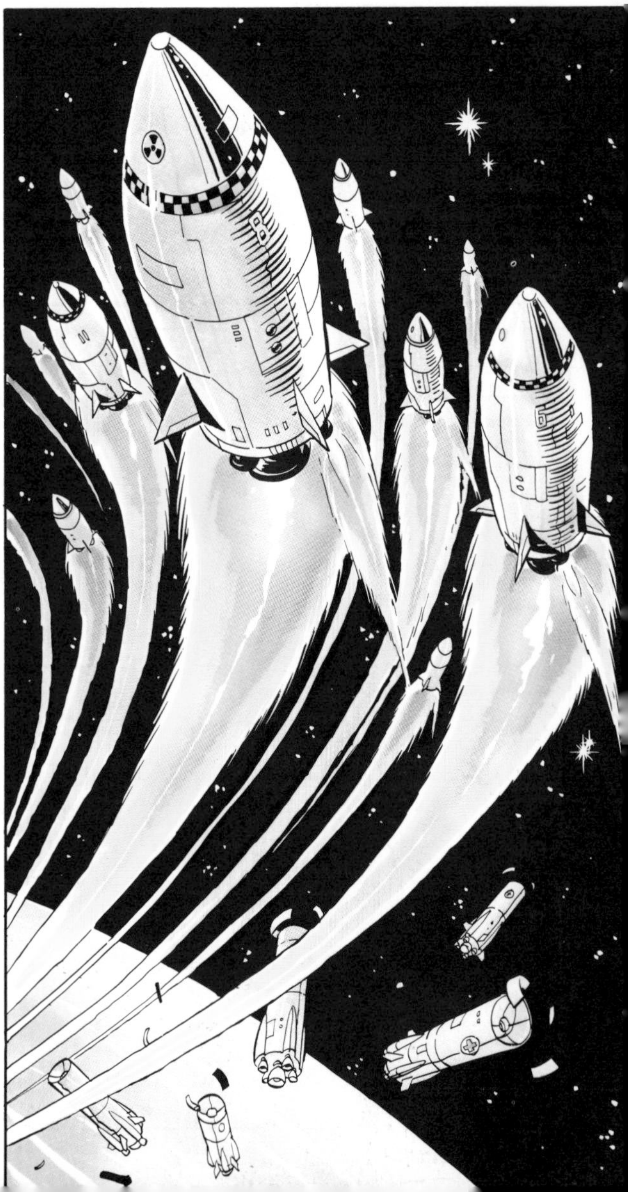

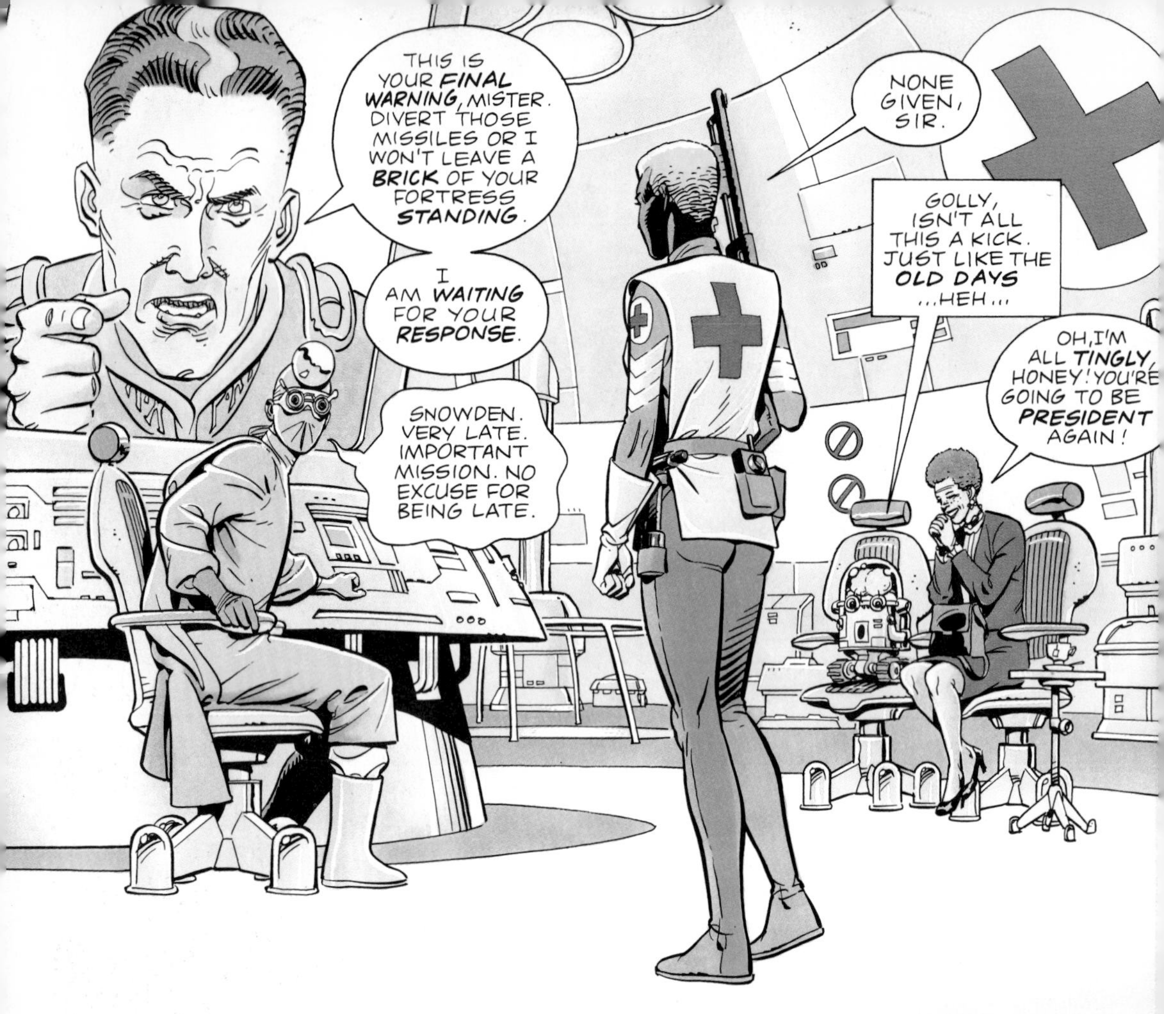
THIS IS YOUR FINAL WARNING, MISTER. DIVERT THOSE MISSILES OR I WON'T LEAVE A BRICK OF YOUR FORTRESS STANDING.
I AM WAITING FOR YOUR RESPONSE.
NONE GIVEN, SIR.
SNOWDEN. VERY LATE. IMPORTANT MISSION. NO EXCUSE FOR BEING LATE.
GOLLY, ISN'T ALL THIS A KICK. JUST LIKE THE OLD DAYS ...HEH...
OH, I'M ALL TINGLY, HONEY! YOU'RE GOING TO BE PRESIDENT AGAIN!

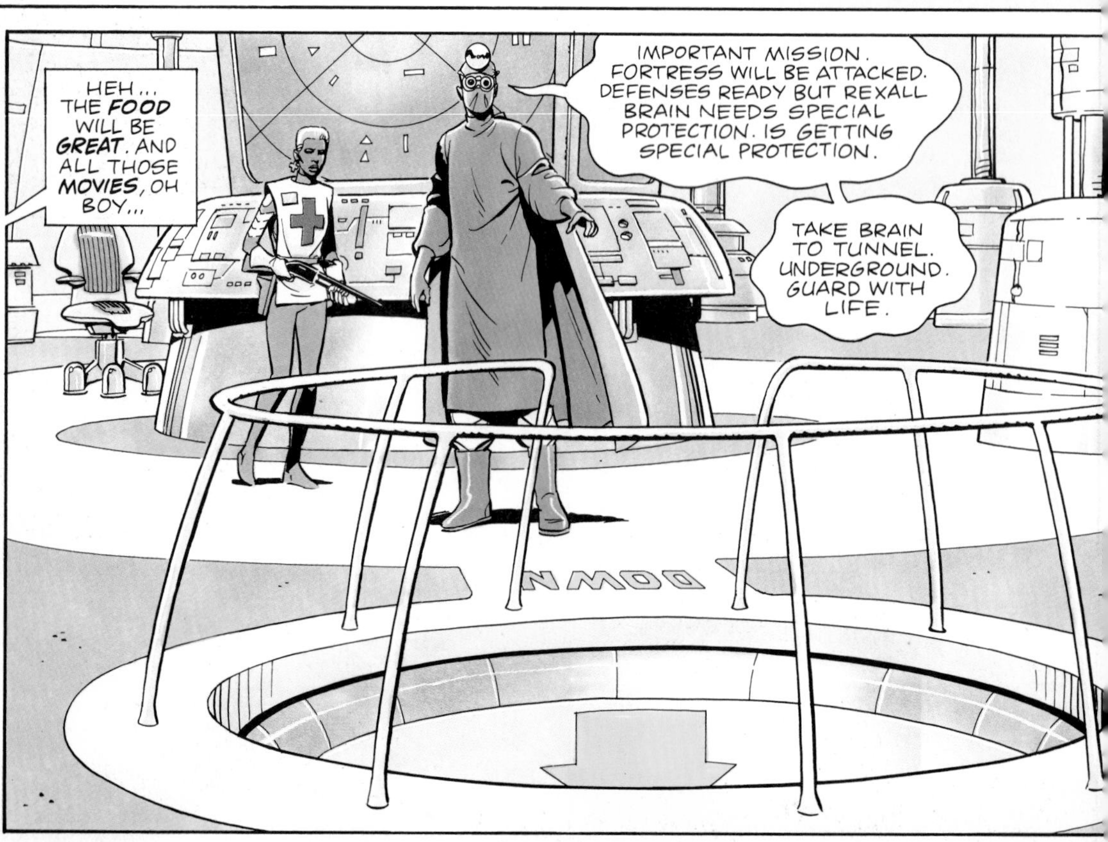
HEH... THE FOOD WILL BE GREAT. AND ALL THOSE MOVIES, OH BOY...
IMPORTANT MISSION. FORTRESS WILL BE ATTACKED. DEFENSES READY BUT REXALL BRAIN NEEDS SPECIAL PROTECTION. IS GETTING SPECIAL PROTECTION.
TAKE BRAIN TO TUNNEL. UNDERGROUND. GUARD WITH LIFE.
DOWN

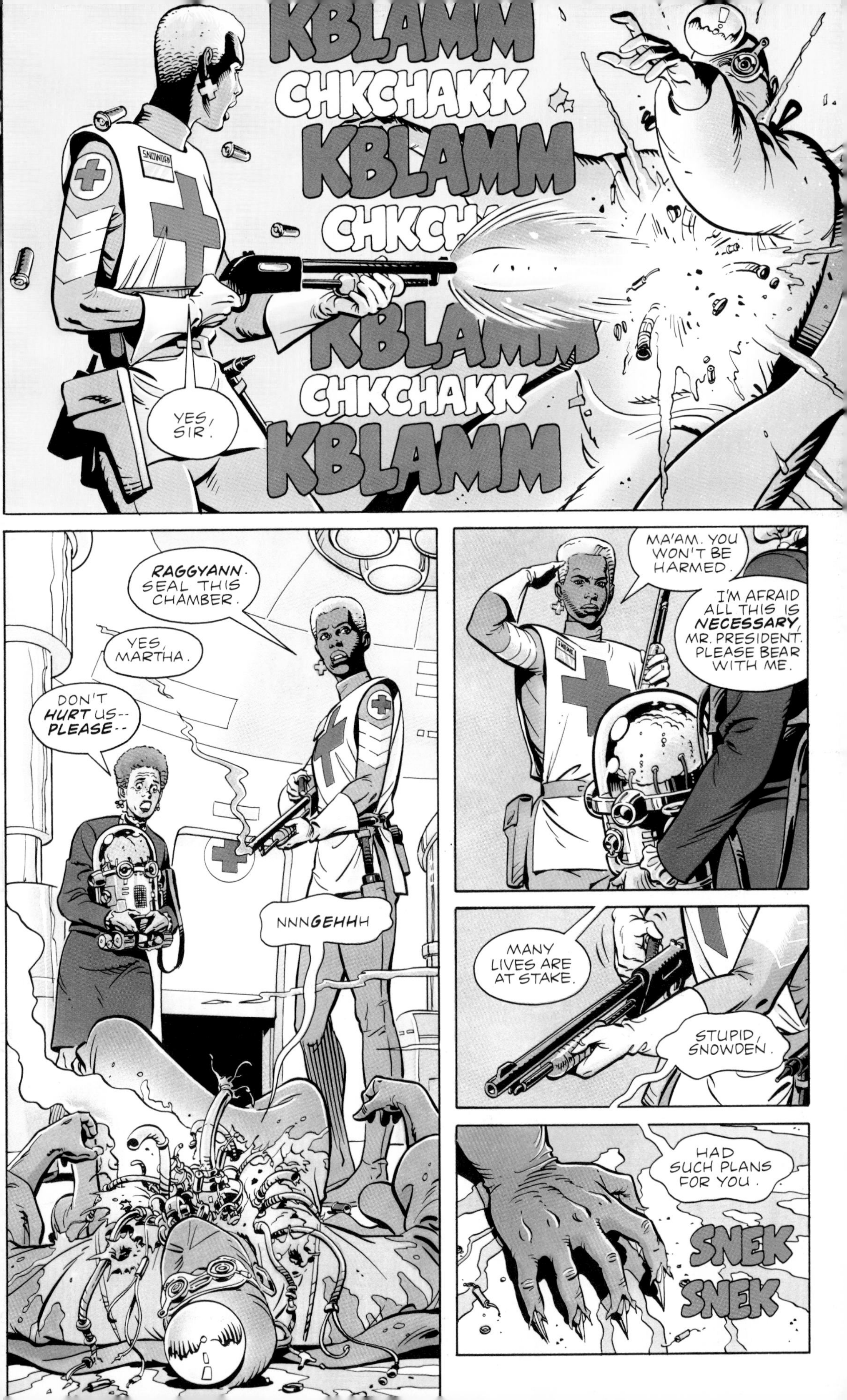
KBLAMM
CHKCHAKK
KBLAMM
CHKCH
YES, SIR.
KBLAMM
CHKCHAKK
KBLAMM
RAGGYANN. SEAL THIS CHAMBER.
YES, MARTHA.
DON'T HURT US-- PLEASE--
NNNGEHHH
MA'AM. YOU WON'T BE HARMED.
I'M AFRAID ALL THIS IS NECESSARY, MR. PRESIDENT. PLEASE BEAR WITH ME.
MANY LIVES ARE AT STAKE.
STUPID, SNOWDEN.
HAD SUCH PLANS FOR YOU.
SNEK
SNEK

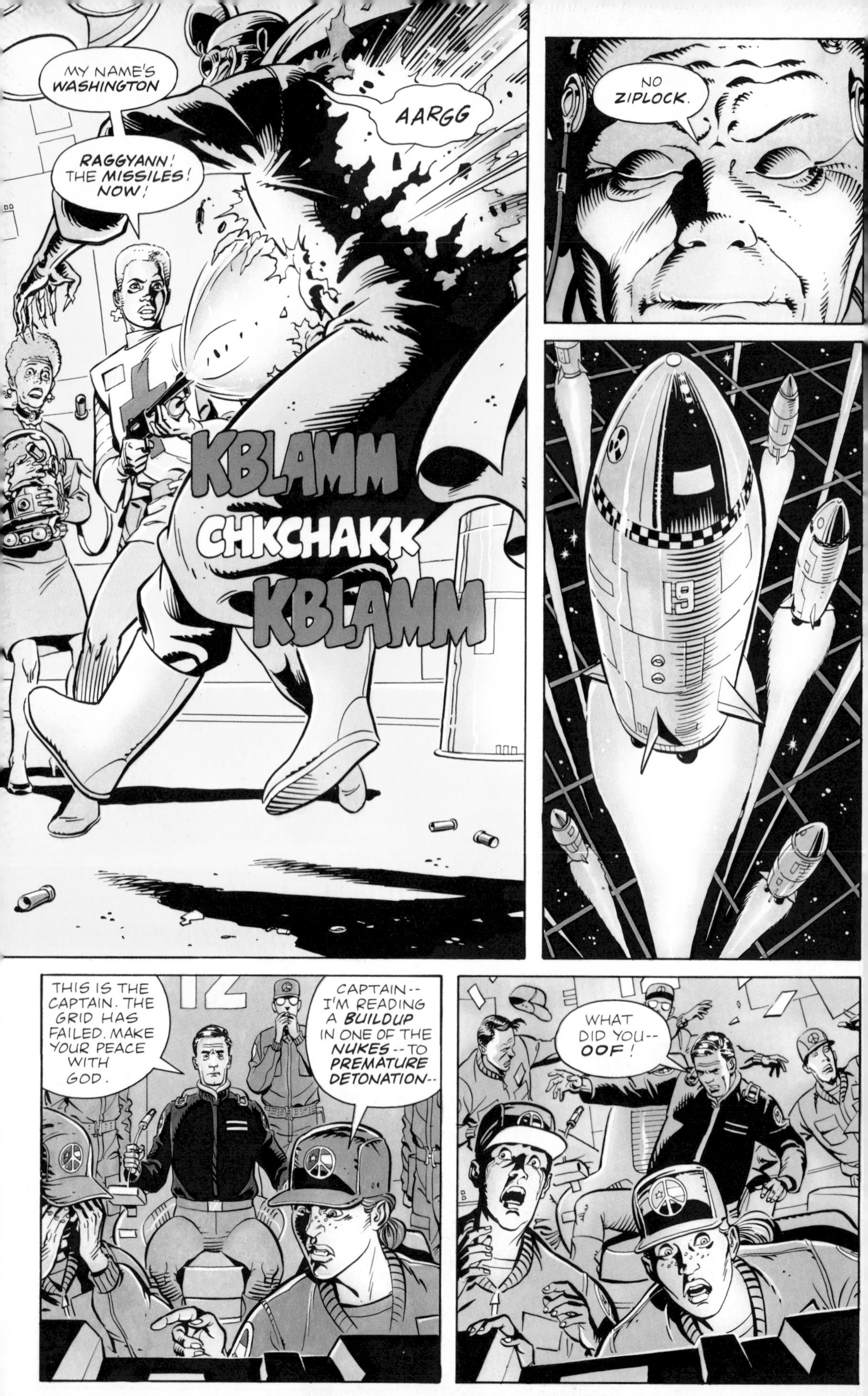
MY NAME'S WASHINGTON
RAGGYANN! THE MISSILES! NOW!
AARGG
KBLAMM
CHKCHAKK
KBLAMM
NO ZIPLOCK.
THIS IS THE CAPTAIN. THE GRID HAS FAILED. MAKE YOUR PEACE WITH GOD.
CAPTAIN-- I'M READING A BUILDUP IN ONE OF THE NUKES--TO PREMATURE DETONATION--
WHAT DID YOU-- OOF!

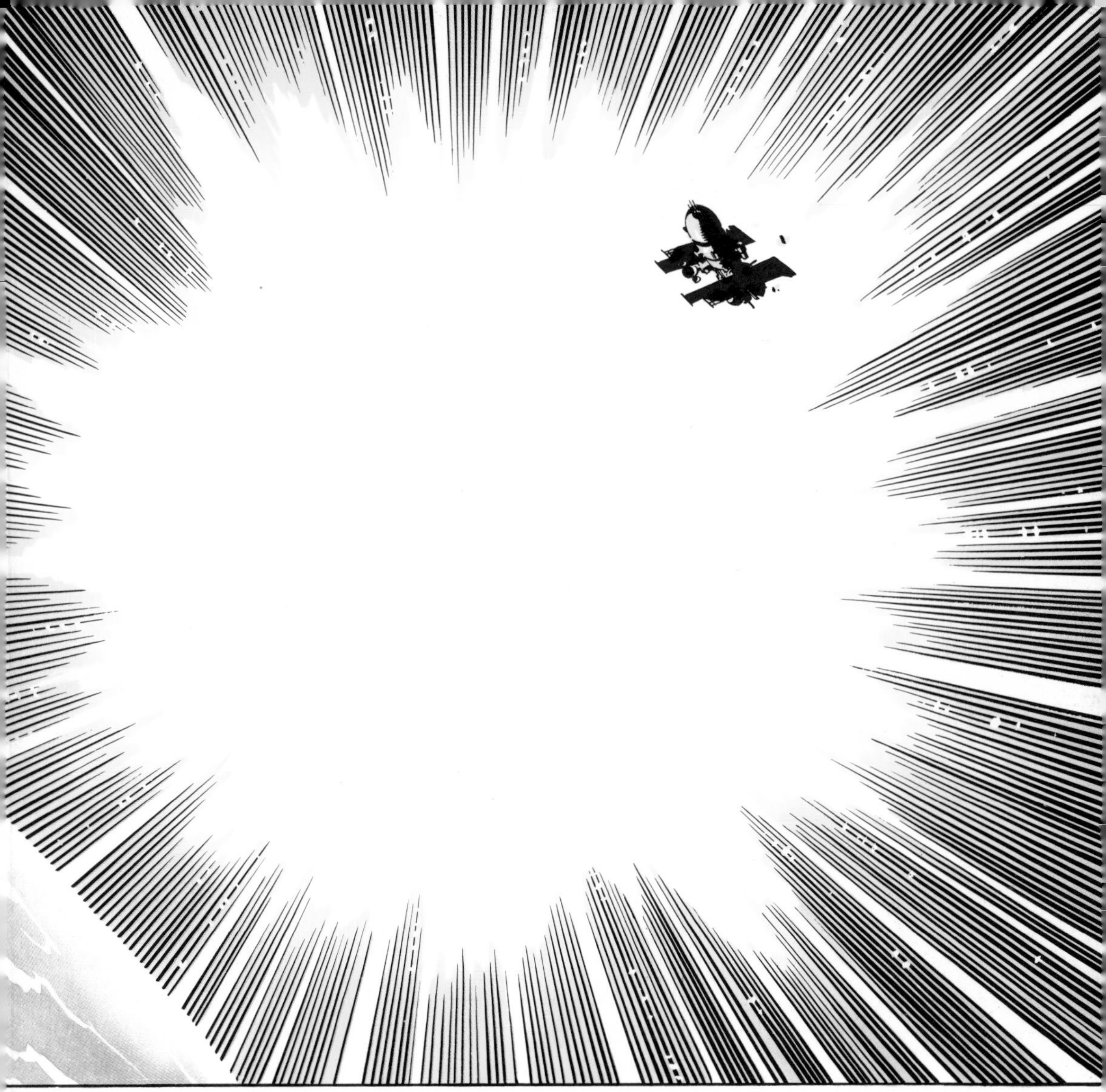

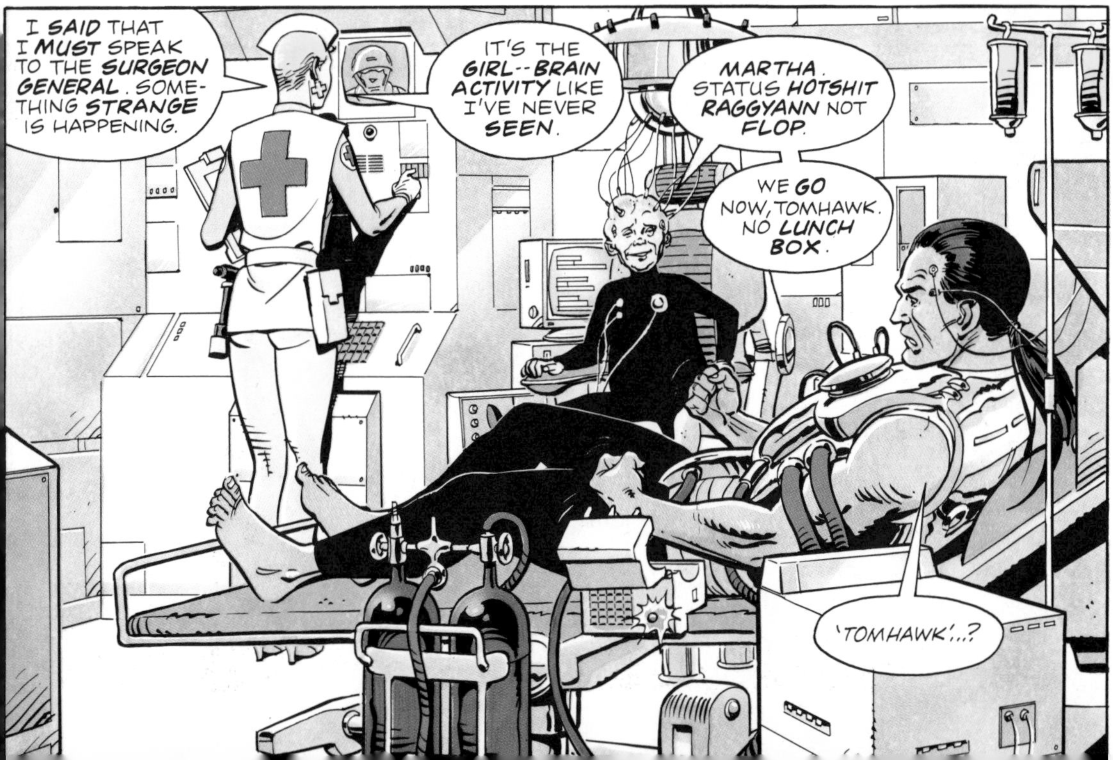
I SAID THAT I MUST SPEAK TO THE SURGEON GENERAL. SOMETHING STRANGE IS HAPPENING.
IT'S THE GIRL--BRAIN ACTIVITY LIKE I'VE NEVER SEEN.
MARTHA. STATUS HOTSHIT RAGGYANN NOT FLOP.
WE GO NOW, TOMHAWK. NO LUNCH BOX.
'TOMHAWK'..?

CRAZY AS IT **SOUNDS**, I THINK SHE'S DOING SOMETHING TO THE **COMPUTER**.

SHE-- AAH

FFT

YOU **DICK**.

THWAAK

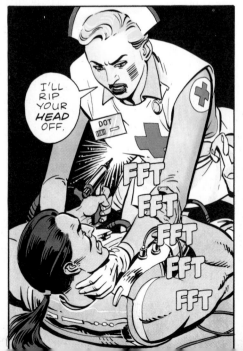

I'LL RIP YOUR **HEAD** OFF.

DOT

FFT
FFT
FFT
FFT
FFT

HEADOFFF

KID-- HELP GET HER **OFF** ME.

NOT **KID**. RAGGYANN.

MARTHA SAID.

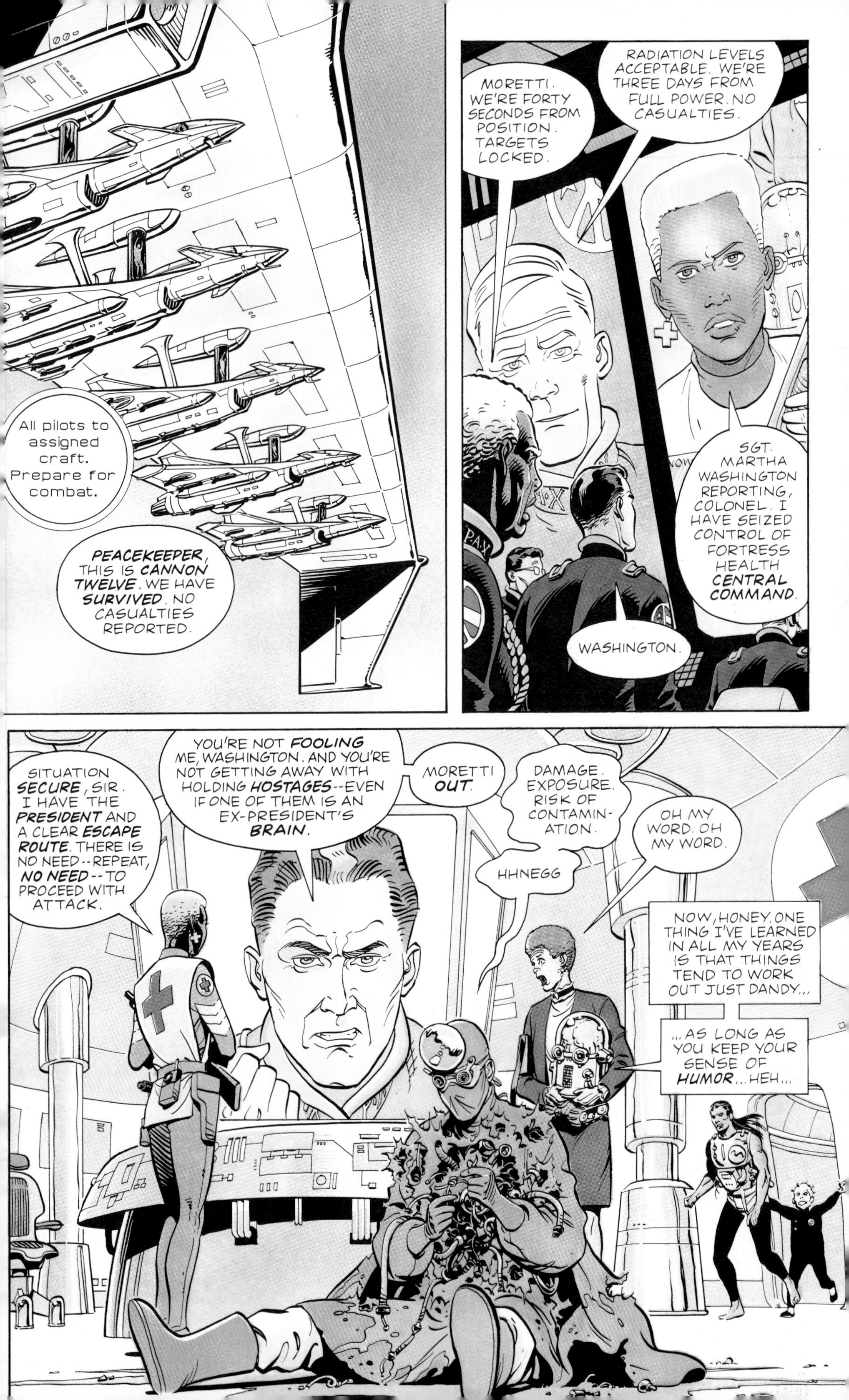
All pilots to assigned craft. Prepare for combat.
PEACEKEEPER, THIS IS CANNON TWELVE. WE HAVE SURVIVED. NO CASUALTIES REPORTED.
MORETTI. WE'RE FORTY SECONDS FROM POSITION. TARGETS LOCKED.
RADIATION LEVELS ACCEPTABLE. WE'RE THREE DAYS FROM FULL POWER. NO CASUALTIES.
SGT. MARTHA WASHINGTON REPORTING, COLONEL. I HAVE SEIZED CONTROL OF FORTRESS HEALTH CENTRAL COMMAND.
WASHINGTON.
SITUATION SECURE, SIR. I HAVE THE PRESIDENT AND A CLEAR ESCAPE ROUTE. THERE IS NO NEED--REPEAT, NO NEED--TO PROCEED WITH ATTACK.
YOU'RE NOT FOOLING ME, WASHINGTON. AND YOU'RE NOT GETTING AWAY WITH HOLDING HOSTAGES--EVEN IF ONE OF THEM IS AN EX-PRESIDENT'S BRAIN.
MORETTI OUT.
DAMAGE. EXPOSURE. RISK OF CONTAMINATION.
HHNEGG
OH MY WORD. OH MY WORD.
NOW, HONEY. ONE THING I'VE LEARNED IN ALL MY YEARS IS THAT THINGS TEND TO WORK OUT JUST DANDY...
...AS LONG AS YOU KEEP YOUR SENSE OF HUMOR... HEH...

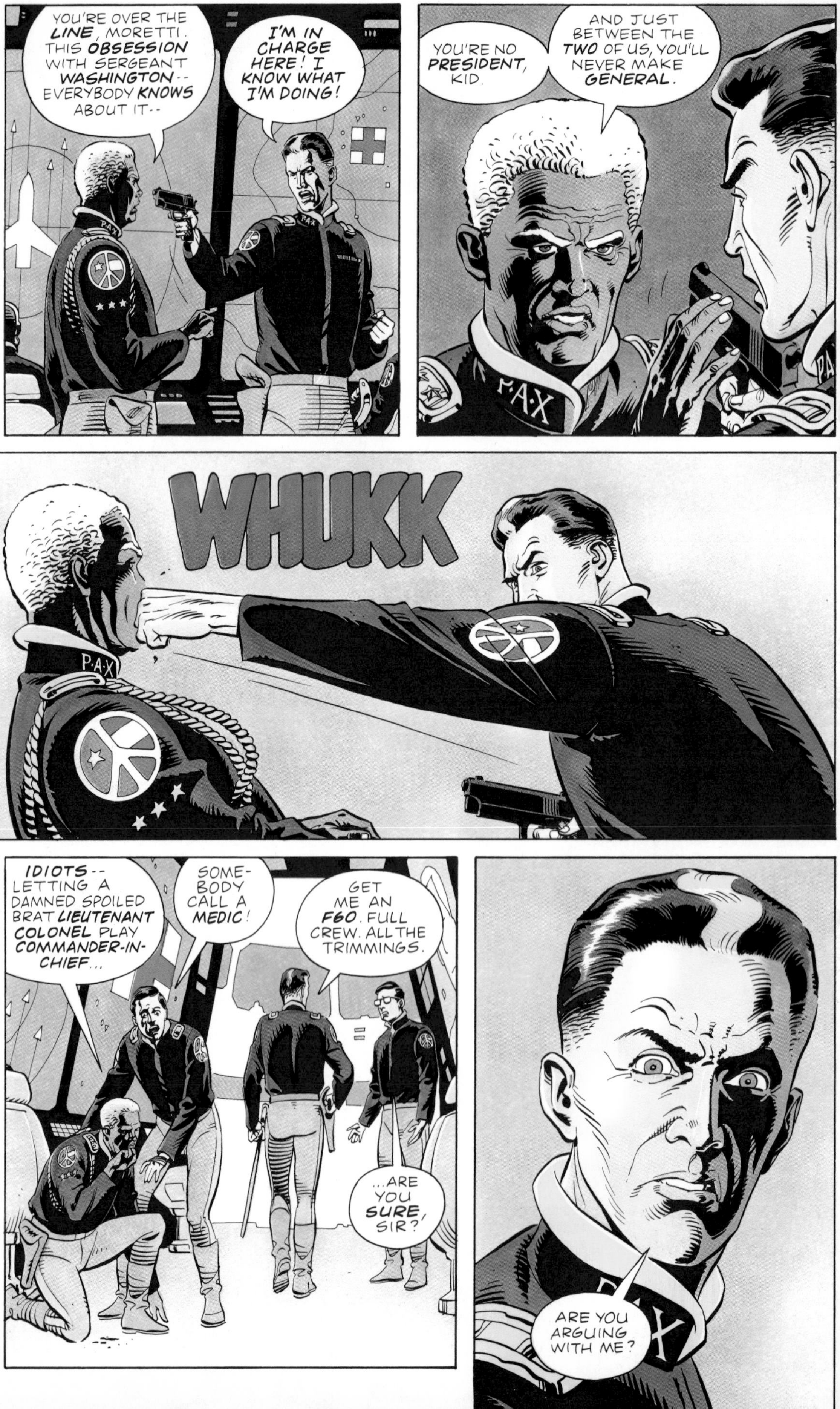

YOU'RE OVER THE LINE, MORETTI. THIS OBSESSION WITH SERGEANT WASHINGTON -- EVERYBODY KNOWS ABOUT IT --
I'M IN CHARGE HERE! I KNOW WHAT I'M DOING!
P·A·X
YOU'RE NO PRESIDENT, KID.
AND JUST BETWEEN THE TWO OF US, YOU'LL NEVER MAKE GENERAL.
P·A·X
WHUKK
P·A·X
IDIOTS -- LETTING A DAMNED SPOILED BRAT LIEUTENANT COLONEL PLAY COMMANDER-IN-CHIEF...
SOME-BODY CALL A MEDIC!
GET ME AN F60. FULL CREW. ALL THE TRIMMINGS.
...ARE YOU SURE, SIR?
ARE YOU ARGUING WITH ME?

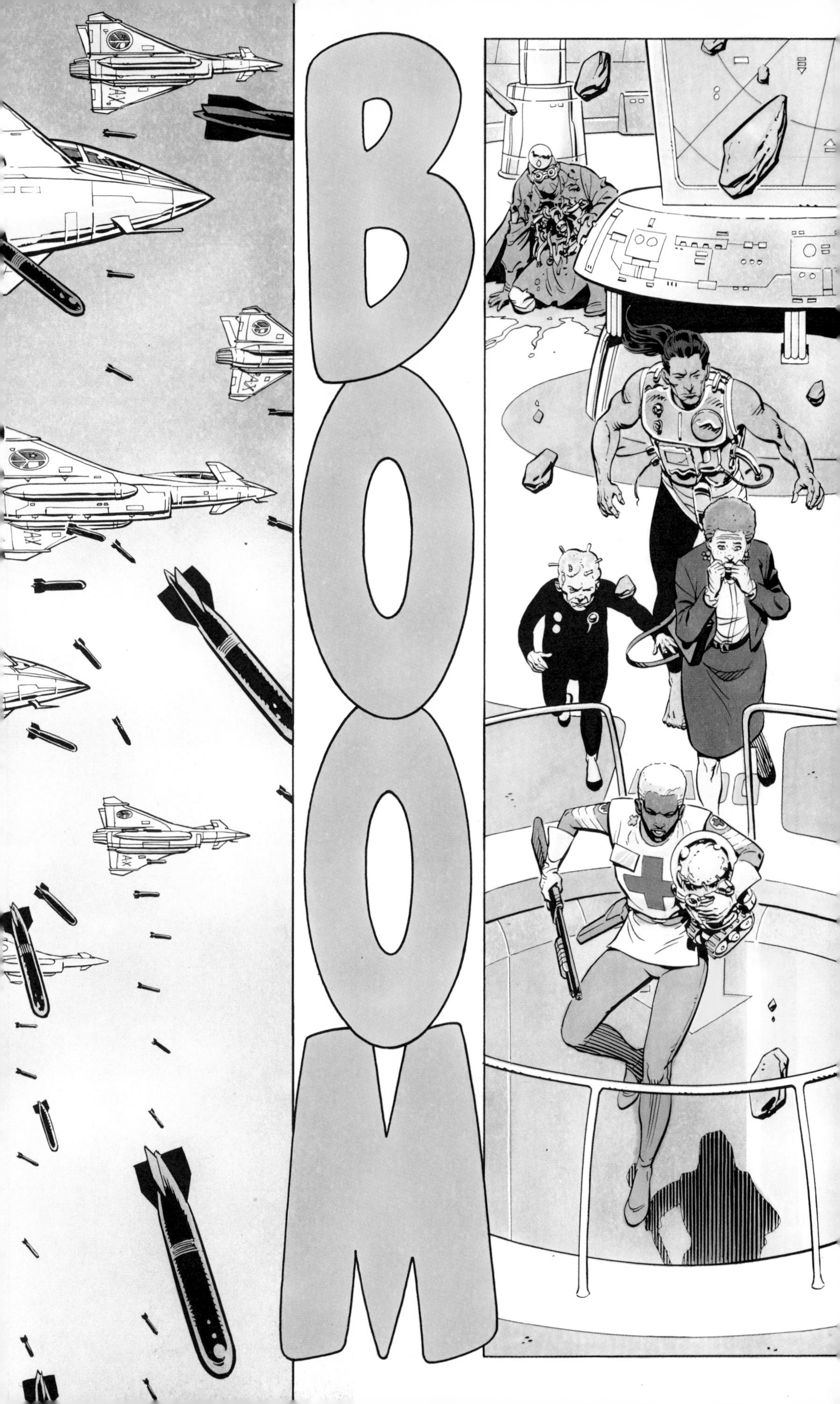
BOOM

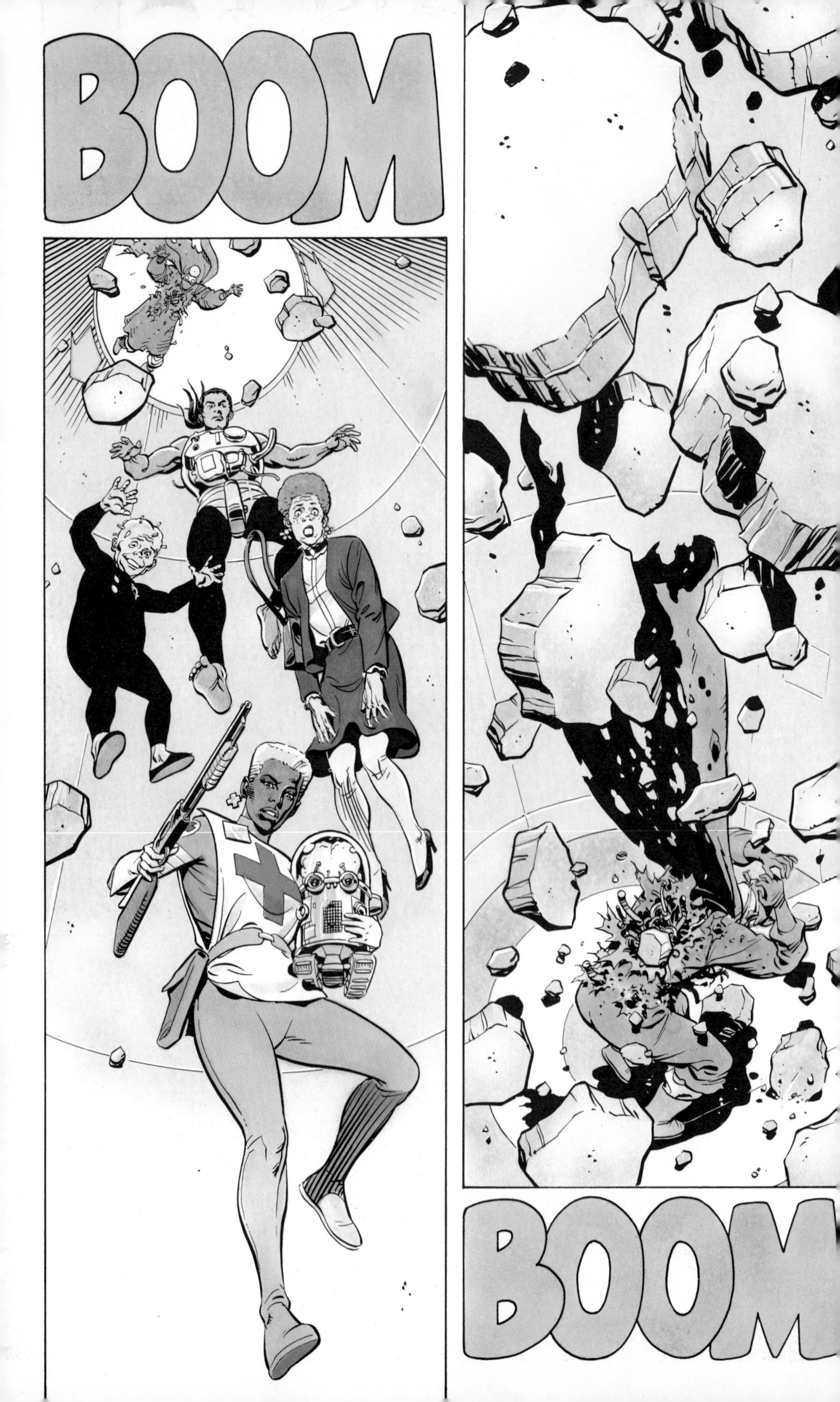
BOOM
BOOM

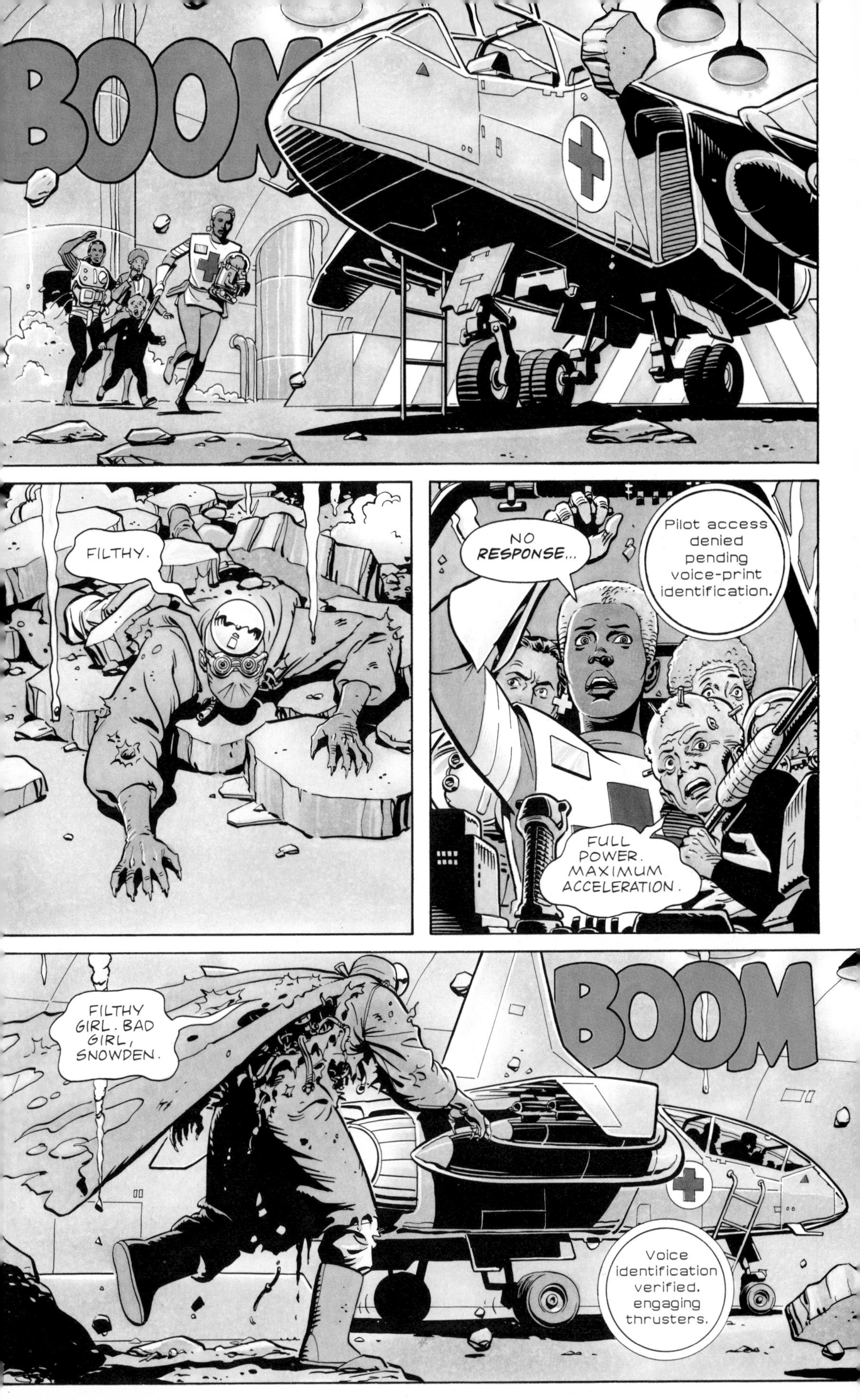
BOOM
FILTHY.
NO RESPONSE...
Pilot access denied pending voice-print identification.
FULL POWER. MAXIMUM ACCELERATION.
FILTHY GIRL. BAD GIRL, SNOWDEN.
BOOM
Voice identification verified. engaging thrusters.

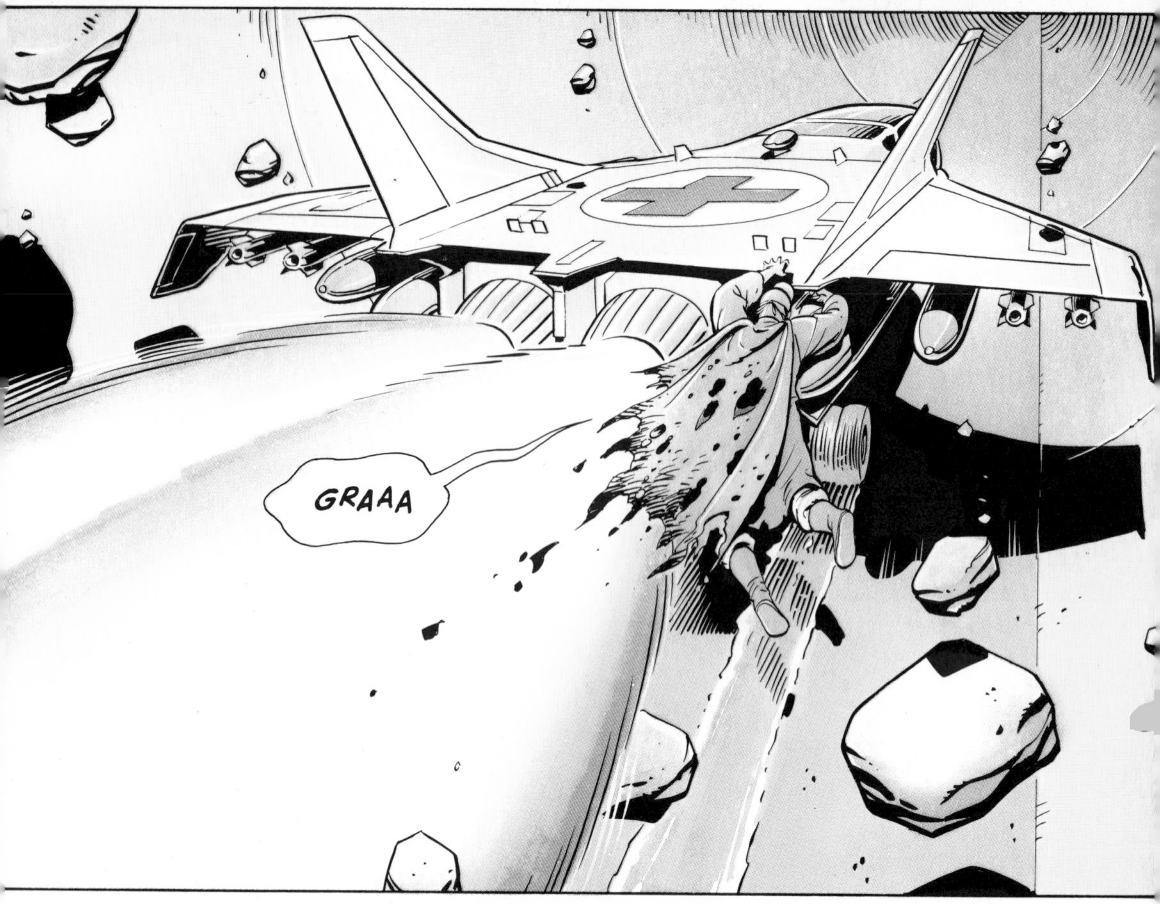
GRAAA

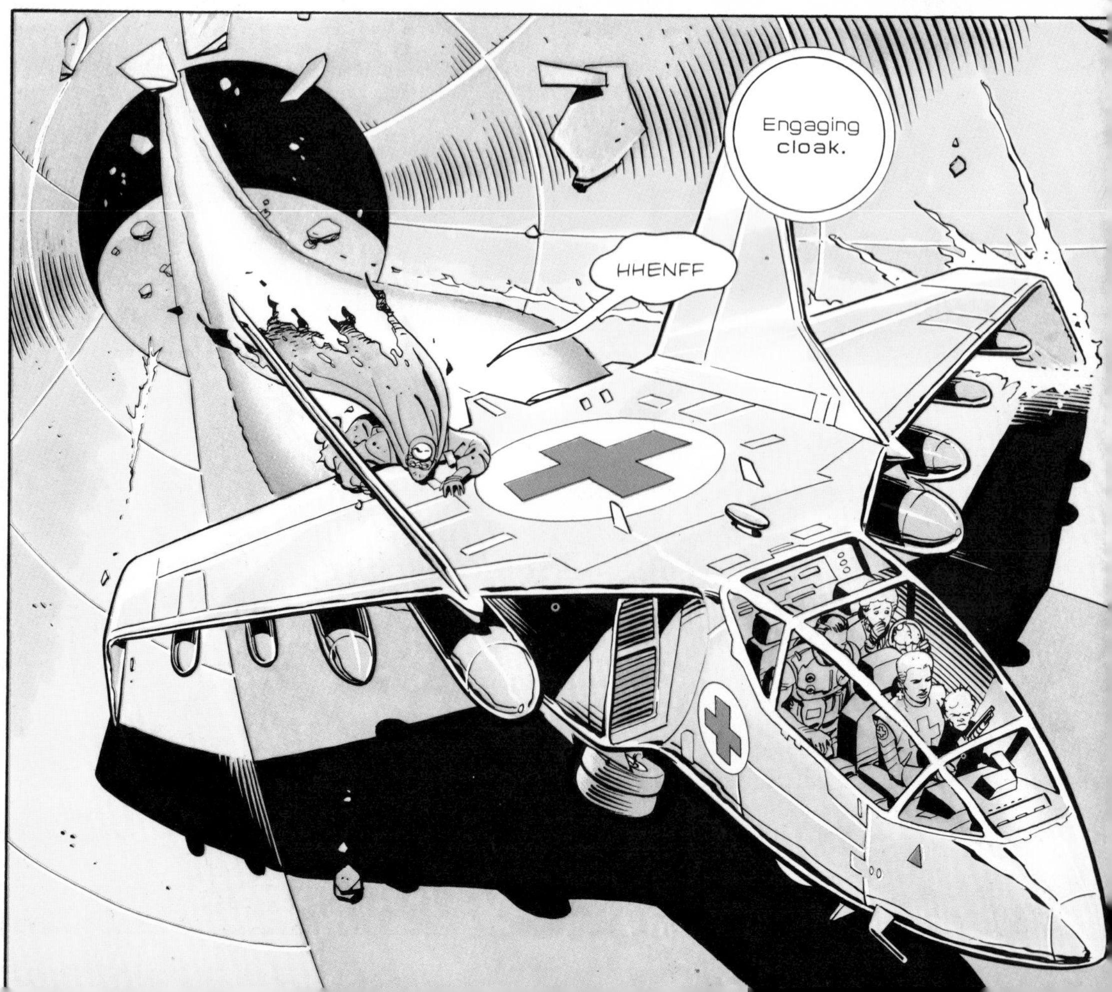
Engaging cloak.
HHENFF

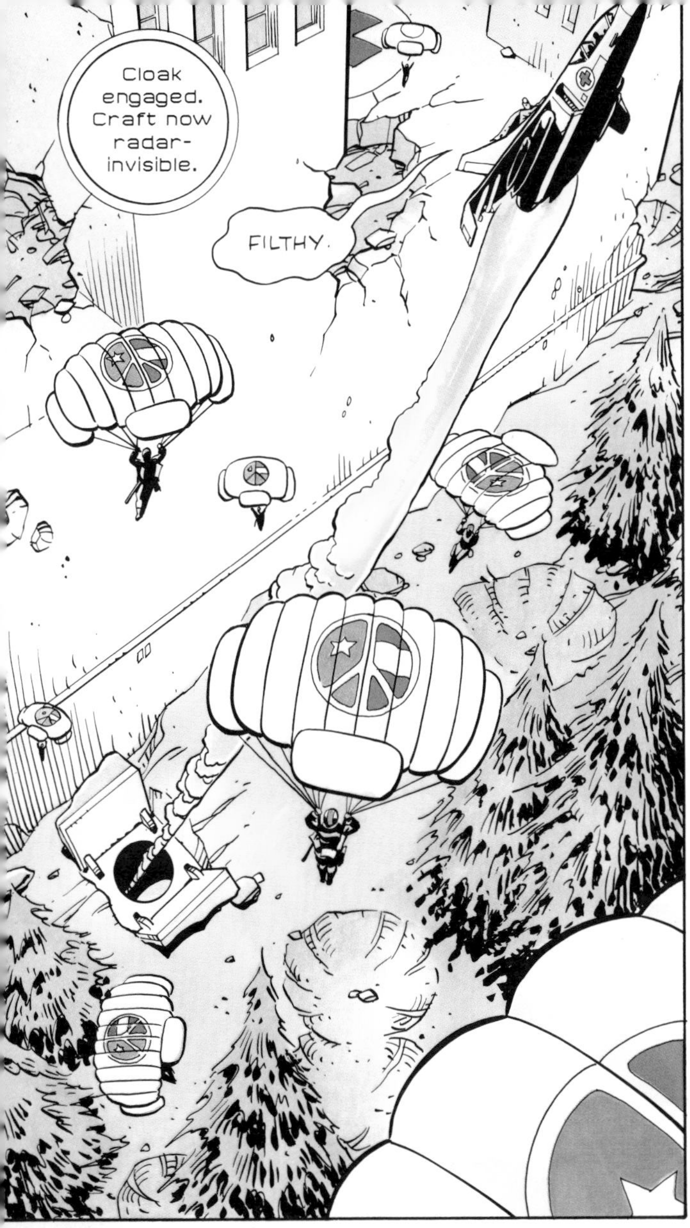
Cloak engaged. Craft now radar-invisible.
FILTHY.

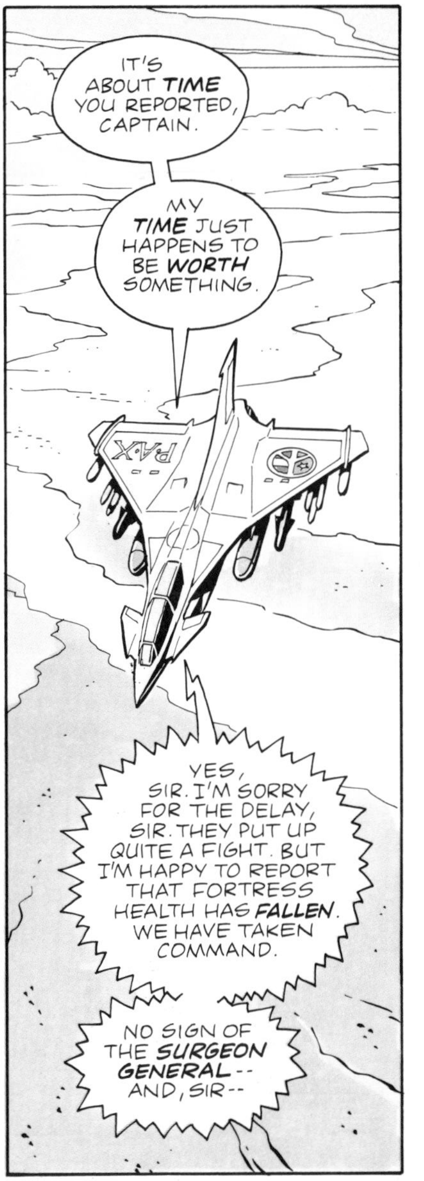
IT'S ABOUT **TIME** YOU REPORTED, CAPTAIN.
MY **TIME** JUST HAPPENS TO BE **WORTH** SOMETHING.
P·A·X
YES, SIR. I'M SORRY FOR THE DELAY, SIR. THEY PUT UP QUITE A FIGHT. BUT I'M HAPPY TO REPORT THAT FORTRESS HEALTH HAS **FALLEN**. WE HAVE TAKEN COMMAND.
NO SIGN OF THE ***SURGEON GENERAL***-- AND, SIR--

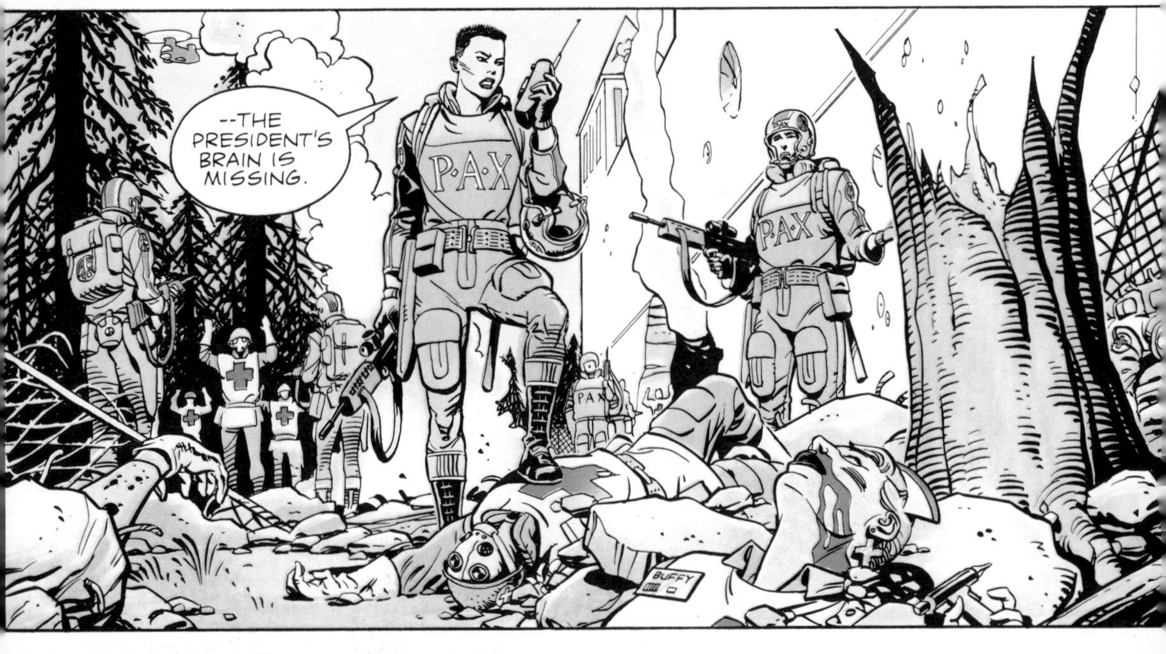
--THE PRESIDENT'S BRAIN IS MISSING.
P·A·X
P·A·X
BUFFY

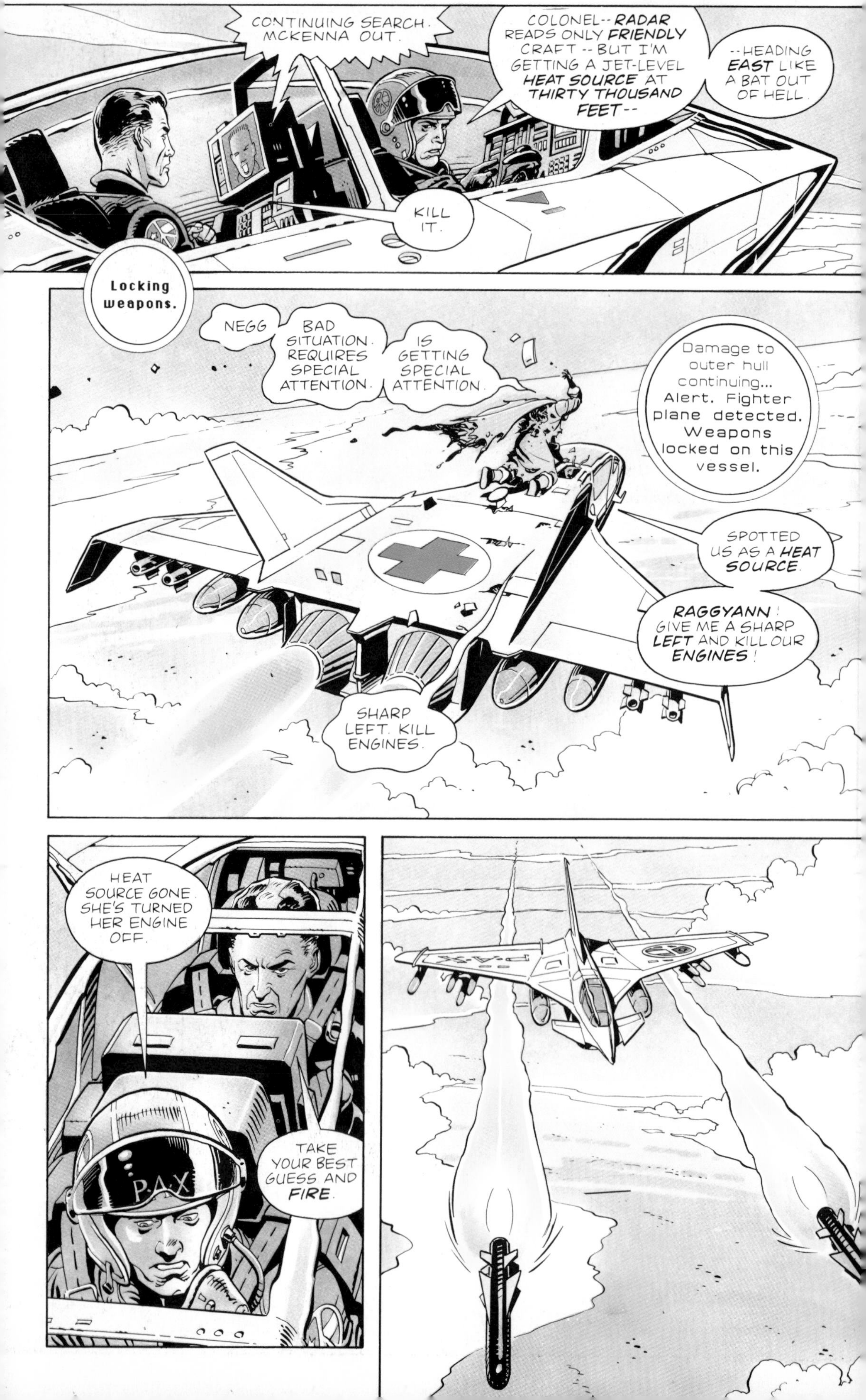
CONTINUING SEARCH. MCKENNA OUT.
COLONEL--RADAR READS ONLY FRIENDLY CRAFT -- BUT I'M GETTING A JET-LEVEL HEAT SOURCE AT THIRTY THOUSAND FEET--
--HEADING EAST LIKE A BAT OUT OF HELL.
KILL IT.
Locking weapons.
NEGG
BAD SITUATION. REQUIRES SPECIAL ATTENTION.
IS GETTING SPECIAL ATTENTION.
Damage to outer hull continuing... Alert. Fighter plane detected. Weapons locked on this vessel.
SPOTTED US AS A HEAT SOURCE.
RAGGYANN! GIVE ME A SHARP LEFT AND KILL OUR ENGINES!
SHARP LEFT. KILL ENGINES.
HEAT SOURCE GONE. SHE'S TURNED HER ENGINE OFF.
TAKE YOUR BEST GUESS AND FIRE.
P.A.X

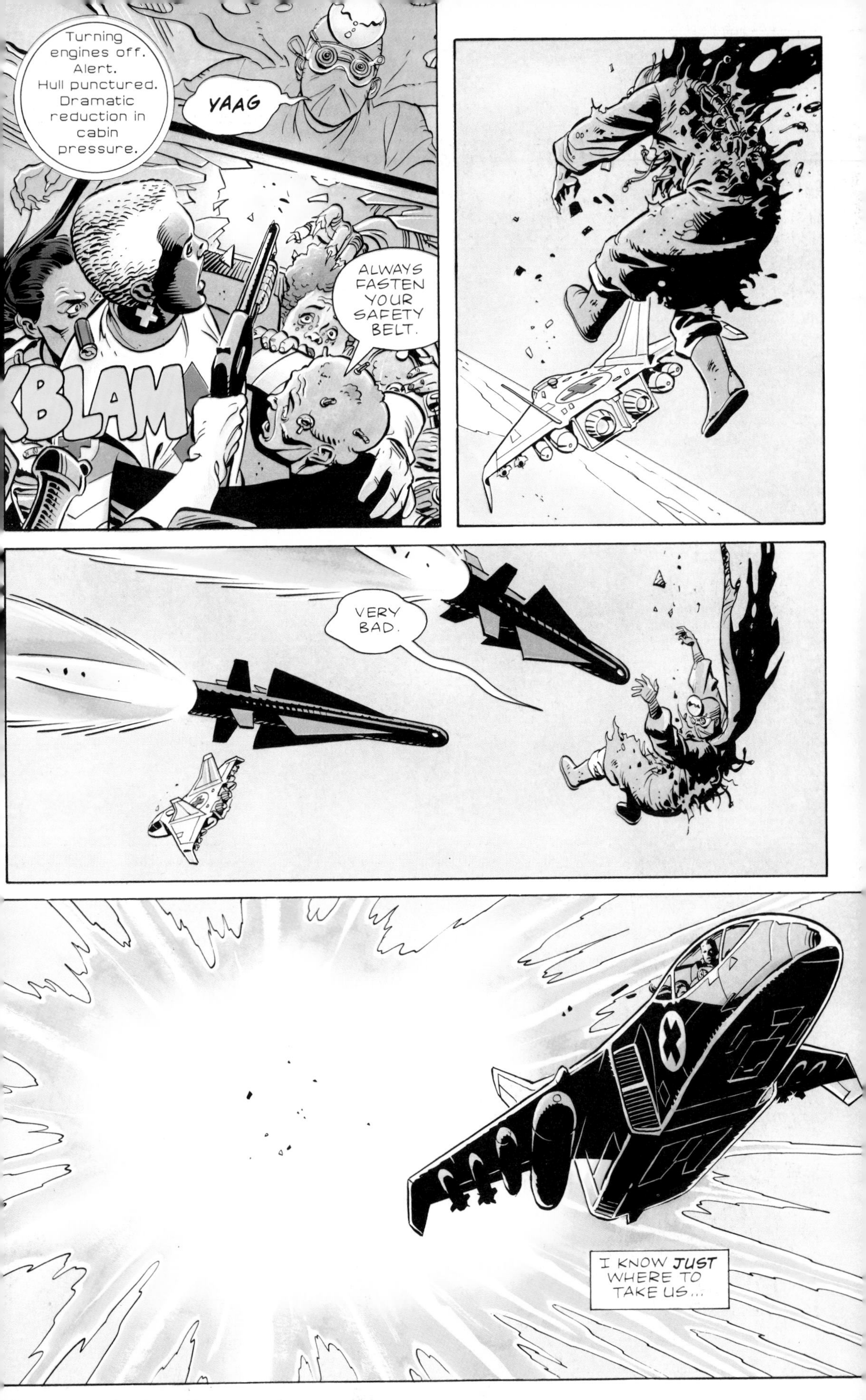

Turning engines off. Alert. Hull punctured. Dramatic reduction in cabin pressure.
YAAG
KBLAM
ALWAYS FASTEN YOUR SAFETY BELT.
VERY BAD.
I KNOW JUST WHERE TO TAKE US...

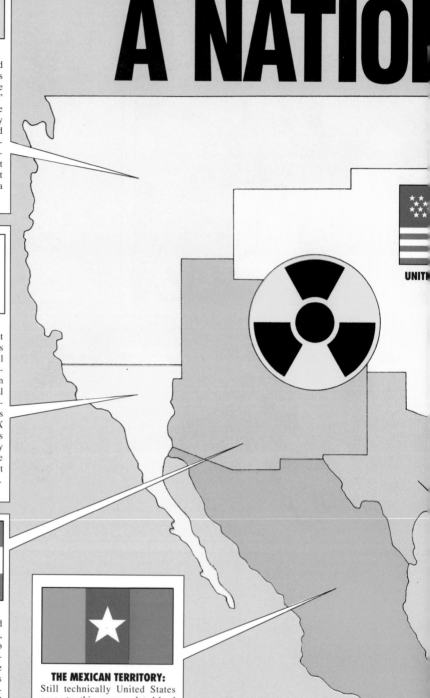

A NATIOI

GOD'S COUNTRY:

The coalition government formed by the Surgeon General and leaders of the New Calvinist Initiative pledges to "lay waste to the impure" and create a smoke-free, drug-free paradise." Prohibited under penalty of death: "bad music, bad food, bad language, contraception, pornography, and adultery." 50,000 battle-hardened Health Enforcement Troops and Pacific Northwest nuclear missile silos provide a formidable military capability.

WONDERLAND:

The world's largest entertainment complex, it used to be the nation's playground. But funny animal robots are on the warpath demanding "cultural autonomy" and an "end to the enslavement of artificial intelligence." Rumors of mass murder and subjugation of humans remain unconfirmed. Should PAX assault Wonderland, a hostage crisis of unheard-of proportions is a likely scenario. Implementation of the "No holds Barred" Amendment could result in the death of millions.

REAL AMERICA:

Fat Boy Burger troops surround multimillion-acre cattlefields, breeding, slaughtering and selling to beef-hungry clients in flagrant defiance of the 94th Amendment. The outlaw fast food conglomerate is well-equipped to defend its territory: its million man army and formidable air force were almost a match for PAX in the Amazon War.

THE MEXICAN TERRITORY:

Still technically United States property, this overpopulated land openly trades with Real America and is Fat Boy's chief source of inexpensive labor. Satellite photos reveal hundreds of illegal cattle-fields, so many that analysts have stopped calling the territory "America's Ireland"; now it's "Burger Heaven." Anti-American sentiment is high, and Mexican-born PAX officers are joining the Fat Boy army in droves. An alliance between the two powers would present an unspeakable threat to the U.S. sovereignty over North America.

UNITE

DIVIDED

THE NEW ENGLAND FEDERATION OF STATES:

Militarily weak, this is the most pacifistic of the new governments, and the most likely to seek reunification with the U.S. Sticking point: the Federation seeks to repeal nearly every Constitutional Amendment passed since 1990. And those Green Mountain eggheads who engineered the schiz-out of the IRS Database in 2009 are bound to be up to more mischief than ever.

THE EAST COAST CAPITALIST DICTATORSHIP

Manhattan strongman Edward Beluga represents no major threat at present to U.S. security. Though strong in conventional forces, Beluga commands no nuclear, chemical or biological capability as yet. Besides, he has his hands full: his troops, weary from the year long Manhattan-Brooklyn War are now fighting block by block against the white gay racist Aryan Thrust, the Black Supremacy Front, and as many as fifty other separatist movements.

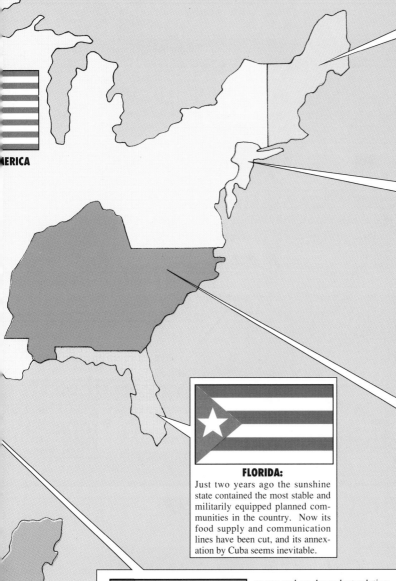

ERICA

FLORIDA:

Just two years ago the sunshine state contained the most stable and militarily equipped planned communities in the country. Now its food supply and communication lines have been cut, and its annexation by Cuba seems inevitable.

THE FIRST SEX CONFEDERACY:

Former First Lady Amanda Nissen, declaring that "everything wrong in the world has been caused by men," emerged as leader in the powerful Southeast Women's Movement, uniting its warring factions to overthrow the governments of the Old South. In her first address, she hit an encouraging note, assuring the U.S. that the Confederacy will seek diplomatic relationships and free trade. The South's abundant farmlands offer a crucial supply of food. Borders remain closed at present to male U.S. citizens. Nissen ordered bans on pornography, marriage, sexist remarks, and "negative role models" in entertainment. Missile silos in the area are abundant but in poor repair. However, a single orbiting laser cannon now answers directly to Nissen, discouraging invasion by PAX.

THE LONE STAR REPUBLIC:

Texas holds fast to its borders—and to its habits. With a platform of "Guns, beef, and beer" Dallas dentist Billy Bob Coolant established a government based on "community standards," rejecting the First, Fifth, and 94th Amendments out of hand. Their warm and co-dependant relationship with Fat Boy Burgers leaves little room for doubt whose side they would stand on if war breaks out between Fat Boy and PAX. Only Texan hatred of Fat Boy porn movies and continuing border skirmishes with the Mexican Territory prevent a full-fledged alliance. Texas commands a 300,000 man army and possesses first-strike nuclear capability on every city in the western hemisphere. The next American president will have to weigh carefully Texan displeasure with the U.S. Constitution as written.

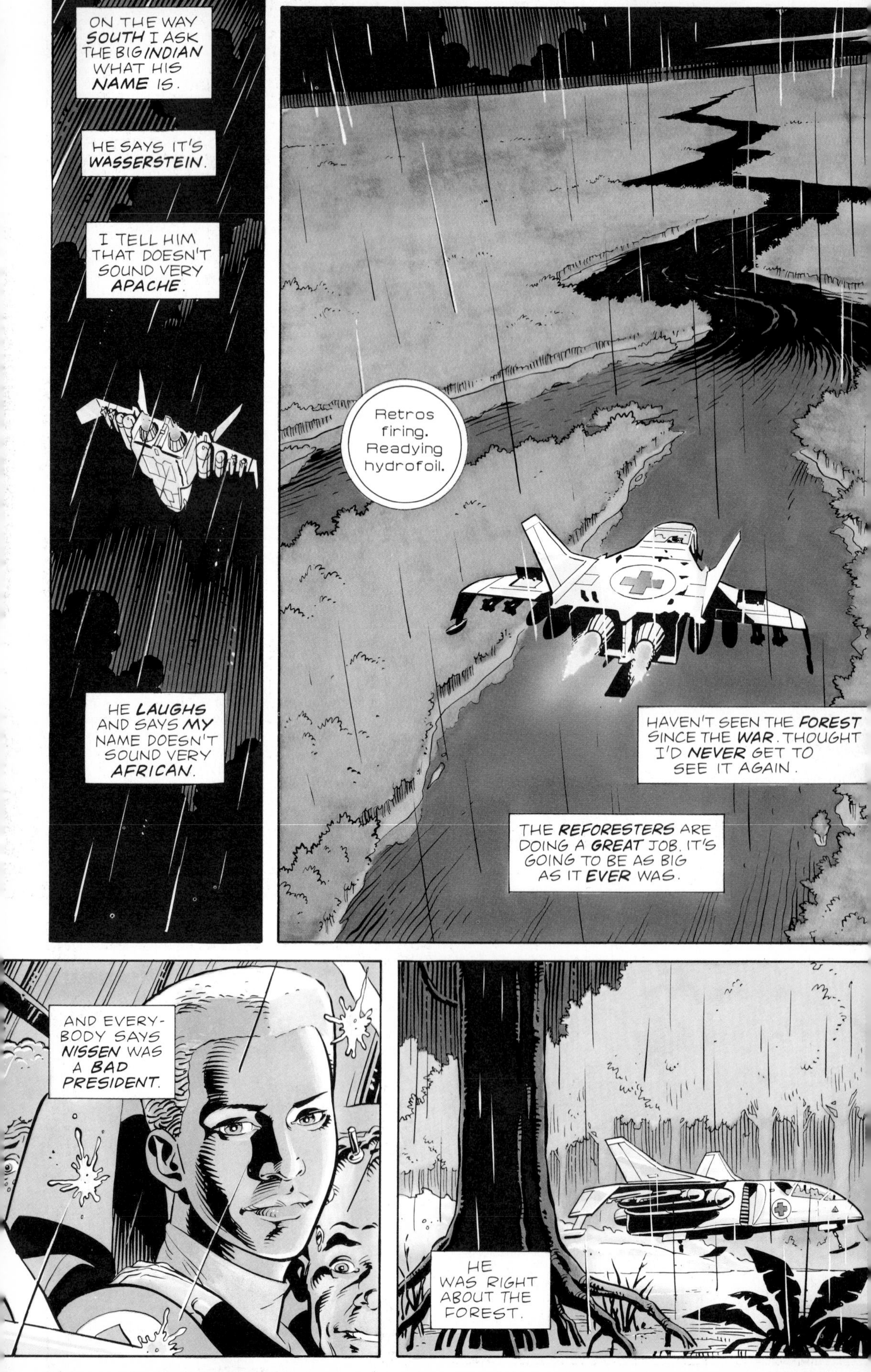

ON THE WAY SOUTH I ASK THE BIG INDIAN WHAT HIS NAME IS.
HE SAYS IT'S WASSERSTEIN.
I TELL HIM THAT DOESN'T SOUND VERY APACHE.
HE LAUGHS AND SAYS MY NAME DOESN'T SOUND VERY AFRICAN.
Retros firing. Readying hydrofoil.
HAVEN'T SEEN THE FOREST SINCE THE WAR. THOUGHT I'D NEVER GET TO SEE IT AGAIN.
THE REFORESTERS ARE DOING A GREAT JOB. IT'S GOING TO BE AS BIG AS IT EVER WAS.
AND EVERYBODY SAYS NISSEN WAS A BAD PRESIDENT.
HE WAS RIGHT ABOUT THE FOREST.

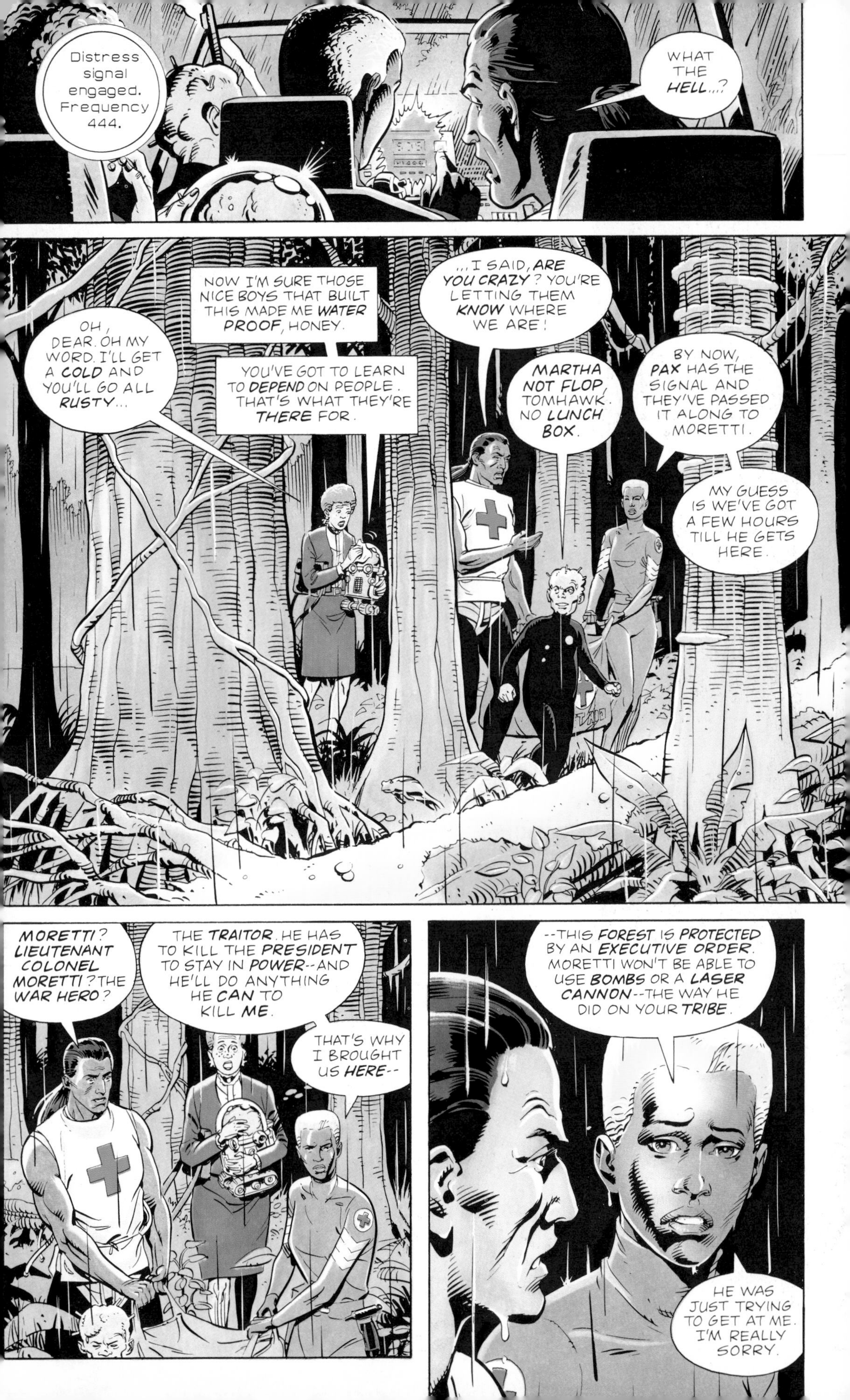
Distress signal engaged. Frequency 444.
WHAT THE HELL...?
NOW I'M SURE THOSE NICE BOYS THAT BUILT THIS MADE ME WATER PROOF, HONEY.
OH, DEAR. OH MY WORD. I'LL GET A COLD AND YOU'LL GO ALL RUSTY...
YOU'VE GOT TO LEARN TO DEPEND ON PEOPLE. THAT'S WHAT THEY'RE THERE FOR.
...I SAID, ARE YOU CRAZY? YOU'RE LETTING THEM KNOW WHERE WE ARE!
MARTHA NOT FLOP, TOMHAWK. NO LUNCH BOX.
BY NOW, PAX HAS THE SIGNAL AND THEY'VE PASSED IT ALONG TO MORETTI.
MY GUESS IS WE'VE GOT A FEW HOURS TILL HE GETS HERE.
MORETTI? LIEUTENANT COLONEL MORETTI? THE WAR HERO?
THE TRAITOR. HE HAS TO KILL THE PRESIDENT TO STAY IN POWER--AND HE'LL DO ANYTHING HE CAN TO KILL ME.
THAT'S WHY I BROUGHT US HERE--
--THIS FOREST IS PROTECTED BY AN EXECUTIVE ORDER. MORETTI WON'T BE ABLE TO USE BOMBS OR A LASER CANNON--THE WAY HE DID ON YOUR TRIBE.
HE WAS JUST TRYING TO GET AT ME. I'M REALLY SORRY.

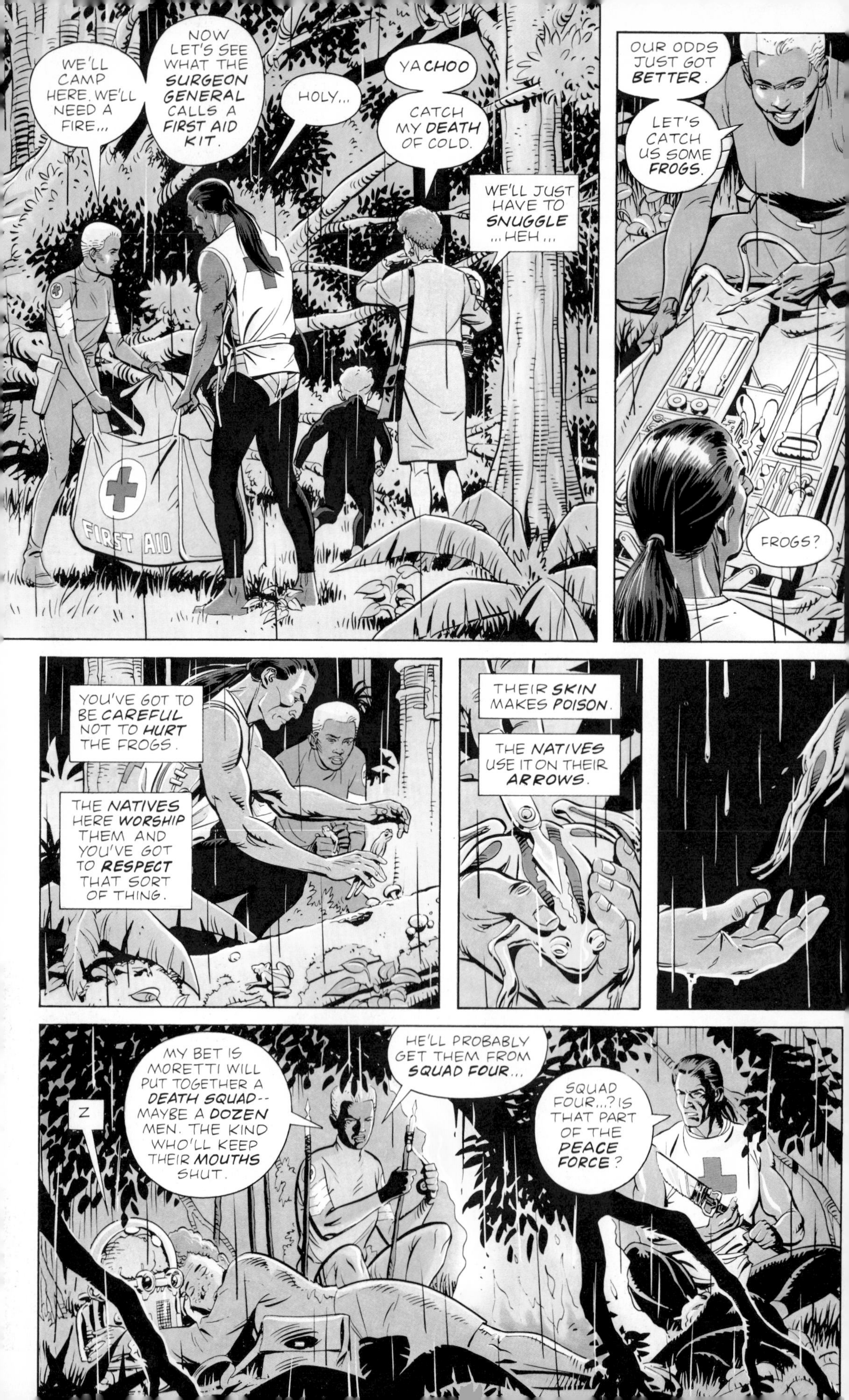
WE'LL CAMP HERE. WE'LL NEED A FIRE...
NOW LET'S SEE WHAT THE SURGEON GENERAL CALLS A FIRST AID KIT.
HOLY...
YACHOO
CATCH MY DEATH OF COLD.
WE'LL JUST HAVE TO SNUGGLE ...HEH...
FIRST AID
OUR ODDS JUST GOT BETTER.
LET'S CATCH US SOME FROGS.
FROGS?
YOU'VE GOT TO BE CAREFUL NOT TO HURT THE FROGS.
THE NATIVES HERE WORSHIP THEM AND YOU'VE GOT TO RESPECT THAT SORT OF THING.
THEIR SKIN MAKES POISON.
THE NATIVES USE IT ON THEIR ARROWS.
Z
MY BET IS MORETTI WILL PUT TOGETHER A DEATH SQUAD-- MAYBE A DOZEN MEN. THE KIND WHO'LL KEEP THEIR MOUTHS SHUT.
HE'LL PROBABLY GET THEM FROM SQUAD FOUR...
SQUAD FOUR...? IS THAT PART OF THE PEACE FORCE?

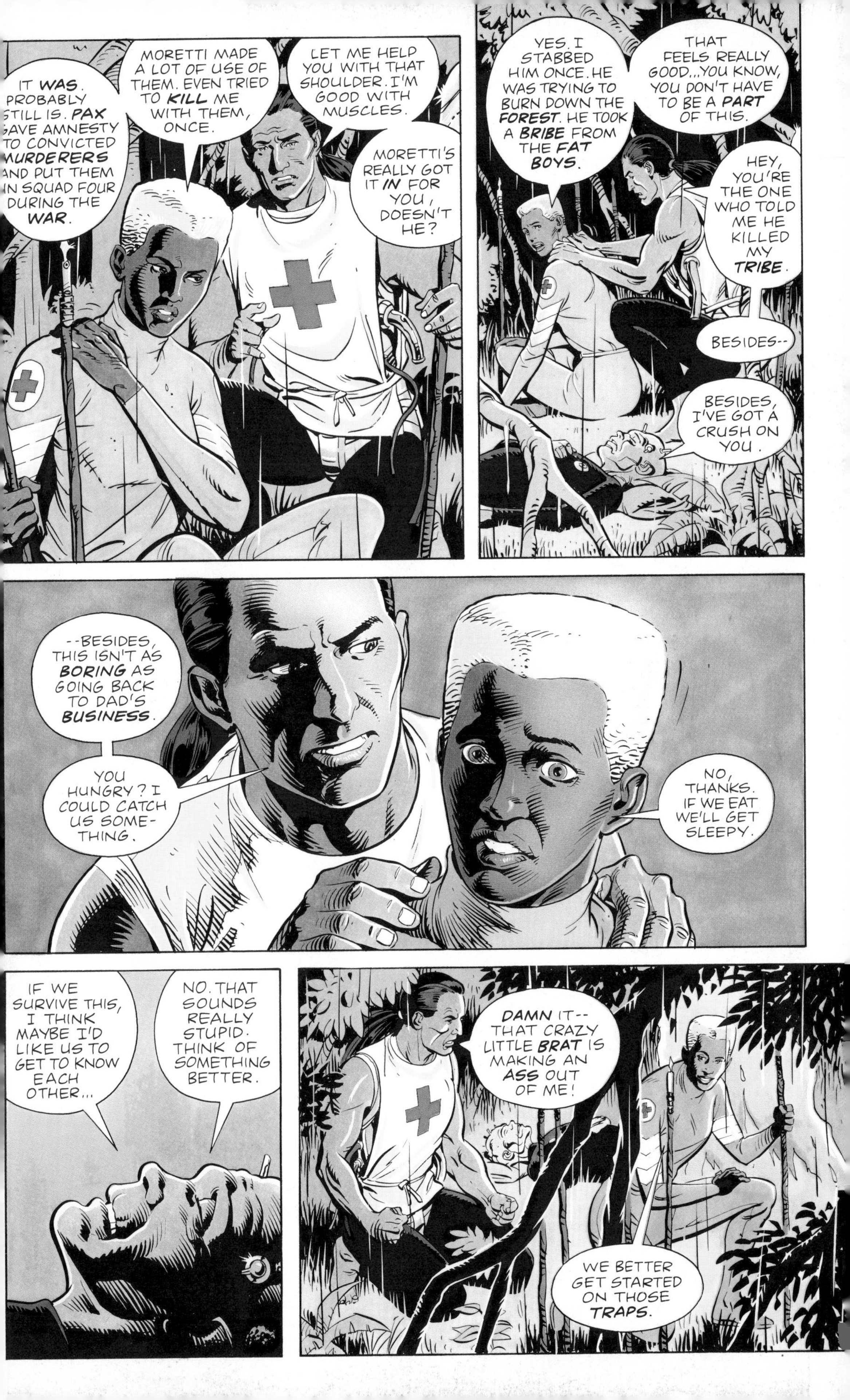

IT WAS. PROBABLY STILL IS. PAX GAVE AMNESTY TO CONVICTED MURDERERS AND PUT THEM IN SQUAD FOUR DURING THE WAR.
MORETTI MADE A LOT OF USE OF THEM. EVEN TRIED TO KILL ME WITH THEM, ONCE.
LET ME HELP YOU WITH THAT SHOULDER. I'M GOOD WITH MUSCLES.
MORETTI'S REALLY GOT IT IN FOR YOU, DOESN'T HE?
YES. I STABBED HIM ONCE. HE WAS TRYING TO BURN DOWN THE FOREST. HE TOOK A BRIBE FROM THE FAT BOYS.
THAT FEELS REALLY GOOD... YOU KNOW, YOU DON'T HAVE TO BE A PART OF THIS.
HEY, YOU'RE THE ONE WHO TOLD ME HE KILLED MY TRIBE.
BESIDES--
BESIDES, I'VE GOT A CRUSH ON YOU.
--BESIDES, THIS ISN'T AS BORING AS GOING BACK TO DAD'S BUSINESS.
YOU HUNGRY? I COULD CATCH US SOME-THING.
NO, THANKS. IF WE EAT WE'LL GET SLEEPY.
IF WE SURVIVE THIS, I THINK MAYBE I'D LIKE US TO GET TO KNOW EACH OTHER...
NO. THAT SOUNDS REALLY STUPID. THINK OF SOMETHING BETTER.
DAMN IT-- THAT CRAZY LITTLE BRAT IS MAKING AN ASS OUT OF ME!
WE BETTER GET STARTED ON THOSE TRAPS.

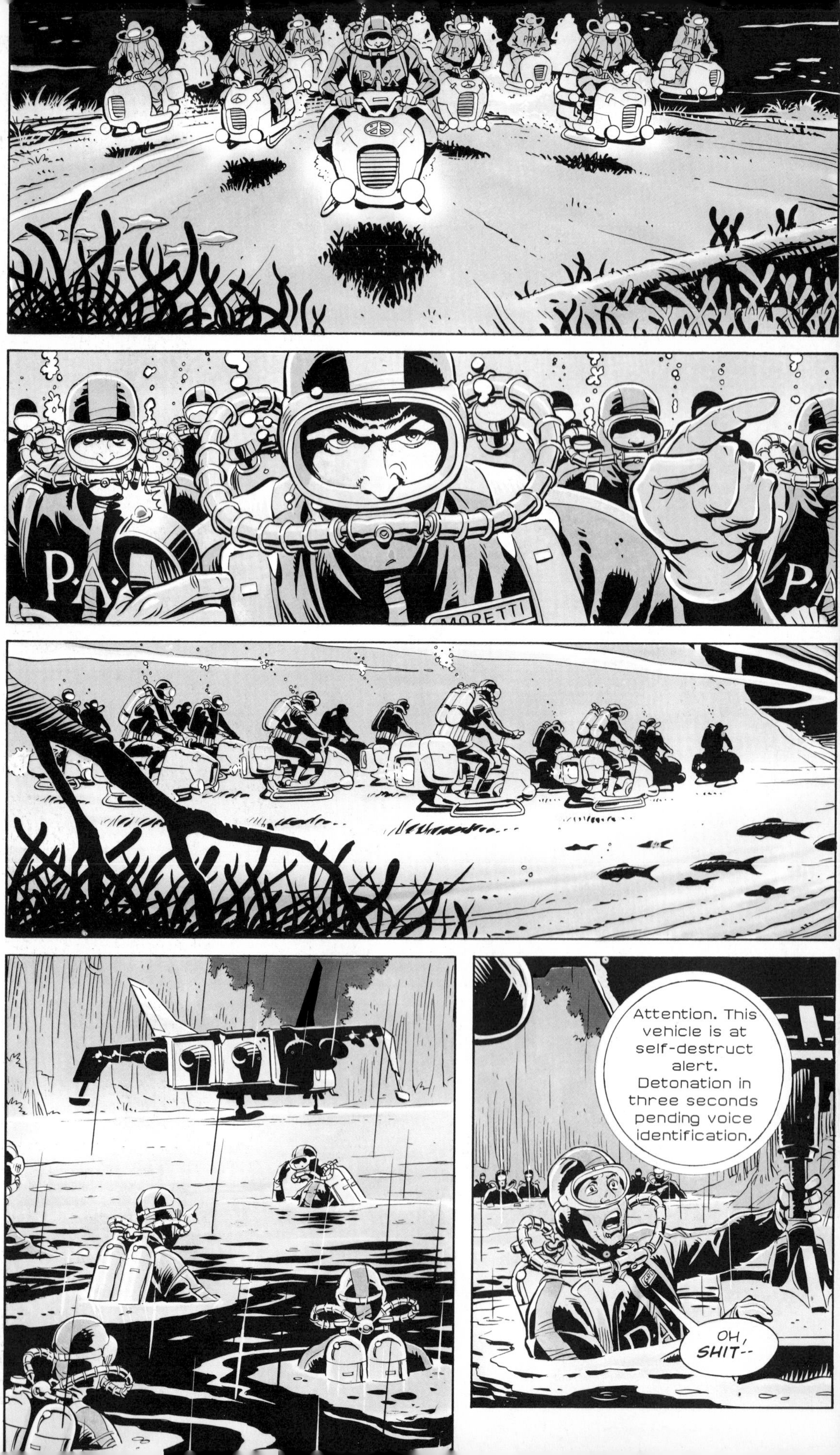
P.A.X
MORETTI
Attention. This vehicle is at self-destruct alert. Detonation in three seconds pending voice identification.
OH, SHIT--

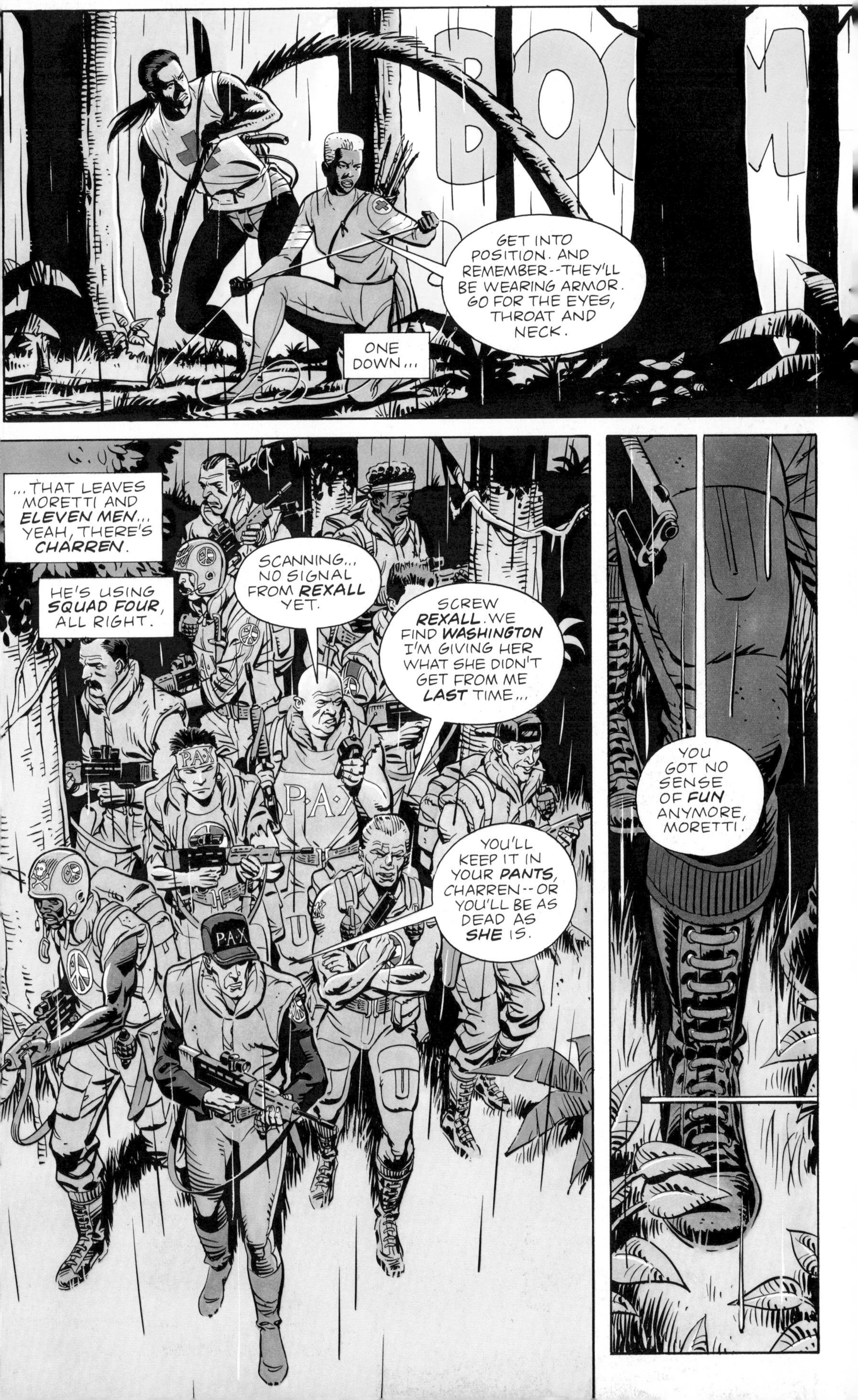
BOOM
GET INTO POSITION. AND REMEMBER--THEY'LL BE WEARING ARMOR. GO FOR THE EYES, THROAT AND NECK.
ONE DOWN...
...THAT LEAVES MORETTI AND ELEVEN MEN... YEAH, THERE'S CHARREN.
HE'S USING SQUAD FOUR, ALL RIGHT.
SCANNING... NO SIGNAL FROM REXALL YET.
SCREW REXALL. WE FIND WASHINGTON I'M GIVING HER WHAT SHE DIDN'T GET FROM ME LAST TIME...
YOU'LL KEEP IT IN YOUR PANTS, CHARREN--OR YOU'LL BE AS DEAD AS SHE IS.
YOU GOT NO SENSE OF FUN ANYMORE, MORETTI.

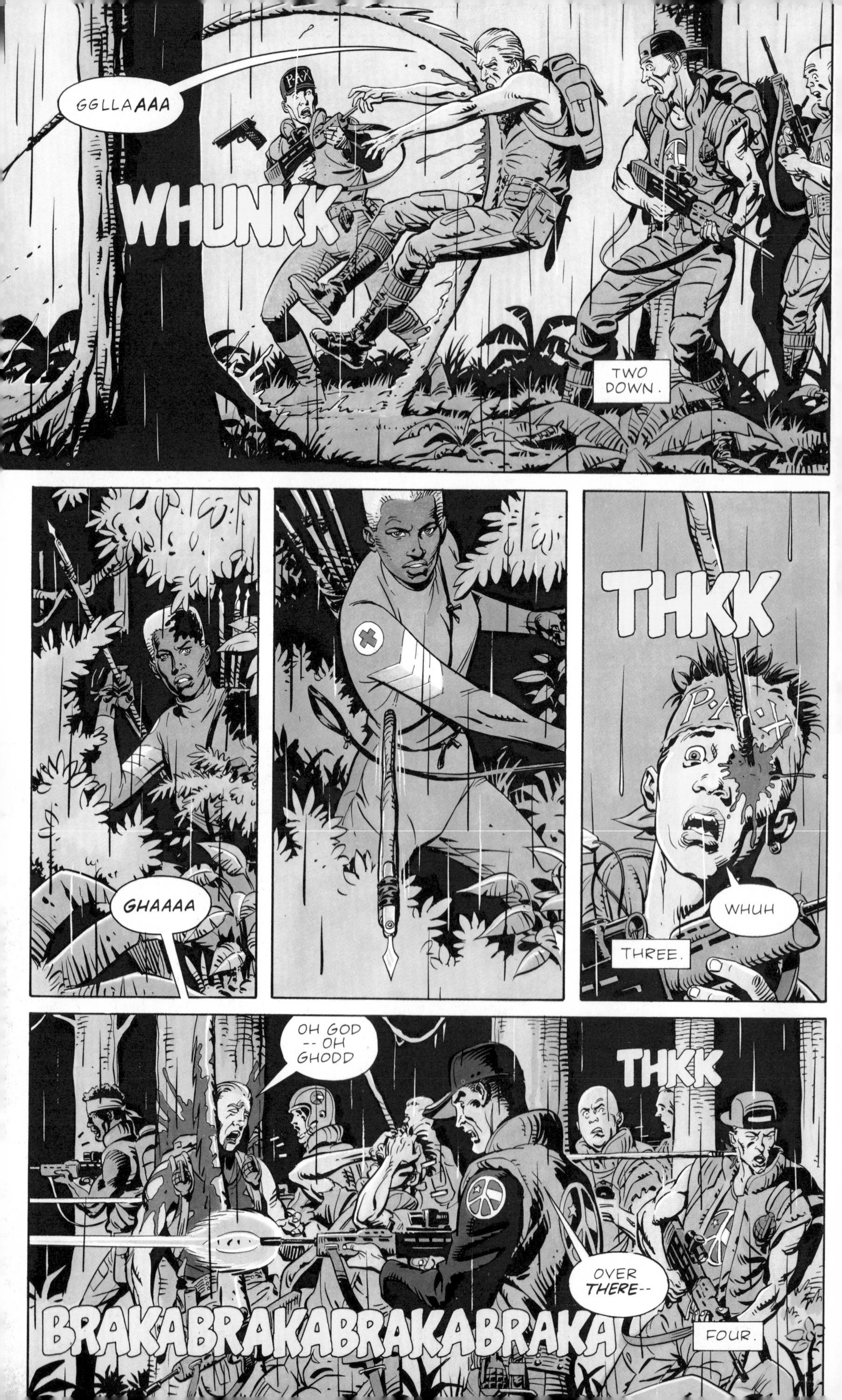
GGLLAAAA
WHUNKK
TWO DOWN.
GHAAAA
THKK
WHUH
THREE.
OH GOD -- OH GHODD
THKK
OVER THERE--
BRAKABRAKABRAKABRAKA
FOUR.

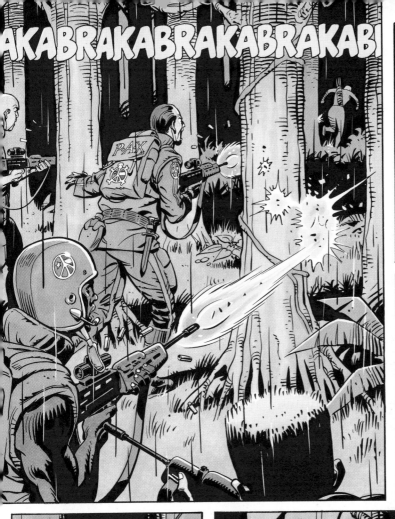

AKABRAKABRAKABRAKABI

OH NO.

NO.

SNAPP

FIVE.

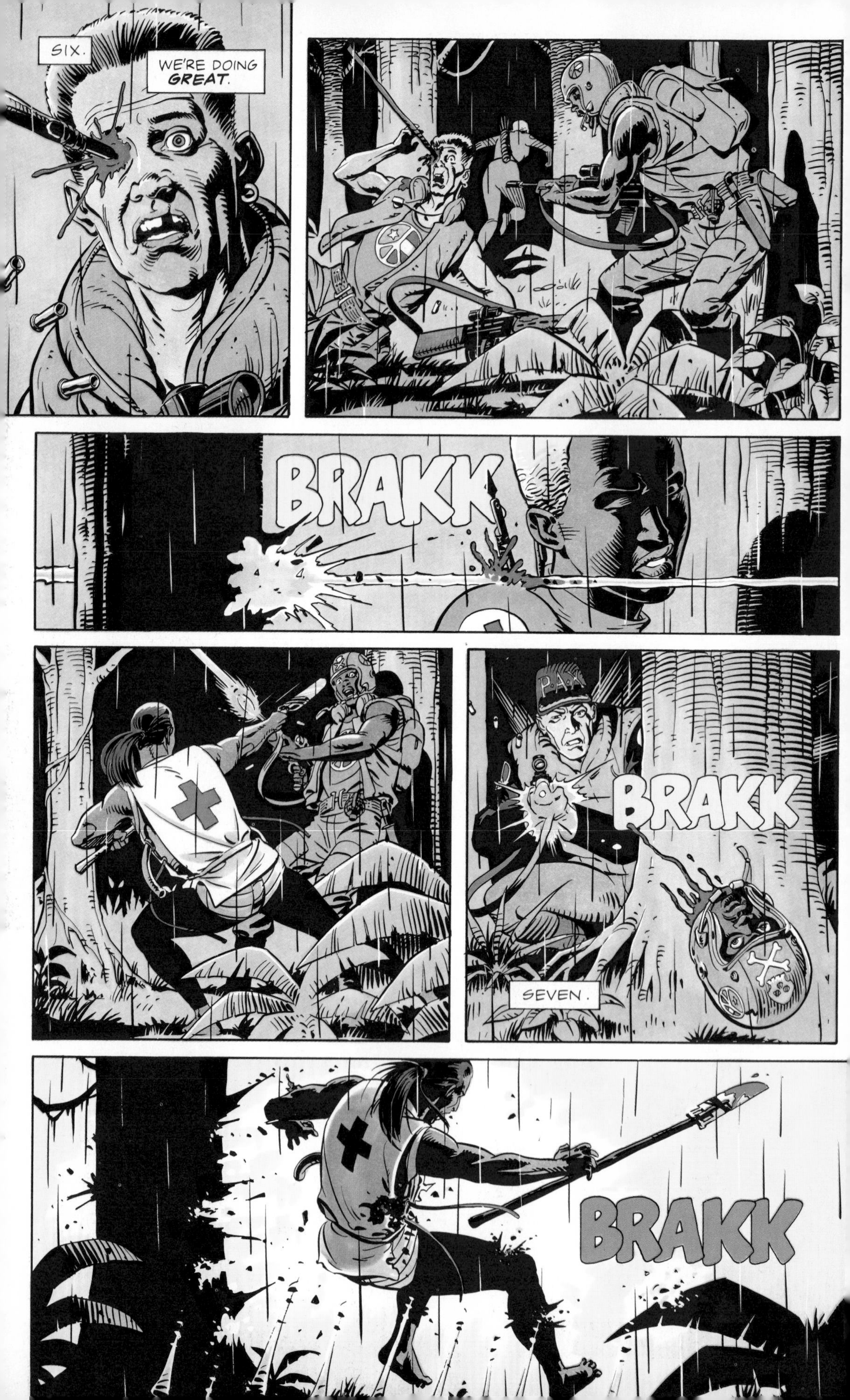
SIX.
WE'RE DOING GREAT.
BRAKK
BRAKK
P.A.X
SEVEN.
BRAKK

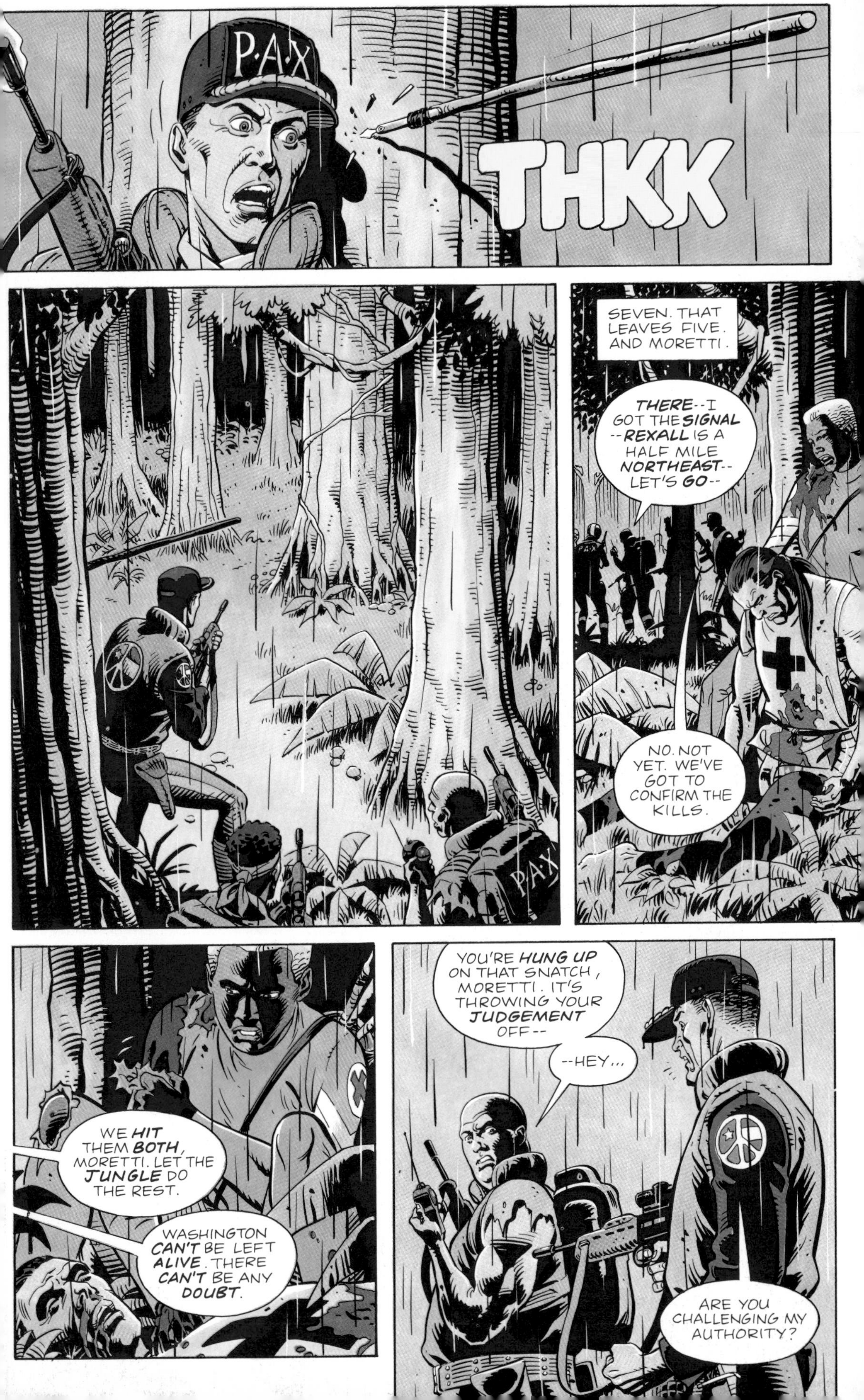
THKK
SEVEN. THAT LEAVES FIVE. AND MORETTI.
THERE--I GOT THE SIGNAL --REXALL IS A HALF MILE NORTHEAST-- LET'S GO--
NO. NOT YET. WE'VE GOT TO CONFIRM THE KILLS.
WE HIT THEM BOTH, MORETTI. LET THE JUNGLE DO THE REST.
WASHINGTON CAN'T BE LEFT ALIVE. THERE CAN'T BE ANY DOUBT.
YOU'RE HUNG UP ON THAT SNATCH, MORETTI. IT'S THROWING YOUR JUDGEMENT OFF--
--HEY...
ARE YOU CHALLENGING MY AUTHORITY?

NO, SIR. FOR THE RECORD, I AM NOT QUESTIONING YOUR AUTHORITY. WE WILL COMPLY WITH WHATEVER ORDER YOU CHOOSE TO GIVE.

...WE MOVE ON PRIMARY TARGET. REXALL. THEN A FINAL SWEEP OF THE AREA.

YES, SIR. WHATEVER YOU SAY.

LET'S *MOVE!*

YOU JUST HOLD ON. JUST HOLD ON. I'LL COME BACK FOR YOU.

SHOULDER'S NO GOOD. WON'T BE ABLE TO USE MY SLING.

NO. GUN'S NO GOOD.

HAVE TO USE THE *RAIN.*

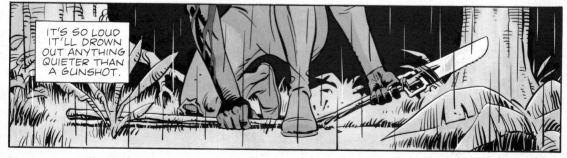

IT'S SO LOUD IT'LL DROWN OUT ANYTHING QUIETER THAN A GUNSHOT.

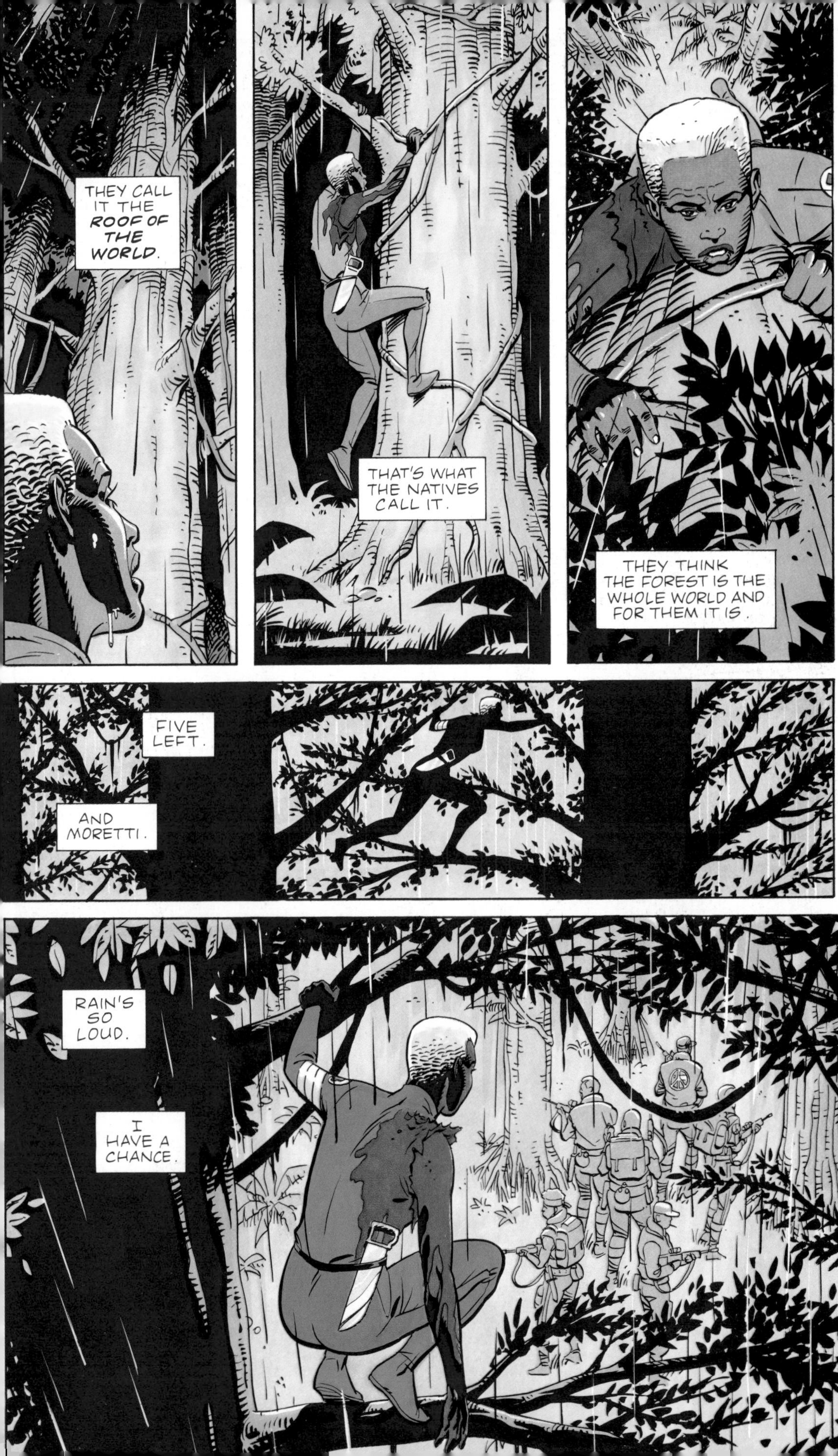
THEY CALL IT THE *ROOF OF THE WORLD*.
THAT'S WHAT THE NATIVES CALL IT.
THEY THINK THE FOREST IS THE WHOLE WORLD AND FOR THEM IT IS.
FIVE LEFT.
AND MORETTI.
RAIN'S SO LOUD.
I HAVE A CHANCE.

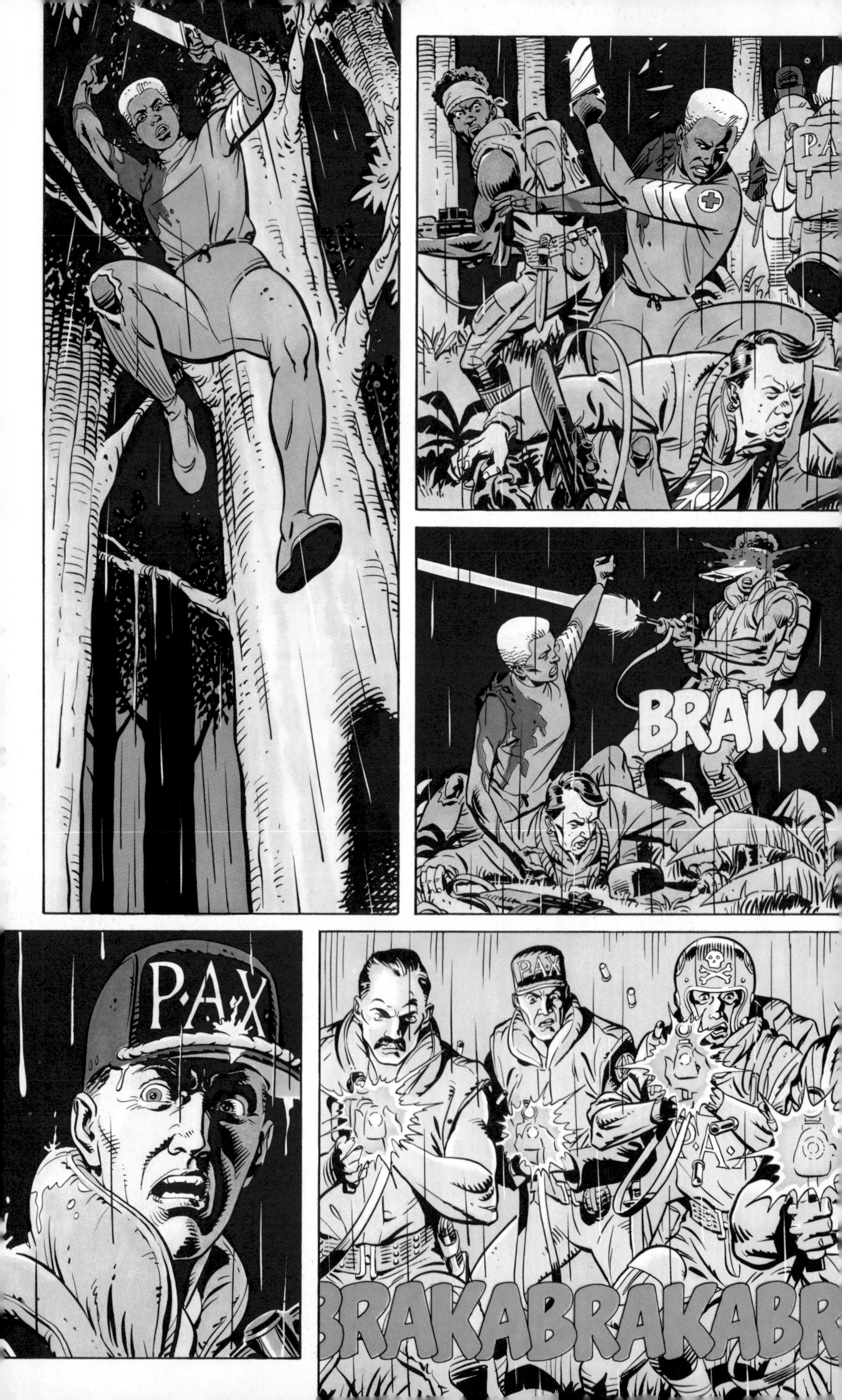
P.A.X
BRAKK
P.A.X
P.A.X
BRAKABRAKABR

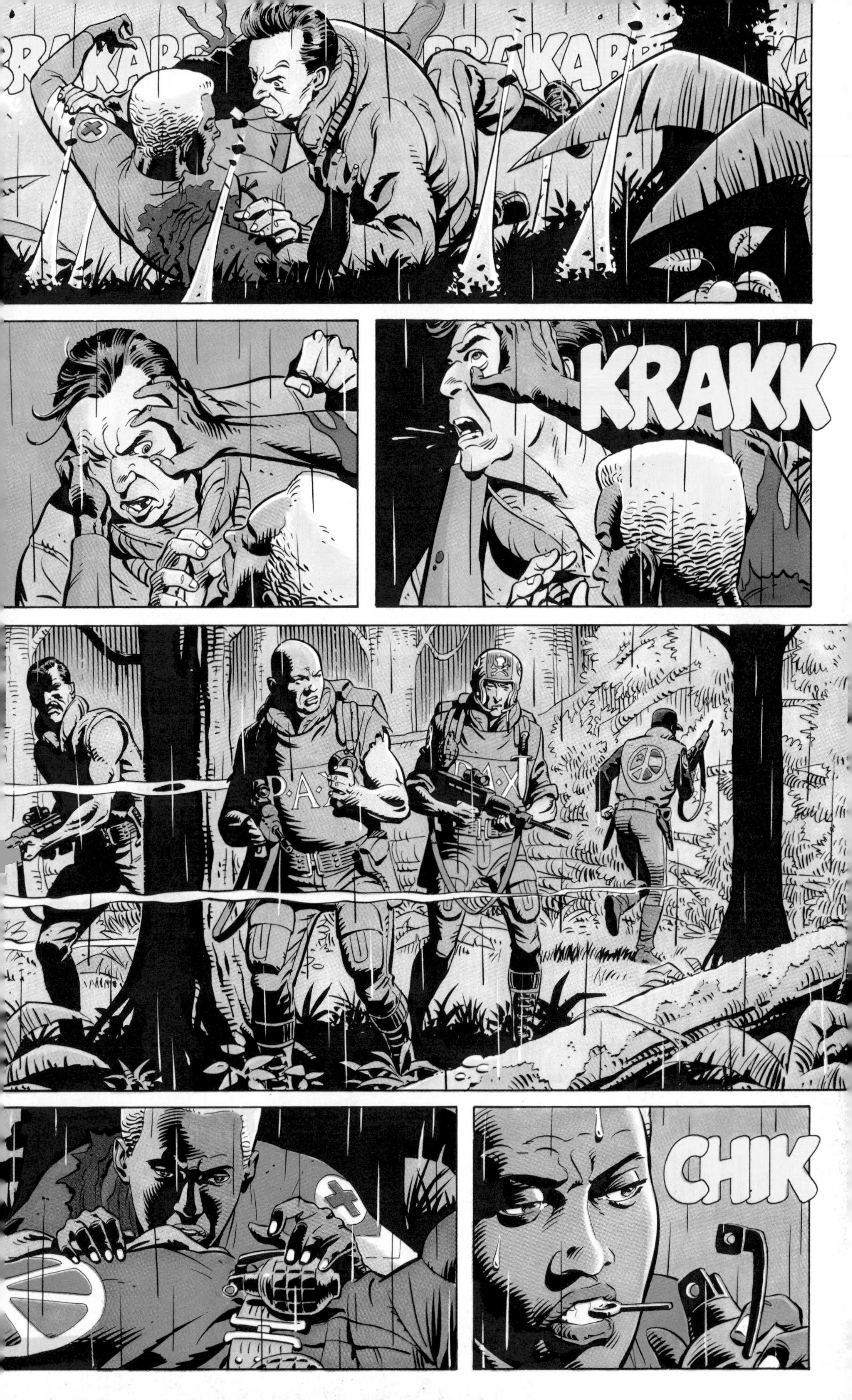
KRAKK
CHIK

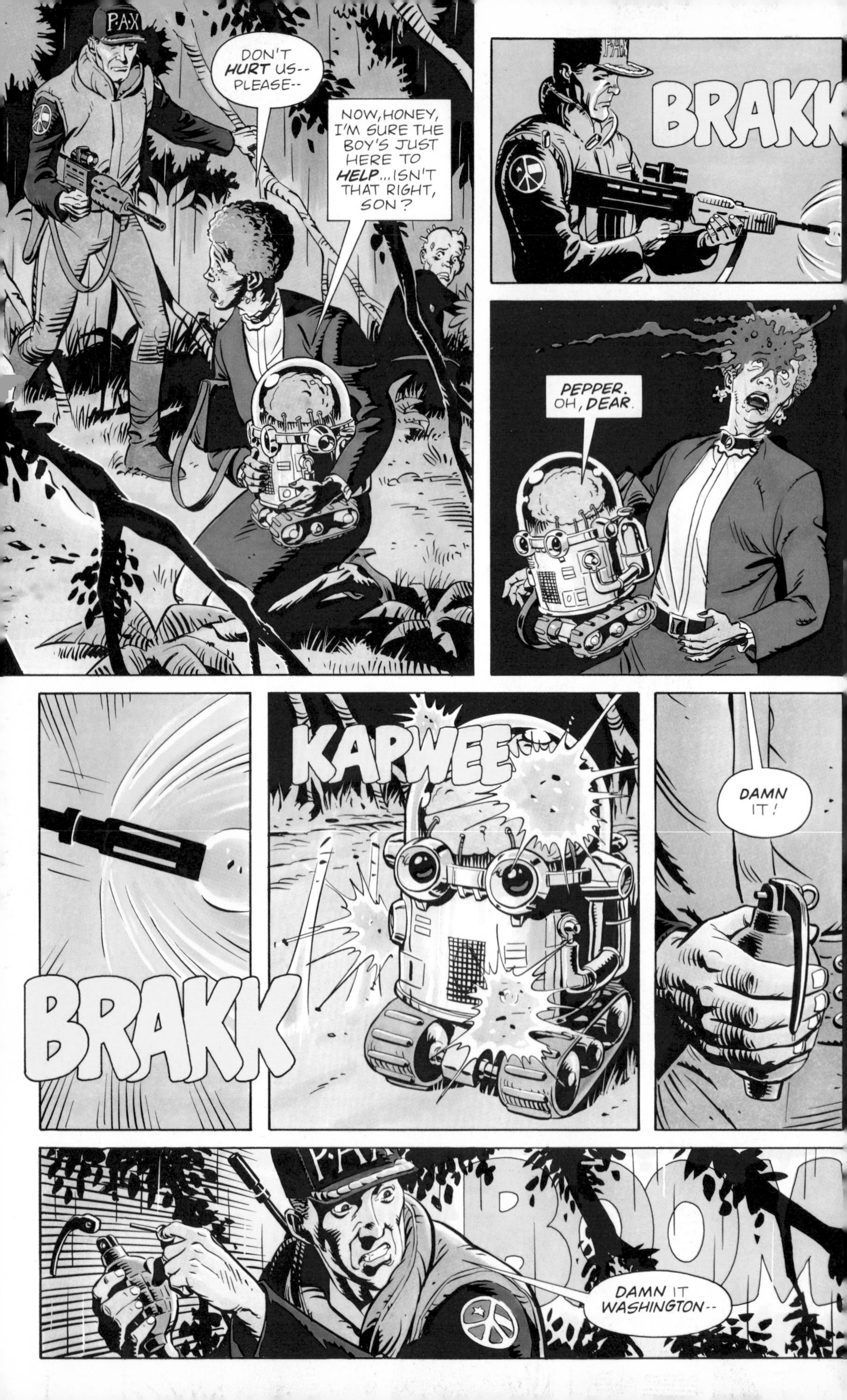
P·A·X
DON'T HURT US-- PLEASE--
NOW, HONEY, I'M SURE THE BOY'S JUST HERE TO HELP...ISN'T THAT RIGHT, SON?
BRAKK
PEPPER. OH, DEAR.
BRAKK
KAPWEE
DAMN IT!
DAMN IT WASHINGTON--

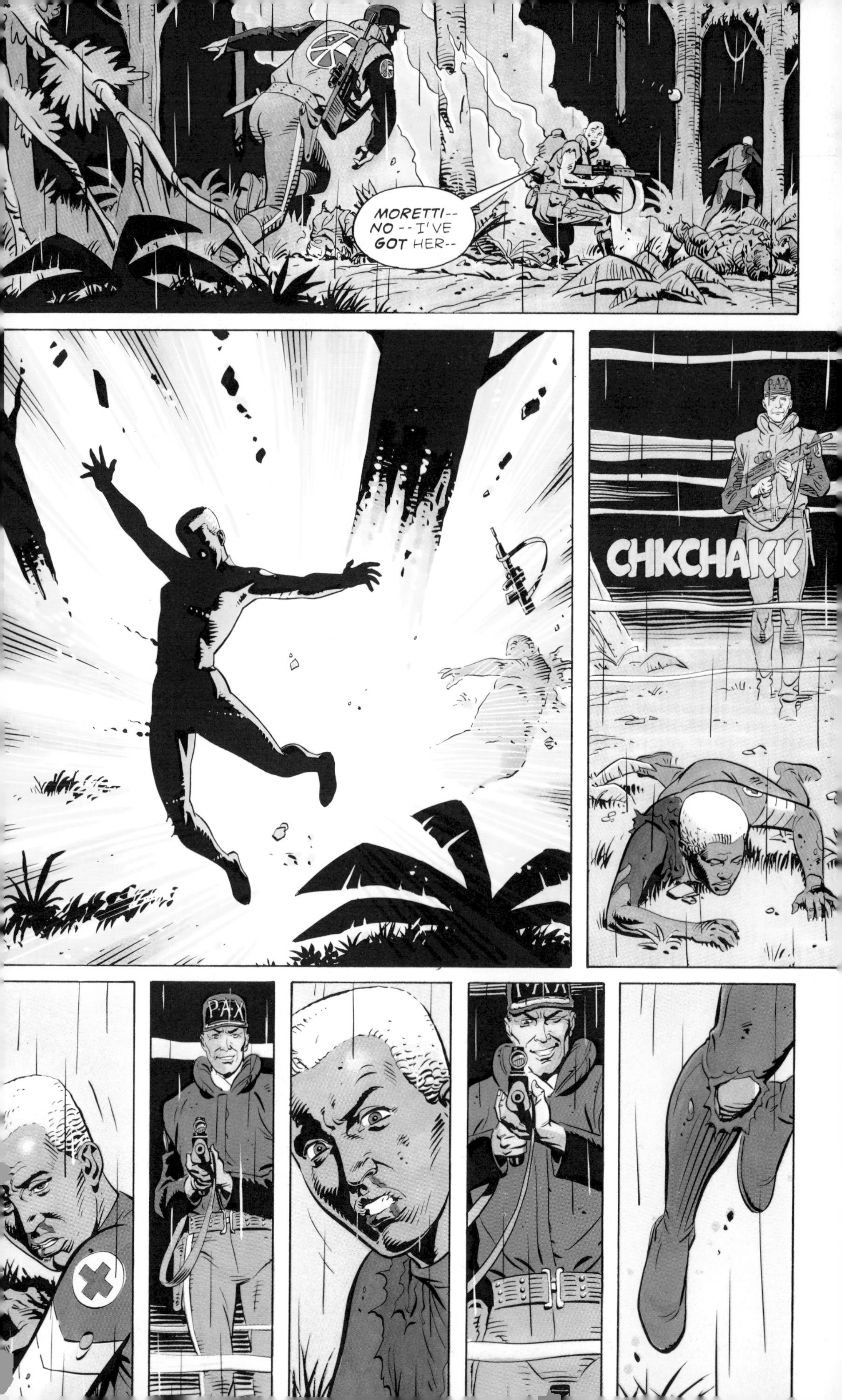
MORETTI--
NO --I'VE
GOT HER--
CHKCHAKK

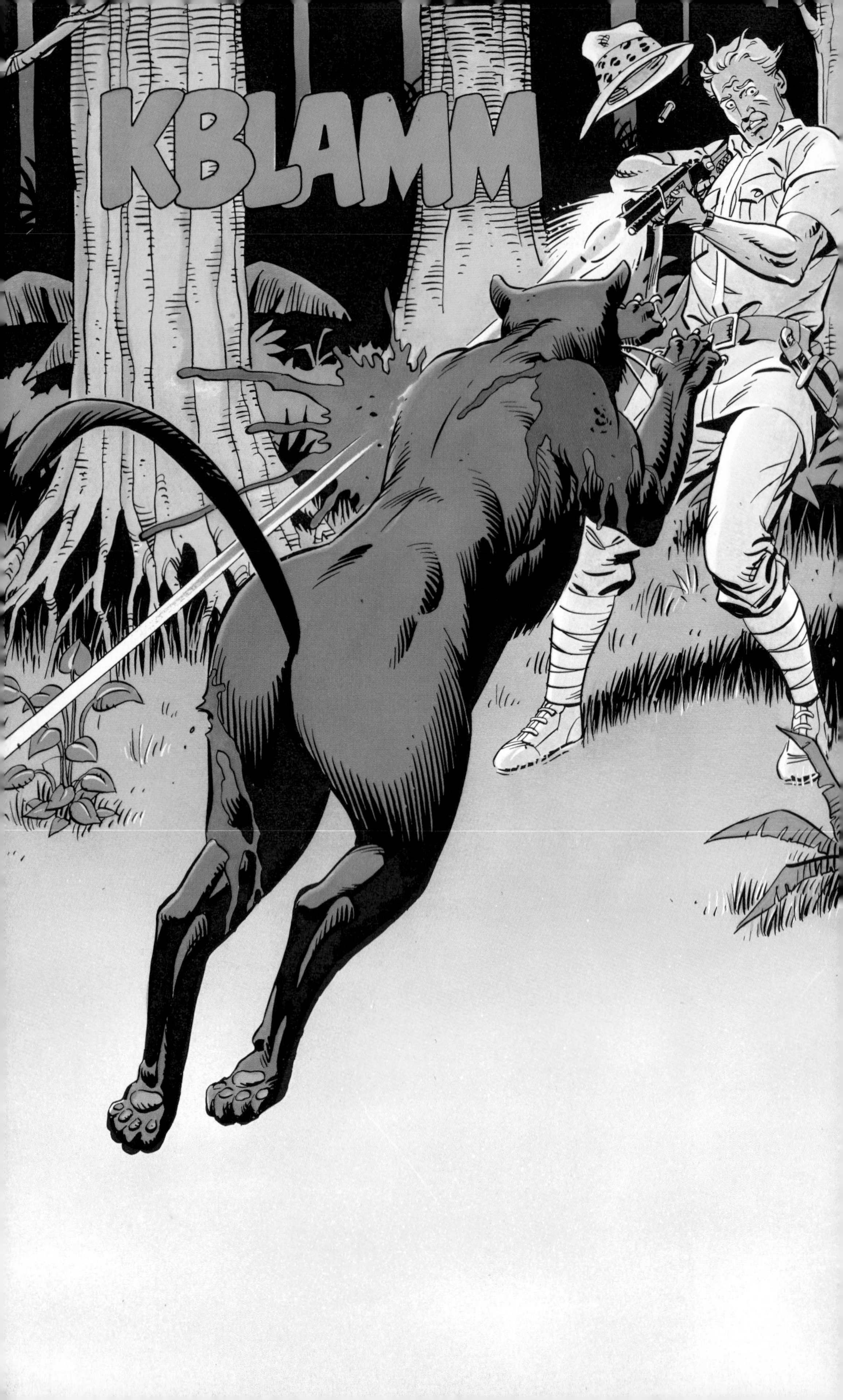
KBLAMM

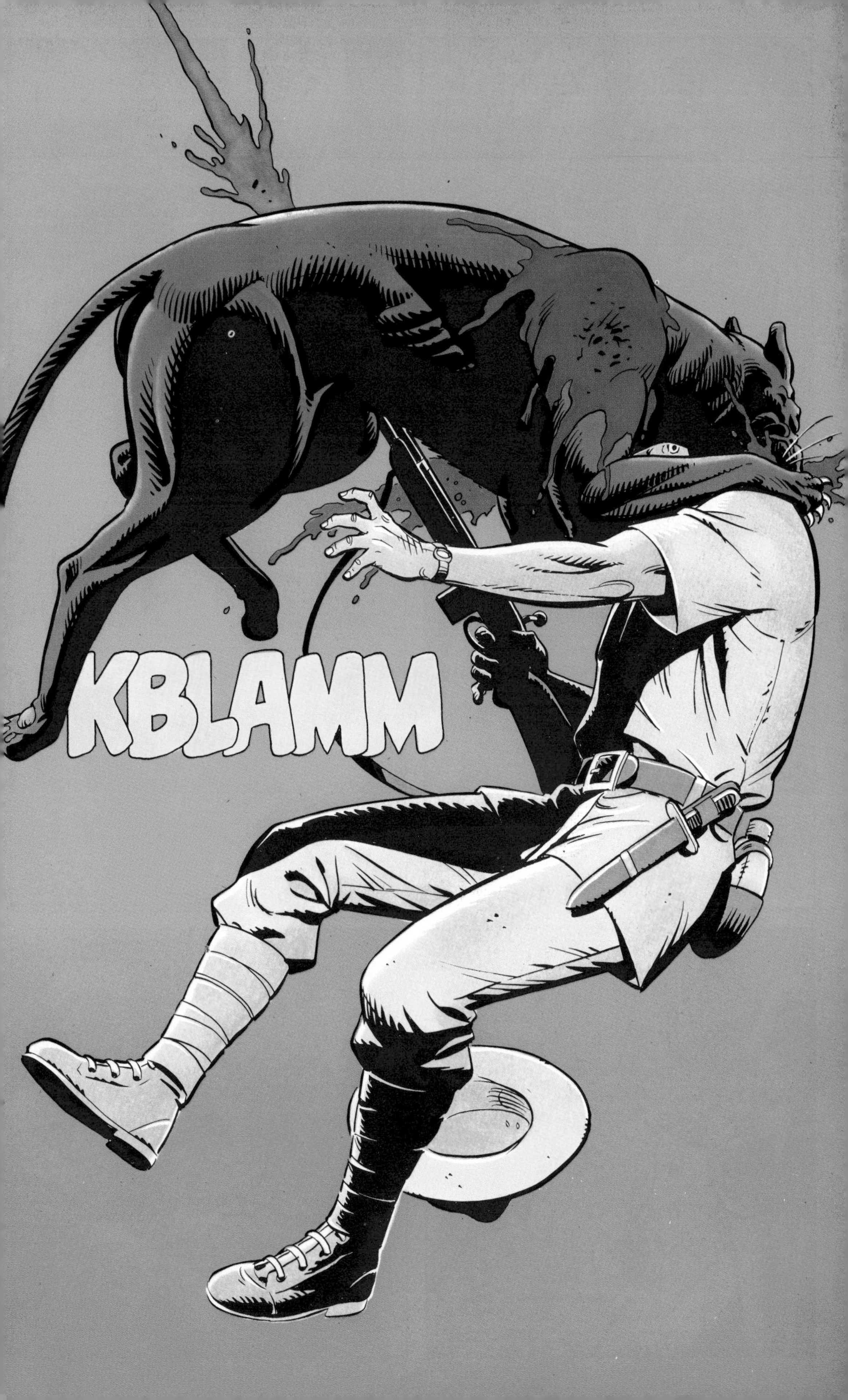
KBLAMM

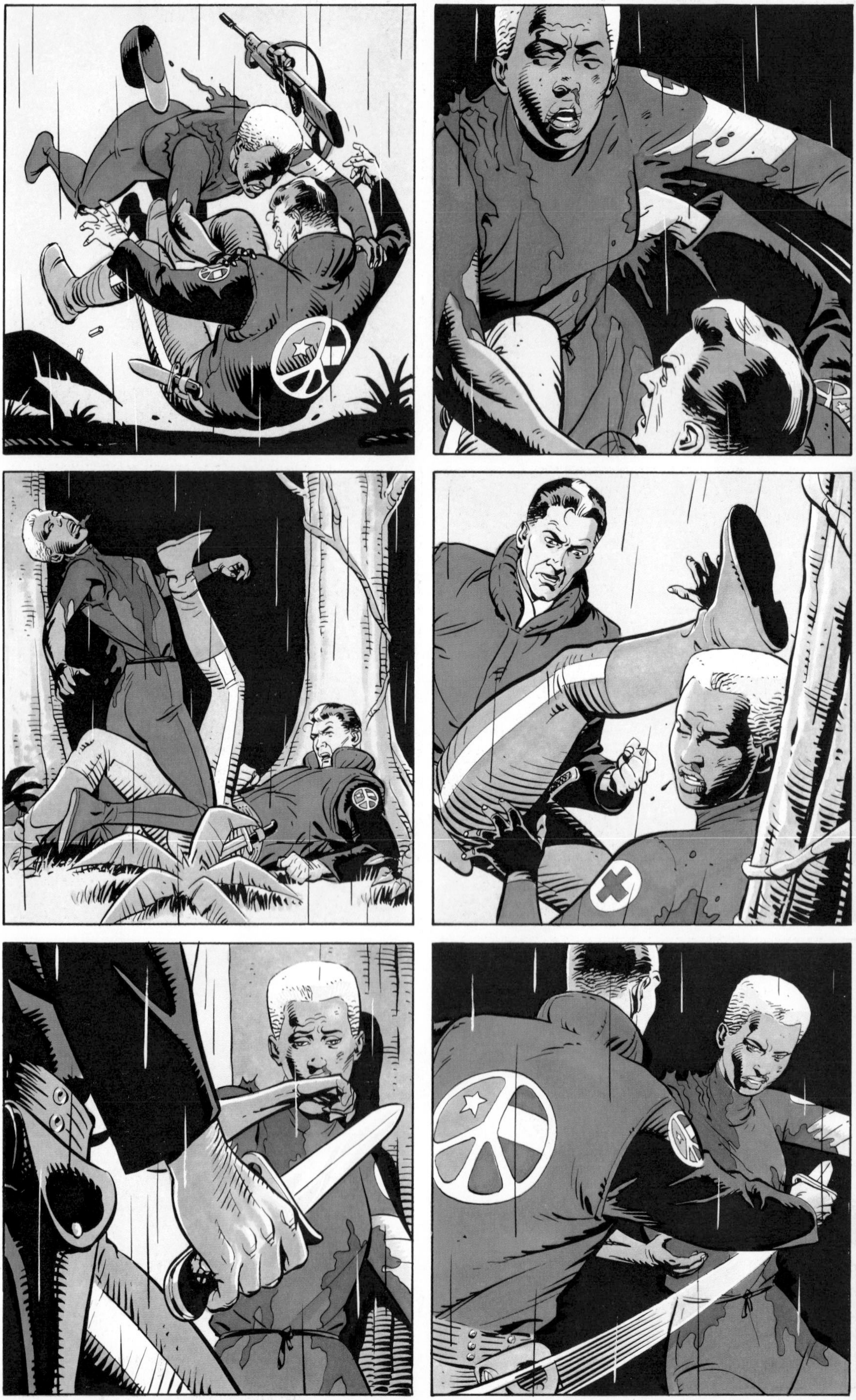

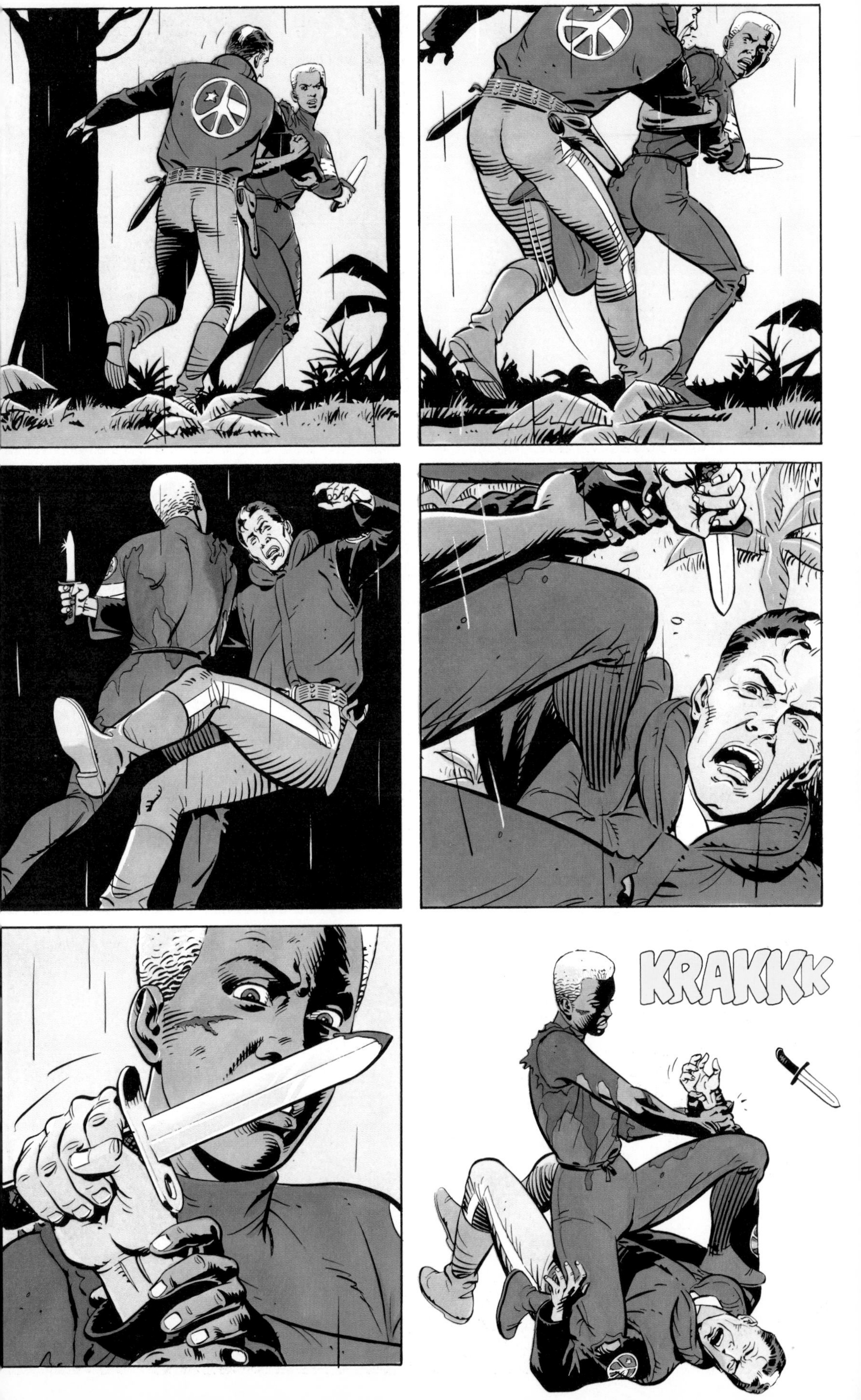
KRAKKK

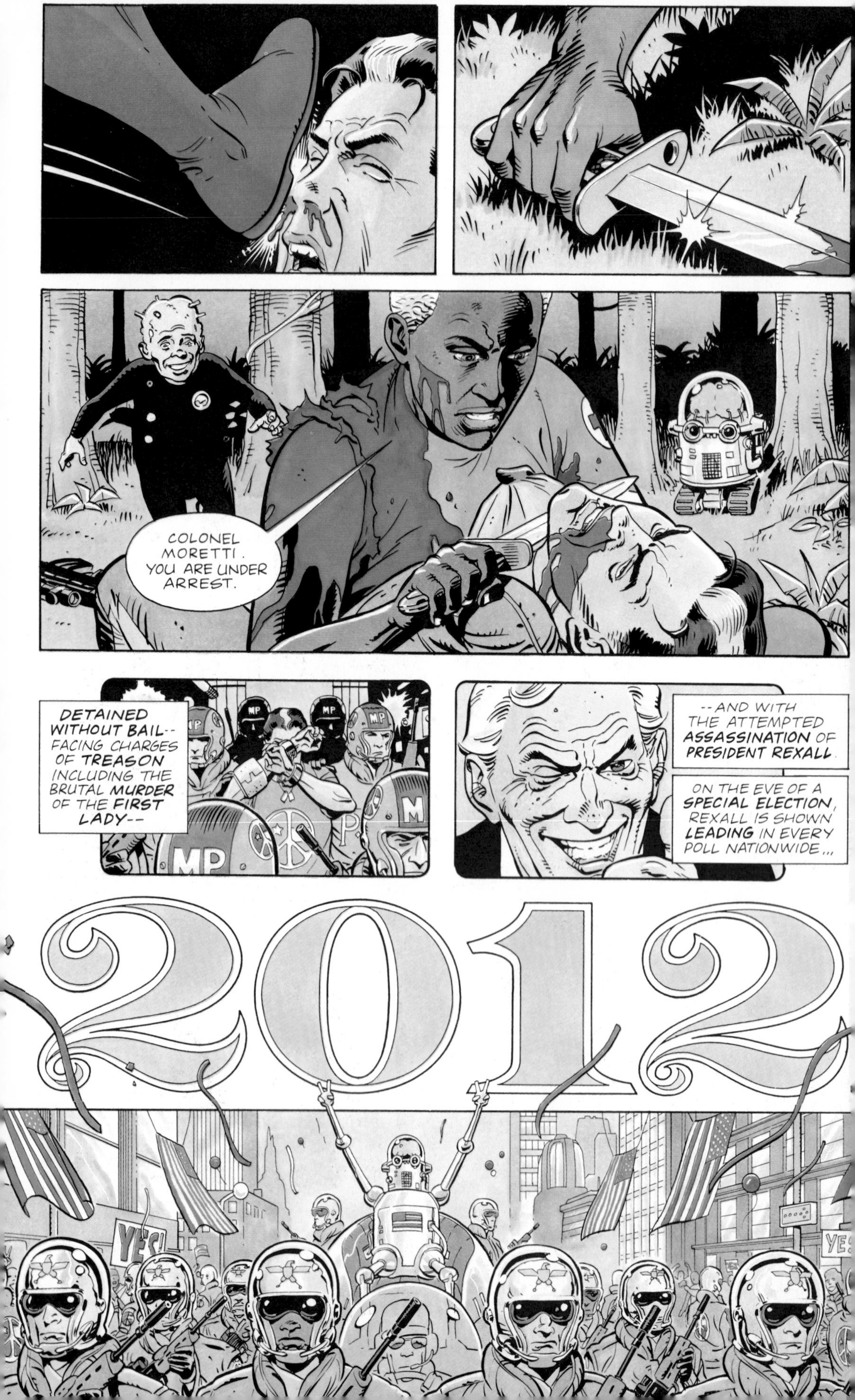
COLONEL MORETTI. YOU ARE UNDER ARREST.
DETAINED WITHOUT BAIL-- FACING CHARGES OF TREASON INCLUDING THE BRUTAL MURDER OF THE FIRST LADY--
MP
--AND WITH THE ATTEMPTED ASSASSINATION OF PRESIDENT REXALL.
ON THE EVE OF A SPECIAL ELECTION, REXALL IS SHOWN LEADING IN EVERY POLL NATIONWIDE...
2012
YES!

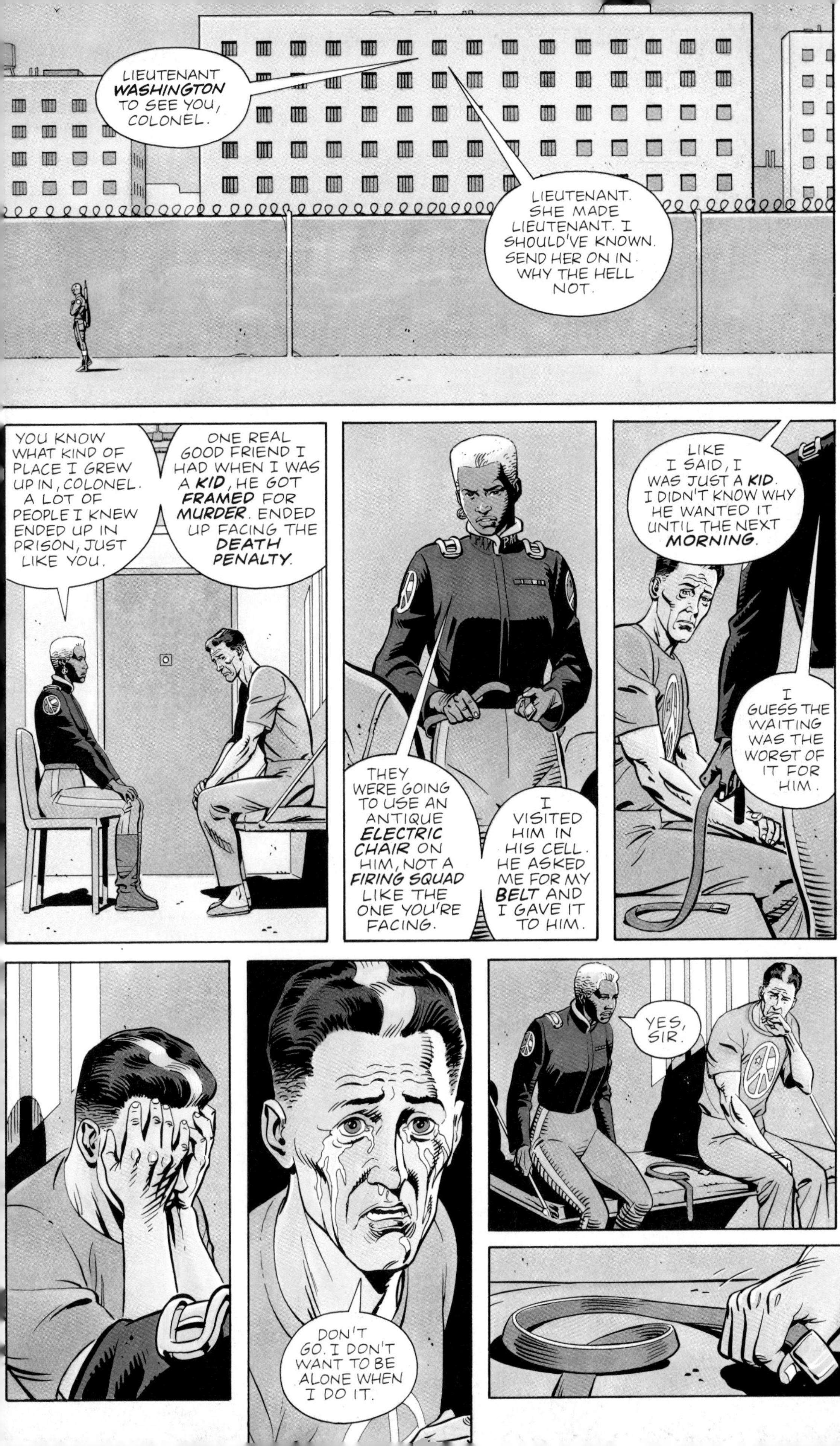
LIEUTENANT WASHINGTON TO SEE YOU, COLONEL.
LIEUTENANT. SHE MADE LIEUTENANT. I SHOULD'VE KNOWN. SEND HER ON IN. WHY THE HELL NOT.
YOU KNOW WHAT KIND OF PLACE I GREW UP IN, COLONEL. A LOT OF PEOPLE I KNEW ENDED UP IN PRISON, JUST LIKE YOU.
ONE REAL GOOD FRIEND I HAD WHEN I WAS A KID, HE GOT FRAMED FOR MURDER. ENDED UP FACING THE DEATH PENALTY.
THEY WERE GOING TO USE AN ANTIQUE ELECTRIC CHAIR ON HIM, NOT A FIRING SQUAD LIKE THE ONE YOU'RE FACING.
I VISITED HIM IN HIS CELL. HE ASKED ME FOR MY BELT AND I GAVE IT TO HIM.
LIKE I SAID, I WAS JUST A KID. I DIDN'T KNOW WHY HE WANTED IT UNTIL THE NEXT MORNING.
I GUESS THE WAITING WAS THE WORST OF IT FOR HIM.
DON'T GO. I DON'T WANT TO BE ALONE WHEN I DO IT.
YES, SIR.

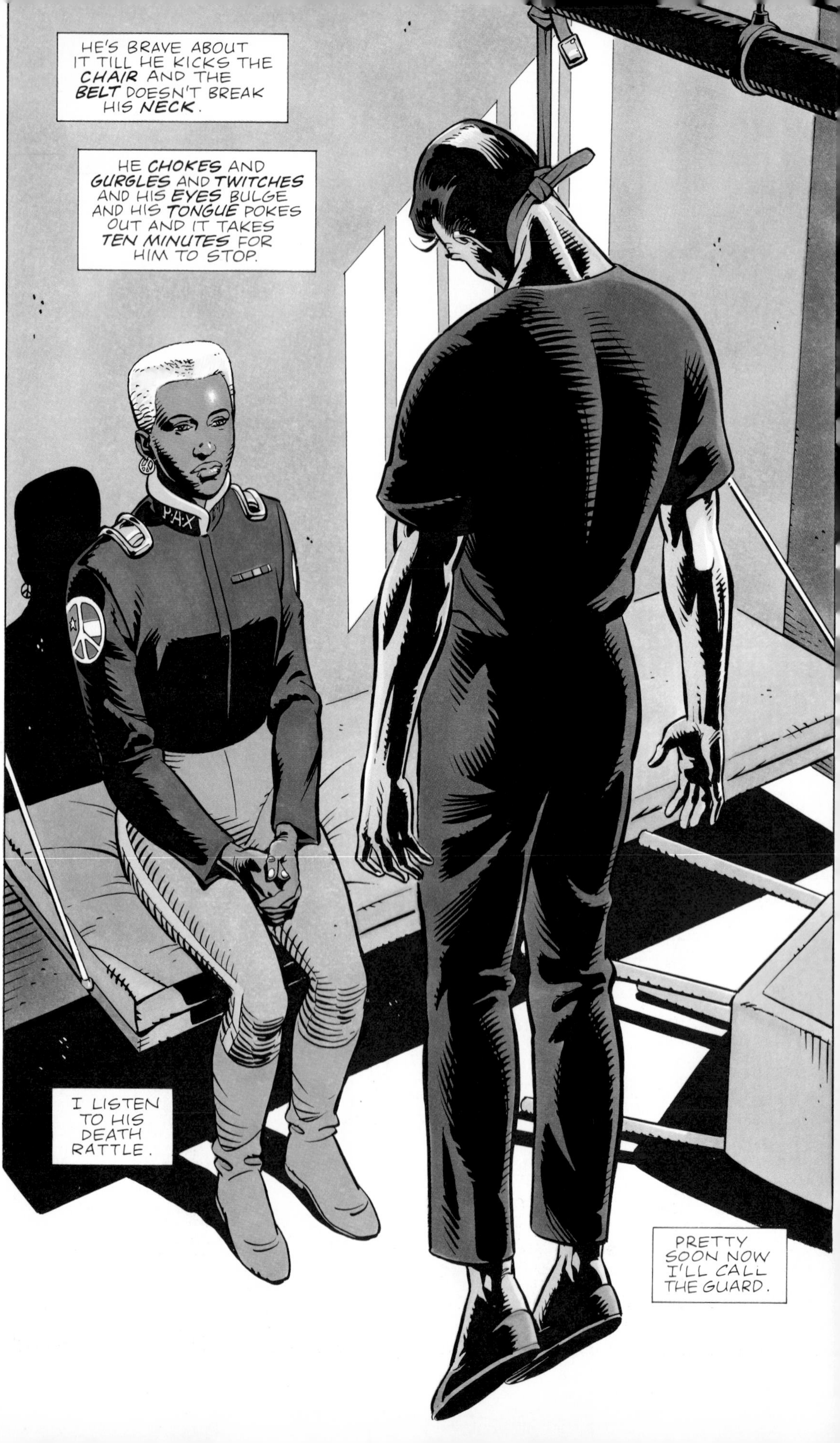
HE'S BRAVE ABOUT IT TILL HE KICKS THE CHAIR AND THE BELT DOESN'T BREAK HIS NECK.
HE CHOKES AND GURGLES AND TWITCHES AND HIS EYES BULGE AND HIS TONGUE POKES OUT AND IT TAKES TEN MINUTES FOR HIM TO STOP.
P·A·X
I LISTEN TO HIS DEATH RATTLE.
PRETTY SOON NOW I'LL CALL THE GUARD.

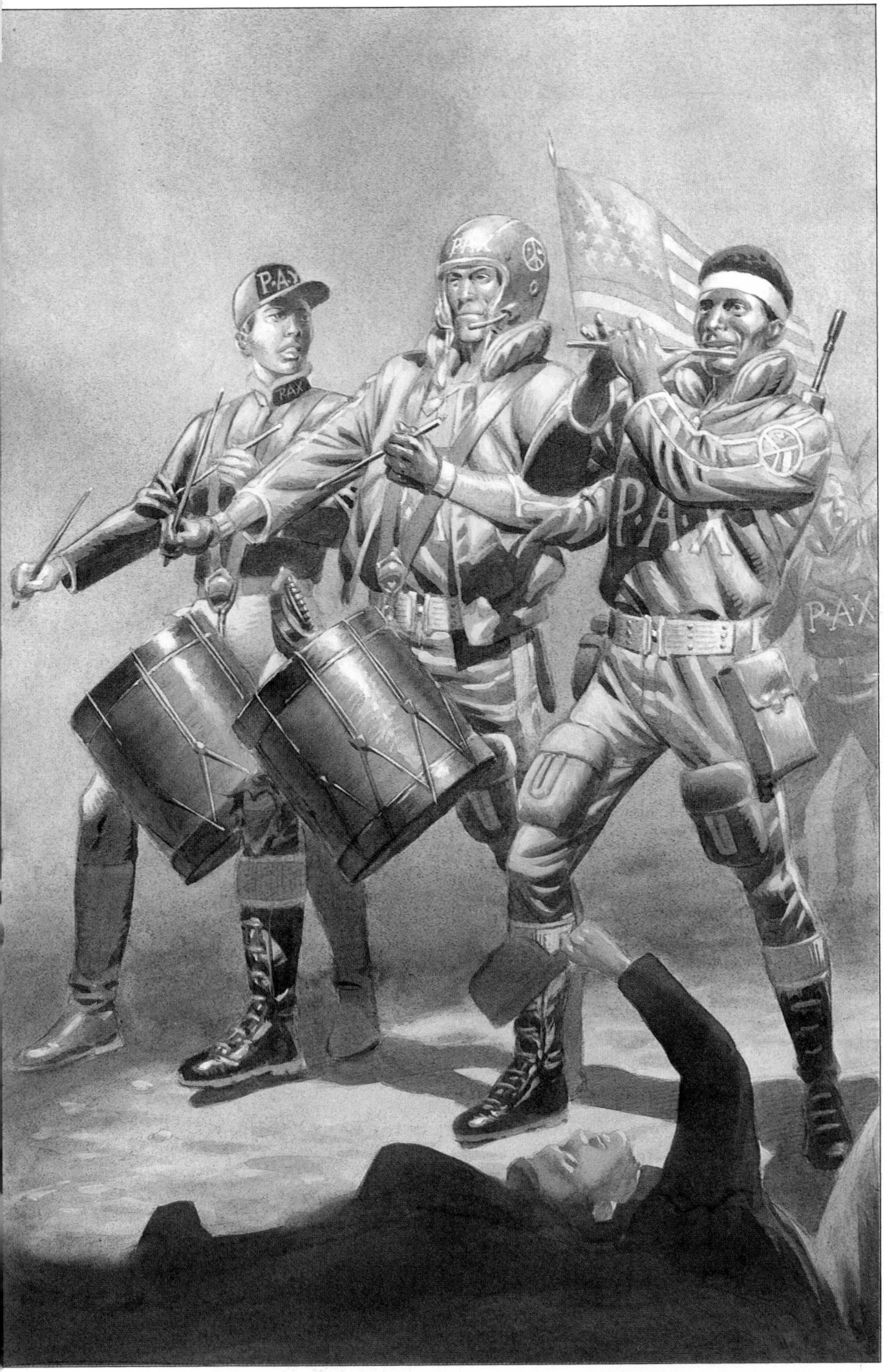
P·A·X
PAX
PAX
P·A·X
P·A·X

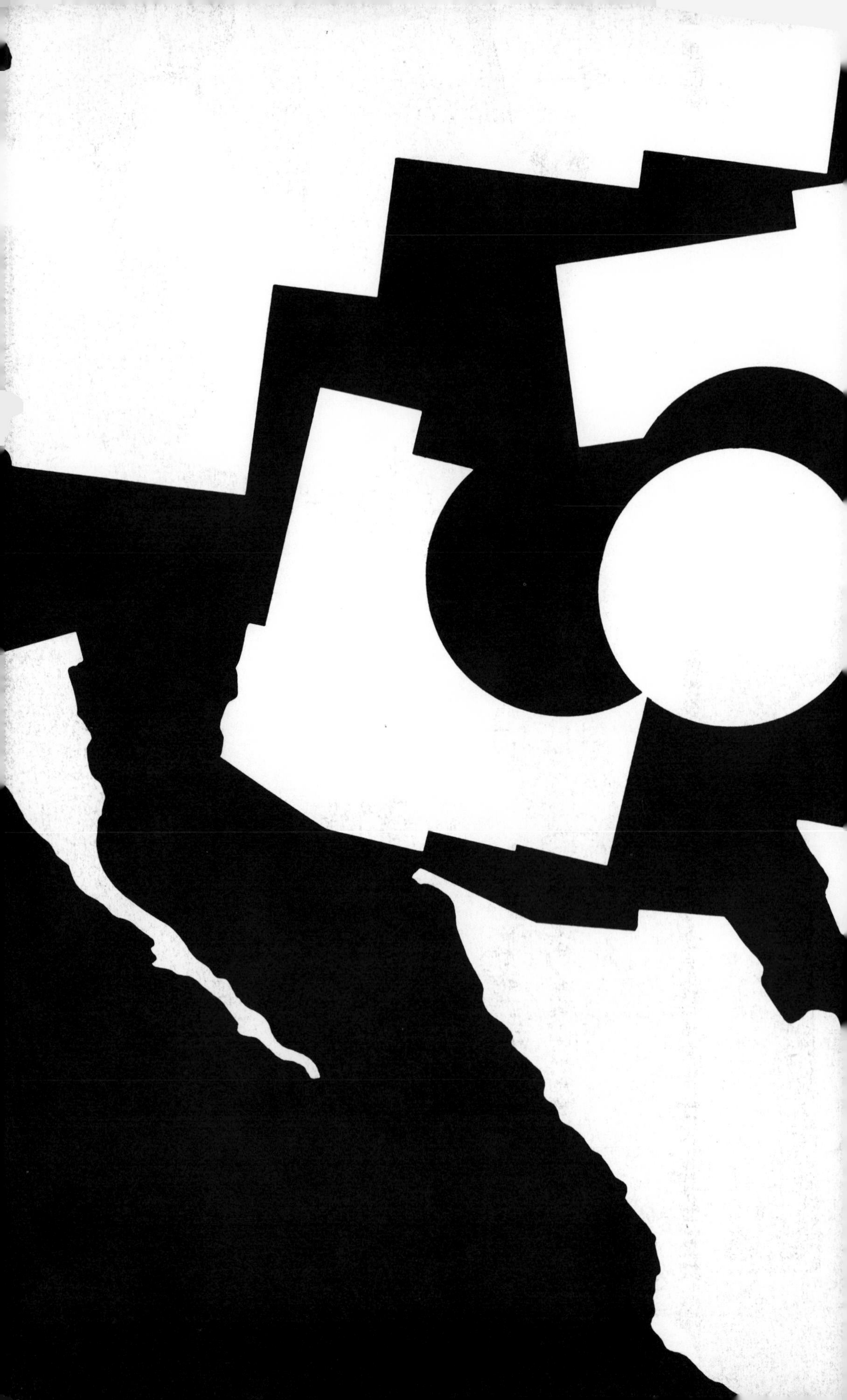

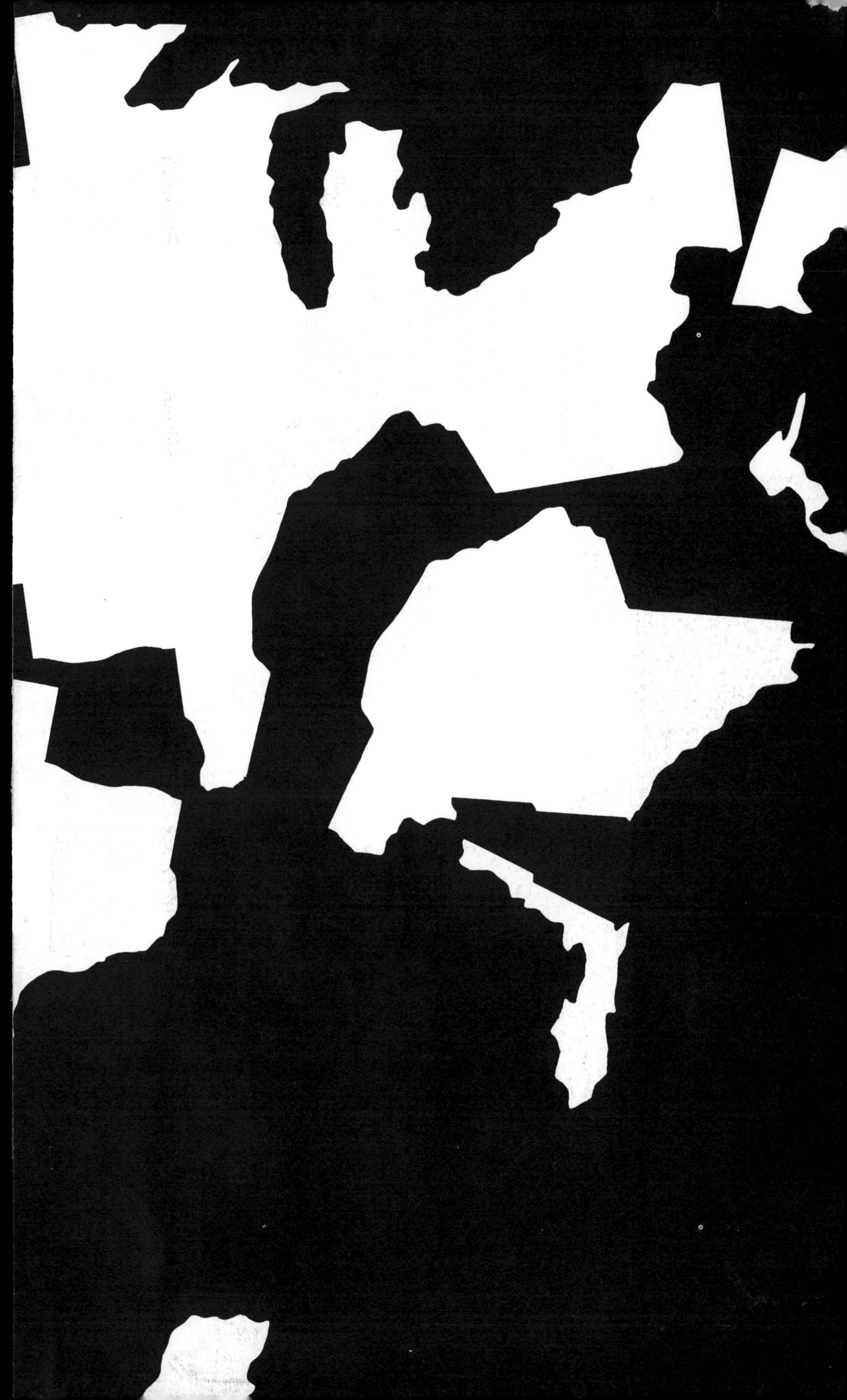